BEST OF HAMLYN ALL COLOUR COOKING

BEST OF HAMLYN
ALL COLOUR
COOKING

HAMLYN

Front cover shows, clockwise from top right:
Spiced Glazed Ham (170), Chocolate Cake (437), Fruit
Baskets (342), Salami and Mozarella Snack Toasts (34).

Title page shows, clockwise from top right:
Walnut-filled Fennel (244), Chelsea Buns (419), Tagliatelle
with Blue Cheese Sauce (320), Stuffed Sardines (83).

Back cover shows, clockwise from top right:
Lancashire Hot Pot (128), Pasta Salad (336), Vegetable
Kebabs (40), Tomato and Orange Soup (1).

The publishers would like to thank the following for
supplying photographs:
Edward Billington (Sugar) Ltd 377, 408, 429; Birds Eye
Wall's Limited 74, 275, 312; British Cheese 328;
Butter Information Council 326; California Raisin
Advisory Board 378, 383, 430; Concentrated Butter 45, 46;
Danish Dairy Board 19, 32, 47, 64, 311, 339, 412;
Egg Marketing 340; Fresh Fruit and Vegetable Information
Bureau 276, 342; The Kellog Company of Great Britain Ltd 373;
Mushroom Growers' Association 25, 31, 73, 261, 265, 266;
Pasta Information Centre 331; Potato Marketing Board 6;
St Ivel 20, 113, 213, 253, 321, 325, 384, 401, 411;
Sun Pat Peanut Butter 269; Twining's Information Service 407;
U.S. Rice Council 289, 292, 301; U.S.A. Peanuts Information
Service 290; John West Foods 341.

Additional photography: Ian O'Leary (Soups and Light Meals
chapter opener); James Jackson (Fish and Shellfish chapter
opener), Paul Williams (Rice and Pasta chapter opener),
Vernon Morgan (Desserts and Puddings chapter opener).

All other photographs from the Octopus Group Picture Library.

Line drawings by Roberta Colgate-Stone, Gay John Galsworthy,
Rob Shone and Lorna Turpin.

Published in 1990 by
The Hamlyn Publishing Group Limited
part of Reed International Books
Michelin House,
81 Fulham Road, London SW3 6RB

Reprinted 1990

ISBN 0 600 57072 X

Produced by Mandarin Offset
Printed in Hong Kong

Contents

Useful Facts and Figures

Notes on metrication

In this book quantities are given in metric and Imperial measures. Exact conversion from Imperial to metric measures does not usually give very convenient working quantities and so the metric measures have been rounded off into units of 25 grams. The table below shows the recommended equivalents.

Ounces	Approx g to nearest whole figure	Recommended conversion to nearest unit of 25	Ounces	Approx g to nearest whole figure	Recommended conversion to nearest unit of 25
1	28	25	9	255	250
2	57	50	10	283	275
3	85	75	11	312	300
4	113	100	12	340	350
5	142	150	13	368	375
6	170	175	14	396	400
7	198	200	15	425	425
8	227	225	16 (1 lb)	454	450

Note: When converting quantities over 16 oz first add the appropriate figures in the centre column, then adjust to the nearest unit of 25. As a general guide, 1 kg (1000 g) equals 2.2 lb or about 2 lb 3 oz. This method of conversion gives good results in nearly all cases, although in certain pastry and cake recipes a more accurate conversion is necessary to produce a balanced recipe.

Liquid measures The millilitre has been used in this book and the following table gives a few examples.

Imperial	Approx ml to nearest whole figure	Recommended ml	Imperial	Approx ml to nearest whole figure	Recommended ml
¼	142	150 ml	1 pint	567	600 ml
½	283	300 ml	1½ pints	851	900 ml
¾	425	450 ml	1¾ pints	992	1000 ml (1 litre)

Spoon measures All spoon measures given in this book are level unless otherwise stated.

Can sizes At present, cans are marked with the exact (usually to the nearest whole number) metric equivalent of the Imperial weight of the contents, so we have followed this practice when giving can sizes.

Oven temperatures The table below gives recommended equivalents.

	°C	°F	Gas Mark		°C	°F	Gas Mark
Very cool	110	225	¼	Moderately hot	190	375	5
	120	250	½		200	400	6
Cool	140	275	1	Hot	220	425	7
	150	300	2		230	450	8
Moderate	160	325	3	Very Hot	240	475	9
	180	350	4				

Notes for American and Australian users

In America the 8-fl oz measuring cup is used. In Australia metric measures are now used in conjunction with the standard 250-ml measuring cup. The Imperial pint, used in Britain and Australia, is 20 fl oz, while the American pint is 16 fl oz. It is important to remember that the Australian tablespoon differs from both the British and American tablespoons; the table below gives a comparison. The British standard tablespoon, which has been used throughout this book, holds 17.7 ml, the American 14.2 ml, and the Australian 20 ml. A teaspoon holds approximately 5 ml in all three countries.

British	American	Australian
1 teaspoon	1 teaspoon	1 teaspoon
1 tablespoon	1 tablespoon	1 tablespoon
2 tablespoons	3 tablespoons	2 tablespoons
3½ tablespoons	4 tablespoons	3 tablespoons
4 tablespoons	5 tablespoons	3½ tablespoons

An Imperial/American guide to solid and liquid measures

Imperial	American	Imperial	American
Solid measures		**Liquid measures**	
1 lb butter or margarine	2 cups	¼ pint liquid	⅔ cup liquid
1 lb flour	4 cups	½ pint	1¼ cups
1 lb granulated or caster sugar	2 cups	¾ pint	2 cups
1 lb icing sugar	3 cups	1 pint	2½ cups
8 oz rice	1 cup	1½ pints	3¾ cups
		2 pints	5 cups (2½ pints)

Note: When making any of the recipes in this book, only follow one set of measures as they are not interchangeable.

Introduction

The Best of Hamlyn All Colour Cooking is a splendidly wide-ranging general cookery book.

It is also a sensibly basic book, its chapters covering the essential kinds of food that all cooks, whether beginners or experienced, need to produce most days of the week. There are separate chapters for soups and light meals, fish and shellfish — a big chapter, acknowledging our heightened awareness of the invaluable part fish can play in a healthy diet — meat and poultry, vegetable and salad recipes, desserts and puddings, and a final chapter with a mouth-watering collection of baking ideas.

Among this book's 466 recipes are some that will widen the repertoire of vegetarian cooks — try Sunflower Okra with Mushrooms (231) or Walnut-filled Fennel (244), for instance — and others to delight lovers of oriental food, whether the delicately-flavoured dishes of China, such as Stir-fried Beef (139) are their preference, or the more robust curry dishes of India, such as Malabar Lamb Curry (148) or Lamb Curry with Yogurt (153) are more to their taste. There are also many recipes for dishes that are quick and easy to prepare, such as Beef, Apricot and Apple Kebabs (140), Poached Pears with Chocolate Sauce (389) and Almond Scones (417). These are a boon for working people and busy parents with families to feed.

Such recipes are quick and easy to find, too, as this book includes preparation and cooking times which, along with the number of servings, are given for every recipe in the book.

Other features which have been included in *The Best of Hamlyn All Colour Cooking* to help its readers include the full-colour photograph which heads each recipe, providing the perfect view of how the finished dish will look when served, elegantly garnished or decorated. Then there is the Cook's Tip which ends each recipe, offering all sorts of helpful information about aspects of cooking techniques, ingredients, time-saving shortcuts and alternative ingredients for those in the recipe. And there is a calorie count provided for each recipe, making healthy and well-balanced meal planning a pleasure rather than a chore.

Each chapter is colour coded, the colour strip running down each page matching the strip behind the chapter title on the Contents page, so that a quick flick through the book will soon identify the chapter wanted.

Together, these features make *The Best of Hamlyn All Colour Cooking* more than just a fine collection of recipes; they turn it into a comprehensive and wide-ranging aid to cooking which will inspire cooks of all ranges of experience and ability.

SOUPS AND LIGHT MEALS

When you're entertaining, the first course is perhaps the most important, setting the scene for what is to follow. Soups are a traditional favourite as they fit so easily into any menu. If you plan to serve a substantial main dish, a light soup such as the Chinese Soup with Fresh Greens is ideal and an elegant Cream of Watercress Soup looks as good as it tastes. Thick soups such as Minestrone or Chestnut Soup are perfect as part of a large menu of small dishes, or when there is likely to be an interval between serving the first and second courses. Substantial soups like White Fish Chowder or Winter Warmer make a meal in themselves, served with a crunchy salad and plenty of crusty bread. Served with a glass of chilled white wine, the delicious range of appetizers based on fish or vegetables make a wonderful start to any meal: try Smoked Trout Paté or Vegetable Terrine, both of which also make a delicious summer lunch and can easily be packed for picnics.

The life of a busy modern family means that often there's only time for a light meal, but it can and should be delicious and satisfying: everyone will enjoy Cheese and Tuna Muffins or Stuffed Pancakes. On cold winter days, tasty savouries like Samosas or Sausage Plait are nutritious and filling. Dishes that can be prepared in advance such as Watercress and Brie Quiche or Potted Prawns are ideal for a later supper after an evening out. The recipes in this chapter offer a variety of ideas for every occasion.

1 | Tomato and Orange Soup

Preparation time
10 minutes

Cooking time
20 minutes

Serves 6

Calories
130 per portion

You will need
1 onion, chopped
2 cloves garlic, crushed
50 g / 2 oz butter or margarine
25 g / 1 oz plain flour
1 (800-g / 28-oz) can chopped
  tomatoes
900 ml / 1½ pints chicken stock
grated rind and juice of 2 oranges
2 teaspoons sugar
salt and pepper

Garnish
150 ml / ¼ pint single cream
grated rind of 1 orange

Fry the onion and garlic in the butter or margarine until softened. Stir in the flour, then the tomatoes. Stirring continuously, add the stock and the orange rind and juice. Reduce the heat and simmer gently for 15 minutes, stirring occasionally. Add the sugar and season to taste. For a smooth soup, blend in a liquidiser.

Pour the soup into individual bowls and garnish each serving with a swirl of cream and a sprinkle of orange rind.

2 | Cream of Watercress Soup

Preparation time
10 minutes

Cooking time
10 minutes

Serves 6

Calories
225 per portion

You will need
1 onion, chopped
2 cloves, garlic, crushed
50 g / 2 oz butter or margarine
50 g / 2 oz plain flour
600 ml / 1 pint chicken stock
600 ml / 1 pint milk
2 bunches of watercress, trimmed
  and chopped
salt and pepper
¼ teaspoon grated nutmeg
juice of ½ lemon
150 ml / ¼ pint single cream
watercress sprigs to garnish

In a saucepan, fry the onion and garlic in the butter or margarine until softened. Reduce the heat and stir in the flour. Gradually add the stock and milk, stirring all the time. Stir in the watercress, salt and pepper, nutmeg and lemon juice. Simmer gently for 5 minutes. Reduce the heat, then stir in the single cream. Reheat without boiling.

Pour the soup into individual soup bowls and garnish each serving with a sprig of watercress.

Freezer Tip

Pour cooled soup into a rigid plastic container, leaving head space for expansion, label and freeze. To serve, dip container in hand-hot water, reheat soup in a saucepan slowly to boiling, stirring frequently.

Cook's Tip

To quickly chop watercress, trim off the stalks and place the leaves in a food processor. Pulse the blades on and off for 1 minute. Remember to utilize your food processor for chopping the onion too.

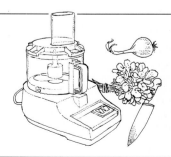

3 | Cheese and Onion Soup

Preparation time
10 minutes

Cooking time
10 minutes

Serves 6

Calories
490 per portion

You will need
2 onions
50 g/ 2 oz butter or margarine
50 g/ 2 oz plain flour
600 ml/ 1 pint chicken stock
600 ml/ 1 pint milk
225 g/ 8 oz matured Cheddar
    cheese, grated
150 ml/¼ pint dry or medium dry
    cider
¼ teaspoon grated nutmeg
salt and pepper

Garnish
grated cheese
croûtons

Chop the onions and cook in the butter or margarine for 3 – 5 minutes until soft. Reduce the heat and stir in the flour. Slowly add first the stock, then the milk, stirring all the time. Bring to the boil and cook for 3–4 minutes. Remove the saucepan from the heat, add the Cheddar and stir until all the cheese has melted. Over a low heat, stir in the cider and seasoning. Do not allow the soup to boil.

Pour the soup into individual bowls and garnish with grated cheese and croûtons.

4 | French Onion Soup

Preparation time
5 minutes

Cooking time
25–30 minutes

Serves 6

Calories
235 per portion

You will need
450 g/ 1 lb onions
50 g/ 2 oz butter or margarine
1 litre/ 1¾ pints beef stock
150 ml/¼ pint dry red wine
salt and pepper
6 slices French bread, buttered
100 g/ 4 oz Cheddar cheese,
    grated

Chop the onions and fry in the butter or margarine until soft and golden brown. Pour in the stock, bring to the boil, then reduce the heat and simmer gently for 25 minutes. Add the wine and seasoning, stir well and heat the soup for a further few minutes.

Put a slice of French bread into each heatproof soup bowl and pour over the soup. When the bread rises to the surface sprinkle the top with the Cheddar, put under a hot grill until golden. Serve immediately

Cook's Tip

To chop an onion, cut a peeled onion in half lengthwise; place the flat side on a chopping board. Holding opposite sides, slice finely first lengthwise, then across.

Cook's Tip

Coarsely grate and freeze small leftover pieces of cheese – they are often useful for recipes such as this one. Pack the cheese in polythene bags, allowing plenty of room in the bag so that the cheese does not become compressed in a lump. Use straight from the freezer.

5 | Chestnut Soup

Preparation time
35 minutes

Cooking time
35 minutes

Serves 4—6

Calories
360–240 per portion

You will need
450 g / 1 lb chestnuts
1 large onion, sliced
40 g / 1½ oz butter
1 medium potato, chopped
3 celery sticks, chopped
1.4 litres / 2½ pints vegetable stock
salt and freshly ground black
   pepper
15 g / ½ oz plain flour
½ teaspoon light brown sugar
pinch of dried mixed herbs
300 ml / ½ pint milk
1 tablespoon dry sherry

For the garnish
croutons (optional)
1 tablespoon chopped parsley
   (optional)

Slit the hard shell of each chestnut. Put the chestnuts into a pan of boiling water and simmer for 20 minutes. Remove the hard shells, rub off the brown skins and roughly chop the chestnuts.

Put the onion and half of the butter into a pan and gently cook until soft. Add the potato, celery, chestnuts, stock, salt and pepper, and bring to the boil. Cover and simmer until the chestnuts are soft. Press through a sieve, or blend in a liquidiser.

Melt the remaining butter, work in the flour and cook for 2 minutes. Stir in the sugar, herbs and chestnut purée, and heat through gently. Add the milk and re-heat, but do not boil. Stir in the sherry and serve, garnished as shown, if you like.

Cook's Tip

If you have a garden, then try drying some herbs for the winter. For example, sage, thyme and tarragon can be tied in bunches and hung in a cool, dry place.

6 | Winter warmer

Preparation time
5 minutes

Cooking time
40 minutes

Serves 4

Calories
355 per portion

You will need
25 g / 1 oz butter
450 g / 1 lb onions, chopped
675 g / 1½ lb potatoes, chopped
900 ml / 1½ pints vegetable stock
1 (280-g / 10-oz) can creamed
   sweetcorn
pinch of mace or nutmeg
2 bay leaves
¼ teaspoon celery salt
pepper
1 (170-g / 6-oz) can evaporated milk
   or single cream
1 tablespoon chopped fennel to
   garnish (optional)

Heat the butter in a large saucepan, add the onions and cook over moderate heat until golden, about 8 minutes. Add the potatoes, stock, sweetcorn, mace or nutmeg, bay leaves, salt and pepper. Bring to the boil, stirring, cover and simmer for 30 minutes or until the potatoes are very soft. Remove the bay leaves. Stir in the evaporated milk or cream, check seasoning, heat through gently and serve in warmed individual bowls. Garnish with fennel, if using.

Cook's Tip

A delicious accompaniment for soup: clean potato peelings, dipped in a thin batter and deep fried until crisp and golden.

7 | Beef Soup with Dumplings

Preparation time
15 minutes

Cooking time
1 hour 20 minutes

Serves 6

Calories
340 per portion

You will need
450 g/ 1 lb braising steak, cubed
25 g/ 1 oz plain flour
50 g/ 2 oz butter or margarine
2 onions, finely chopped
2 cloves garlic, crushed
1 teaspoon marjoram
1 teaspoon paprika
salt and pepper
1.15 litres/ 2 pints beef stock

For the dumplings
2 day-old bread rolls
6 tablespoons lukewarm milk
1 onion, finely chopped
1 tablespoon oil
2 tablespoons chopped parsley
salt and pepper
1 egg

Coat the beef in flour. Melt the fat in a large saucepan, add the onion and garlic and fry for 3 minutes. Add the meat and fry until browned on all sides. Add the marjoram and seasoning. Gradually blend in the stock, bring to the boil, reduce the heat and simmer for 1 hour. Cut the rolls into thin slices and soften with the warmed milk. Cook the onion in the oil. Mix together the bread, onion, parsley, seasoning and egg. With wet hands, form the mixture into six small balls.

Add the dumplings to the soup and simmer for a further 15 minutes. Serve each portion of soup with a dumpling.

Freezer Tip

Before adding the dumplings, cool soup quickly and freeze. Make and freeze the dumplings separately. To reheat, bring the soup to the boil, add the defrosted dumplings, and cook as above.

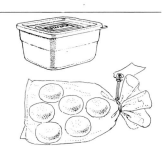

8 | Bacon and Split Pea Soup

Preparation time
10 minutes, plus overnight soaking

Cooking time
1 hour 10 minutes

Serves 6

Calories
295 per portion

You will need
100 g/ 4 oz split peas
1 small turnip
1 carrot
2 leeks
2 tablespoons oil
8 rashers rindless smoked streaky bacon, diced
1.4 litres/ 2½ pints ham or chicken stock
salt and pepper
½ teaspoon dried mixed herbs
150 ml/ ¼ pint single cream
1 tablespoon chopped parsley to garnish

Cover the split peas with cold water and soak them overnight. Drain well. Dice the turnip and carrot. Slice the leeks into rings.

Cook the vegetables in the oil for 5 minutes, add the bacon and continue cooking for a few minutes. Add the stock and split peas. Season well with salt, pepper and the mixed herbs. Simmer gently for an hour. Blend the soup in a liquidiser until smooth.

Return the soup to the saucepan and reheat over a low heat. Stir in the cream. Pour into individual soup bowls and garnish each serving with chopped parsley.

Cook's Tip

Reserve the cooking liquid from a joint of bacon or gammon for this soup. Omit the streaky bacon. Cool and chill the liquid, then skim off any fat before use.

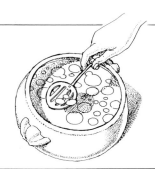

9 | Gazpacho

Preparation time
25 minutes, plus chilling

Serves 6

Calories
162 per portion

You will need
2 small slices brown bread, crusts removed and torn
600 ml / 1 pint tomato juice
2 garlic cloves, peeled
½ cucumber, peeled and chopped
1 red and 1 green pepper, cored, seeded and chopped
1 large onion, finely chopped
750 g / 1½ lb tomatoes, skinned, seeded and chopped
4 tablespoons olive oil
2 tablespoons red wine vinegar
salt and pepper
¼ teaspoon dried marjoram
¼ teaspoon dried basil
1 tablespoon chopped fresh parsley

For the garnish
croûtons
sliced stuffed green olives
chopped cucumber, peppers and spring onions

Place the bread in a blender with the tomato juice and garlic, leave for 5 minutes, then purée until smooth.

Add the cucumber, peppers, onion, tomatoes, olive oil, vinegar, salt and pepper to taste, marjoram and basil, blending well. Transfer to a chilled soup tureen.

Chill at least 1 hour. Sprinkle with parsley and serve with small bowls of croûtons, olives, cucumber, peppers and onion to garnish. Crusty French bread is a good accompaniment.

Cook's Tip

To make croûtons, fry bread cubes in hot oil for 1 minute until golden and crisp. Drain well on paper towels, then sprinkle with salt. When cool, store in a tight container until ready to use.

10 | Chilled Provençal Soup

Preparation time
10 minutes, plus cooling

Cooking time
15 minutes

Serves 4

Calories
188 per portion

You will need
2 tablespoons olive oil
2 garlic cloves, peeled and crushed
2 small aubergines, cubed
450 g / 1 lb tomatoes, skinned and chopped
2 courgettes, sliced
2 tablespoons tomato purée
300 ml / ½ pint water
salt and pepper to taste
grated Parmesan cheese, to serve

For the sauce
2 bunches fresh basil, chopped
4 garlic cloves, peeled
2 tablespoons chopped pine nuts
50 g / 2 oz Parmesan cheese, grated
125 ml / 4 fl oz olive oil

Heat the oil and fry the garlic for 1 minute. Add the aubergines, tomatoes and courgettes. Stir well, reduce the heat and cook, covered, for 5 minutes. Add the tomato purée, water and seasoning. Bring to the boil, then simmer for 5 minutes, until the vegetables are tender.

Meanwhile, to make the sauce, place the basil, garlic, nuts and cheese in a liquidizer and blend until finely ground. Blend in the oil gradually.

Pour the vegetable mixture into the individual bowls and leave to cool. When cold, stir basil sauce into each bowl and sprinkle with Parmesan cheese.

Cook's Tip

Pine nuts are pale oval seeds from the Mediterranean Stone Pine. They are a traditional ingredient in this basil sauce, also known as pesto sauce. Buy pine nuts in small quantities as they do not keep well.

11 | *Borscht*

Preparation time
10 minutes

Cooking time
1 hour

Serves 6

Calories
60 per portion

You will need
450 g / 1 lb raw beetroot
2 carrots
1 onion
bay leaf
1.15 litres / 2 pints beef stock
salt and pepper
150 ml / ¼ pint natural yogurt to
    garnish

Grate or finely chop the beetroot. Finely chop one carrot and the onion. Grate the second carrot. Put the vegetables, bay leaf, stock and seasoning into a saucepan. Bring to the boil, reduce the heat and simmer for 1 hour. Taste the soup and adjust the seasoning.

Pour the borscht into individual soup bowls and top each serving with a spoonful of natural yogurt.

12 | *Minestrone*

Preparation time
25 minutes, plus
overnight soaking

Cooking time
1 hour 15 minutes

Serves 6

Calories
220 per portion

You will need
50 g / 2 oz dried haricot beans
1 onion, chopped
1 clove garlic, crushed
2 tablespoons oil
4 rashers rindless bacon, diced
1 (425-g / 15-oz) can tomatoes
1.15 litres / 2 pints chicken stock
1 leek, cut into rings
2 carrots, diced
¼ small white cabbage, finely
    shredded
salt and pepper
50 g / 2 oz pasta shapes
1 tablespoon grated Parmesan
    cheese to serve

Cover the haricot beans with plenty of cold water and soak overnight. Drain. Fry the onion and garlic in the oil in a large saucepan, then add the bacon and continue cooking for a further few minutes.

Stir in the tomatoes, stock and haricot beans, then bring to the boil, cover and simmer gently for 45 minutes. Add the leek, carrot and white cabbage and continue simmering for a further 15 minutes. Season to taste, add the pasta and cook for 10 minutes, or until the pasta is tender but firm.

Pour the minestrone into individual soup bowls and sprinkle each serving with Parmesan cheese.

Cook's Tip

Traditional borscht contains shredded cabbage and cubes of beef. Dice braising steak and add to the soup with the beetroot. Add the cabbage for the last 15 minutes cooking time.

Cook's Tip

To save on soaking time, substitute 1 (425-g / 15-oz) can white cannellini beans for the dried haricot beans. Add the drained canned beans to the soup with the pasta.

13 | Seafood Soup

Preparation time
15 minutes

Cooking time
30 minutes

Serves 6

Calories
245 per portion

You will need
600 ml / 1 pint water
350 g / 12 oz haddock
1 bay leaf
1 lemon, cut into wedges
salt and pepper
1 onion, chopped
2 cloves garlic, crushed
1 tablespoon oil
25 g / 1 oz plain flour
600 ml / 1 pint milk
350 g / 12 oz cooked peeled
   prawns and bottled mussels
   (mixed)
$\frac{1}{4}$ teaspoon ground mace
2 tablespoons lemon juice
2 tablespoons dry white wine
   (optional)
4 tablespoons single cream
croûtons to garnish

Bring the water, haddock, bay leaf, lemon wedges and seasoning to the boil and simmer gently for 15 minutes. Drain the fish, reserving the cooking liquid. Discard the bay leaf and lemon wedges. Skin, bone and flake the fish.

In a large saucepan, cook the onion and garlic in the oil until softened. Reduce the heat, add the flour, then gradually pour in the milk, stirring all the time. Add the seafood, mace, lemon juice, wine (if using) and seasoning to taste, simmer for 5 minutes, then add the fish and simmer for a further 5 minutes. Remove from heat. Stir in the cream. Garnish each serving with croûtons.

14 | White Fish Chowder

Preparation time
10 minutes

Cooking time
25–30 minutes

Serves 6

Calories
295 per portion

You will need
2 rashers bacon
450 g / 1 lb coley, haddock or cod
50 g / 2 oz butter or margarine
4 medium potatoes, peeled and
   diced
2 leeks, sliced into rings
50 g / 2 oz button mushrooms
600 ml / 1 pint milk
salt and pepper
pinch of grated nutmeg
1 (227-g / 8-oz) can tomatoes
1 tablespoon chopped parsley to
   garnish

Dice the bacon and fry in its own fat until crisp; remove from the pan. Cut the fish into small pieces, removing skin and bones.

Heat the butter or margarine in a saucepan, then add the fish, potato, leek and mushrooms. Cook for 2 minutes. Add the milk, then simmer gently for 15–20 minutes. Season with salt and pepper and the nutmeg. Stir in the bacon and tomatoes and heat through gently.

Pour the chowder into individual soup bowls and garnish with freshly chopped parsley.

Cook's Tip

Mace is the outer covering of the nutmeg. It is used to season savoury dishes like pâtés, baked meats and soups.

Freezer Tip

Frozen cod steaks are ideal for this chowder. Defrost for about 15 minutes, then cut into cubes and cook while still partially frozen.

15 | Soup with Fresh Greens

Preparation time
15 minutes

Cooking time
10–15 minutes

Serves 4

Calories
50 per portion

You will need
1.2 litres/2 pints water
1 onion, sliced
3 cloves garlic, sliced
3 tablespoons pounded dried
    shrimps
½ teaspoon shrimp paste
    (optional)
2 teaspoons soy sauce
1 teaspoon salt
225 g/8 oz fresh green leaves,
    washed (see Cook's Tip)

Put the water, onion and garlic in a large pan and bring to the boil. Lower the heat, then add the shrimps, shrimp paste, if used, soy sauce and salt. Stir well, then add the green leaves.

Boil for 5 minutes, taste and adjust the seasoning, then pour into a warmed soup tureen. Serve hot.

16 | Chicken and Sweetcorn Soup

Preparation time
10 minutes

Cooking time
20–25 minutes

Serves 4

Calories
120 per portion

You will need
900 ml/1½ pints clear broth (see
    Cook's Tip recipe 10) with a
    little of the cooked chicken
    reserved
350 g/12 oz sweetcorn kernels
salt and pepper
2 teaspoons cornflour (optional)
1 tablespoon water (optional)
chopped spring onions to garnish
    (optional)

Pour the skimmed stock into a large pan and add 225 g/8oz of the sweetcorn. Bring to the boil, add salt and pepper to taste, cover and simmer for 15 minutes. Blend the soup in a liquidizer or food processor until smooth, then return to the pan.

Reheat the soup and decide whether it is thick enough for your liking. If not, blend the cornflour with the water and stir it into the soup, then bring to the boil. Add the remaining sweetcorn and the reserved chopped chicken from preparing the stock. Simmer for 5 minutes, then taste and adjust the seasoning before serving, garnished with spring onions if liked.

Cook's Tip

This is an everyday soup which is quick and very easy to make. The dried shrimps can be pounded at home or bought ready-powdered, and the soup can be varied by adding different fresh green vegetable leaves: watercress, sorrel, spinach, cabbage, pea leaves or mustard leaves.

Cook's Tip

Crisp prawn crackers make a very tasty accompaniment to this soup.

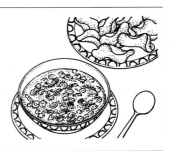

17 | *Grilled Grapefruit*

Preparation time
5 minutes, plus 10
minutes standing time

Cooking time
5 minutes

Serves 4

Calories
85 per portion

You will need
2 grapefruit
50 g / 2 oz brown sugar
2 tablespoons rum, brandy or
  vermouth
few sprigs of mint to decorate

Halve the grapefruit, loosen the segments from the skin
and from the centre with a grapefruit knife or other sharp
knife, so they are easy to remove. Sprinkle each half with
sugar. Pour over the rum, brandy or vermouth. Leave to
stand for 10 minutes to allow the sugar and alcohol to
soak right through the grapefruit.

Cook the grapefruit halves under a hot grill for about 5
minutes. Serve immediately decorated with a sprig of
fresh mint.

18 | *Melon and Black Grape Cocktail*

Preparation time
10 minutes, plus 1
hour to chill

Serves 4

Calories
50 per portion

You will need
1 small honeydew melon
225 g / 8 oz black grapes
2 teaspoons mint sauce
1 teaspoon caster sugar
few sprigs of mint to decorate

Halve the honeydew melon and scoop out the seeds. Use
a melon baller to remove the fruit in neat balls into a bowl.
Halve and remove the seeds from the black grapes. Add
the grape halves to the melon, then add the mint sauce
and sugar.

Cover the cocktail and chill for about an hour, tossing
occasionally. Check the flavour, adding a little more
sugar if required.

Serve the cocktail in glasses and decorate with fresh
mint.

Cook's Tip

*Using a sharp pointed knife,
cut around the middle of
the grapefruit in towards
the centre in a zig-zag
pattern. Pull the halves
apart gently. This sort of
edge is called vandyke.*

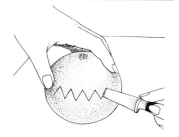

Cook's Tip

*For special occasions, frost
the tops of the glasses by
dipping the rims lightly in
beaten egg white then
sugar.*

19 | Vegetable Terrine

Preparation time
25 minutes

Cooking time
1 hour

Oven temperature
180 C, 350 F, gas 4

Serves 4

Calories
305 per portion

You will need
450 g / 1 lb carrots (peeled weight)
225 g / 8 oz broccoli
350 g / 12 oz cauliflower florets
salt and pepper
2 eggs
75 g / 3 oz Danish Havarti cheese,
   grated
1 teaspoon mild mustard
100 g / 4 oz fresh white
   breadcrumbs
75 g / 3 oz Danish Buko soft cheese
   with garlic
¼ teaspoon ground coriander
sage leaves to garnish (optional)

Line and butter a 900-g / 2-lb loaf tin. Cook the vegetables separately in boiling salted water until just tender. Drain, rinse in cold water and cool separately. Purée the cauliflower in a liquidiser until smooth. Add 1 egg, the Havarti cheese, mustard, seasoning and 50 g / 2 oz of the breadcrumbs. Turn into the prepared tin and smooth the surface. Arrange the broccoli in small florets on top. Liquidise the carrots until smooth. Add the remaining egg, seasoning, the garlic-flavoured cheese, coriander and the remaining breadcrumbs. Mix thoroughly. Spoon carefully over the broccoli and smooth the surface. Cover with buttered greaseproof paper and aluminium foil. Bake for 45–50 minutes or until firm. Remove from the oven and stand for 10 minutes. Turn out carefully, garnish and serve with a tomato sauce (see below).

20 | Stuffed Aubergines

Preparation time
10 minutes

Cooking time
45 60 minutes

Oven temperature
200 C, 400 F, gas 6

Serves 4

Calories
305 per portion

You will need
2 tablespoons oil
2 onions, chopped
2 cloves garlic, crushed
225 g / 8 oz cooked haricot beans
   (or use canned beans)
2 tomatoes, chopped
1 teaspoon basil
1 teaspoon thyme
2 teaspoons tomato purée
salt and pepper
2 aubergines
1 (397-g / 14-oz) can chopped
   tomatoes
225 g / 8 oz low-fat hard cheese,
   grated (for example Shape
   cheese)
watercress to garnish

Heat the oil in a saucepan. Add the onions and garlic and cook until soft but not browned. Stir in beans, tomatoes, herbs and tomato purée. Season well.

Cut the aubergines in half lengthways. Scoop out the flesh, chop this and add it to the beans; cook gently for 10 minutes. Meanwhile, parboil the aubergine shells for 5 minutes, drain well and fill with the bean mixture. Pour the tomatoes into a baking dish and arrange the aubergines on top. Sprinkle with cheese, cover with foil and bake for 20 minutes. Remove foil and cook for 15 minutes more. Garnish with watercress and serve with brown rice or potatoes.

Cook's Tip

To make a tomato sauce, place 2 (397-g / 14-oz) cans tomatoes with their juices in a pan. Add 50 g / 2 oz butter, 2–3 teaspoons sugar, a few drops of Tabasco and salt and pepper and mash the tomatoes as the mixture comes to the boil. Cook for 8–10 minutes until blended and thickened. Press through a sieve to remove seeds. Reheat as required.

Cook's Tip

A quick way of scooping out and chopping aubergines: cut in half and cut the middle criss-cross with a sharp knife. Carefully cut out the flesh or scoop out with a spoon.

21 | Smoked Trout Pâté

Preparation time
20 minutes, plus
chilling

Serves 4–6

Calories
210 per portion

You will need
75 g / 3 oz butter or margarine,
    softened
2 smoked trout, skinned and
    flaked
1 teaspoon finely grated lemon
    rind
150 ml / ¼ pint single cream
1 tablespoon horseradish sauce
1 teaspoon chopped fresh dill, or
    ½ teaspoon dried
1 teaspoon chopped fresh parsley
1–2 tablespoons lemon juice
pepper or cayenne pepper
lemon slices to garnish

Cream the butter until it is soft, then beat in the fish. Gradually incorporate the remaining ingredients until the pâté is smooth and light.

Alternatively, place all the ingredients in a liquidizer or food processor and work until smooth.

Spoon into individual pots or one large bowl. Cover with cling film and chill until ready to serve. Serve with lemon slices.

22 | Smoked Mackerel and Cream Cheese Pâté

Preparation time
20 minutes

Serves 4

Calories
607 per portion

You will need
350 g / 12 oz smoked mackerel
    fillets, skinned and flaked
75 g / 3 oz butter, softened
175 g / 6 oz full fat soft cheese
2 teaspoons lemon juice
1 tablespoon chopped fresh
    chives
pepper
4 small bay leaves to garnish

Cream together the butter and cheese, then stir in the fish, lemon juice, chives and pepper to taste. Beat until the mixture is smooth.

Divide the pâté between four individual ramekin dishes. Place a bay leaf in each dish to garnish. Serve with wholemeal toast if liked.

Cook's Tip

When time is short, this pâté can be served at room temperature as soon as it is made. If you don't have any dill, increase the amount of parsley or use finely chopped chives or spring onion tops.

Cook's Tip

Another attractive way to present this pâté is with a layer of melted butter poured over the top of each portion. Press a bay leaf into each before the butter sets. Cool, then cover with cling film. Refrigerate for up to two days.

23 | Potted Prawns

Preparation time
20 minutes, plus 30 minutes to chill

Cooking time
5 minutes

Serves 4

Calories
555 per portion

You will need
4 spring onions
450 g / 1 lb peeled cooked prawns
150 ml/¼ pint mayonnaise
2 teaspoons horseradish sauce
2 tablespoons lemon juice
pinch of cayenne
salt and pepper
100 g / 4 oz butter

Garnish
whole prawns
watercress sprigs
curly endive (optional)

Thinly slice the spring onions. Place 225 g/8 oz prawns in a liquidiser, add the mayonnaise, horseradish, spring onions and lemon juice. Blend the mixture to a paste. Mix the remaining prawns into the paste. Add the cayenne, salt and pepper. Press the prawn mixture into individual ramekins.

Melt the butter in a small saucepan, then pour it over the potted prawns, dividing the quantity evenly between the ramekins. Refrigerate until the butter is firm, about 30 minutes.

Garnish the potted prawns with whole prawns, watercress, and curly endive, if liked, and serve with hot buttered toast.

24 | Quick Taramasalata

Preparation time
10 minutes, plus 1 hour to chill

Serves 4

Calories
305 per portion

You will need
100 g / 4 oz smoked cod's roe
75 g / 3 oz fresh white bread
2 tablespoons milk
large clove of garlic, crushed
100 ml / 4 fl oz olive oil
juice of ½ lemon

Garnish
lemon slices
parsley sprigs

To retain pink flecks, skin the roe rather than scoop out the middle. Trim the crusts from the bread and soak the slices in the milk for 15 minutes, remove and squeeze dry. Mash with the cod's roe and crushed garlic.

Place the mixture in a liquidiser. Pour in the oil gradually, while blending, then add the lemon juice and blend until smooth. Chill for an hour before serving.

Garnish with lemon slices and parsley sprigs and serve the taramasalata with a selection of packeted savoury snacks and a green salad.

Microwave Tip

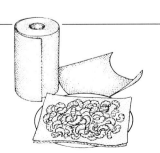

To defrost prawns, spread over a double thickness of absorbent kitchen paper. Cover with absorbent kitchen paper and cook on full power for about 3 minutes (for 450 g / 1 lb).

Cook's Tip

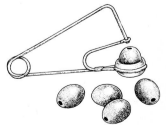

Serve stoned black olives and warm pitta bread with the taramasalata. To quickly stone olives use a cherry stoner.

25 | Mushrooms Indienne

Preparation time
10 minutes, plus 30 minutes to chill

Serves 4

Calories
100 per portion

You will need
150 ml/¼ pint soured cream or natural yogurt
1–2 teaspoons curry paste
1 tablespoon sieved mango chutney
salt and pepper
1 dessert apple, peeled, cored and chopped
175 g/6 oz button mushrooms
Chinese leaves, shredded
4 lemon slices to garnish

Mix together the cream and curry paste according to taste. Add the chutney, seasoning, apple and mushrooms and mix well. Chill for at least 30 minutes before serving.

Pile each portion on to a bed of shredded Chinese leaves and garnish with a twist of lemon.

Cook's Tip

Instead of the curry paste, you can use curry powder but halve the quantity. Cook the powder in a little butter in a small pan for 3 minutes before adding to the cream.

26 | Peanut Dip with Crudités

Preparation time
15–20 minutes

Cooking time
5 minutes

Serves 6

Calories
190 per portion

You will need
2 tablespoons sunflower oil
1 onion, finely chopped
2 cloves garlic, crushed
½ teaspoon chilli powder
1 teaspoon ground cumin
1 teaspoon ground coriander
6 tablespoons crunchy peanut butter
6 tablespoons water
1 teaspoon shoyu
1 teaspoon lemon juice

For the crudités
1 small cauliflower
1 bunch of radishes
1 red pepper, deseeded
6 celery sticks
6 carrots

Heat the oil in a small saucepan, add the onion and fry for a few minutes until softened. Add the garlic and spices, stir and cook for 1 minute. Mix in the peanut butter, then gradually blend in the water, stirring until thickened. Add the shoyu and lemon juice, stir well and leave to cool.

Break the cauliflower into florets and halve the radishes if large. Cut the remaining vegetables into long thin pieces.

Turn the dip into a small dish, place on a large plate and surround with the crudités.

Cook's Tip

Wholemeal grissini – Italian breadsticks – make excellent dippers, much favoured by children. If serving the dip for a child's party, eliminate the spices.

27 | Individual Onion Quiches

Preparation time
20 minutes

Cooking time
35 minutes

Oven temperature
200 C, 400 F, gas 6

Serves 4

Calories
625 per portion

You will need
225 g / 8 oz plain flour
pinch of salt
100 g / 4 oz margarine
2 tablespoons cold water

For the filling
2 large onions, sliced into rings
2 tablespoons oil
2 eggs
150 ml / ¼ pint milk
salt and pepper
100 g / 4 oz Cheddar cheese,
   grated

Garnish
onion rings (optional)
coriander sprigs (optional)

Sift the flour and salt into a mixing bowl. Rub in the fat until the mixture resembles fine breadcrumbs. Gradually add the water and form the mixture into a ball. Put the pastry on a lightly floured board. Roll it out and use to line four 11-cm / 4½-in quiche rings or flan dishes.

Cook the onion rings in the oil until soft. Beat the eggs lightly, then beat in the milk, season and add the cheese. Divide the onions equally amongst the quiches. Pour over the egg mixture.

Bake the quiches in a moderately hot oven for 30 minutes.

28 | Avocado Dip

Preparation time
10 minutes, plus 15 minutes to chill

Serves 4

Calories
130 per portion

You will need
1 onion
1 green chilli
1 tomato
2 avocados
juice of 1 lemon
1 or 2 cloves garlic, crushed
salt and pepper

Finely chop the onion. Slit, deseed, rinse, dry and finely chop the green chilli. Peel, deseed and chop the tomato.

Peel and stone the avocados. Mash to a chunky consistency in a bowl. Add the lemon juice, onion, garlic and chilli. Mix thoroughly, then season to taste with salt and pepper. Stir in the chopped tomato, then transfer the dip to a serving bowl or four individual bowls.

Chill for at least 15 minutes. Serve with taco chips, salted crisps, or vegetable crudités.

Freezer Tip

Place the cooled quiches on a baking tray, covered with cling film. Put in freezer until hard, then pack into two polythene bags, seal, label and return to the freezer. Use within 1 month.

Cook's Tip

Wash your hands well after handling chillies and do not rub your eyes when cutting them. The juice can irritate skin. Remove the hot seeds inside, and rinse the chillies under cold running water.

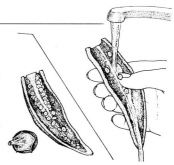

29 | Puff Pastry with Leeks

Preparation time
15 minutes

Cooking time
20 minutes

Oven temperature
220C, 425F, Gas 7

Serves 4

Calories
748 per portion

You will need
1 × 375-g /13-oz packet frozen
    puff pastry, thawed
1 egg, beaten
parsley sprigs to garnish

For the filling
50 g / 2 oz butter
350 g / 12 oz white part of leeks,
    thinly sliced and well washed
juice of ½ lemon
salt and pepper
150 ml / ¼ pint double cream

Roll out the pastry to a rectangle 26 × 150 cm / 10 × 6 inches. Cut into four pieces, each 13 × 7 ½ / 5 × 3 inches.

Score each piece lightly in a diamond pattern and brush the tops with the beaten egg. Place on a moistened baking sheet and bake in a preheated oven for 20 minutes until puffed and golden on top.

Meanwhile, prepare the filling. Melt the butter and cook the leeks for 10 minutes until soft but not browned. Add the lemon juice and salt and pepper to taste and stir well. Add the cream, bring to the boil, stirring constantly and cook for 2–3 minutes until lightly thickened.

When the pastry slices are cooked, remove from the oven and cut each one in half horizontally. Divide the leek mixture between the bottom halves of the pastry slices, then replace the pastry top. Garnish with parsley sprigs and serve at once.

Cook's Tip

Don't be tempted to use single cream to make the creamy leek filling or it may curdle when boiled.

30 | Leek Terrine with Walnuts and Feta

Preparation time
25 minutes, plus
chilling

Cooking time
10 minutes

Serves 6

Calories
264 per portion

You will need
20 small young leeks, roots and
    most of green parts trimmed
radicchio or other chicory leaves
75 g / 3 oz Feta cheese, crumbled
50 g / 2 oz walnut halves,
    chopped
salt and pepper

For the dressing
4 tablespoons olive oil
2 tablespoons walnut oil
2 tablespoons wine vinegar
2 tablespoons English mustard

Split the leeks horizontally to within 5 cm / 2 inches of the root end. Wash well. Boil the leeks in salted water for 10 minutes or until tender.

Layer a 450 g / 1 lb loaf tin with the leeks laid head to tail alternately, sprinking each layer with salt and pepper to taste. Place another tin inside the first, pressing down the leeks. Invert both tins so the liquid drains out. Chill for at least 4 hours with a 1 kg / 2 lb weight on top.

Meanwhile, to make the dressing, mix together all the ingredients and season with salt and pepper to taste. Set aside until needed.

Carefully turn out the leek terrine. Using a very sharp knife, cut into 6 thick slices. Place each slice on a plate and surround with the salad leaves. Scatter the walnuts and Feta cheese on top of the salad. Spoon over some dressing and serve.

Cook's Tip

This is an ideal dish for a dinner party because both the terrine and dressing can be made a day ahead and kept overnight in the refrigerator. Let the terrine come to room temperature before serving.

31 | Mushroom Vols-au-Vent

Preparation time
20 minutes

Cooking time
35 minutes

Oven temperature
220 C, 425 F, gas 7

Makes 12

Calories
130 per vol-au-vent

You will need
12 frozen puff pastry vol-au-vent cases
beaten egg to glaze

For the filling
1 tablespoon oil
1 onion, finely chopped
100 g / 4 oz carrot, diced
225 g / 8 oz mushrooms, sliced
2 tablespoons plain flour
200 ml / 7 fl oz skimmed milk
¼ teaspoon dried sage
salt and pepper
75 g / 3 oz Sage Derby cheese, cubed
salad ingredients to garnish

Place the vol-au-vent cases on a dampened baking tray. Brush with beaten egg and bake in a hot oven for 15–20 minutes, or as directed on the packet.

Heat the oil and cook the onion and carrot slowly in a covered pan for 5 minutes. Add the mushrooms and cook for a further 3 minutes. Stir in the flour and cook for 1 minute. Gradually add the milk and bring to the boil, stirring. Add the sage, seasoning and cheese. Spoon into the cooked vol-au-vent cases and serve at once, garnished with salad ingredients.

32 | Feta Parcels

Preparation time
30 minutes

Cooking time
35 minutes

Oven temperature
180 C, 350 F, gas 4

Makes 6

Calories
570 per parcel

You will need
150 g / 5 oz butter
1 large onion, chopped
675 g / 1½ lb frozen chopped spinach, defrosted and drained
225 g / 8 oz feta cheese
2 bunches spring onions, chopped
25 g / 1 oz chopped parsley
1 tablespoon dill
salt and pepper
2 eggs, beaten
10 sheets filo pastry

Melt 25 g / 1 oz of the butter and cook the onion for 5 minutes until softened. Place the spinach in a bowl, crumble the cheese over it, then stir in the spring onions, parsley, dill, seasoning and eggs and mix well.

Melt the remaining butter. Unwrap the filo pastry sheets. Place one on the work surface and brush with some of the butter, cover with a second sheet and brush with butter. Continue until 5 sheets have been brushed with butter. Brush the top sheet. (Cover any pastry not being used with a cloth.) Cut the layered pastry into three, widthways. Divide half of the spinach mixture between the strips leaving a 2.5-cm / 1-in border down the long edges. Fold in the long edges, brush with butter and fold up the short edges to make parcels 13 × 9 cm / 5 × 3½ in. Place on a baking tray, mark the tops and brush with butter.

Repeat with the remaining filo pastry sheets and spinach mixture. Bake for 25–30 minutes until golden.

Cook's Tip

Don't save vols-au-vent for parties and weddings. With interesting fillings they make tasty suppers or quick starters for unexpected guests. Children enjoy them too, particularly if they can choose their own fillings.

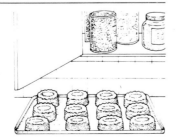

Cook's Tip

Filo pastry is available in continental delicatessens and large supermarkets. If it's not to hand, the parcels may be made with puff pastry instead. Use 1 (368-g / 13-oz) packet, defrosted. Cut it in half and roll each piece to a rectangle 30 × **37.5 cm / 12 × 15 in. The parcels will be slightly smaller.**

33 | Cheese and Tuna Muffins

Preparation time
10 minutes

Cooking time
15–20 minutes

Oven temperature
190C, 375F, Gas 5

Makes 8

Calories
233 per portion

You will need
4 wholemeal or cheese muffins, split
1 onion, peeled and sliced into rings
2 × 200-g / 7-oz cans tuna in brine, drained and flaked
50 g / 2 oz alfalfa sprouts
3 tablespoons mayonnaise
3 tablespoons soured cream
3 tablespoons sunflower seeds
salt and pepper
75 g / 3 oz Cheddar cheese, grated
2 tomatoes, thinly sliced

Toast the muffins on their cut sides under a preheated hot grill. Place on a large baking sheet and top each with an equal quantity of the onion.

Mix the tuna with the alfalfa sprouts, mayonnaise, soured cream, sunflower seeds and salt and pepper to taste, blending well. Spread equally over the muffin halves. Sprinkle with the cheese and top each with a slice of tomato.

Cook in a preheated oven for 15–20 minutes until golden, bubbly and heated through. Serve while still hot.

34 | Salami and Mozzarella Snack Toasts

Preparation time
15 minutes

Cooking time
10 minutes

Makes 4

Calories
274 per portion

You will need
4 thick slices crusty bread
100 g / 4 oz salami, rinded and thinly sliced
4 tomatoes, skinned and sliced
salt and pepper
1 green or yellow pepper, cored, seeded and sliced
75 g / 3 oz Mozzarella cheese, thinly sliced
1 teaspoon dried mixed herbs
4–8 small black olives
parsley sprigs to garnish

Place the bread under a preheated hot grill and toast until golden on one side.

Turn the bread slices over and cover with the salami and tomatoes, adding salt and pepper to taste.

Top with the pepper slices and cheese. Sprinkle with the herbs, and place under a preheated moderate grill and toast for 10 minutes until cooked through and bubbly. Serve hot, topped with the black olives and garnished with parsley sprigs.

Cook's Tip

To reduce the calories in this tasty snack, use low-fat mayonnaise. Also, Dutch Edam cheese contains fewer calories than Cheddar, a high-fat cheese.

Cook's Tip

Vary the flavour of this Italian-style snack each time you make it by using a different type of salami. Supermarkets stock excellent choices from France as well as Italy.

35 | Stuffed French Bread

Preparation time
25 minutes

Serves 3

Calories
631 per portion

You will need
1 large long crusty French stick
25 g / 1 oz butter, softened
2 lettuce leaves, shredded
3 slices Mortadella, rinded and rolled
25 g / 1 oz salami, rinded and rolled into cornets
50 g / 2 oz smoked cheese, rinded and sliced
50 g / 2 oz blue cheese, sliced
1 hard-boiled egg, shelled
1 large beefsteak tomato

For the coleslaw
100 g / 4 oz white cabbage, grated
25 g / 1 oz onion, grated
1 small carrot, grated
1 stick celery, chopped
1 tablespoon raisins
3 walnut halves, roughly chopped
3–4 tablespoons mayonnaise

To make the coleslaw, mix the cabbage with the onion, carrot, celery, raisins, walnuts and mayonnaise. Mix well.

Slice the loaf in half horizontally. Butter the inside of the loaf thinly. Spread the coleslaw along the length of the bottom half of the loaf and top with the lettuce, Mortadella, salami, smoked cheese, blue cheese, sliced egg and tomato, arranging attractively.

Press firmly together and cut vertically into 3 thick sections to serve.

36 | Baked Continental Loaf

Preparation time
10 minutes

Cooking time
15–20 minutes

Oven temperature
190C, 375F, Gas 5

Serves 4

Calories
395 per portion

You will need
1 long crusty loaf of bread
50 g / 2 oz butter, softened
1 garlic clove, peeled and crushed
8 slices quick-melting cheese
8 slices cooked Continental-style ham
8 slices garlic sausage
2 tomatoes, thinly sliced

Make eight crosswise cuts equally along the length of the loaf almost to the base.

Cream the butter with the garlic and spread thinly between the slices of bread. Place a slice of cheese, ham, garlic sausage and tomato in each cut. Press gently together to re-form the loaf shape.

Cover the loaf loosely with foil. Place in a preheated oven and cook for 10–15 minutes.

Remove the top of the foil and cook for a further 5 minutes or until golden and bubbly. Pull apart or cut between the slices of bread to serve

Cook's Tip

Give this snack an Oriental flavour by substituting shredded Chinese leaves for the cabbage, bean-sprouts for the celery and water chestnuts for the onions. Water chestnuts are available canned in most supermarkets.

Cook's Tip

Using a wholemeal loaf of bread adds extra flavour as well as valuable dietary fibre.

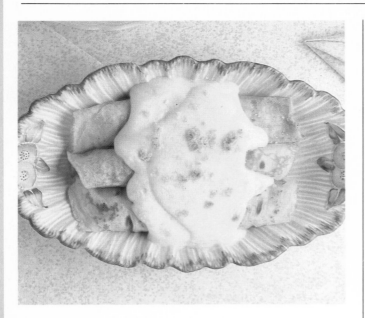

37 | Stuffed Pancakes

Preparation time
50 minutes

Cooking time
1 hour 5 minutes

Oven temperature
200 C, 400 F, gas 6

Serves 5

Calories
705 per portion

You will need
For the batter
100 g/4 oz plain flour
pinch of salt
1 egg, plus 1 yolk, beaten
300 ml/½ pint milk
1 tablespoon vegetable oil
50 g/2 oz lard or oil for frying

For the filling
10 leeks, trimmed, slit and washed

For the sauce
75 g/3 oz butter or margarine
75 g/3 oz plain flour
1 litre/1¾ pints milk
salt and pepper
125 g/5 oz Parmesan cheese,
grated

To make the batter, place all the ingredients in a liquid-iser and blend until smooth. Use to make 10 pancakes (see Cook's Tip). Set the leeks in a steamer over a pan of boiling water. Cover and cook for 10 minutes until tender. Set aside. To make the sauce, melt the butter or margarine in a saucepan over a low heat, then add the flour. Cook for 2 minutes, stirring. Gradually add the milk and bring the sauce to the boil, stirring constantly. Simmer gently for 2–3 minutes. Season to taste. Cool a little and add 100 g/4 oz of the cheese.

Place a leek and a little sauce on each pancake. Roll up and arrange in a greased, ovenproof dish. Pour over remaining sauce and sprinkle with the 25 g/1 oz cheese. Bake in a moderately hot oven for 25–30 minutes.

Cook's Tip

For good pancakes use a frying pan that does not stick. Grease with oil, heat slowly until very hot, then pour in a little batter. Tilt pan to cover the base, cook to set, turn the pancake and brown the second side.

38 | Frittata

Preparation time
15 minutes

Cooking time
7 minutes

Serves 2

Calories
310 per portion

You will need
25 g/1 oz butter
4 eggs, beaten
275 g/10 oz spinach, cooked and
lightly chopped, or 100 g/4 oz
frozen spinach, cooked
3 firm tomatoes, peeled and
coarsely chopped
100 g/4 oz cooked potatoes, diced,
or 75 g/3 oz cooked brown rice
salt and pepper
1 teaspoon chopped sage or
¼ teaspoon dried sage
few drops of Tabasco sauce

Heat half the butter in a large frying pan until sizzling. Pour in the beaten eggs and stir for a few seconds. Allow the eggs to settle in the pan and then distribute the spinach, tomatoes and potatoes or rice evenly over the surface. Sprinkle with salt, pepper, sage and Tabasco sauce. Cook gently for about 4 minutes until the underside is set and golden brown. Gently lift the edge with a fish slice to check. When the underside is done, tip the omelette out on to a large plate so that the cooked side is on top.

Add the remaining butter to the pan and melt, coating the base. Slide the omelette back into the pan and cook the other side for about 3 minutes. Cut into quarters and serve hot or cold.

Cook's Tip

Butter burns more readily than oil and must be carefully watched while melting. To alleviate this problem, use a mixture of butter and oil when frying the frittata.

39 | Corn Fritters

Preparation time	**You will need**
10 minutes	40 g / 1½ oz wholemeal flour
	225 g / 8 oz canned sweetcorn,
Cooking time	drained
15 minutes	2 tablespoons snipped chives
	2 eggs, beaten
	3 tablespoons water
Serves 4	25 g / 1 oz butter
	225 g / 8 oz mushrooms, sliced
Calories	225 g / 8 oz tomatoes, peeled and
235 per portion	chopped
	1 tablespoon chopped parsley
	salt and pepper
	vegetable oil for cooking

Put the flour in a bowl, stir in the sweetcorn and chives, reserving a small quantity for garnish, and beat in the eggs. Add enough water to make a thick batter and transfer to a jug.

Heat the butter in a saucepan and cook the mushrooms for 3 minutes. Stir in the tomatoes, parsley and salt and pepper and set aside.

Heat a little vegetable oil in a heavy-based frying pan or griddle until hot. Pour spoonfuls of the batter on to the pan and cook quickly until golden underneath and just set on top. Turn over and quickly cook the other side. Drain on absorbent kitchen paper and keep warm while cooking the remaining batter.

Towards the end of cooking, return the mushroom mixture to the heat and warm through gently. Serve the fritters topped with the mushroom mixture and garnished with the reserved snipped chives.

Cook's Tip

Only a little oil is needed for cooking the fritters, so either brush it on with a bristle brush or use a pad of absorbent kitchen paper to rub it on, taking care not to burn your fingers!

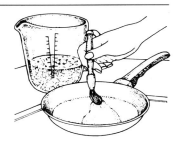

40 | Vegetable Kebabs

Preparation time	**You will need**
15 minutes	450 g / 1 lb small new potatoes,
	scrubbed
Cooking time	1 medium green pepper,
25 minutes	deseeded
	1 large aubergine, cubed
Serves 4	450 g / 1 lb small onions
	8 bay leaves
Calories	16 button mushrooms
270 per portion	4 tablespoons olive oil
	juice of ½ lemon
	1 clove garlic, crushed
	1 teaspoon tomato purée
	½ teaspoon oregano
	salt and pepper

Cook the potatoes for 5 minutes in boiling water. Drain thoroughly. Cut the pepper into chunks. Thread the potatoes, pepper, aubergine, onions, bay leaves and mushrooms on to 8 skewers.

Mix together the oil, lemon juice, garlic, tomato purée, oregano and salt and pepper. Brush the kebabs all over with this mixture and cook them on a barbecue for about 10 minutes each side, basting with more of the oil mixture during cooking. Alternatively cook the kebabs under a moderately hot grill for a similar time, turning once.

Cook's Tip

Serve the kebabs with a barbecue sauce. Sauté 1 onion and 1 clove garlic with 1 celery stick in a little oil. Add 175 g / 6 oz canned chopped tomatoes, 1 tablespoon tomato purée, 1 teaspoon prepared mustard, 1 teaspoon *soy sauce and 1 teaspoon brown sugar. Simmer for 20 minutes. Serve hot.*

41 | Eggs Mimosa

Preparation time
20 minutes

Cooking time
30 minutes

Serves 6

Calories
322 per portion

You will need
12 hard-boiled eggs, shelled and
 quartered
50 g / 2 oz butter
2 Spanish onions, peeled and
 thinly sliced
50 g / 2 oz plain flour
600 ml / 1 pint milk
salt and pepper
2 tablespoons chopping fresh
 parsley to garnish

Separate the yolks from the whites of the hard-boiled
eggs and pass the yolks through a nylon sieve. Place in
separate bowls, cover and keep warm.

Melt the butter and sweat the onions gently until soft,
but not browned.

Stir in the flour and cook for 2–3 minutes. Remove
from the heat and gradually stir in the milk. Cook, stirring,
until the sauce comes to the boil, then simmer gently for
4–5 minutes. Add salt and pepper to taste.

Arrange the egg whites in the base of a serving dish,
then pour over the sauce. Cover with the sieved egg yolk,
then make a pattern with the parsley to garnish. Serve at
once.

42 | Eggs Stuffed with Peppers

Preparation time
15 minutes

Cooking time
5 minutes

Serves 4
as a starter

Calories
60 per portion

You will need
4 hard-boiled eggs, shelled
1 small red pepper, cored and
 seeded
2 tablespoons olive oil
2 teaspoons capers, well drained
 and finely chopped
4 teaspoons finely chopped fresh
 parsley
2 anchovy fillets, finely chopped
1 teaspoon Dijon mustard
salt and pepper
shredded lettuce to serve

Cut the eggs in half and remove the yolks. Sieve the yolks
into a bowl through a fine nylon sieve.

Plunge the pepper into a pan of boiling salted water
and cook for 5 minutes. Drain and dry with a paper towel.
Cut sixteen strips from the pepper and finely chop the remainder.

Add the chopped pepper to the egg yolks with the olive
oil, capers, parsley, anchovies, mustard and salt and pepper to taste. Mix well.

Spoon the mixture into the egg white halves and top
each with two strips of pepper. Serve the eggs on a bed
of shredded lettuce.

Cook's Tip

*Use the back of a wooden
spoon to push the yolks
through the sieve. If you don't
have a fine nylon sieve, the
egg yolks can be finely
chopped with a sharp knife.*

Cook's Tip

*This versatile recipe is suitable
for serving as a light lunch
dish for two with a salad, or
as part of a buffet for a party.
The stuffed eggs can be
prepared up to six hours in
advance. Cover and chill until
ready to serve.*

43 | *Classic Greek Salad*

Preparation time
15 minutes, plus 30–60 minutes to stand

Serves 4

Calories
125 per portion

You will need
1 medium onion, sliced and
    separated into rings
1 tablespoon olive oil
1 tablespoon wine vinegar
salt and pepper
4 tomatoes, thinly sliced
½ cucumber, peeled and diced
10–12 black olives (optional)
100 g/4 oz feta cheese or other
    white, crumbly cheese, diced

Put the onion into a bowl with the oil, vinegar and a little salt and pepper. Mix well, then leave to stand for 30–60 minutes to allow the onion to soften slightly. Stir occasionally.

Add the tomatoes, cucumber, olives and cheese, mixing gently to distribute all the ingredients. Serve at once.

44 | *Smoked Cheese and Nut Salad*

Preparation time
15 minutes

Serves 6

Calories
270 per portion

You will need
50 g/2 oz hazelnuts, coarsely
    chopped
6 tablespoons vegetable oil
2 tablespoons wine vinegar
salt and pepper
pinch of cayenne
½ teaspoon prepared English
    mustard
½ teaspoon sugar
1 crisp lettuce, shredded
1 head radicchio, separated into
    leaves
2 dessert apples
1 tablespoon lemon juice
150 g/5 oz German smoked
    cheese, cut into 1-cm/½-inch
    cubes
watercress to garnish

To make the dressing, toast the chopped hazelnuts under a medium grill until evenly browned. Cool. Put oil, vinegar, salt and pepper, cayenne, mustard and sugar into a screwtop jar, add the hazelnuts and shake for 1 minute until well mixed.

Arrange the lettuce and radicchio on 6 individual plates. Cut the apples into 1-cm/½-in cubes, toss in the lemon juice and arrange with the cubes of cheese on top of the salad. Spoon the dressing over the cheese and apple just before serving and garnish with sprigs of watercress.

Cook's Tip

Feta cheese has a salty, distinct flavour which perfectly complements the other ingredients in this salad. Alternatively, you can use another mild, crumbly cheese such as Cheshire. For a creamy texture, try mozzarella.

Cook's Tip

An unusual colourful starter using radicchio. The same quantities will serve 2–3 as a main meal salad.

45 | Watercress and Brie Quiche

Preparation time
25 minutes

Cooking time
50 minutes

Oven temperature
200 C, 400 F, gas 6
then
180 C, 350 F, gas 4

Serves 6

Calories
445 per portion

You will need
For the pastry
100 g/4 oz plain flour
100 g/4 oz wholemeal flour
½ teaspoon salt
50 g/2 oz concentrated butter,
    softened
25 g/1 oz lard
about 3 tablespoons water

For the filling
275 g/10 oz ripe Brie cheese
300 ml/½ pint milk
100 g/4 oz watercress, trimmed
3 eggs, beaten
1 teaspoon mustard powder
freshly ground black pepper

Sift the flours and salt into a bowl or food processor, adding the bran remaining in the sieve to the bowl. Rub in the fats or process until the mixture resembles breadcrumbs. Add just enough water to mix to a firm dough. Roll out on a lightly floured surface and use to line a 23-cm/9-in loose-bottomed flan tin. Bake blind in a moderately hot oven for 10 minutes (see Cook's Tip).

Meanwhile remove the rind from the Brie. Dice the cheese, place in a saucepan with the milk and stir over a low heat until blended. Remove from the heat, stir in the watercress, beaten eggs, mustard and seasoning. Pour into the flan case and cook in a moderate oven for 35 minutes. Cool slightly before removing from the tin.

Cook's Tip

To bake blind, line the pie shell with greaseproof paper and fill with baking beans. Bake in a moderately hot oven for 10 minutes, then remove paper and beans. Proceed as in the recipe above. If, however, the pie shell is to have a cold (or separately cooked) filling, bake for 15 minutes with the beans, and a further 5 minutes after the beans and paper have been removed.

46 | Rainbow Quiche

Preparation time
25 minutes

Cooking time
35 40 minutes

Oven temperature
220 C, 425 F, gas 7
then
190 C, 375 F, gas 5

Serves 4

Calories
555 per portion

You will need
For the pastry
100 g/4 oz wholemeal flour
50 g/2 oz plain flour
pinch of salt
50 g/2 oz concentrated butter,
    softened
2 tablespoons poppy seeds
2 3 tablespoons water

For the filling
15 g/½ oz concentrated butter
1 red onion, sliced
175 g/6 oz red, green or yellow
    pepper, deseeded and sliced
1 courgette, sliced
1 tablespoon chopped basil
freshly ground black pepper
100 g/4 oz Cheddar cheese, grated
1 tomato, sliced
3 eggs
150 ml/¼ pint single cream
basil leaves to garnish (optional)

Mix the flours and salt in a large bowl and rub in the butter. Stir in the poppy seeds and enough water to mix to a firm dough. Roll out and use to line a 19-cm/7½-in flan tin. Melt the butter for the filling in a large pan and fry the onion, pepper and courgette until softened. Place in the flan case with the basil, black pepper, grated cheese and tomato. Beat the eggs and cream and pour over. Cook in a hot oven for 15 minutes, reducing to moderately hot for a further 15 minutes, until set. Garnish with basil if liked.

Cook's Tip

If possible, do use the red or purple onion, and red, yellow or green peppers, or even a combination, to make this quiche live up to its name.

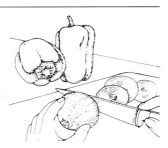

47 | Blue Cheese Soufflé

Preparation time
15 minutes

Cooking time
30 35 minutes

Oven temperature
200 C, 400 F, gas 6

Serves 4

Calories
310 per portion

You will need
40 g / 1½ oz butter
25 g / 1 oz plain flour
300 ml / ½ pint milk
pinch of grated nutmeg
4 egg yolks
100 g / 4 oz Danish blue cheese, crumbled
3 egg whites
salt and pepper

Melt the butter in a pan and use a little to brush the inside of a 1.4-litre/2½-pint soufflé dish. Stir the flour into the remaining butter; cook for 1 minute. Gradually stir in the milk, bring to the boil and cook for 2 minutes, stirring constantly. Add the nutmeg and allow to cool slightly. Beat in the egg yolks and cheese. Whisk the egg whites until stiff, lightly fold into the sauce and season to taste.

Turn into the prepared soufflé dish and cook in a moderately hot oven for 25–30 minutes until well risen and golden brown. Serve at once with green vegetables or a salad.

48 | Surprise Soufflé

Preparation time
20 minutes

Cooking time
1 hour

Oven temperature
190 C, 375 F, gas 5

Serves 4

Calories
475 per portion

You will need
4 large carrots, thickly sliced
3 large potatoes, peeled and cut into 1-cm/½-in dice
1 small turnip, cut into 1-cm/½-in dice
1 large onion, chopped
salt and pepper
8 tomatoes, peeled and deseeded
25 g / 1 oz butter
25 g / 1 oz plain flour
½ teaspoon mustard powder
300 ml / ½ pint milk
3 eggs, separated
100 g / 4 oz Cheddar cheese, grated
1 tablespoon chopped parsley to garnish (optional)

Cook the carrots, potatoes, turnip and onion in a pan of boiling salted water for 15 minutes. Drain and season to taste, then place in a 1.75-litre/3-pint ovenproof soufflé dish. Purée the tomatoes with a little seasoning and pour over the vegetables.

Melt the butter in a pan over a low heat, then add the flour and mustard powder. Cook for 2 minutes, stirring. Gradually add the milk and bring the sauce to the boil, stirring constantly. Simmer gently for 2–3 minutes. Allow it to cool slightly, then beat in the egg yolks and cheese. Whisk the egg whites until stiff and fold into the sauce. Pour the sauce over the vegetables in the soufflé dish. Bake in a moderately hot oven for about 40 minutes until risen and golden. Garnish with parsley before serving, if using.

Cook's Tip

When serving a soufflé, use a large serving spoon to reach down to the lightly cooked mixture at the bottom of the dish. Each portion should also include some of the crust.

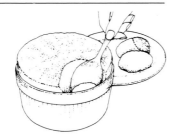

Cook's Tip

The surprise in this soufflé is the vegetable mixture at the bottom of the dish, which makes the soufflé sufficiently substantial to serve on its own.

49 | *Samosas*

Preparation time
20–25 minutes

Cooking time
25–30 minutes

Makes 10

Calories
255 per samosa

You will need
225 g/8 oz minced beef or lamb
1 onion, finely chopped
1 small pepper, deseeded and
    finely chopped
1 small carrot, diced
1 small potato, diced
2 cloves garlic, crushed
1½ tablespoons garam masala
salt and pepper
225 g/8 oz self-raising flour
4 tablespoons oil, plus oil for
    deep frying
1 egg
2 tablespoons water

Cook the meat and onion gently until the fat runs. Add the vegetables and seasoning and simmer for 10 minutes, stirring frequently. Leave to cool.

Sift the flour and a pinch of salt into a bowl. Mix in the 4 tablespoons oil, the egg and water to make a dough. Knead gently on a lightly floured surface until smooth. Divide into ten equal portions and roll out each portion to a 13-cm/5-in square. Place some of the filling in the middle of each square. Dampen the edges with water, fold one top corner over to the opposite corner and seal the edges to form a triangular pasty.

Heat the oil for deep frying and fry the samosas, a few at a time, for about 5 minutes or until golden. Drain on absorbent kitchen paper and keep warm while cooking the remainder. Garnish the samosas as illustrated and serve hot with a cucumber raita. (See Cook's Tip below.)

50 | *Sausage Plait*

Preparation time
10–15 minutes

Cooking time
40–45 minutes

Oven temperature
190 C, 375 F, gas 5

Serves 4

Calories
790 per portion

You will need
1 (368-g/13-oz) packet frozen
    puff pastry, defrosted
beaten egg to glaze

For the filling
450 g/1 lb sausagemeat
1 onion, finely chopped
1 tablespoon chutney
1 teaspoon dried sage
salt and pepper

Roll out the pastry to an oblong measuring 25 cm × 35 cm/10 × 14 in. Mix all the filling ingredients together, season well. Arrange the filling down the middle of the pastry. Cut the edges of the pastry diagonally into 2.5-cm/1-in strips, up to the filling. Fold these strips of pastry over the filling to form a plait, dampening the edges with water in order to hold them in place.

Brush with a little beaten egg and bake in a moderately hot oven for 40–45 minutes. Serve hot or cold, with a salad.

Cook's Tip

To make a raita, coarsely grate ¼ cucumber. Put in a sieve, sprinkle with salt and drain over a bowl. Squeeze out liquid, then mix with 150 ml/¼ pint chilled natural yogurt and 1 teaspoon chopped mint.

Cook's Tip

Add 100 g/4 oz finely diced mature Cheddar cheese to the filling. Continue as above.

51 | Spanish-style Omelette

Preparation time
20 minutes

Cooking time
15 minutes

Serves 4

Calories
387 per portion

You will need
50 g / 2 oz butter
1 large onion, peeled and sliced
100 g / 4 oz bacon, rinded and chopped
225 g / 8 oz cooked potatoes, peeled and diced
1 red pepper, cored, seeded and chopped
1 green pepper, cored, seeded and chopped
4 eggs, beaten
salt and pepper
1 teaspoon dried marjoram
50 g / 2 oz Cheddar cheese, grated
6 stuffed green olives, sliced
1 teaspoon paprika

Melt the butter and fry the onion and bacon until crisp and lightly browned.

Add the potatoes and peppers and cook for 2 minutes. Beat the eggs with salt and pepper to taste and the marjoram. Pour into the pan and cook until the mixture is almost set.

Sprinkle with the cheese, olives and paprika. Place under a preheated hot grill for 3 minutes until golden. Serve hot, with warm crusty bread and a salad.

Cook's Tip

This colourful omelette is filling enough to make a light meal. Serve it with crusty white bread and a salad with an olive oil and vinegar dressing.

52 | Piperade Tomatoes

Preparation time
10 minutes, plus cooling

Cooking time
20 minutes

Makes 4

Calories
264 per portion

You will need
4 large tomatoes, preferably Mediterranean
50 g / 2 oz butter
2 rashers streaky bacon, rinded and chopped
1 shallot, peeled and finely chopped
1 small red or green pepper, cored, seeded and diced
4 eggs, lightly beaten
salt and pepper
lettuce leaves to serve

Slice the tops off the tomatoes, and reserve as lids. Scoop out the insides of the tomatoes (a grapefruit knife makes this very easy) and chop up the flesh.

Melt 25 g / 1 oz butter and fry the bacon, shallot and pepper for 5 minutes. Add the tomato flesh and simmer for 10 minutes, stirring occasionally, until reduced to a thick purée.

In another pan, melt the remaining butter and pour in the eggs. Cook gently, stirring until the eggs are scrambled. Stir the piperade mixture into the scrambled eggs and add salt and pepper to taste. Leave to cool.

Fill the tomato cases with the cold piperade and replace the lids. Serve on a bed of lettuce.

Cook's Tip

Piperade, sautéed peppers with scrambled eggs, is a classic dish from the Basque region of Spain along the Pyrenees mountains. These Mediterranean-style tomatoes can be served either as a starter or light main course.

FISH AND SHELLFISH

Many people are discovering that fish is the perfect food. Not only is it delicious, and quick to cook, fish is good for you as well. Low in calories but highly nutritious and easy to digest, fish dishes get top marks in a healthy diet. The naturally fine flavour and delicate texture of white fish is the basis of dishes such as Buttery Fried Plaice with Fried Parsley or Haddock Crumble, which are easy to prepare and good to eat. These are perfect for family meals, but versatile fish is the centrepiece of some classic dishes too, such as Plaice Veronique and Haddock and Spinach Roulade. Many of the recipes in this chapter are ideal for entertaining: try Salmon with Caper and Parsley Sauce, or Halibut with Raisins and Olives for a special dinner party.

There are recipes here for fish that's steamed, baked, fried and grilled. This versatility of cooking method extends to the way fish combines so well with other flavourings, in Smoked Haddock and Orange Kebabs with Rice, for example, or Whiting and Fennel Soufflés. For a summer lunch or supper dish, introduce Mediterranean specialities such as Prawn Risotto or Squid with Herbs. Many of the most exciting recipes for fish come from Oriental cooks, who place great value on nutritious fresh foods that can be speedily cooked. Try tender Fillets of Sole with Mushrooms then move on to more adventurous ideas such as Braised Fish with Black Bean Sauce.

53 | Haddock Crumble

Preparation time
20 minutes

Cooking time
30 minutes

Oven temperature
200 C, 400 F, gas 6

Serves 4

Calories
740 per portion

You will need
675 g/ 1½ lb haddock fillets
6 tablespoons water
salt and pepper
For the sauce
1 small onion, chopped
50 g/ 2 oz butter
40 g/ 1½ oz plain flour
600 ml/ 1 pint milk
juice of ½ lemon
50 g/ 2 oz mature Cheddar cheese, grated
For the topping
50 g/ 2 oz butter or margarine
100 g/ 4 oz plain flour
50 g/ 2 oz jumbo oats
1 tablespoon chopped fresh dill
knob of butter
dill sprig to garnish

Put the haddock, water and seasoning in a pan. Cover and poach for 5 minutes. Reserve any liquor and flake the fish, discarding skin. Fry onion in butter for 3 minutes, then add the flour. Gradually stir in the milk. Bring the sauce to the boil, add the lemon juice, seasoning and strained fish liquor. Simmer for 2 minutes. Add the cheese and fish to the sauce, then pour into an ovenproof dish.

Rub the fat into the flour until the mixture resembles fine breadcrumbs. Stir in oats, dill and seasoning. Spread on top of the fish. Dot with butter and bake in a moderately hot oven for 30 minutes or until the crumble is golden. Garnish with dill.

54 | Plaice Véronique

Preparation time
10 minutes

Cooking time
15 minutes

Oven temperature
190 C, 375 F, gas 5

Serves 4

Calories
315 per portion

You will need
8 medium plaice fillets, skinned
salt and pepper
150 ml/ ¼ pint dry white wine
1 tablespoon lemon juice
100 g/ 4 oz seedless grapes, plus
  a few extra to garnish
  (optional)
25 g/ 1 oz butter or margarine
25 g/ 1 oz plain flour
150 ml/ ¼ pint milk

Roll up each fillet skinned side inwards. Place the fish rolls in a greased ovenproof dish. Season the fish with salt and pepper, pour over the wine and lemon juice. Cover and bake in a moderately hot oven for about 15 minutes, or until the fish flakes easily when tested with the point of a knife. Transfer the fish to a serving dish and keep warm. Reserve the cooking liquor for the sauce.

Place the grapes in boiling water, boil for one minute, then drain. Heat the butter or margarine over a gentle heat, add the flour, then gradually add the milk, seasoning and reserved cooking liquor, stirring continuously. Bring the sauce to the boil, reduce the heat and simmer gently for 2 minutes, stirring occasionally. Pour the sauce over the fish and garnish with the grapes adding a few unblanched grapes if you like. Serve at once.

Cook's Tip

To skin fish fillets, place skin side down on a board. Rub salt on your fingers to hold the tail end. With a sharp knife cut at an acute angle, using a sawing motion between the flesh and skin.

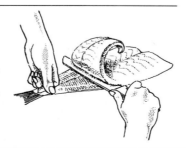

Microwave Tip

Arrange the rolls round a shallow dish. Cover with cling film and microwave for 5 minutes on full power. Mix in remaining ingredients, cover and cook for 5 minutes. Add grapes, cook 1 minute and serve.

55 | Hake Paprika

Preparation time
15 minutes

Cooking time
30–35 minutes

Oven temperature
190C, 375F, Gas 5

Serves 4

Calories
286 per portion

You will need
75 g / 3 oz butter
2 large onions, peeled and sliced
3 canned pimientos, drained and
    chopped
4 hake portions, thawed if frozen
salt and pepper
300 ml / ½ pint plain yogurt
2 teaspoons paprika

For the garnish
croûtons
parsley sprigs

Melt 50 g / 2 oz of the butter and fry the onions for 5 minutes until softened. Add the pimientos and mix well.

Spoon half of the onion mixture into a greased oven-proof dish. Top with the fish and sprinkle with salt and pepper to taste. Dot with the remaining butter. Place in a preheated oven and cook, uncovered, for 15 minutes.

Top with the remaining onion mixture. Mix the yogurt with the paprika and pour over the fish. Bake for a further 10–15 minutes. Garnish with croûtons and parsley sprigs. Serve at once.

Cook's Tip

Substitute haddock or whiting portions for the hake. Using Greek yogurt will produce a richer sauce.

56 | Halibut with Raisins and Olives

Preparation time
10 minutes

Cooking time
20 minutes

Serves 4

Calories
428 per portion

You will need
4 small halibut steaks, or 2 large
    steaks, halved
seasoned plain flour
4 tablespoons olive oil for frying
2 garlic cloves, peeled and
    crushed
2 small onions, peeled and
    chopped
2 sticks celery, chopped
50 g / 2 oz seedless raisins
100 g / 4 oz stoned green olives
125 ml / 4 fl oz white wine
salt and pepper
celery leaves to garnish

Wash the halibut and pat dry with paper towels. Toss in seasoned flour, shaking off any excess.

Heat the oil and fry the fish for 10–12 minutes, turning once, until golden brown and cooked through. Transfer the fish to a serving plate and keep warm.

Add the garlic, onion and celery to the pan and fry for 5 minutes until softened. Add the raisins, olives, wine and salt and pepper to taste. Cook for a further 5 minutes.

Pour the sauce over the fish. Serve at once, garnished with celery leaves.

Cook's Tip

Halibut, a flat fish, has a firm but tender flesh. It can become dry, however, it is best to prepare this dish just before serving rather than trying to keep it warm for a long time.

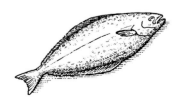

57 | Prawn Cutlets

Preparation time
10 minutes

Cooking time
2–3 minutes

Serves 2

Calories
230 per portion

You will need
8 Dublin Bay or large king prawns
  in their shells
1 tablespoon dry sherry
1 egg, beaten
2 tablespoons cornflour
oil for deep frying
fresh coriander leaves to garnish

Clean, de-vein and split the prawns to make cutlets (see Cook's Tip). Sprinkle with the sherry, dip in the egg and coat in the cornflour. Repeat the coating once more.

Heat the oil to 180 C/350 F and deep-fry the prawns for 2–3 minutes. Drain on absorbent kitchen paper and serve at once garnished with fresh coriander. Serve plain or with soy sauce.

58 | Steamed Whole Fish

Preparation time
about 45 minutes

Cooking time
12 minutes

Serves 4

Calories
380 per portion

You will need
3 slices root ginger, chopped
2 teaspoons salt
1.25 kg/2½ lb small fish (trout,
  sole or mackerel for example)
3 tablespoons soy sauce
1½ teaspoons sugar
1 tablespoon wine vinegar
2 tablespoons oil
2–3 rashers bacon, shredded
3–4 large dried Chinese
  mushrooms, soaked for 20
  minutes, drained, stemmed and
  shredded
4 spring onions, chopped

Mix the ginger and salt and rub over the fish inside and out; leave for 30 minutes.

Mix the soy sauce with the sugar, vinegar and oil, pour over the fish and leave for 15 minutes.

Place the fish on a heatproof dish and spoon over the marinade. Sprinkle with the bacon, mushrooms and spring onions. Place on a rack in a wok or large pan containing water. Cover and steam vigorously for 12 minutes. The fish is cooked when it will flake easily using chopsticks. Serve hot.

Cook's Tip

To make prawn cutlets, hold the prawns firmly by the tail and remove the shell, leaving the tail shell intact. Cut the prawns in half lengthways almost through to the tail and remove the dark intestinal vein. Then flatten the prawns.

Cook's Tip

This Chinese quick-steaming method of cooking fish is ideal for fresh whole fish or fillets of larger fish such as salmon, sea bream or striped bass.

59 | Stuffed Plaice Rolls

Preparation time
20 minutes

Cooking time
20–25 minutes

Oven temperature
180 C, 350 F, gas 4

Serves 4

Calories
390 per portion

You will need
8 small plaice fillets, skinned
100 g/4 oz white breadcrumbs
grated rind and juice of 1 lemon
1 tablespoon chopped fresh dill
50 g/2 oz cream cheese
salt and pepper
1 egg, lightly beaten
25 g/1 oz butter or margarine
25 g/1 oz plain flour
300 ml/½ pint milk
150 ml/¼ pint dry white wine

Garnish
dill sprigs
lemon twists

Put the fillets on a board, skinned side uppermost. Mix together the breadcrumbs, lemon rind and juice, dill, cream cheese, salt and pepper. Mix in enough egg to make a soft consistency. Place a spoonful of the stuffing on to each fillet and roll up. Place in an ovenproof dish and cover with greased foil. Bake in a moderate oven for 20–25 minutes.

To make the sauce, melt the butter or margarine over a gentle heat, add the flour, then gradually add the milk and wine and bring the sauce to the boil, stirring continuously. Reduce the heat and simmer gently for 2 minutes. Season to taste and pour over the stuffed plaice fillets. Garnish with fresh dill and lemon twists and serve immediately.

60 | Baked Stuffed Trout

Preparation time
10 minutes

Cooking time
20–25 minutes

Oven temperature
200 C, 400 F, gas 6

Serves 4

Calories
445 per portion

You will need
1 onion, finely chopped
25 g/1 oz butter or margarine
100 g/4 oz frozen chopped
  spinach
100 g/4 oz fresh brown
  breadcrumbs
50 g/2 oz flaked almonds,
  roughly chopped
grated rind of 1 lemon
¼ teaspoon grated nutmeg
salt and pepper
1 egg, lightly beaten
4 medium trout, cleaned, washed
  and dried
2 tablespoons olive oil

Garnish
lime twists
dill sprigs

Cook the onion in the butter or margarine until soft. Cover the spinach with boiling water, boil for 2 minutes, drain and squeeze dry. Mix together the onion, spinach, breadcrumbs, almonds, grated lemon rind, nutmeg and seasoning. Combine this stuffing with the egg. Divide into four and use to fill the cavity in each fish.

Place the fish in a shallow ovenproof dish, brush with the oil and bake in a moderately hot oven for 20–25 minutes or until the flesh flakes easily. Serve immediately, garnished with lime twists and fresh dill.

Cook's Tip

To make lemon twists, thinly slice a lemon and cut a slit in to the centre of each slice. Twist the slices from the cuts.

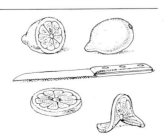

Freezer Tip

To freeze whole fish, like mackerel or trout, stuff the body cavity with a small roll of foil so that the fish stays a good shape. Remove the foil, stuff the fish (if required) and cook straight from frozen.

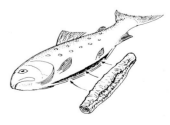

61 | Kippers with Lemon Butter

Preparation time
10 minutes

Cooking time
5–8 minutes

Serves 4

Calories
375 per portion

You will need
8 kipper fillets
1 small onion, thinly sliced
75 g / 3 oz butter
grated rind and juice of ½ lemon
1 tablespoon chopped parsley
salt and pepper

Garnish
lemon twists
parsley sprigs

Skin the kippers and remove any obvious bones. Brush a grill grid with oil, place the kippers on top and arrange the onion rings on top.

Beat the butter until pale and creamy, then gradually work the rind and juice of the lemon into the butter. Beat in the parsley and seasoning. Dot the lemon butter over the fish.

Grill the kippers for 5–8 minutes. Garnish with lemon twists and parsley sprigs, and serve with a fresh green salad and wholemeal bread.

62 | Quick Tuna Bake

Preparation time
10 minutes

Cooking time
20–25 minutes

Oven temperature
200 C, 400 F, gas 6

Serves 4

Calories
480 per portion

You will need
2 (198-g / 7-oz) cans tuna, drained
4 spring onions, chopped
1 (425-g / 15-oz) can mushroom soup
100 g / 4 oz Cheddar cheese, grated
1 teaspoon chopped fresh dill
¼ teaspoon Worcestershire sauce
salt and pepper
225 g / 8 oz fresh brown breadcrumbs
knob of butter
dill sprig to garnish

Flake the tuna and mix together with the onion, soup, cheese, dill, Worcestershire sauce, salt and pepper.

Pour some of the fish sauce into an ovenproof dish. Add a layer of breadcrumbs, followed by a layer of sauce. Continue layering in this fashion until all the ingredients have been used up. Finish with a layer of breadcrumbs on the top, dot the surface with the butter and bake in a moderately hot oven for 20–25 minutes. Serve immediately, garnished with a sprig of dill and accompanied by a green salad.

Cook's Tip

To make an interesting, crunchy green salad, include some bean sprouts, fine strips of celery and sliced avocado with the lettuce and other traditional ingredients.

Cook's Tip

A quick way of 'chopping' spring onions: wash and trim them, then hold them over a bowl and snip them up from green end toward the root.

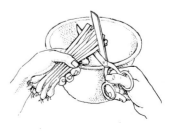

63 | *Fish Bake*

Preparation time
35 minutes

Cooking time
35 45 minutes

Oven temperature
190 C, 375 F, gas 5

Serves 4

Calories
300 per portion

You will need
450 g/1 lb white fish fillet, skinned
3 tablespoons oil
1 onion, sliced
1 green pepper, deseeded and
    diced
2 celery sticks, chopped
salt and pepper
1 tablespoon cider vinegar
1 (397-g/14-oz) can chopped
    tomatoes
100 g/4 oz fresh breadcrumbs
grated rind of 1 lemon
50 g/2 oz cheese, grated
2 tablespoons chopped parsley
lemon twist to garnish

Cut the fish fillets into chunks and place in an ovenproof dish. Heat the oil in a small pan, add the onion, pepper and celery and cook until soft but not browned. Spoon the mixture over the fish, season to taste and pour on the vinegar and tomatoes.

Mix all the topping ingredients, seasoning to taste. Spoon this topping over the tomatoes, then bake in a moderately hot oven for about 30 minutes, until golden brown. Serve piping hot, with brown rice or baked potatoes and a crisp salad.

Cook's Tip

Add some chopped peanuts or walnuts to the topping and stir in some chopped fresh herbs if you like. Suitable fish are haddock, plaice, cod, coley or whiting.

64 | *Haddock and Spinach Roulade*

Preparation time
30 minutes

Cooking time
25 minutes

Oven temperature
200 C, 400 F, gas 6

Serves 4

Calories
480 per portion

You will need
350 g/12 oz smoked haddock
150 ml/¼ pint milk
25 g/1 oz butter
25 g/1 oz plain flour
175 g/6 oz soft cheese with black
    pepper
2 hard-boiled eggs, chopped
450 g/1 lb frozen chopped spinach,
    defrosted
4 eggs, separated
salt
¼ teaspoon grated nutmeg
75 g/3 oz brie, rind removed
25 g/1 oz dried breadcrumbs

Line and grease a 33 × 23 cm/13 × 9-in Swiss roll tin. To make the filling, poach the haddock in the milk for 10 minutes. Drain and reserve 200 ml/7 fl oz of the cooking liquid, or make it up to this amount with extra milk. Flake fish. Whisk the butter, flour and cooking liquid over low heat until boiling. Stir in half the soft cheese, fish and eggs.

For the roulade, cream the remaining soft cheese with the spinach, egg yolks, salt and nutmeg. Cut the Brie into small pieces and stir in. Whisk the egg whites until stiff and fold in, adding the breadcrumbs, a spoonful at a time. Pour into the tin; bake for 8–10 minutes.

Reheat the filling. Turn the roulade out on to grease-proof paper, spread the filling over quickly and, with the aid of the paper, roll up the roulade. Serve at once.

Cook's Tip

After adding the roulade mixture to the tin, tilt it quickly so that the mixture flows into all the corners.

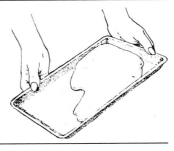

65 | Buttery Fried Plaice with Fried Parsley

Preparation time
10 minutes

Cooking time
20 minutes

Serves 6

Calories
532 per portion

You will need
plain flour for coating
salt and pepper
6 fillets of plaice, well trimmed
175 g / 6 oz butter
12 large parsley sprigs

Season the flour with the salt and pepper, then dip the fillets in it. Shake off any excess flour.

Melt half the butter and fry the fillets for 3 minutes on each side; if they are very large they may take a little longer. Add more of the butter if necessary, as flour-coated fish tends to soak up the fat. Remove from pan and keep warm on a serving platter. Fry in batches if necessary.

Add any remaining butter to the pan and raise the heat. Add the parsley and toss in the butter over a high heat, for 3–4 minutes until it becomes crispy.

Pour the parsley and juices over the fish and serve. Glazed carrots and baked potatoes are good accompanying vegetables.

Cook's Tip

This is a simple French way of pan-frying fish. The butter will become brown when frying the parsley but this adds an extra flavour. In France, it is called 'beurre noir', black butter.

66 | Plaice in Sweet and Sour Sauce

Preparation time
10 minutes

Cooking time
20 minutes

Serves 4

Calories
280 per portion

You will need
4 plaice fillets, about 175 g /6 oz each
100 g / 4 oz button mushrooms, wiped and sliced
1 red pepper, cored, seeded and very thinly sliced
2 tablespoons flaked almonds
1 tablespoon cornflour
4 tablespoons orange juice
grated rind of 1 orange
1 tablespoon light brown sugar
1 tablespoon clear honey
1 tablespoon cider vinegar
1 tablespoon tomato purée
1 tablespoon soy sauce
1 tablespoon sweet sherry
1 tablespoon oil
1 tablespoon Tabasco sauce

Cut four pieces of foil 20 × 30 cm / 8 × 12 inches and brush the centres with a little oil. Place each fillet on a piece of foil. Scatter the mushrooms, pepper and almonds over them. Bring up the sides of the foil and make a dish shape.

To make the sauce, put the cornflour into a bowl and gradually stir in the orange juice. Stir in the remaining ingredients with salt and pepper to taste.

Pour the sauce over the fish. Fold and seal the edges of the foil firmly to make watertight parcels. Place them in a steamer or colander over a pan of boiling water for 20 minutes, or until the fish flakes easily.

Cook's Tip

If you don't have a steamer or colander, the fish parcels can be cooked between two heatproof plates over a pan of boiling water. You will either have to cook the fish one at a time, or use four saucepans at once.

67 | Fish Balls

Preparation time
10 minutes

Cooking time
10 minutes

Serves 4

Calories
245 per portion

You will need
450 g/ 1 lb white fish, for
  example, hake, whiting, or cod
50 g/ 2 oz fresh white
  breadcrumbs
25 g/ 1 oz sesame seeds
1 egg, lightly beaten
1 teaspoon Worcestershire sauce
1 tablespoon soy sauce
2 tablespoons tomato ketchup
1 tablespoon chopped parsley
salt and pepper
oil for frying

Garnish
tomato rose
parsley sprig

Skin the fish and chop the flesh, removing any bones. Mix the chopped fish with the remaining ingredients. Take small spoonsful of the fish mixture and roll into balls the size of marbles.

Heat the oil in a saucepan and fry the fish balls a few at a time for 3–4 minutes or until golden. Drain on absorbent kitchen paper and keep warm until all the fish balls are cooked.

Serve hot with boiled rice and stir-fried vegetables, garnishing with a tomato rose and parsley sprig.

68 | Seafood Curry

Preparation time
20 minutes

Cooking time
25–30 minutes

Serves 4

Calories
260 per portion

You will need
450 g/ 1 lb white fish fillets, for
  example, haddock, coley or
  whiting, skinned
1–2 tablespoons oil
2 onions, finely chopped
2 cloves garlic, crushed
1 green pepper, deseeded and
  diced
2 tablespoons curry powder
2 teaspoons chilli powder
25 g/ 1 oz plain flour
600 ml/ 1 pint hot water
100 g/ 4 oz cooked mussels
100 g/ 4 oz peeled cooked prawns
4 tomatoes, peeled, deseeded
  and quartered
salt and pepper

Garnish
whole prawns
coriander sprigs

Cut the fish into cubes. Heat the oil in a frying pan, add the onions, garlic and pepper and fry until softened, but not browned. Add the spices and flour and cook gently. Gradually add the water, stirring all the time. Bring the mixture to the boil, reduce the heat and simmer gently, then add the white fish and cook for 15 minutes.

Add the mussels, prawns and tomatoes, season to taste and continue cooking for a further 5–10 minutes.

Garnish with whole prawns and coriander sprigs and serve at once with boiled rice and poppadums.

Cook's Tip

To prevent this fish mixture sticking to your hands as you shape it, dampen your hands with cold water. If the mixture begins to stick, dampen your hands again.

Cook's Tip

If you cook poppadums in a frying pan, use two fish slices to prevent them from curling up as they cook.

69 | Fish Molee

Preparation time
10 minutes

Cooking time
20–25 minutes

Serves 4

Calories
400 per portion

You will need
675 g/1½ lb cod fillet, skinned and
   cut into 4 pieces
2 tablespoons plain flour
4 tablespoons oil
2 onions, sliced
2 garlic cloves, crushed
1 teaspoon turmeric
4 green chillies, finely chopped
2 tablespoons lemon juice
175 ml/6 fl oz thick coconut milk
   (see Cook's Tip recipe 3)
salt

Coat the fish with the flour. Heat the oil in a frying pan, add the fish and fry quickly on both sides. Remove with a slotted spoon and set aside.

Add the onion and garlic to the pan and fry until soft and golden. Add the turmeric, chillies, lemon juice, coconut milk and salt to taste. Simmer, uncovered for 10 minutes or until thickened.

Add the fish and any juices, spoon over the sauce and cook gently for 2–3 minutes, until tender.

70 | Trout with Salted Cabbage

Preparation time
15 minutes

Cooking time
13 minutes

Serves 4

Calories
240 per portion

You will need
2 tablespoons oil
1 onion, chopped
2.5 cm/1 inch piece root ginger,
   peeled and shredded
4 trout, cleaned
150 ml/¼ pint chicken stock (see
   Cook's Tip)
25 g/1 oz pickled cabbage,
   chopped
25 g/1 oz canned bamboo shoots,
   drained and sliced
1 tablespoon soy sauce
2 teaspoons dry sherry

Heat the oil in a wok or deep frying pan, add the onion and ginger and cook for 1 minute. Add the trout and fry for 1 minute on each side, until browned.

Stir in the stock, then add the cabbage, bamboo shoots, soy sauce and sherry. Cook for 10 minutes, basting the fish occasionally.

Transfer to a warmed serving dish and garnish as shown if liked. Serve at once.

Cook's Tip

When buying fish fillets or steaks, look for a fresh cut appearance, firm elastic flesh that does not separate easily from the bones and, of course, a mild, pleasant odour.

Cook's Tip

For home-made chicken stock, break up a carcass and put in a large saucepan with a quartered onion, bayleaf and mace blade. Cover with water and bring to the boil. Simmer for 2–3 hours, then strain.

71 | Stir-Fried Fish with Vegetables

Preparation time
5 minutes, plus 15 minutes standing time

Cooking time
4 minutes

Serves 4

Calories
220 per portion

You will need
450 g/1 lb cod fillet, skinned and cut into wide strips
1 teaspoon salt
1 tablespoon oil
2 rashers back bacon, shredded
50 g/2 oz cooked peas
50 g/2 oz cooked sweetcorn
6 tablespoons chicken stock or water
2 teaspoons dry sherry
2 teaspoons soy sauce
1 teaspoon sugar
1 teaspoon cornflour
1 teaspoon water

Sprinkle the fish fillets with the salt and leave to stand for 15 minutes.

Heat the oil in a frying pan, add the fish and bacon and stir-fry for 3 minutes. Add the remaining ingredients, except the cornflour and water, and bring to the boil. Blend the cornflour with the water and stir in. Cook for 1 minute.

Serve at once, garnished as shown if liked.

72 | Steamed Mussels

Preparation time
40 minutes

Cooking time
10–15 minutes

Serves 6

Calories
250 per portion

You will need
1 kg/2¼ lb mussels
100 g/4 oz ghee
1 large onion, chopped
2 garlic cloves, chopped
2 teaspoons desiccated coconut
2 teaspoons salt
1 teaspoon turmeric
1 teaspoon chilli powder
1 teaspoon black pepper
150 ml/¼ pint vinegar
450 g/1 lb natural yogurt
2 teaspoons garam masala
juice of 2 lemons

Prepare the fish as in the Cook's Tip. Heat the ghee, add the onion and garlic and fry for 5 minutes. Add the coconut and salt and fry until browned. Add the turmeric, chilli powder and pepper and fry for 1 minute. Add the vinegar and shellfish, cover and bring to the boil; cook for about 5 minutes or until the shells open, then remove from the heat.

Remove the empty half shells and discard. Arrange the remainder in a serving dish. Pour the cooking liquid into a liquidizer or food processor with the yogurt and garam masala and blend for 1 minute. Reheat until hot but not boiling. Pour over the shellfish, sprinkle with lemon juice and serve at once.

Cook's Tip

In Chinese cooking fish is often stir-fried with vegetables that retain their colour and nutritional value. Fresh, dried and pickled vegetables are used, as are numerous soy bean-based products from bean curd to soy sauce flavourings. The recipe above combines fish with peas, sweetcorn and soy sauce.

Cook's Tip

Scrub the mussels under cold running water and pull away the black hairs known as the 'beard' with a sharp tug. Leave to soak for 30 minutes. Discard any mussels that are not tightly shut or that do not shut quickly when tapped.

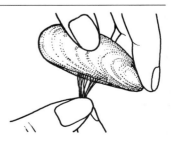

73 | Russian Fish Plait

Preparation time
30–35 minutes, plus
30 minutes to cool fish

Cooking time
35–40 minutes

Oven temperature
220 C, 425 F, gas 7

Serves 4

Calories
390 per portion

You will need
1 (227-g/8-oz) packet frozen puff
  pastry, defrosted
beaten egg to glaze

For the filling
20 g/$\frac{3}{4}$ oz margarine
20 g/$\frac{3}{4}$ oz plain flour
150 ml/$\frac{1}{4}$ pint milk
1 tablespoon chopped parsley
freshly ground black pepper
2 hard-boiled eggs, chopped
100 g/4 oz smoked haddock,
  cooked and flaked
75 g/3 oz button mushrooms,
  sliced

For the garnish
lemon and cucumber slices
parsley sprigs

Whisk the margarine, flour, milk, parsley and a pinch of pepper in a medium saucepan over a moderate heat until the sauce thickens, then cook gently for 1 minute. Add the chopped eggs and flaked haddock. Cool.

Roll out the pastry to a 30-cm/12-in square. Lift on to a damp baking tray. Place the filling in a 10-cm/4-in wide panel down the centre and scatter over the mushrooms. Brush the pastry edges with beaten egg and cut from the filling to the edge in 1-cm/$\frac{1}{2}$-in wide strips down both sides. Fold the strips over the filling to resemble a plait. Glaze and bake in a hot oven for 30–35 minutes. Serve hot or cold, garnished with lemon and cucumber twists and sprigs of parsley.

Cook's Tip

You can easily omit the small amount of fish in this recipe and increase the quantity of egg or mushrooms. This is delicious served hot or it travels well, packed up cold, for an unusual picnic dish.

74 | Neptune Flans

Preparation time
20 minutes

Cooking time
40–45 minutes

Oven temperature
200 C, 400 F, gas 6

Makes 4

Calories
655 per flan

You will need
1 (396-g/14-oz) packet frozen
  shortcrust pastry, defrosted

For the filling
1 (198-g/7-oz) packet frozen
  buttered smoked haddock
1 (198-g/7-oz) packet frozen
  haddock or cod steaks
salt and pepper
1 tablespoon chopped parsley
2 eggs, beaten
300 ml/$\frac{1}{2}$ pint milk
2 tablespoons double cream

For the garnish
2 tomato slices, halved
4 lemon slices, halved
parsley sprigs

Roll out the pastry on a lightly floured surface and use to line four individual fluted flan rings, placed on a baking tray. Poach the fish in simmering water for about 15 minutes, until cooked. Drain and flake well, then season and stir in the parsley. Divide the fish evenly between the flan cases. Beat the eggs and milk together and stir in the cream. Pour into the flans and cook in a moderately hot oven for 25–30 minutes, until set and golden brown. Garnish and serve with a crisp green salad.

Cook's Tip

For a special occasion, substitute 100 g/4 oz smoked salmon for the smoked haddock, adding it to the poached haddock or cod in the flan cases. Garnish each flan with red lumpfish caviar.

75 | *Parmesan Smokies*

Preparation time
10 minutes

Cooking time
20–25 minutes

Oven temperature
200C, 400F, Gas 6

Serves 4

Calories
479 per portion

You will need
450 g / 1 lb Arbroath Smokies,
  boned and skinned
300 ml / ½ pint water
1 fresh tarragon sprig
50 g / 2 oz butter
50 g / 2 oz plain flour
300 ml / ½ pint milk
150 ml / ¼ pint single cream
4 tablespoons dry white wine
50 g / 2 oz Cheddar cheese,
  grated
50 g / 2 oz Parmesan cheese,
  grated
salt and pepper
25 g / 1 oz fine fresh breadcrumbs

Poach the fish with the water and tarragon for 5 minutes until tender. Remove from the liquid and finely flake. Reserve 150 ml / ¼ pint poaching liquid.

Melt the butter and stir in the flour. Cook for 3 minutes, stirring, then stir in the milk, poaching liquid and cream and continue cooking, without boiling, until the sauce thickens.

Remove from the heat and stir in the fish, wine, Cheddar cheese and half the Parmesan cheese. Season to taste. Spoon into individual ovenproof dishes and top with the breadcrumbs and remaining cheese.

Cook for 10–15 minutes until golden and crisp. Serve at once.

Cook's Tip

Arbroath Smokies are small, lightly smoked Scottish haddock, highly praised for their fine flavour and texture. If unavailable, smoked haddock is a good substitute.

76 | *Fried Whitebait*

Preparation time
10 minutes

Cooking time
12–15 minutes

Serves 4

Calories
715 per portion

You will need
500 g / 1 lb whitebait
100 g / 4 oz plain flour
salt and pepper
oil for deep frying

For the garnish
1 lemon, quartered
watercress sprigs

Sort through the whitebait, discarding any crushed or broken ones.

Season the flour with salt and pepper to taste and put in a shallow plate. Heat the oil to 180–190C / 350–375F or until a cube of bread browns in 30 seconds. Take a quarter of the fish and toss them in the flour, making sure they are well covered. Shake off any surplus flour and fry for 2 minutes. Drain the fish on paper towels and fry the remaining three batches.

When all the fish are cooked, check the oil temperature, re-heat and crisp all the whitebait for 2 minutes. Drain again, then pile them on to a serving dish and garnish with lemon and watercress. Serve as a starter with thin brown bread and butter if liked.

Cook's Tip

Whitebait are miniature oily fish eaten whole, including the heads. To make a spicier dish, stir paprika or cayenne pepper to taste into the seasoned flour. If the fish need washing, use ice cold water and pat dry.

77 | Chinese Steamed Trout

Preparation time
10 minutes

Cooking time
15 minutes

Serves 4

Calories
350 per portion

You will need
1 tablespoon sesame oil
1 tablespoon light soy sauce
1 tablespoon dry sherry
2 rainbow trout, about 1 kg/2 lb
    total weight, cleaned
4 garlic cloves, sliced
6 spring onions, shredded
5 cm/2 inch piece root ginger,
    shredded
2 tablespoons dry white vermouth
2 tablespoons oil

Mix together the sesame oil, soy sauce and sherry and use to brush the inside and skin of the fish. Mix together the garlic, spring onions and ginger and place a quarter of the mixture inside each fish.

Place the fish on a heatproof plate, scatter over the remaining garlic mixture and pour over the vermouth and oil. Put the plate in a wok or steamer and steam vigorously for 15 minutes, or until the fish are tender.

Arrange on a warmed serving dish, pour over the juices and serve at once.

78 | Coconut Fish

Preparation time
10 minutes

Cooking time
15 minutes

Serves 4

Calories
450 per portion

You will need
2 tablespoons oil
4 green chillies, seeded and
    chopped
2 garlic cloves, chopped
2.5 cm/1 inch piece root ginger,
    finely chopped
100 g/4 oz creamed coconut
1 kg/2 lb thick haddock fillets,
    skinned and cubed
salt
juice of 2 lemons

Heat the oil in a large frying pan, add the chillies, garlic and ginger and fry for 3 minutes. Add the creamed coconut and, when bubbling, add the fish and salt to taste. Stir well.

Cook for 3—4 minutes, stirring and breaking up the fish as it cooks. As soon as all the fish is cooked through, pour in the lemon juice, stir well and serve.

Cook's Tip

If you do not have a Chinese steamer, place the food on a heatproof plate which fits into a wok with a lid. Place a strip of foil under the plate to enable it to be lifted in and out of the wok with ease.

Cook's Tip

Coconut is much used in food in southern India. It is particularly good with fish in this dish which is simple to make and not too chilli hot. Serve it with boiled rice and moong dhal.

79 | *Scallop Shells*

Preparation time
10 minutes

Cooking time
15 minutes

Serves 4

Calories
274 per portion

You will need
2 tablespoons oil
1 small onion, peeled and finely
  chopped
1–2 garlic cloves, peeled and
  crushed
8–10 large scallops, removed from
  shells
1 tablespoon plain flour
salt and pepper
225 g / 8 oz button mushrooms,
  wiped and quartered
1 tablespoon lemon juice
4–5 tablespoons fine white
  breadcrumbs
3 tablespoons chopped fresh
  parsley

Heat the oil and fry the onion and garlic for 3 minutes until softened.

Meanwhile, separate the orange roes from the scallops, then cut each scallop horizontally in half. Lightly dust with the flour and season to taste with the salt and pepper.

Add the scallops to the mushrooms and cook for 5–6 minutes until tender, then add the roes and lemon juice. Cook for a further 3 minutes, stirring gently.

Heat the remaining oil, and fry the breadcrumbs for 3 minutes until crisp. Stir in the parsley.

To serve, spoon the scallop mixture into four heated scallop shells and top with the crisp crumbs. Serve at once.

80 | *Moules à la Crème*

Preparation time
15 minutes

Cooking time
20 minutes

Serves 4

Calories
353 per portion

You will need
2.25 litres / 4 pints fresh mussels,
  well scrubbed
300 ml / ½ pint water
2 tablespoons oil
25 g / 1 oz butter
2 onions, peeled and chopped
2 garlic cloves, peeled and
  crushed
150 ml / ¼ pint dry white wine
2 tablespoons chopped fresh
  parsley (optional)
150 ml / ¼ pint double cream
salt and pepper
parsley sprigs to garnish

Place the mussels and water in a large saucepan, cover and cook over a high heat for 5–6 minutes until all the shells open. Discard any that do not open.

Strain the mussels, reserving the cooking liquid. Remove and discard the mussels' top shells.

Heat the oil and butter and fry the onions and garlic for 5 minutes until soft. Add 150 ml / ¼ pint reserved liquid and cook for a further 8 minutes.

Add the wine and parsley if liked. Bring almost to the boil, then return the mussels and add the cream. Warm through and season to taste with salt and pepper. Serve in individual bowls, garnished with parsley sprigs.

Cook's Tip

If your scallops aren't sold with their shells, ask a fishmonger if he has any spare. Scrub them well before using. You can also buy scallop shells in cookware shops. Alternatively, use individual ramekins.

Cook's Tip

Place an empty bowl on the table for everyone to put the shells in as they eat the mussels. The mussels can be eaten with a fork or scooped out of the half shells with another shell, used as a spoon. Give everyone a soup *spoon for eating the sauce at the bottom of the bowl. Finger bowls for cleaning your hands are also useful.*

81 | Spiced Prawns in Coconut

Preparation time
5 minutes

Cooking time
15 minutes

Serves 4

Calories
280 per portion

You will need
4 tablespoons oil
1 large onion, sliced
4 garlic cloves, sliced
2 teaspoons ground coriander
1 teaspoon turmeric
1 teaspoon chilli powder
½ teaspoon ground ginger
½ teaspoon salt
pepper to taste
2 tablespoons vinegar
200 ml/⅓ pint coconut milk (see
    Cook's Tip)
2 tablespoons tomato purée
450 g/1 lb peeled prawns

Heat the oil in a wok or deep frying pan, add the onion and garlic and fry gently until soft and golden.

Mix the spices together in a bowl, add the salt and pepper, stir in the vinegar and mix to a paste. Add to the wok and fry for 3 minutes, stirring constantly.

Stir in the coconut milk and tomato purée and simmer for 5 minutes. Stir in the prawns and heat through for 2–3 minutes, until well coated with sauce. Serve at once garnished as shown if liked.

82 | Hot Jumbo Prawns

Preparation time
10 minutes

Cooking time
6 minutes

Serves 4

Calories
370 per portion

You will need
1 teaspoon very finely chopped
    root ginger
3 spring onions, chopped
12 giant Pacific prawns, shelled
3 tablespoons self-raising flour
pinch of salt
½–1 teaspoon chilli powder
½ teaspoon paprika
3 teaspoons dry sherry
1 egg, beaten
1 tablespoon chopped fresh
    coriander
oil for deep frying
tomato roses and coriander leaves
    to garnish

Mix together the ginger, spring onions and prawns. Place the flour, salt, chilli powder to taste and paprika in a bowl. Add the sherry and egg and beat to a smooth batter. Fold in the coriander and prawn mixture.

Heat the oil to 160 C/325 F and deep fry half the battered prawns for 2–3 minutes, until golden. Drain on absorbent kitchen paper and keep hot while frying the remainder.

Arrange on a warmed serving dish and garnish with coriander leaves and tomato roses. Serve at once.

Cook's Tip

Coconut milk can be bought in a very convenient form as coconut granules. Simply make up a thin or thick coconut milk following the packet instructions.

Cook's Tip

To make a tomato rose, thinly pare all the skin from a tomato, taking care to keep it in one piece. Tightly curl the skin into a circle and use at once.

83 | Stuffed Sardines

Preparation time
10 minutes

Cooking time
6–8 minutes

Makes 6

Calories
236 per portion

You will need
350 g / 12 oz sardines, cleaned
salt and pepper
lemon wedges and parsley sprigs
    to garnish

For the stuffing
4 tablespoons chopped fresh
    parsley
50 g / 2 oz breadcrumbs
1 tablespoon lemon juice
1 tablespoon grated Parmesan
    cheese
25 g / 1 oz butter, melted
salt and pepper

Wash the sardines and pat dry. Sprinkle well with salt and pepper.

To make the stuffing, mix together the parsley, bread-crumbs, lemon juice, Parmesan cheese, butter and salt and pepper to taste.

Fill the cavity of each fish with a little stuffing.

Place the sardines under a preheated hot grill for 6–8 minutes, turning once, until cooked through and flesh flakes easily.

Cook's Tip

**The stuffing can be made a
day ahead but do not stuff the
sardines until ready to grill.
Leaving the fish overnight
with the stuffing inside can be
a health hazard, even if the
fish are in the refrigerator.**

84 | Seafood Casserole

Preparation time
10 minutes

Cooking time
20–25 minutes

Serves 4

Calories
191 per portion

You will need
4 tablespoons olive oil
2 garlic cloves, peeled and
    crushed
2 onions, peeled and chopped
2 small red peppers, cored,
    seeded and chopped
900 g / 2 lb mixed seafood, cut
    into pieces or steaks
4 tomatoes, skinned and sliced
300 ml ½ pint white wine
100 g / 4 oz whole button
    mushrooms, wiped
salt and pepper
toasted French bread to serve

Heat the oil and gently fry the garlic and onions for 5 minutes. Add the red peppers and cook for 2 minutes. Add the fish and stir to coat in oil.

Add the tomatoes, wine, mushrooms and salt and pepper to taste. Bring to the boil, then simmer, uncovered, for 15–20 minutes until the fish is tender.

Serve hot with toasted French bread and a salad.

Cook's Tip

**The key to success with this
Mediterranean-style recipe is
to use a variety of seafood,
including shellfish and firm
white fish. Red mullet,
scampi, cod, hake, sole and
prawns are all ideal.**

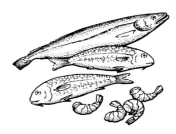

85 | *Plaice Gougère*

Preparation time
10 minutes

Cooking time
1 hour

Oven temperature
200 C, 400 F, gas 6

Serves 4

Calories
760 per portion

You will need
1 medium onion, sliced
150 g/5 oz butter
175 g/6 oz plain flour
300 ml/½ pint milk
350 g/12 oz plaice fillets, skinned
    and cut into strips
100 g/4 oz canned sweetcorn
100 g/4 oz mushrooms, sliced
3 tablespoons cider
2 tablespoons natural yogurt
salt and pepper
300 ml/½ pint water
4 eggs, beaten
75 g/3 oz Cheddar cheese, grated
1 tablespoon dry breadcrumbs
chopped parsley

Cook the onion in 25 g/1 oz of the butter for 8 minutes until golden. Stir in 25 g/1 oz of the flour and cook for 1 minute. Remove the pan from the heat and gradually stir in the milk. Bring to the boil, stirring, and cook for 1 minute. Stir in the fish, sweetcorn, mushrooms, cider, yogurt and salt and pepper.

Melt the remaining butter in a saucepan with the water. Bring to the boil, take off the heat and immediately beat in the remaining flour until just smooth. Beat in the eggs a little at a time, then stir in the cheese. Spoon the paste round the edge of a greased 1.15-litre/2-pint ovenproof dish. Spoon the fish sauce into the middle, sprinkle with the breadcrumbs and bake for 40–45 minutes or until crisp and golden. Scatter parsley on top and serve immediately.

Cook's Tip

A gougère makes a marvellous lunch dish, virtually complete in itself (though you can add a salad from this book if you like). Don't be put off by the choux pastry. It is very easy to make.

86 | *Goujon Salad*

Preparation time
20 minutes

Cooking time
12–15 minutes

Serves 4

Calories
520 per portion

You will need
1 iceberg lettuce, shredded
1 bunch spring onions, chopped
1 red pepper, deseeded and cut
    into strips
¼ cucumber, halved lengthways
    and sliced
2 tablespoons sunflower oil
1 tablespoon lemon juice
150 ml/¼ pint soured cream
2 tablespoons snipped chives
8 small sole fillets, skinned
1 large egg
1 tablespoon water
salt and pepper
about 150 g/5 oz dry white or
    wholewheat breadcrumbs for
    coating
oil for deep frying

Mix the lettuce, onions, pepper and cucumber together. Beat together the oil and lemon juice. In a separate bowl mix together the soured cream and chives. Cut the fish fillets diagonally into strips about 1 cm/ ½ in wide. Beat the egg with the water and season generously with salt and pepper. Coat the fish in the egg mixture, drain, then toss in the breadcrumbs to coat.

Heat the oil to 180 C, 350 F, add the goujons a few at a time and cook until crisp and golden. Drain on absorbent kitchen paper. Keep hot while cooking the remaining goujons. Pour the oil and vinegar dressing over the salad and toss well. Place the goujons on a warmed plate and serve with the salad. Serve the soured cream sauce separately.

Cook's Tip

Red peppers (which are simply ripe green peppers) are a good source of vitamins A and C. Look for plump, firm pods with bright colour. To deseed, slice off the top, then cut round the pith to remove the core and seeds cleanly.

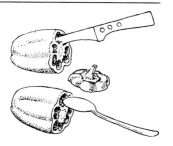

87 | Sole with Saté Sauce

Preparation time
35 minutes

Cooking time
20 minutes

Serves 4

Calories
750 per portion

You will need
1 teaspoon each of coriander, cumin and fennel seeds, crushed
2 garlic cloves, crushed
100 g/4 oz crunchy peanut butter
1 teaspoon dark soft brown sugar
2 green chillies, seeded and chopped
150 g/5 oz creamed coconut
3 tablespoons lemon juice
25 g/1 oz butter
1 shallot, finely chopped
1 tablespoon each of chopped chives, tarragon and parsley
grated rind of ½ lemon
8 Dover or lemon sole fillets
1 egg, beaten
4–5 tablespoons fresh breadcrumbs

To make the sauce, heat a wok or frying pan, add the crushed seeds and stir-fry for 2 minutes. Add the garlic, peanut butter, sugar, chillies and creamed coconut dissolved in 450 ml/¾ pint water, stir well and cook gently for 7–8 minutes. Stir in the lemon juice and keep warm.

Melt the butter in a pan, add the shallot and cook for 1 minute. Stir in the herbs and lemon rind. Cool slightly, then divide between the fish. Roll up each fillet, secure with wooden cocktail sticks, dip in egg, then coat in breadcrumbs. Deep fry for 4–5 minutes until golden. Drain and serve with the sauce.

Cook's Tip

This fish dish is particularly enhanced by the addition of fresh herbs, which bring out its delicate flavour. The secret of using fresh herbs is that they should be gathered and cooked immediately, so that the flavour is captured in the food and not lost during storage.

88 | Pineapple Prawn Curry

Preparation time
15 minutes

Cooking time
15 minutes

Serves 4

Calories
450 per portion

You will need
2 garlic cloves
1 small onion, quartered
2 green chillies, chopped
50 g/2 oz butter
1 bunch spring onions, chopped
450 g/1 lb raw peeled prawns
1 large green pepper, cored, seeded and coarsely chopped
150 ml/¼ pint double cream
salt
1 small pineapple, cut into chunks

Put the garlic, onion and green chillies in a liquidizer or food processor and work to a paste.

Melt the butter in a large frying pan, add the spring onions, prawns and green pepper and cook, stirring constantly until the prawns turn pink. Add the prepared paste and fry, stirring, for 2 minutes.

Add the cream, a spoonful at a time, and when it has all been incorporated, season with salt to taste. Stir in the pineapple. Cover and simmer for 5 minutes, then serve at once.

Cook's Tip

This pale creamy prawn curry should be cooked at the last possible moment for freshness. The pineapple helps to give the curry a little bite or acidity. Use fresh pineapple – canned is too sweet and bland.

89 | Baked Spiced Fish

Preparation time
10 minutes plus
overnight marinating

Cooking time
30 minutes

Oven temperature
180 C, 350 F, gas 4

Serves 4

Calories
180 per portion with
white fish (400 per
portion with oily fish)

You will need
250 ml/8 fl oz natural yogurt
1 onion, chopped
1 garlic clove, chopped
1 teaspoon grated root ginger
1 tablespoon vinegar
1½ teaspoons ground cumin
pinch of chilli powder
1 kg/2 lb whole fish or 675 g/
  1½ lb fish fillets (see Cook's
  Tip)
juice of 1 lemon
1 teaspoon salt

For the garnish
lemon slices
fresh coriander leaves

Put a quarter of the yogurt, the onion, garlic, ginger, vinegar, cumin and chilli powder in a liquidizer or food processor and blend to a smooth sauce. Add the remaining yogurt.

Score the fish and place in an ovenproof dish. Rub with lemon juice and sprinkle with the salt. Pour over the yogurt marinade, cover and leave to marinate overnight.

Cover the fish with foil and bake for 30 minutes. Serve hot, garnished with lemon slices and coriander leaves.

90 | Crab Omelette

Preparation time
10 minutes

Cooking time
about 1–2 minutes

Serves 3–4

Calories
360–270 per portion

You will need
2 spring onions
4 eggs, beaten
salt
3 tablespoons oil
2 slices root ginger, shredded
175 g/6 oz crab meat
1 tablespoon sake or dry sherry
1 tablespoon soy sauce
2 teaspoons sugar

For the garnish (optional)
½ lettuce, shredded
tomato water-lily (see Cook's Tip)
seedless grape

Cut the white part of the spring onions into 2.5-cm/1-inch lengths. Chop the green part finely and beat into the eggs with salt to taste.

Heat the oil and add the white spring onions and the ginger, then the crab and sake or sherry. Stir-fry for a few seconds, then add the soy sauce and sugar.

Lower the heat, pour in the egg mixture and cook for a further 30 seconds. Transfer to a warmed serving plate, garnish with shredded lettuce and a tomato water-lily with a grape on top. Serve at once.

Cook's Tip

When selecting the fish for this dish you will find that whole fish give the best results – try bream, snapper or flounder for example. You can use an oily fish such as mackerel but increase the amount of vinegar to 2 tablespoons. If using fillets, select cod or a similar chunky fish, or use fish steaks.

Cook's Tip

To make a tomato water-lily, make zig-zag cuts around the middle of a tomato using a small, sharp knife. Make sure the cuts go right through to the centre. Separate the two halves carefully.

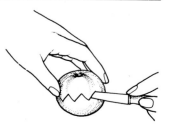

91 | Prawns with Tamarind

Preparation time
10 minutes, plus 1 hour
for the tamarind paste

Cooking time
about 10 minutes

Serves 4

Calories
300 per portion

You will need
225 g/8 oz tamarind
100 ml/4 fl oz water
1 small red pepper, cored, seeded
  and chopped
25 g/1 oz small onions, chopped
2 garlic cloves, chopped
1 red chilli, seeded and chopped
1 tablespoon ground lemon grass
6 tablespoons oil
4 teaspoons caster sugar
2 teaspoons lime juice
salt
450 g/1 lb unpeeled
  Mediterranean prawns, heads
  left on and de-veined through
  the shell

To make the tamarind paste, place the tamarind and water in a small pan and bring to the boil. Cover and simmer for 10 minutes. Remove from the heat and leave to stand, covered, for 1 hour. Mash, then sieve into a bowl. Reserve 3 tablespoons and use the remainder for another dish (see Cook's Tip).

Place the red pepper, onions, garlic, chilli and lemon grass in a liquidizer or food processor and blend. Heat the oil, add the pepper mixture and stir-fry for 5 minutes. Gradually blend in the tamarind paste, sugar, lime juice and salt to taste. Add the prawns and stir-fry for 5 minutes or until the prawns are just firm to the touch. Serve at once.

Cook's Tip

**The tamarind paste can be
stored in the refrigerator for
use in other dishes for up to 2
weeks.**

92 | Pickled Haddock Steaks

Preparation time
15 minutes, plus 12
hours chilling time

Cooking time
about 20 minutes

Serves 4

Calories
340 per portion

You will need
4 tablespoons oil
4 (225-g/8-oz) haddock steaks
2 onions, chopped
1 garlic clove, peeled
2.5 cm/1 inch piece root ginger,
  peeled
1 tablespoon coriander seeds
4 green chillies, seeded
5 tablespoons wine vinegar
½ teaspoon turmeric
4 curry leaves (see Cook's Tip)
salt

Heat the oil in a large frying pan, add the fish and fry on both sides until browned. Remove with a slotted spoon and set aside. Add the onions to the pan and fry until soft.

Put the garlic, ginger, coriander seeds, chillies and 1 tablespoon vinegar into a liquidizer or food processor and work to a paste. Add to the pan with the turmeric, curry leaves and salt to taste and fry for 3–4 minutes.

Add the remaining vinegar, bring to simmering point, stir well and add the fish. Cook, uncovered, for 3–4 minutes, until tender.

Place the fish in a dish, pour over all the juices and leave to cool. Cover and keep in the refrigerator for at least 12 hours. Serve cold.

Cook's Tip

**Curry leaves, or kari patta, are
the aromatic leaves of the
sweet nim tree, available
dried. They release an
appetising smell when
cooked.**

93 | *Plaice and Lime Pinwheels*

Preparation time
20 minutes

Cooking time
10–13 minutes

Makes 8

Calories
472 per portion

You will need
75 g / 3 oz butter, softened
2 tablespoons chopped fresh
 chives
40 g / 1½ oz fresh white
 breadcrumbs
grated rind of 1 lime
4 tablespoons lime juice
salt and pepper
8 plaice fillets, skinned

For the garnish
lime twists
fresh chives or dill

Beat the butter with the chives until soft and creamy. Add the breadcrumbs, lime rind and enough lime juice to make a stuffing with a good spreading consistency. Add salt and pepper to taste.

Divide the stuffing in four parts and spread the plaice fillets with the stuffing. Roll up from the wide end and secure each with a wooden cocktail stick.

Place in a greased flameproof dish and sprinkle with the remaining lime juice. Place under a preheated hot grill and cook for 5 minutes. Turn over and grill for a further 5–8 minutes. Serve at once garnished with lime twists and chives or dill.

94 | *Poached Trout*

Preparation time
5 minutes

Cooking time
10–12 minutes

Serves 4

Calories
312 per portion

You will need
4 rainbow trout, about 350 g /
 12 oz each, cleaned
150 ml / ¼ pint dry cider
a few parsley stalks
1 onion, peeled and sliced
2 slices lemon
6 black peppercorns
150 ml / ¼ pint double cream
salt and pepper
parsley sprigs and lemon slices to
 garnish

Simmer the trout in the cider with the parsley stalks, onions, lemon and peppercorns, covered, for 10–12 minutes until the fish are just cooked and the flesh flakes easily. Transfer the fish to a serving plate and keep warm.

Strain the cooking liquid and bring it rapidly to the boil. Immediately lower the heat, stir in the cream and heat through. Remove from the heat and season with salt and pepper to taste.

Pour the sauce over the fish. Serve garnished with the parsley sprigs and lemon slices.

Cook's Tip

Use 1½ slices bread to make the breadcrumbs. Cut off the crusts and either process in a food processor or rub along a grater set in a bowl. You can also use wholemeal breadcrumbs.

Cook's Tip

If you decide to clean the fish yourself rather than having the fishmonger do it, wash out any blood along the back-bone. If not removed, the cooked fish can have a bitter taste.

95 | Crab in Black Bean Sauce

Preparation time
6 minutes

Cooking time
12 minutes

Serves 4

Calories
260 per portion

You will need
2 tablespoons oil
2 tablespoons salted black beans, coarsely chopped
2 garlic cloves, crushed
2 tablespoons chopped root ginger
4 spring onions, chopped
225 g/8 oz lean minced pork
1 large cooked crab, cut into pieces
2 tablespoons dry sherry
300 ml/½ pint chicken stock
2 eggs, beaten
1–2 teaspoons sesame oil
spring onion flowers to garnish

Heat the oil in a wok or deep frying pan, add the black beans, garlic, ginger and spring onions and fry briskly for 30 seconds. Add the pork and brown quickly for 1 minute. Add the crab, sherry and stock and boil rapidly for 8-10 minutes.

Combine the eggs and sesame oil and stir into the wok. Stir for 30 seconds, until the egg has cooked in strands. Transfer to a warmed serving dish and garnish with spring onion flowers. Serve at once.

96 | Prawns with Almonds

Preparation time
4 minutes

Cooking time
7 minutes

Serves 4

Calories
300 per portion

You will need
75 g/3 oz blanched almonds
350 g/12 oz peeled prawns
2 teaspoons cornflour
1 heaped teaspoon finely chopped root ginger
1 small garlic clove, crushed
2 tablespoons oil
1 celery stick, finely chopped
2 teaspoons soy sauce
2 teaspoons sherry
2 tablespoons water
pepper
spring onion flowers to garnish

Brush a frying pan with oil, add the almonds, then heat and toss until golden. Drain well.

Place the prawns in a bowl with the cornflour, ginger and garlic and mix well.

Heat the oil in the pan, add the prawn mixture and celery and stir-fry for 2–3 minutes. Add the soy sauce, sherry, water and pepper to taste. Bring to the boil, add the almonds and heat for 30 seconds. Serve hot, garnished with spring onion flowers.

Cook's Tip

Crab in Black Bean Sauce comes from southern China, where minced pork is often added to a fish dish to extend the dish. The salted black beans give a traditional flavour. The crab is cooked in the shell to protect the meat during cooking – the easiest way of eating it is with the fingers!

Cook's Tip

Prawns with Almonds has the traditional delicacy of Chinese food. It is flavoured with fresh root ginger – a knobbly root with a sandy coloured skin. Cut off the knobs and peel just as you would a small potato.

97 | Crispy Skin Fish

Preparation time
10 minutes, plus 3½
hours standing time

Cooking time
about 10 minutes

Serves 4

Calories
270 per portion

You will need
675 g/1½ lb small fish
3–4 slices root ginger, chopped
1 tablespoon salt
1½ tablespoons plain flour
oil for deep frying

Slit the fish along the belly, clean and rinse thoroughly but leave the heads and tails intact. Rub the fish inside and out with the ginger and salt. Leave for 3 hours. Rub with the flour and leave for a further 30 minutes.

Heat the oil to 180 C/350 F and deep-fry the fish in batches for 3–4 minutes, or until crisp and golden. Drain on absorbent kitchen paper and serve hot.

98 | Dry Fried Herring

Preparation time
about 20 minutes

Cooking time
30 minutes

Serves 4

Calories
260 per portion

You will need
about 1 teaspoon chilli powder
1½ teaspoons turmeric
1 teaspoon ground ginger
1 teaspoon garlic powder or paste
salt and pepper
450 g/1 lb herring fillets, cut into
  5-cm/2-inch pieces
oil for frying
1 lemon, sliced to garnish

Mix together the chilli powder, turmeric, ginger, garlic and salt and pepper to taste. Rub this mixture into the fish and set aside to marinate for 10–15 minutes.

Heat a little oil and fry the fish in two batches until golden brown. Remove and drain the fish. Serve hot, garnished with lemon slices.

Cook's Tip

This recipe is suitable for small fish such as whiting, herring and small trout. Make sure the fish are fried until really crisp for success.

Cook's Tip

The herring is a bony, delicately flavoured fish and because of this it is generally fried rather than made into a curry. Cut the herring into pieces with or without the roe as liked.

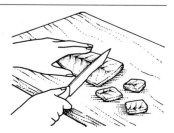

99 | *Mackerel with Cherries*

Preparation time
5 minutes

Cooking time
10 minutes

Serves 4–6

Calories
284 per portion

You will need
100–175 g / 4–6 oz red cherries, stoned and chopped
4 tablespoons red wine
4 tablespoons water
1–2 teaspoons sugar
4–6 fresh mackerel fillets
pepper
lemon twists and parsley sprigs to garnish

Simmer the cherries in the wine and water for 10 minutes until soft. Add sugar to taste keeping the flavour tart. Cool for 1 minute, then purée in a liquidizer or food processor or mash with a fork. Return to the pan and keep warm while cooking the fish.

Meanwhile, season the mackerel with pepper to taste and cook under a preheated low grill for 5 minutes on each side until cooked through and the flesh flakes easily.

Transfer to warmed serving plates and serve at once with the hot cherry sauce, garnished with lemon and parsley.

100 | *Honey and Vegetable Mackerel*

Preparation time
15 minutes

Cooking time
30 minutes

Oven temperature
190C, 375F, Gas 5

Serves 2

Calories
725 per portion

You will need
2 mackerel, about 450 g / 1 lb each, cleaned and heads removed
2 tablespoons clear honey
1 carrot, peeled and cut into matchstick strips
1 stick celery, cut into matchstick strips
1 × 5 cm / 2 inch slice fresh root ginger, peeled and cut into matchstick strips
salt and pepper
1 tablespoon wine vinegar
1 tablespoon soy sauce

Place the mackerel on a large piece of greased foil. Brush with the honey and sprinkle with the carrot, celery and ginger. Sprinkle with salt and pepper to taste, the wine vinegar and soy sauce.

Fold over the foil to enclose the fish completely, then place on a baking sheet. Place in a preheated oven and cook for 30 minutes or until tender. Remove from the foil to serve.

Cook's Tip

When cherries aren't in season, use a 425-g / 15-oz can of red cherries, well drained. If they are too sweet, omit the sugar from the sauce and add 1–2 teaspoons lemon juice instead.

Cook's Tip

The fish packets can be prepared in advance and kept in the refrigerator until ready to cook. Crimp the edges of the foil tightly so none of the delicious juices ooze out.

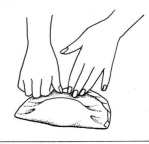

101 | Herrings with Soured Cream Sauce

Preparation time
15 minutes

Cooking time
12 minutes

Serves 4

Calories
435 per portion

You will need
4 fresh herrings
1 tablespoon oil
1 tablespoon white wine vinegar
salt and pepper
4 spring onions, chopped
300 ml/½ pint soured cream
1 teaspoon mustard powder
cayenne
1 tablespoon chopped fresh dill

Garnish
cayenne
halved lemon slices
1 teaspoon chopped fresh dill,
 plus a few sprigs

Scale and gut the herrings. Wash the insides and outsides of the fish and pat dry. Cut slits down both sides of each fish. Brush the fish with oil, then spoon the vinegar into the slits and season the fish generously.

Heat the grill to medium heat and grill the herrings on one side for 6 minutes. Turn the fish over, brush with a little more oil and cook for a further 6 minutes. Transfer the herrings to a serving plate and keep warm.

Mix the remaining ingredients together. Pour the sauce into a small serving bowl, and sprinkle with cayenne and dill. Garnish the fish with halved lemon slices and sprigs of dill and serve with the sauce.

Cook's Tip

To make your own soured cream, add 1–2 tablespoons lemon juice to 150 ml/¼ pint single cream.

102 | Salmon Mousse

Preparation time
15 minutes, plus 1
hour to chill

Serves 4

Calories
365 per portion

You will need
1 tablespoon gelatine
2 tablespoons hot water
1 (213-g/7½-oz) can salmon
150 ml/¼ pint natural yogurt
150 ml/¼ pint mayonnaise
1 tablespoon tomato ketchup
salt and pepper
2 egg whites

Garnish
orange slices
lime slices
parsley sprigs
dill sprigs

Sprinkle the gelatine on to the hot water in a bowl. Stand the bowl over a saucepan of simmering water and stir until dissolved.

Flake the salmon into a bowl, remove any remaining bones, and add the natural yogurt. Stir in the mayonnaise, then the tomato ketchup, gelatine and seasoning. Whisk the egg whites until stiff but not dry and fold into the salmon mixture. Pour the mixture into a serving bowl and chill for an hour or until set.

Garnish the mousse with orange and lime slices, dill and parsley sprigs and serve with triangles of toast and a salad.

Cook's Tip

The mousse can be set in a fish-shaped mould for elegant presentation. Serve turned out on a flat serving platter.

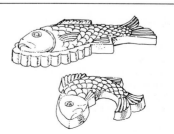

103 | *Salmon with Caper and Parsley Sauce*

Preparation time
10 minutes

Cooking time
25 minutes

Serves 4

Calories
401 per portion

You will need
2 salmon steaks, 225 g / 8 oz each
salt and pepper
300 ml / ½ pint dry white wine
2 bay leaves
2 shallots, peeled and chopped
2 celery sticks, chopped
celery leaves to garnish

For the sauce
50 g / 2 oz butter
2 garlic cloves, peeled and
  crushed
2 tablespoons capers, drained and
  chopped
4 tablespoons chopped fresh
  parsley

Wipe the salmon steaks and sprinkle on both sides with salt and pepper. Place the wine, bay leaves, shallots and celery in a shallow pan and bring to a simmer. Add the salmon steaks, cover and poach for 12–15 minutes until the fish is cooked through.

Remove the salmon from the liquid, place on a warmed serving plate and keep warm. Strain the liquid and reserve.

To make the sauce, melt the butter and cook the garlic, capers and parsley for 1 minute. Add salt and pepper to taste and 125 ml / 4 fl oz of the poaching liquid. Bring to the boil. Pour over the salmon and serve at once, garnished with celery leaves.

Cook's Tip

The salmon steaks are cooked through when the flesh flakes easily if tested with the tip of a knife. Do not poach in boiling water or the cooked fish will be tough.

104 | *Chilled Salmon Steaks*

Preparation time
15 minutes

Cooking time
20 minutes

Oven temperature
180C, 350F, Gas 4

Serves 4

Calories
501 per portion

You will need
4 salmon steaks, 175 g / 6 oz each
salt and pepper
1 lemon
4 sprigs parsley or dill
4 tablespoons dry white wine
1 small cucumber, diced
about 150 ml / ¼ pint mayonnaise

For the garnish
lettuce
dill or parsley sprigs

Put the salmon steaks in a greased ovenproof dish and sprinkle with salt and pepper.

Grate the rind from the lemon and reserve for the sauce. Thinly slice the lemon and place one slice on top of each steak. Place a herb sprig on top of each salmon steak and pour the wine over. Cover the dish with foil and bake in a preheated oven for 20 minutes until the salmon is cooked but not dry. Leave to cool.

To make the sauce, place the cucumber in a bowl. Stir in the mayonnaise with any salmon cooking liquid, the reserved lemon rind and salt and pepper to taste. Add more mayonnaise if you want a larger quantity of sauce.

To serve, carefully remove the skin and the central bone from the salmon, keeping the steaks whole. Arrange the steaks on individual serving plates. Spoon cucumber sauce over each salmon steak where the bone has been removed. Garnish with lettuce and herbs.

Cook's Tip

This chilled fish dish is ideal for summer entertaining. The salmon steaks and poaching liquid can be kept separately, covered, in the refrigerator for a day. For variety, use halibut, cod or turbot instead of salmon.

105 | *Squid with Herbs*

Preparation time
about 10 minutes

Cooking time
2 minutes

Serves 4

Calories
230 per portion

You will need
1 kg/2 lb prepared baby squid (see
  Cook's Tip)
salt
pepper
4 tablespoons olive oil
3–4 cloves garlic, thickly sliced
2 tablespoons chopped thyme
1 tablespoon chopped parsley
juice of ½ lemon

For the garnish
lemon slices
tiny bunches of thyme

Cut the squid into slices; cut the tentacles in half if they are large. Season with salt and pepper to taste.

Heat the oil in a wok, add the garlic and cook gently until browned, then discard the garlic by removing with a slotted spoon. Increase the heat, add the squid and cook briskly for just under 1 minute. Sprinkle with the herbs and lemon juice. Serve immediately, garnished with lemon and tiny bunches of thyme.

106 | *Stir-Fried Squid with Vegetables*

Preparation time
30 minutes

Cooking time
about 10 minutes

Serves 4

Calories
270 per portion

You will need
400 g/14 oz squid, cleaned
2 slices root ginger, chopped
1 tablespoon sake or dry sherry
1 tablespoon cornflour
15 g/½ oz dried wood ears,
  soaked for 20 minutes
4 tablespoons vegetable oil
2 spring onions, chopped
225 g/8 oz cauliflower or broccoli
  florets
2 carrots, cut into diamond
  shaped chunks
1 teaspoon salt
1 teaspoon sugar
1 teaspoon sesame oil

Cut the prepared squid into rings and thin slices. Place in a bowl with half the ginger, the sake or sherry and corn-flour. Mix well and leave to stand for 20 minutes. Meanwhile, drain the wood ears and break into small pieces, discarding the hard bits.

Heat 2 tablespoons of the oil in a wok or frying pan, add the spring onions and remaining ginger, then the cauli-flower or broccoli, carrots and wood ears. Stir, then add the salt and sugar and continue cooking until the vege-tables are tender, adding a little water if necessary. Re-move from the pan with a slotted spoon and drain.

Heat the remaining oil in the pan, add the squid and stir-fry for about 1 minute. Return the vegetables to the pan, add the sesame oil and mix well. Serve hot.

Cook's Tip

To prepare squid, draw back the rim of the body pouch to locate the quill-shaped pen and pull free to discard. Separate the body from the tentacles by pulling gently apart just below the eyes – the inedible head and ink-sack will come away together. Slip a finger under the skin and peel it away gently.

Cook's Tip

The squid's ink sacs contain a dark brown liquid, which can be used as a basis for a sauce in which to cook it.

107 | Spicy Prawns

Preparation time
8 minutes

Cooking time
15–20 minutes

Serves 4–6

Calories
280–190 per portion

You will need
450 g/1 lb peeled prawns
1 teaspoon ground coriander
1 heaped tablespoon chopped
     parsley
1 egg, beaten
40 g/1½ oz fresh wholewheat
     breadcrumbs
3 tablespoons oil
2 onions, finely chopped
1 garlic clove, crushed
¼ teaspoon chilli powder
½ teaspoon ground ginger
¼ teaspoon ground bay leaves
150 ml/¼ pint hot water
juice of 1 lemon

Mince the prawns and mix with the coriander and parsley. Divide and shape into walnut-sized balls; dip into the egg and coat in the breadcrumbs. Set aside.

Heat 2 tablespoons of the oil in a frying pan, add the prawn balls and fry until golden. Remove and keep warm. Heat the remaining oil, add the onions and fry until brown. Stir in the garlic, chilli, ginger and ground bay leaves and cook, stirring, for about 5 minutes.

Add the hot water, bring to the boil, then simmer for 8–10 minutes. Stir in the lemon juice. Serve the sauce with the prawn balls.

108 | Prawns in Chilli Sauce

Preparation time
6 minutes

Cooking time
6 minutes

Serves 4

Calories
140 per portion

You will need
1 tablespoon oil
3 spring onions, chopped
2 teaspoons chopped root ginger
225 g/8 oz peeled prawns
100 g/4 oz mangetout
½ teaspoon chilli powder
1 teaspoon tomato purée
¼ teaspoon salt
½ teaspoon sugar
1 tablespoon dry sherry
½ teaspoon sesame oil
whole prawns in shell to garnish

Heat the oil in a wok or deep frying pan, add the spring onions and ginger and stir-fry for 30 seconds. Add the prawns, mangetout, chilli powder, tomato purée, salt, sugar and sherry and stir-fry briskly for 5 minutes. Sprinkle over the sesame oil and serve at once, garnished with whole prawns.

Cook's Tip

Spicy Prawns has the pungent, hot flavour of Indian food. Serve with rice and a green salad for a main meal.

Cook's Tip

Prawns in Chilli Sauce originates from the western Szechuan region of China, where the emphasis is on hotness of food combined with pungent flavoured vegetables. Serve with plain rice or noodles.

109 | Fillets of Sole with Mushrooms

Preparation time
20 minutes

Cooking time
5–10 minutes

Serves 3–4

Calories
300–220 per portion

You will need
450 g/1 lb sole fillets
1 egg white
1 tablespoon cornflour
oil for deep frying
225 g/8 oz button mushrooms, sliced
2–3 spring onions, shredded
1 slice root ginger, shredded
1 teaspoon sugar
1 teaspoon salt
1 tablespoon soy sauce
1 tablespoon sake or dry sherry
100 ml/4 fl oz fish stock
1 teaspoon sesame oil

Halve the fish fillets if they are large. Mix in a bowl with the egg white and cornflour. Heat the oil in a wok or deep frying pan and deep fry the fish until golden and crisp; drain on absorbent kitchen paper.

Pour off all but 2 tablespoons of the oil in the pan. Add the mushrooms, spring onions and ginger. Stir-fry for 30 seconds, then add the salt, sugar, soy sauce, sherry and stock. Bring to the boil, add the fish and simmer for 2 minutes. Sprinkle over the sesame oil and serve hot.

Cook's Tip

This dish is not unlike the French Filets de Sole Bonne Femme. The fish can be skinned if liked, but leaving the skin on helps to keep the fish intact during cooking.

110 | Fish and Bean Curd Casserole

Preparation time
20 minutes

Cooking time
15–20 minutes

Serves 4

Calories
220 per portion

You will need
450 g/1 lb firm white fish fillets
1 tablespoon cornflour
2 tablespoons water
1 egg white
450 g/1 lb firm bean curd or tofu
a few Chinese or Cos lettuce leaves
3 tablespoons sake or dry sherry
2 tablespoons light soy sauce
1 teaspoon sugar
2 slices root ginger, peeled
3 spring onions, chopped
salt and pepper
300 ml/½ pint clear broth (see Cook's Tip recipe 10)
50 g/2 oz cooked ham, chopped
1 teaspoon sesame oil

Cut the fish into small pieces. Mix the cornflour to a paste with 2 tablespoons cold water, then mix with the egg white and use to coat the fish. Cut the bean curd into small cubes.

Line a flameproof casserole with the Chinese leaves or lettuce. Add the bean curd and fish pieces with the sherry, soy sauce, sugar, ginger, spring onions and salt and pepper to taste. Pour over the broth and sprinkle with the ham. Bring to the boil, cover, reduce the heat and simmer for 15–20 minutes.

Sprinkle with the sesame oil and serve at once.

Cook's Tip

An easy way to separate an egg: break the egg over a saucer or shallow dish. Place an egg-cup (or small glass) over the yolk. Holding the egg-cup in place, tilt the saucer and pour off all the white into a small bowl.

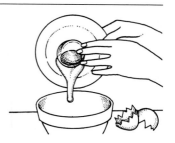

111 | Braised Prawns

Preparation time
5 minutes plus 1–2 hours marinating time

Cooking time
about 5 minutes

Serves 4

Calories
180 per portion

You will need
1 teaspoon salt
1 egg white
2 tablespoons cornflour
225 g/8 oz raw peeled prawns
225 g/8 oz lard
2 tablespoons dry sherry
4 tablespoons stock
1 tablespoon water
1 teaspoon sesame oil

Mix the salt with the egg white and 1 tablespoon of the cornflour. Add the prawns and leave to marinate in the refrigerator for 1–2 hours.

Heat the lard in a pan. Add the prawns and stir to separate them, then lift out with a slotted spoon. Pour off the excess lard, leaving a small amount in the pan. Add the sherry, stock and prawns and bring to the boil. Dissolve the remaining cornflour in the water and add to the pan, stir until thickened. Add the sesame oil and serve.

112 | Soy-Braised Cod or Halibut Steaks

Preparation time
15 minutes

Cooking time
about 12 minutes

Serves 4

Calories
260 per portion

You will need
50 g/2 oz lard
3–4 spring onions, chopped
2–3 slices root ginger, chopped
450 g/1 lb cod or halibut steaks, quartered
2 tablespoons sherry
2 tablespoons soy sauce
1 tablespoon sugar
100 ml/4 fl oz water
1 tablespoon cornflour dissolved in 1½ tablespoons water
1 teaspoon sesame oil
shredded spring onion to garnish

Melt the lard in a pan over a high heat. Add the spring onions and ginger and stir-fry for a few seconds. Add the fish pieces and stir very gently to separate. Add the sherry and bring to the boil, then stir in the soy sauce, sugar and water. Simmer for about 10 minutes.

Add the cornflour mixture and simmer until thickened. Add the sesame oil and serve hot, garnished with shredded spring onion.

Cook's Tip

Braised Prawns can be served either hot or cold. Serve on a bed of shredded lettuce.

Cook's Tip

Any other firm white fish may be used for this recipe, such as haddock, whiting or plaice. Use fish steaks or fillets, depending upon the fish type.

113 | Whiting and Fennel Soufflés

Preparation time
40 minutes

Cooking time
20 25 minutes

Oven temperature
220 C, 425 F, gas 7

Serves 6

Calories
285 per soufflé

You will need
225 g/8 oz whiting fillets
150 ml/¼ pint milk
½ onion, chopped
1 small carrot, chopped
1 bay leaf
1 head fennel, with a few leaves
50 g/2 oz butter
75 g/3 oz plain flour
150 ml/¼ pint single cream
2 eggs, separated
salt and pepper
pinch of cayenne
100 g/4 oz low-fat hard cheese,
   grated (for example Shape
   cheese)

Poach the fish in the milk with the onion, carrot and bay leaf for 10 minutes. Cool. Trim the fennel, cut into four and simmer in water for about 8 minutes, until soft. Keeping the cooking water, drain and chop the fennel. Drain the fish (reserving the milk for the sauce) and flake. Discard the flavouring vegetables. Make a thick sauce: melt the butter in a pan, stir in the flour then gradually add the milk, cream and 150 ml/¼ pint of the fennel water, stirring continuously. Beat in the yolks, and stir in the fish and fennel. Season well and add the cayenne. Whisk the egg whites until stiff and fold into the fish mixture. Divide the mixture between six individual soufflé dishes (each holding about 150 ml/¼ pint) and sprinkle with cheese. Bake for 20–25 minutes.

Cook's Tip

Fish is an excellent food, low in carbohydrate and high in protein. All fish are a good source of B vitamins and minerals such as iodine and calcium.

114 | Prawn Risotto

Preparation time
15 minutes

Cooking time
38 43 minutes

Serves 4

Calories
375 per portion

You will need
1 onion, chopped
2 tablespoons oil
1 clove garlic, crushed
1 red pepper, deseeded and diced
225 g/8 oz long-grain brown rice
750 ml/1¼ pints water
salt and pepper
100 g/4 oz frozen cut French
   beans
225 g/8 oz peeled cooked prawns
4 tablespoons grated Parmesan
   cheese

Cook the onion in the oil with the garlic until soft but not browned. Add the pepper and rice and cook for 3 minutes, stirring frequently. Pour in the water and add seasoning to taste. Bring to the boil, cover and simmer gently for 30 minutes. Add the beans and prawns, without stirring in, re-cover and continue to cook for 5–10 minutes. When most of the liquid has been absorbed and the beans are just cooked, stir in the Parmesan cheese and serve at once.

Cook's Tip

On the fishmonger's slab, look for prawns with firm unbroken heads and tails that are intact and undamaged. They should have a mild fresh sea smell with no trace of ammonia.

115 | Steamed Sweet and Sour Fish

Preparation time
10 minutes

Cooking time
12–15 minutes

Serves 4

Calories
150 per portion

You will need
1 large whole plaice, cleaned
salt
2 (2.5-cm/1-inch) pieces root
   ginger, shredded
3 spring onions, sliced

For the sauce
150 ml/¼ pint fish or chicken
   stock
1 tablespoon soy sauce
1 tablespoon sugar
1 tablespoon wine vinegar
1 tablespoon dry sherry
1 tablespoon tomato purée
1 teaspoon chilli sauce
pinch of salt
1 tablespoon cornflour

Score the fish by making 3 diagonal cuts on each side. Rub the fish with salt and sprinkle with the ginger and spring onions. Put on an ovenproof plate and place in a steamer. Steam for 12–15 minutes until tender.

Meanwhile, make the sauce. Mix all the ingredients except the cornflour, together in a small pan. Bring to the boil and cook for 1 minute. Blend the cornflour with 2 tablespoons water and stir into the sauce. Cook, stirring until thickened.

Carefully lift the plaice on to a serving dish and spoon over the sauce. Serve hot.

Cook's Tip

Fresh or frozen plaice can be used for this recipe. Garnish with fresh coriander leaves and tomato flowers if liked.

116 | Braised Fish with Black Bean Sauce

Preparation time
20 minutes

Cooking time
10–15 minutes

Serves 4

Calories
260 per portion

You will need
3 tablespoons black beans (see
   Cook's Tip)
2 tablespoons oil
2 spring onions, chopped
2.5 cm/1 inch piece root ginger,
   chopped
1 small red pepper, cored, seeded
   and chopped
2 celery sticks, chopped
2 tablespoons soy sauce
2 tablespoons dry sherry
4 cod or haddock cutlets, each
   weighing 150 g/5 oz
shredded spring onion to garnish

Soak the black beans in warm water for 10 minutes; drain.

Heat the oil in a wok or deep frying pan, add the spring onions, ginger, red pepper and celery and stir-fry for 1 minute. Stir in the soy sauce and sherry. Place the fish on top of the vegetables and simmer for 5–10 minutes until almost tender, depending upon the thickness of the fish. Spoon over the black beans and cook for 2 minutes.

Arrange the fish on a warmed serving dish and spoon the sauce over. Serve hot, garnished with shredded spring onion.

Cook's Tip

Black beans are salted, fermented beans with a strong, salty flavour. They are sold in packs or by weight in Chinese supermarkets. They must be soaked for 5–10 minutes before use.

117 | Smoked Mackerel and Orange Kebabs with Rice

Preparation time
5 minutes

Cooking time
10 minutes

Serves 4

Calories
184 per portion

You will need
1 × 175-g / 6-oz packet par-cooked long-grain rice
salt
1 tablespoon butter
juice and grated rind of ½ orange
4 smoked mackerel fillets, about 175 g / 6 oz each, skinned
1 teaspoon lemon juice
pepper
3 large oranges, peeled and segmented
2 tablespoons blanched almonds, toasted
1 bunch watercress, trimmed to garnish

Cook the rice in boiling, salted water for 10 minutes, or until just tender. Drain and stir in the butter, orange juice and orange rind. Keep warm.

Meanwhile, cut the mackerel fillets crosswise into 2.5 cm / 1 inch strips and toss in the lemon juice. Sprinkle with pepper.

Thread the mackerel strips and orange segments alternately on to four skewers. Grill on a preheated hot grill for 5 minutes, turning the skewers once.

Just before serving, stir the toasted almonds into the rice. Serve the fish skewers on the rice, garnished with watercress sprigs.

Cook's Tip

To toast the almonds, place them in a single layer on a baking sheet under a hot grill for about 2 minutes, until golden. Use a long-handled wooden spoon to stir at least once.

118 | Smoked Haddock Mousse

Preparation time
20 minutes, plus chilling

Cooking time
12 minutes

Serves 4

Calories
275 per portion

You will need
450 g / l lb smoked haddock fillets, broken into pieces
300 ml / ½ pint milk
pepper
25 g / 1 oz butter
25 g / 1 oz plain flour
150 ml / ¼ pint double cream
2 tablespoons chopped fresh parsley
3 tablespoons dry white wine
15 g / ½ oz gelatine
1 tablespoon lemon juice
few drops anchovy essence
cucumber slices to garnish

Poach the haddock in the milk and pepper for 6–8 minutes until tender. Remove the haddock from the liquid and discard the skin and any bones. Reserve 150 ml / ¼ pint poaching liquid. Melt the butter, then stir in the flour and cook for 3 minutes, stirring. Add the reserved liquid and cream and continue cooking until the sauce boils and thickens. Add the parsley and haddock.

Meanwhile, place the wine in a small bowl and sprinkle the gelatine on top. Place in a pan of simmering water until the gelatine dissolves. Stir in the lemon juice, anchovy essence and pepper to taste, then fold into the fish mixture.

Spoon into a wetted 1.2 litre / 2 pint mould. Smooth the surface, then cover with cling film and chill until set.

To serve, unmould and garnish with cucumber slices.

Cook's Tip

To unmould, place a serving plate on top of the mould and turn over, giving a sharp shake halfway over. If not unmoulded, dip the mould in hot water. Do not leave for more than a few seconds or the design will disappear.

119 | *Fish Ragoût*

Preparation time
15 minutes

Cooking time
20–25 minutes

Oven temperature
200 C, 400 F, gas 6

Serves 4

Calories
180 per portion

You will need
450 g / 1 lb cod, coley or haddock
 fillets, skinned
1 onion, sliced into rings
1 clove garlic, crushed
1 green pepper, deseeded and
 sliced into rings
100 g / 4 oz button mushrooms
1–2 tablespoons oil
1 (400-g / 14-oz) can of chopped
 tomatoes
150 ml / ¼ pint dry white wine
½ teaspoon chopped fresh basil
salt and pepper

Garnish
fresh basil leaves
1 tablespoon chopped parsley

Rinse the fish, cut it into cubes, then put into an ovenproof dish. Fry the onion, garlic, pepper and mushrooms in the oil for 2–3 minutes, then add to the fish. Mix together the tomatoes, wine, basil, salt and pepper. Pour over the fish mixture. Cover the dish with foil and bake in a moderately hot oven for 20–25 minutes.

Serve immediately with parslied boiled rice, garnishing with fresh basil leaves and chopped parsley.

120 | *Fish Cakes*

Preparation time
20 minutes

Cooking time
20 minutes

Serves 4

Calories
390 per portion

You will need
225 g / 8 oz coley, cubed
knob of butter
salt and pepper
225 g / 8 oz mashed potatoes
100 g / 4 oz Cheddar cheese,
 grated
25 g / 1 oz plain flour
1 egg, lightly beaten
100 g / 4 oz fresh white
 breadcrumbs
oil for frying

Garnish
lemon slices
lime slices
parsley sprigs

Place the fish on a buttered flameproof plate, season and cover with foil. Steam over a pan of boiling water for 10–15 minutes or until the fish flakes easily.

Flake the fish and mix with the potato and cheese. Season, divide the mixture into eight portions and pat each into a round cake. Coat the fish cakes in the flour, dip into the egg and then into the breadcrumbs. Heat the oil in a frying pan and fry the fish cakes until golden brown on the underside, then turn and cook until golden on the other side. Drain on absorbent kitchen paper.

Garnish the fish cakes with lemon and lime slices and parsley sprigs.

Cook's Tip

Fresh basil tastes significantly superior to its dried counterpart. Grow your own in a pot indoors, positioned on a light windowsill – purchase in plant form or nurture from seed.

Freezer Tip

For real speed, use instant mashed potato. Freeze the cakes before frying – put them on a baking tray covered with cling film and open freeze. Pack in freezer bags when hard.

121 | Crunchy Fish Pie

Preparation time
15–20 minutes

Cooking time
35–45 minutes

Oven temperature
190C, 375F, gas 5

Serves 4

Calories
725 per portion

You will need
50 g/2 oz butter or margarine
50 g/2 oz plain flour
600 ml/1 pint milk
salt and pepper
¼ teaspoon dill weed
1 (198-g/7-oz) can tuna,
 drained and flaked
100 g/4 oz peeled, cooked
 prawns
2 tablespoons lemon juice

For the topping
175 g/6 oz wholemeal flour
50 g/2 oz oatmeal
100 g/4 oz butter
salt and pepper

Garnish
2 whole cooked prawns
parsley sprigs

Melt the butter or margarine over a low heat, stir in the flour, cook for 2 minutes, then gradually add the milk, stirring all the time. Bring the sauce to the boil, simmer gently for a few minutes. Add the seasoning, dill weed, tuna, prawns and lemon juice. Pour into an ovenproof dish.

Place the flour, oatmeal, butter and seasoning in a bowl. Using your fingertips, rub the fat into the dry ingredients until the mixture resembles fine bread-crumbs. Spoon over the fish mixture and bake in a moderately hot oven for 30–40 minutes. Serve hot, garnished with whole prawns and parsley.

Microwave Tip

Whisk the butter, flour and milk and cook in a micro-wave on full power for 8–10 minutes, whisk again. Add seafood, microwave for 3–5 minutes, then transfer to serving dish, top and grill until brown.

122 | Fish Envelopes

Preparation time
15 minutes

Cooking time
20–25 minutes

Oven temperature
220C, 425F, gas 7

Serves 4

Calories
585 per envelope

You will need
450 g/1 lb smoked haddock,
 skinned and boned
1 large onion, chopped
50 g/2 oz butter or margarine
2 hard-boiled eggs, chopped
2 tablespoons chopped parsley
2 tablespoons natural yogurt
salt and pepper
1 (368-g/13-oz) packet frozen
 puff pastry, defrosted
beaten egg to glaze

Garnish
watercress sprigs
tomato lily

Grease two baking trays. Cut the fish into small pieces and cook with the onion in the butter or margarine for 5 minutes. Mix the hard-boiled eggs, parsley, yogurt and seasoning with the fish and onion. Leave to cool while preparing the pastry envelopes.

Divide the pastry into four and roll into 18-cm/7-in squares. Divide the fish mixture between the squares, keeping it well in the centre. Dampen the edges of the pastry with a little water and bring the four corners to the centre, pressing well together to seal. Glaze the pastry envelopes with beaten egg, transfer to the baking trays and bake in a hot oven for 15–20 minutes, until golden. Serve immediately, garnished with watercress and a tomato lily.

Microwave Tip

Defrost frozen puff pastry in the microwave. Unwrap and place on double thick absorbent kitchen paper. Allow 1 minute on full power, turning once.

123 | Fish au Gratin

Preparation time
15 minutes

Cooking time
12–16 minutes

Serves 4

Calories
205 per portion

You will need
50 g/ 2 oz fresh white
   breadcrumbs
4 fresh cod steaks
salt and pepper
25 g/ 1 oz butter or margarine
50 g/ 2 oz Cheddar cheese, grated
$\frac{1}{4}$ teaspoon mustard powder
lemon twists to garnish

Spread the breadcrumbs on a sheet of foil and grill until golden and crunchy, then leave to cool.

Season the cod steaks generously with salt and pepper on each side. Dot the butter or margarine over one side of the fish. Turn the grill on to medium heat. Place the cod steaks buttered side up on a sheet of foil and grill for 6–8 minutes. Turn them over, mix together the breadcrumbs, cheese, mustard and seasoning to taste, sprinkle over the fish and grill for a further 6–8 minutes.

Place the cod steaks in a hot serving dish, garnish with lemon twists and serve at once with jacket potatoes and a green vegetable.

124 | Haddock in Cider

Preparation time
20 minutes

Cooking time
30 minutes

Oven temperature
180 C, 350 F, gas 4

Serves 4

Calories
320 per portion

You will need
10 shallots, peeled
100 g/ 4 oz button mushrooms
1–2 tablespoons oil
2 celery sticks, thinly sliced
1 green pepper, deseeded and
   diced
4 fresh haddock steaks
salt and pepper
300 ml/ $\frac{1}{2}$ pint dry cider
25 g/ 1 oz butter or margarine
25 g/ 1 oz plain flour
150 ml/ $\frac{1}{4}$ pint single cream
chopped parsley to garnish

Fry the shallots and mushrooms in the oil until golden. Transfer to a casserole dish. Add the celery and pepper to the pan and cook for a few minutes. Add to the casserole. Place the haddock steaks in the casserole, season with salt and pepper. Pour over the cider and bake in a moderate oven for 25 minutes or until the fish flakes easily when tested with the point of a knife. Transfer the fish and vegetables to a serving plate, cover and keep warm. Carefully drain off the cooking liquor. Melt the butter or margarine in a small saucepan, add the flour, then gradually add the cooking liquor, stirring continuously. Bring the sauce to the boil, season to taste, reduce the heat and simmer gently for 1–2 minutes. Stir in the cream and reheat without boiling. Pour the sauce over the fish, garnish with chopped parsley and serve immediately.

Cook's Tip

A quick way to make breadcrumbs: take a large piece of bread and rub it on the coarse side of a grater.

Cook's Tip

To avoid runny eyes when peeling shallots or pickling onions, peel them in a bowl of water. Drain and discard the skin when all are peeled.

MEAT AND POULTRY

The range of recipes devised for meat and poultry is vast. This chapter includes a selection of the best, using all kinds and cuts of meat and a variety of cooking methods.

Steaks and chops are high-quality cuts that can be grilled or fried with mouth-watering results, especially if served with a complementary sauce, as in Marsala Steaks, Noisettes Niçoise or Pork Chops with Spicy Mustard Cream. Less expensive cuts can be equally delicious if braised with vegetables. All over the world cooks have invented variations on the tender, tasty stew to make a nutritious, filling dish: from the inimitable Irish Stew to Chilli con Carne, from Hungarian Goulash to Malabar Lamb Curry, the international spectrum is reflected here.

Meat is an important part of a balanced diet, as it is rich in protein, essential vitamins and iron. Today's health-conscious cook will value dishes such as Stuffed Peppers, Stir-fried Liver with Spinach and Beef, Apricot and Apple Kebabs which are highly nutritious and cooked to reduce the fat content of meat as far as possible.

Chicken naturally takes a major place in the repertoire of all good cooks – low in fat but full of protein, chicken is at the basis of classics like Coq au Vin as well as family favourites like Chicken and Leeks. These and many more exciting recipes are included in this chapter.

125 | Marsala Steaks

Preparation time
10 minutes

Cooking time
10–15 minutes

Serves 4

Calories
784 per portion

You will need
2 rump steaks, about 225 g / 8 oz
   each
salt and pepper
50 g / 2 oz butter
4 teaspoons olive oil
100 g / 4 oz mushrooms, wiped
   and finely chopped
50 g / 2 oz smooth pâté
4 tablespoons Marsala
6 tablespoons brandy
thyme sprigs to garnish

Sprinkle the steaks on both sides with salt and pepper to taste.

Heat the butter and oil and fry the steaks for 2–4 minutes on each side until browned and cooked to your liking. Keep warm.

Add the mushrooms to the pan and cook on a high heat for 1 minute, stirring constantly. Add the pâté and Marsala and stir until well mixed and hot. Add salt and pepper to taste and spread the mixture over the steaks. Return them to the frying pan.

Warm the brandy and pour over the steaks at the table. Carefully ignite the brandy and serve when the flames have extinguished. Garnish with sprigs of thyme.

126 | Beef in Cream Sauce

Preparation time
5 minutes

Cooking time
8 minutes

Serves 4

Calories
175 per portion

You will need
1 tablespoon oil
2 onions, peeled and thinly sliced
3–4 slices beef for beef olives, cut
   into matchstick strips
1 tablespoon soy sauce
2 tablespoons single cream
salt and pepper
parsley sprigs and tomato slices
   to garnish

Heat the oil and fry the onions for 4 minutes, stirring, until lightly browned. Push to one side of the pan. Tilt the pan to let the juices run out of the onions and over the base.

Add the meat strips and stir-fry for 2–3 minutes until evenly browned. Mix with the onions, then add the soy sauce and stir in the cream and salt and pepper to taste. Heat through gently, without boiling. Serve at once, garnished with parsley.

Cook's Tip

For variety, use sirloin steak instead of rump steak. Both cuts are tender and suitable for quick pan-frying.

Cook's Tip

Beef for beef olives are thin slices of lean beef available from supermarkets. These slices are usually rolled around a stuffing and braised. Otherwise, ask your butcher for beef suitable for quick cooking, such as topside.

127 | Beef Cobbler

Preparation time
20 minutes

Cooking time
2 hours 25 minutes

Oven temperature
160 C, 325 F, gas 3 and
220 C, 425 F, gas 7

Serves 4

Calories
750 per portion

You will need
575 g/ 1¼ lb stewing or braising
    steak, cut into cubes
25 g/ 1 oz plain flour
1 teaspoon dried mixed herbs
salt and pepper
1 onion, chopped
3 tablespoons oil
100 g/ 4 oz baby carrots
2 parsnips, quartered and sliced
600 ml/ 1 pint beef stock
100 g/ 4 oz frozen peas

For the topping
225 g/ 8 oz self-raising flour
pinch of salt
50 g/ 2 oz butter or margarine
1 egg, beaten plus extra to glaze
3 tablespoons milk

Toss the meat in a mixture of the flour, herbs and seasoning. Cook in the oil until browned. Transfer to a casserole. Cook the onion in the oil until soft and add to the casserole with the carrots, parsnips and beef stock. Season to taste. Cover and cook in a moderate oven for 2 hours until the meat is cooked. Stir in the peas.

Sift the flour and salt into a bowl, rub in the fat until the mixture resembles fine breadcrumbs. Stir in the beaten egg and enough milk to make a soft dough. Roll out on a lightly floured work surface to about 2.5 cm/1 in thick. Cut into rounds using a 5-cm/2-in scone cutter. Place the cobblers on top of the meat in the casserole, increase the oven heat and bake for 15 minutes.

Freezer Tip

If you intend freezing the cooked cobbler, then first line the casserole dish with double-thick cooking foil, making sure there are no cracks or gaps and allowing plenty of overlap round the rim.

Cook the casserole and cobbler in the lined dish, then cool and lightly cover. Freeze until hard. When solid, the cobbler in foil can be removed from the dish, packed in extra foil, labelled and stored.

128 | Lancashire Hot Pot

Preparation time
10 minutes

Cooking time
2 hours

Oven temperature
160 C, 325 F, gas 3 and
200 C, 400 F, gas 6

Serves 4

Calories
705 per portion

You will need
675–1 kg/ 1½–2 lb middle or best
    end neck of lamb
4 lambs' kidneys, skinned and
    cored
2 carrots, sliced
1 small turnip, diced
2 onions, chopped
salt and pepper
450 g/ 1 lb potatoes, sliced
300 ml/ ½ pint lamb or beef stock
25 g/ 1 oz butter or margarine
1 teaspoon chopped parsley to
    garnish

Cut the lamb and the kidneys into neat pieces and place in alternate layers with the carrot, turnip and onion in a casserole. Season with salt and pepper.

Finish the hot pot with layers of sliced potatoes. Pour over the stock and dot the top with small pieces of butter or margarine. Cover the casserole with a lid and place in a moderate oven for about 2 hours until the meat is cooked. Uncover the casserole for the last half an hour and increase the oven temperature to moderately hot to brown the top layer of potatoes.

Serve immediately garnished with chopped parsley.

Cook's Tip

To core kidneys, cut them in half, then use kitchen scissors to snip out the white cores.

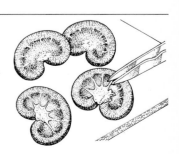

129 | Chilli con Carne

Preparation time
10 minutes

Cooking time
30–35 minutes

Serves 4

Calories
435 per portion

You will need
1 tablespoon oil
1 onion, chopped
2 cloves garlic, crushed
450 g/ 1 lb minced beef
15 g/½ oz plain flour
salt
2 teaspoons chilli powder
1 (400-g/ 14-oz) can tomatoes
300 ml/½ pint beef stock
1 (425-g/ 15-oz) can red kidney
   beans
chopped parsley to garnish

Heat the oil in a frying pan and cook the onion and garlic until soft. Add the minced beef and cook until brown all over. Mix in the flour, salt to taste, chilli powder, tomatoes and beef stock. Stir the mixture well and bring to the boil. Reduce the heat and simmer gently for 30 minutes, stirring occasionally.

Drain the kidney beans, add to the chilli and cook for a further 5–10 minutes or until the kidney beans are heated through.

Serve the chilli on a bed of boiled rice. Garnish with parsley.

130 | Moussaka

Preparation time
30 minutes

Cooking time
1 hour 40 minutes

Oven temperature
180 C, 350 F, gas 4

Serves 4

Calories
630 per portion

You will need
2 aubergines, thinly sliced
salt and pepper
3 tablespoons oil
3 onions, thinly sliced
6 tomatoes, peeled
450 g/ 1 lb minced beef or lamb
1 tablespoon plain flour
1 tablespoon tomato purée
300 ml/½ pint beef stock
1 teaspoon dried mixed herbs
40 g/ 1½ oz butter or margarine
40 g/ 1½ oz plain flour
600 ml/ 1 pint milk
75 g/ 3 oz Cheddar cheese, grated
chopped parsley to garnish

Sprinkle the aubergines with salt to remove bitter juices and leave covered while preparing the other vegetables. Heat the oil in a frying pan and cook the onion until soft. Remove from the pan and set aside. Slice the tomatoes.

Rinse the aubergine, then dry on absorbent kitchen paper and fry in the pan, a few slices at a time, until golden on each side. Drain.

Fry the meat until browned. Stir in the flour, tomato purée, stock, herbs and seasoning. Bring to the boil, then simmer for 15 minutes. Make a cheese sauce with the remaining ingredients, as instructed in recipe 110. Layer the meat and vegetables in an ovenproof dish, then top with the cheese sauce. Bake in a moderately hot oven for 1 hour.

Garnish the moussaka with chopped parsley and serve, accompanied by a mixed salad.

Cook's Tip

Dried red kidney beans need overnight soaking and rapid boiling for 3–5 minutes, then about 1 hour's simmering. They can be used half-cooked in chilli. Add extra liquid and cook until tender.

Cook's Tip

A quick way to make cheese sauce: put all ingredients, except cheese, in a saucepan and heat slowly to boiling point, whisking continuously. Stir in cheese.

131 | Stuffed Peppers

Preparation time
20 minutes

Cooking time
about 40 minutes

Serves 4

Calories
470 per portion

You will need
5 tablespoons oil
1 onion, finely chopped
2 teaspoons ground coriander
1 teaspoon ground cumin
½ teaspoon chilli powder
350 g/12 oz minced beef
3 tablespoons long-grain rice
salt
4 large green or red peppers,
   sliced lengthways, cored and
   seeded
1 (400-g/14-oz) can tomatoes

Heat 3 tablespoons of the oil in a pan. Add the onion and fry until golden. Add the spices and cook for 2 minutes. Add the minced beef and fry, stirring, until browned. Add the rice and salt to taste and cook for 2 minutes. Leave to cool, then fill the pepper shells with the mixture.

Heat the remaining oil in a pan just large enough to hold the peppers. Add the peppers, pour a little of the tomato juice into each pepper and the remaining juice and tomatoes into the pan, seasoning with salt to taste. Bring to simmering point, cover and cook for about 25 minutes, until the rice is tender.

132 | Coriander Beef with Aubergine

Preparation time
20 minutes

Cooking time
about 2¼ hours

Serves 6

Calories
500 per portion

You will need
75 ml/3 fl oz oil
2 onions, finely sliced
2.5 cm/1 inch piece root ginger,
   chopped
3 garlic cloves, chopped
3 tablespoons ground coriander
½ teaspoon hot chilli powder
1 kg/2 lb lean boneless beef, cut
   into 4-cm/1½-inch cubes
475 ml/16 fl oz beef stock
1 large aubergine, cut into
   4-cm/1½-inch cubes
675 g/1½ lb tomatoes, chopped
1 (400-g/14-oz) can chick peas,
   drained
salt and pepper
1 teaspoon garam masala (see
   Cook's Tip recipe 67)

Heat the oil, add the onion and cook for 10 minutes until tender. Add the ginger, garlic, coriander and chilli powder, then cook for 2 minutes. Stir in the beef and brown for 5 minutes, turning frequently.

Add the stock, bring to the boil, reduce the heat, cover and simmer for 1½ hours.

Stir in the aubergine, cover and simmer for 20 minutes. Add the tomatoes and chick peas, cover and simmer for a further 10 minutes, then season to taste with salt and pepper. Stir in the garam masala and serve at once.

Cook's Tip

Serve this dish with a simple side salad accompaniment, naan bread and yogurt.

Cook's Tip

Sprinkling aubergine cubes with salt draws out any bitter juices and also prevents the aubergine absorbing too much oil. Rinse thoroughly through, or the cubes will taste salty.

133 | Veal Chops with Marjoram Sauce

Preparation time
10 minutes

Cooking time
35 minutes

Serves 4

Calories
289 per portion

You will need
4 large veal chops, about 255 g /
   8 oz each
25 g / 1 oz butter
1 tablespoon oil
1 onion, peeled and finely
   chopped
1 garlic clove, peeled and crushed
3 tablespoons chicken stock
3 tablespoons dry vermouth
1 tablespoon chopped fresh
   marjoram, or 1 teaspoon dried
salt and pepper
4 tablespoons double cream

Heat the butter and oil and fry the chops over moderate heat for 4 minutes on each side. Remove the chops and keep warm.

Fry the onion and garlic for 3 minutes, stirring occasionally, then pour in the stock and vermouth and stir well. Return the chops to the dish and add the marjoram and salt and pepper to taste.

Bring the sauce to the boil, then cover the dish, lower the heat and simmer for 20 minutes.

Increase the heat, bring the sauce to the boil again to reduce the liquid slightly. Add the cream and heat through. Adjust the seasoning if necessary and serve.

Cook's Tip

You are more likely to get veal chops from a butcher than at a supermarket. These meaty chops are very popular in Italy.

134 | Veal Scallopini Mirabeau

Preparation time
20 minutes, plus
chilling

Cooking time
10 minutes

Serves 4

Calories
501 per portion

You will need
2 veal cutlets, about 275 g / 10 oz
   each, boned
25 g / 1 oz plain flour
1 egg, beaten
75 g / 3 oz fine dry white
   breadcrumbs, sieved
4–6 tablespoons butter
2 tablespoons olive oil
anchovy fillets, drained and each
   cut in half lengthways
stuffed olives, sliced
1 lemon, cut into wedges

Cut each veal cutlet across the grain into two thin slices horizontally. Lay the pieces between two sheets of greaseproof paper and pound until thin. Sprinkle with a little flour.

Place the egg in one shallow dish and the breadcrumbs in another. Dip the veal in the egg, draining carefully, then roll in the breadcrumbs, patting the coating on firmly. Chill for at least 30 minutes.

Heat the butter and olive oil in a frying pan large enough to hold all the veal in a single layer. When the butter is foaming, fry the veal over moderate heat for 3–5 minutes on one side, then turn over and arrange a lattice of anchovy strips on each piece. Place an olive slice in each lattice opening and continue cooking for a further 3–5 minutes, or until the breadcrumbs are crisp and golden and the veal is cooked, but still juicy.

Transfer to a heated serving dish. Serve garnished with lemon wedges.

Cook's Tip

The veal should be pounded thinly but not so thin that the breadcrumb coating is nearly the same thickness as the veal. Lay the slices between two sheets of greaseproof paper and flatten gently with a meat mallet or rolling pin.

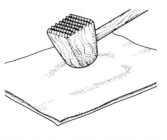

135 | *Beef and Orange Kebabs*

Preparation time
10 minutes

Cooking time
15 minutes

Serves 4

Calories
235 per portion

You will need
500 g / 1 lb frying steak, cut into
  bite-sized pieces
2–3 tomatoes, quartered
½ green pepper, cored, seeded
  and cut into pieces
½ red pepper, cored, seeded
  and cut into pieces
125 g / 4 oz button mushrooms
1 onion, cut into segments
2 tablespoons oil
grated rind and juice of 1 orange
1 tablespoon soy sauce
pepper
watercress to garnish

Thread the meat and vegetables alternately on to long skewers, starting with tomato.

Mix together the oil, orange rind and juice, sugar, soy sauce and pepper to taste, and use to coat the kebabs, brushing on with a pastry brush. Cook under a preheated moderate grill, about 7.5 cm / 3 inches away from the heat, for 15 minutes. Brush the kebabs with the oil and orange mixture after 10 minutes and turn over. Garnish with watercress.

Serves with crusty French bread and a green salad.

Cook's Tip

You can substitute boneless chicken or pork for these kebabs. The marinade is suitable for either, but if you use chicken, reduce the cooking time by 1–2 minutes per side.

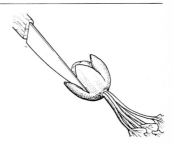

136 | *Beef and Radish Salad*

Preparation time
15 minutes

Serves 4

Calories
515 per portion

You will need
1 bunch radishes, with leaves
450 g / 1 lb cold rare roast beef
50 g / 2 oz walnut halves, broken

For the dressing
4 tablespoons walnut or olive oil
2 tablespoons orange juice
1 tablespoon wine vinegar
salt and pepper

Thinly slice the beef and cut into strips about 4 × 1 cm / 1½ × ½ inch and place in a bowl.

Select a few of the best radishes to make 'roses' for garnishing. Thinly slice the remaining radishes and add to the beef with the walnuts.

To make the dressing, mix all the ingredients together and pour over the salad. Toss until well coated.

Arrange in a serving dish. Spoon the beef and radish salad in the centre and garnish with the radish roses and radish leaves.

Cook's Tip

To make radish 'roses', make long cuts from the top of each radish to within 1 cm / ½ inch of the base. Leave in a bowl of iced water or in the refrigerator for several hours until they open out.

137 | Veal Escalopes with Ham and Cheese

Preparation time
15 minutes

Cooking time
12–15 minutes

Serve 4

Calories
418 per portion

You will need
4 teaspoons plain flour
salt and pepper
4 veal escalopes, about 175 g / 6 oz each
2 tablespoons olive oil
25 g / 1 oz butter
100 g / 4 oz Parma ham, chopped
2 teaspoons chopped fresh marjoram, or ½ teaspoon dried
2 tablespoons Parmesan cheese, grated
4 tablespoons Marsala
fresh marjoram or parsley to garnish

Place the flour on a plate and season with salt and pepper. Coat the veal escalopes with the flour, shaking off any excess.

Heat the oil and butter and fry the veal quickly on both sides until golden brown.

Divide the ham between the four escalopes and sprinkle with marjoram and cheese. Stir the Marsala into the pan juices and spoon over the veal.

Cover and cook gently for 3–4 minutes until the cheese has melted. Serve hot, garnished with marjoram.

138 | Veal in Lemon Sauce

Preparation time
10 minutes

Cooking time
8–10 minutes

Serves 4

Calories
313 per portion

You will need
2 veal fillets, about 350 g / 12 oz each, thinly sliced
4 tablespoons seasoned flour
2 tablespoons olive oil
50 g / 2 oz butter
4 tablespoons lemon juice
4 tablespoons chicken stock or water
salt and pepper
chopped fresh parsley and lemon slices to garnish

Toss the veal in seasoned flour, shaking off any excess. Heat the oil and half the butter and fry the veal quickly on both sides, for 2–3 minutes, until lightly browned. Remove the veal from the pan and keep warm.

Reduce the heat and stir the lemon juice and stock into the pan, scraping down any sediment. Add salt and pepper to taste. Add the remaining butter to the pan, tilting it until the butter has melted.

Return the veal to the pan and reheat gently. Transfer to a warmed serving dish and sprinkle with chopped parsley. Garnish with lemon slices.

Cook's Tip

Use sage if marjoram isn't available. Both herbs are oftened partnered with veal.

Cook's Tip

When squeezing fresh lemon juice, first roll the lemon on the work surface, pressing firmly. This breaks down the membranes inside and yields more juice.

139 | *Stir-fried Beef*

Preparation time
10 minutes, plus
marinating

Cooking time
20 minutes

Serves 4

Calories
419 per portion

You will need
450 g / 1 lb fillet of beef, thinly
 sliced
2 tablespoons soy sauce
4 teaspoons cornflour
salt
1 garlic clove, peeled and finely
 chopped
1 cm / ½ inch piece fresh root
 ginger, peeled and finely
 chopped
2 tablespoons oil
300 ml / ½ pint chicken stock
2 tablespoons dry sherry
6 tablespoons milk
8 spring onions, thinly sliced
spring onion tassels to garnish

Cut the beef into 1 cm / ½ inch wide strips. Mix together 1 tablespoon soy sauce, 1 teaspoon of the cornflour and a pinch of salt. Toss the beef in this marinade, cover and leave at room temperature for about 2 hours.

Heat the oil in a wok or large frying pan and fry the garlic and ginger over moderately high heat, stirring, for 1 minute. Add the stock, sherry and remaining soy sauce. Stir and bring to the boil, then lower the heat and simmer the sauce for 10 minutes.

Increase the heat again, add the beef, any marinade and the spring onions to the sauce. Stir-fry for 3 minutes. Pour the milk on to the remaining cornflour and stir to make a smooth paste. Add to the sauce, bring to the boil and stir-fry for 1–2 minutes until it thickens. Serve hot garnished with spring onion tassels.

Cook's Tip

Serve with tumeric-flavoured rice. Cook 175–225 g / 6–8 oz long-grain rice in boiling salted water with 1 teaspoon tumeric. Drain and keep hot until ready to serve. To make spring onion tassels curl decoratively, place in ice water for 5-10 minutes after slicing both ends.

140 | *Beef, Apricot and Apple Kebabs*

Preparation time
25 minutes

Cooking time
25–30 minutes

Makes 4

Calories
209 per portion

You will need
450 g / 1 lb thin beef topside
25 g / 1 oz butter
1 onion, peeled and chopped
100 g / 4oz fresh white
 breadcrumbs
½ teaspoon dried thyme
2 tablespoons chopped fresh
 parsley
salt and pepper
2 teaspoons lemon juice
1 egg, beaten
12 fresh apricots, skinned and
 stoned
3 green dessert apples, cored and
 cut into eighths
4 bay leaves
1 × 375-g / 13-oz can cook-in
 barbecue sauce

Spread the beef flat and cut into 12 strips about 4 cm / 1½ inches wide. Melt the butter and fry the onion for 5 minutes. Remove from the heat, stir in the breadcrumbs, thyme, parsley and salt and pepper to taste. Bind together with the lemon juice and egg. Divide the stuffing equally between the beef strips and roll up.

Thread the stuffed beef rolls on to four skewers, alternating with the apricots, apple slices and bay leaves. Brush with the barbecue sauce.

Place under a preheated moderate grill and cook for 20–25 minutes, turning frequently and basting with the sauce. Serve hot with any remaining barbecue sauce.

Cook's Tip

To stone fresh apricots, halve lengthways along the slight indentation. Turn the halves in opposite directions, then pull them apart and lift out the stone. A 482-g / 1-lb can apricot halves may be used instead.

141 | Roast Duck with Orange Sauce

Preparation time
20 minutes

Cooking time
2–2½ hours

Oven temperature
190 C, 375 F, gas 6

Serves 6

Calories
200 per portion

You will need
1 (1.75-2.25-kg/ 4-5 lb) duck
salt
300 ml/½ pint chicken stock

For the sauce
1 onion, finely chopped
1 tablespoon oil
25 g/ 1 oz plain flour
150 ml/¼ pint orange juice
2 tablespoons brandy (optional)
salt and pepper

Garnish
orange slices
watercress sprigs

Weigh the duck and calculate the cooking time. Allow 30 minutes per 450 g/1 lb. Rub the salt over the duck. Place the duck on a wire rack in a roasting tin and roast in a moderately hot oven for the calculated time.

Remove the duck from the oven and place on a hot serving dish to keep warm. Pour off the fat and reserve any juices from the tin.

To make the sauce: fry the onion in the oil until soft, add the flour and gradually blend in the orange juice, stock and reserved juices. Bring the sauce to the boil, reduce the heat and simmer gently for 2 minutes, then add the brandy, if using, and seasoning.

Serve the duck garnished with orange slices and watercress sprigs and serve the sauce separately.

142 | Roast Beef

Preparation time
5 minutes

Oven temperature
220 C, 425 F, gas 7
OR 160 C, 325 F, gas 3

Calories
200 per 100 g/ 4 oz
portion lean roast beef

You will need
1 joint of beef (see notes below)
50 g/ 2 oz lard or dripping, if
needed
salt and pepper

Beef can be either quick roasted at a high temperature of 220 C, 425 F, gas 7, or slow roasted at 160 C, 325 F, gas 3. Quick roasting should only be used for prime cuts of beef such as fillet, rib, topside or sirloin. Slow roasting can be used for prime cuts, aitchbone and best brisket. When quick roasting beef, allow 15 minutes per 450 g/1 lb plus 15 minutes for a rare joint, 20 minutes per 450 g/1 lb plus 20 minutes for medium rare and 25 minutes per 450 g/ 1 lb plus 25 minutes for a well done joint. When slow roasting beef, allow 25 minutes per 450 g/1 lb plus 25 minutes for a rare joint, 30 minutes per 450 g/1 lb plus 30 minutes for medium rare and 35 minutes per 450 g/1 lb plus 35 minutes for a well done joint. Allow 100–175 g/ 4–6 oz beef from a boneless joint per person and 175– 225 g/6–8 oz of beef from a joint on the bone. Weigh the joint and calculate the cooking time.

Spread fat over all surfaces of lean joints. Place the joint in a roasting tin and season. Roast for the calculated time, basting regularly. Transfer the meat to a hot serving plate and keep warm. Serve with gravy, Yorkshire pudding (see Cook's Tip below) and vegetables.

Microwave Tip

For a really crisp skin and moist, tender flesh, cook duck in microwave oven for 25 minutes, turning dish once. Remove from dish and cook on rack in roasting tin in a very hot oven for a further 25 minutes.

Cook's Tip

To make Yorkshire pudding: blend 100 g/4 oz plain flour, 1 egg and 150 ml/¼ pint milk until smooth. Stir in 150 ml/ ¼ pint milk and water mixed. Heat a little of the fat from roasting tin in 1 large tin or 12 bun tins.

Pour in batter and cook in hot oven for 20–40 minutes until risen and brown. For extra light and crisp Yorkshire puddings use 2 eggs.

143 | Irish Stew

Preparation time
20 minutes

Cooking time
2 hours

Serves 4

Calories
685 per portion

You will need
2 tablespoons oil
450 g/ 1 lb potatoes, thinly sliced
675–1 kg/ 1½–2 lb middle or scrag
   end neck of lamb or mutton
3 onions, thinly sliced
salt and pepper
900 ml/ 1½ pints lamb stock
chopped parsley to garnish

Heat the oil in a large saucepan and brown the sliced potatoes. Remove the potatoes and reserve. Cut the lamb or mutton into neat joints, then layer the lamb, onion and potato in the saucepan, seasoning each layer well. Pour over the stock and bring the stew slowly to the boil. Reduce the heat, cover with a lid and simmer gently for 2 hours or until the meat is cooked.

   Garnish the stew with parsley and serve with seasonal vegetables.

144 | Hungarian Goulash

Preparation time
15 minutes

Cooking time
2½–3 hours

Oven temperature
160 C, 325 F, gas 3

Serves 4

Calories
495 per portion

You will need
25 g/ 1 oz plain flour
¼ teaspoon mustard powder
1 tablespoon paprika
salt and pepper
575 g/ 1¼ lb stewing or braising
   steak, cut into cubes
3 tablespoons oil
2 onions, sliced into rings
1 red pepper, deseeded and
   sliced
1 green pepper, deseeded and
   sliced
450 g/ 1 lb tomatoes, peeled and
   quartered
600 ml/ 1 pint beef stock
150 ml/ ¼ pint soured cream
1 tablespoon chopped parsley to
   garnish

Mix together the flour, mustard, paprika, salt and pepper and toss the meat cubes in the mixture. Heat the oil in a frying pan and cook the cubes of meat until brown on all sides. Transfer to a casserole. Gently fry the onions and peppers in the remaining fat until soft, and add to the casserole with the tomatoes and beef stock.

   Mix the ingredients together well. Cover the casserole with a lid and cook in a moderate oven for 2–2½ hours or until the meat is tender.

   Pour the soured cream over the meat and serve immediately, garnished with chopped parsley.

Cook's Tip

Always trim excess fat from lamb before casseroling. If the casserole looks greasy, leave to stand for 5 minutes, then use a large flattish spoon to skim off the fat.

Microwave Tip

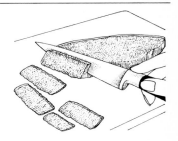

Only tender meats microwave well. Use rump steak, cut across the grain into small thin slices. Flour the meat, then mix in all ingredients. Microwave on full power for 20 minutes.

145 | Lamb with Rosemary

Preparation time
6 minutes

Cooking time
10 minutes

Serves 4

Calories
189 per portion

You will need
2 teaspoons oil
1 onion, peeled and finely chopped
2 garlic cloves, peeled and crushed
2–3 large lamb chump chops, trimmed and cubed
2 teaspoons soy sauce
1 sprig fresh rosemary, finely chopped, or 1 teaspoon dried
2 teaspoons cornflour blended with 3 tablespoons water
150 ml / ¼ pint hot lamb stock or water

Heat the oil and stir-fry the onion for 2 minutes, then stir in the garlic. Push the mixture to one side of the pan and add the meat. Stir-fry for 3–4 minutes until evenly browned. Push to one side and tilt the pan so the fat runs out of the meat. Drain off this excess fat.

Mix the meat with the onions and move back into the centre of the pan. Add the soy sauce and the rosemary and stir-fry for a few seconds. Transfer to warmed serving plates using a slotted spoon and keep warm.

Pour the blended cornflour into the pan and stir to release any pan juices. Add the stock and simmer, stirring, until thickened.

Spoon the thickened sauce over the meat. Serve at once, garnished with rosemary.

Cook's Tip

Cornflour is the thickening agent in the sauce. Be sure to taste the sauce before taking it off the heat and spooning over the sauce. The cornflour needs sufficient cooking so it doesn't taste raw.

146 | Greek Cinnamon Lamb

Preparation time
10 minutes, plus chilling

Cooking time
7–8 minutes

Serves 4
as a starter

Calories
390 per portion

You will need
125 g / 4 oz Greek yogurt
2 tablespoons olive oil
2 tablespoons chopped fresh mint
1 garlic clove, peeled and crushed
2 tablespoons honey
¼ teaspoon ground cinnamon
salt and pepper
450 g / 1 lb lamb neck fillet, trimmed and cut into small cubes
8 bay leaves
lemon wedges to garnish

Mix together the yogurt, oil, mint, garlic, honey, cinnamon and salt and pepper to taste, blending well. Add the lamb and stir to coat. Cover and chill for 4 hours.

Drain the lamb from the marinade with a slotted spoon and thread on to four small skewers with the bay leaves.

Cook under a preheated hot grill or over glowing coals on a barbecue for 7–8 minutes, basting frequently with the marinade, until cooked through.

Serve hot garnished with lemon wedges and with any remaining marinade drizzled over.

Cook's Tip

Do not substitute dried mint for fresh in this recipe. If fresh mint isn't available, use another fresh herb such as coriander or parsley. The finely grated rind of a large orange is another suitable alternative.

147 | Lamb Kebab

Preparation time
10 minutes, plus
overnight chilling time

Cooking time
10 minutes

Serves 4

Calories
450 per portion

You will need
300 g/10 oz natural yogurt
1 tablespoon ground coriander
½ teaspoon chilli powder
1 tablespoon oil
salt
675 g/1½ lb boned leg of lamb,
    cubed
4 onions
2 red peppers
4 tomatoes
2 tablespoons finely chopped
    fresh coriander leaves

Put the yogurt, coriander, chilli, oil and salt to taste in a large bowl. Add the meat, mix well, cover and chill overnight in the refrigerator.

Cut the onion into quarters and separate the layers. Core and seed the peppers and cut into squares and cut the tomatoes in half.

Thread the onion, lamb and red pepper alternately on to 8 skewers, beginning and ending each kebab with a tomato half. Cook under a preheated hot grill for about 10 minutes, turning frequently and basting with any remaining marinade as necessary. Sprinkle with chopped coriander to serve.

148 | Malabar Lamb Curry

Preparation time
10 minutes

Cooking time
1 hour

Serves 4

Calories
470 per portion

You will need
3 tablespoons oil or ghee
2 onions, finely chopped
1 teaspoon turmeric
1 tablespoon ground coriander
1 teaspoon ground cumin
2 teaspoons chilli powder
½ teaspoon ground cloves
12 curry leaves
675 g/1½ lb boned leg of lamb,
    cubed
1 tablespoon coarsely grated fresh
    cococnut
300 ml/½ pint water
1 teaspoon salt

Heat the oil or ghee in a pan, add the onions and fry until golden. Stir in the turmeric, coriander, cumin, chilli powder, cloves and curry leaves and fry for 1–2 minutes.

Add the meat and coconut and fry, stirring, until well browned. Pour in the water and add the salt. Cover and simmer for 45 minutes or until the lamb is tender. Turn on to a warmed serving dish and serve hot.

Cook's Tip

Serve the kebabs with a finger bowl – make it effective by adding a few drops of lemon juice and make it look decorative by floating a few flower heads on the surface.

Cook's Tip

This is a southern Indian curry which is delicious served with rice, poppadoms, chutneys and a Pineapple Raita: beat a little salt and sugar into a bowl of natural yogurt, stir in some pineapple chunks and a finely chopped green chilli.

149 | Stir-Fried Lamb with Noodles

Preparation time
15 minutes, including soaking time

Cooking time
8 minutes

Serves 4–6

Calories
330–220 per portion

You will need
100 g/4 oz cellophane noodles
1 tablespoon oil
3 spring onions, chopped
2.5 cm/1 inch piece root ginger, chopped
2 garlic cloves, sliced
2 celery sticks, chopped
450 g/1 lb very lean lamb, thinly sliced
1 red pepper, cored, seeded and sliced
2 tablespoons light soy sauce
2 tablespoons dry sherry
150 ml/¼ pint stock
2 teaspoons sesame oil

Soak the noodles in warm water for about 10 minutes; drain.

Heat the oil in a wok or frying pan, add the spring onions, ginger and garlic and stir-fry for 1 minute. Add the celery and lamb and cook for 2 minutes. Add the red pepper, soy sauce and sherry and bring to the boil. Stir in the stock and noddles and simmer for 5 minutes. Sprinkle with the sesame oil.

Serve at once, garnished as shown if liked.

150 | Lamb with Extra Onions

Preparation time
15 minutes

Cooking time
about 1–1¼ hours

Serves 4–6

Calories
700–480 per portion

You will need
675 g/1½ lb boneless shoulder of lamb, cubed
5 large onions
100 g/4 oz ghee
6 garlic cloves, peeled
1 piece root ginger
1 tablespoon chilli powder
2 teaspoons ground coriander
2 teaspoons ground cumin
2 teaspoons black pepper
1½ teaspoons turmeric
2 teaspoons salt
350 g/12 oz natural yogurt
300 ml/½ pint beef stock
6 green chillies, chopped
1 tablespoon fenugreek seeds
2 tablespoons chopped fresh mint

Place the lamb in a bowl. Purée 1 onion in a liquidizer or food processor and add to the lamb.

Heat the ghee, add the lamb mixture and fry on all sides. Slice the remaining onions, garlic and ginger. Remove the lamb with a slotted spoon and set aside. Add the sliced onions, garlic and ginger and fry gently for 4–5 minutes. Meanwhile, mix the ground spices and salt with the yogurt. Add to the pan, increase the heat and add the lamb, stirring constantly. Add the stock, bring to the boil, cover and simmer for 40 minutes.

Add the chillies, fenugreek and mint and simmer for a further 5–10 minutes. Serve hot.

Cook's Tip

Use lean boneless leg of lamb or lamb neck fillets for this dish – removing any visible fat and cutting the flesh in thin slices.

Cook's Tip

This recipe is called Goscht Dopiaza in Indian, which is roughly translated as 'meat with double onions' since the Hindu word for onion is piaz and the word for two is do (pronounced dough). Onions form a crucial part of virtually **all Indian curry dishes and, in fact, many Indians regard onions as vegetables in themselves.**

151 | Lamb with Chilled Cucumber Sauce

Preparation time
10 minutes

Cooking time
10 minutes

Serves 4

Calories
517 per portion

You will need
8 noisettes of lamb
8 slices bread, crusts removed
40 g / 1½ oz butter

For the sauce
½ cucumber, peeled and grated
150 ml / ¼ pint unsweetened plain
 yogurt
½ tablespoon chopped fresh mint
salt and pepper

To make the sauce, mix together all the ingredients. Cover and chill until ready to serve.

Cook the noisettes under a preheated hot grill for 2–3 minutes on either side, then about 7 minutes on a lower setting until done to desired taste.

Meanwhile, cut the bread into rounds with a biscuit cutter. Melt the butter, then fry the bread until golden on each side. Drain well on paper towels and sprinkle with salt.

To serve, place two fried bread rounds on each plate and top with noisettes. Serve hot with the chilled sauce.

152 | Noisettes Niçoise

Preparation time
10 minutes

Cooking time
10 minutes

Serves 4

Calories
290 per portion

You will need
8 noisettes of lamb
2 onions, peeled and finely
 chopped
2 garlic cloves, peeled and finely
 chopped
4 tomatoes, skinned and chopped
1 tablespoon oil
salt and pepper
8 black olives

Cook the noisettes under a preheated hot grill for 2–3 minutes on either side, then 7 minutes on a lower setting until done to desired taste.

Meanwhile, heat the oil and fry the onions and garlic for 5 minutes until tender. Add the tomatoes and salt and pepper to taste. Continue cooking until the tomatoes are heated through and tender.

Transfer the noisettes to a heated serving dish and spoon over the tomato mixture. Add the olives and serve at once.

Cook's Tip

This refreshing sauce, also called raita, is often served as a cooling accompaniment with hot, spicy curries. If you have time, sprinkle the grated cucumber with salt and leave for 30 minutes for all excess liquid to drain off. If time is short, put the cucumber in a sieve and squeeze out as much liquid as possible with the back of a wooden spoon.

Cook's Tip

You can ask your butcher to make the noisettes or do it yourself. Remove the bone from loin or best end of neck chops. Roll the meat into a neat round with the fat on the outside. Tie with string.

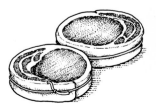

153 | Lamb Curry with Yogurt

Preparation time
15 minutes

Cooking time
about 1¼ hours

Serves 4

Calories
450 per portion

You will need
4 tablespoons oil
3 onions, chopped
6 cardamoms
5 cm/2 inch cinnamon stick
1½ tablespoons ground coriander
2 tablespoons ground cumin
½ teaspoon turmeric
½ teaspoon ground cloves
1–2 teaspoons chilli powder
½ teaspoon grated nutmeg
2 tablespoons water
1 tablespoon paprika
300 g/10 oz natural yogurt
675 g/1½ lb boned leg of lamb, cubed
1 large tomato, skinned and chopped
salt

Heat the oil in a large pan, add the onions, cardamoms and cinnamon and fry until the onions are golden. Stir in the coriander, cumin, turmeric, cloves, chilli powder and nutmeg. Fry until dry, then add the water and cook, stirring, for 5 minutes, adding a little more water if needed.

Add the paprika and slowly stir in the yogurt. Add the lamb, tomato and salt to taste and mix well. Bring to simmering point, cover and cook for 1 hour or until the meat is tender.

154 | Dry Lamb Curry

Preparation time
10–15 minutes

Cooking time
about 50 minutes

Serves 4

Calories
450 per portion

You will need
3 tablespoons oil
225 g/8 oz onions, finely chopped
6 cloves
6 cardamoms
2.5 cm/1 inch cinnamon stick
2 green chillies, finely chopped
675 g/1½ lb boned leg of lamb, cut into strips
2 teaspoons ground coriander
1 teaspoon ground cumin
300 g/10 oz natural yogurt
2 tablespoons chopped fresh coriander leaves
3 curry leaves
salt
1 teaspoon garam masala

Heat the oil in a pan, add the onions and fry until soft. Add the cloves, cardamoms and cinnamon and fry for 1 minute, then add the chillies and lamb. Fry for a further 10 minutes, turning the lamb to brown on all sides.

Add the remaining ingredients, except garam masala, seasoning with salt to taste. Stir well, bring to simmering point and cook, uncovered, for 40 minutes until the meat is tender and the liquid has evaporated. Stir in the garam masala and serve.

Cook's Tip

Curry comes from the Tamil word for a relish. It has been used as a convenient shorthand in the West for dishes, particularly stews, made of meat, fish or vegetables, cooked with spices and served with rice or Indian breads. True curries were born in southern India. They belong to those regions where rice is the staple food and where the climate is hot and humid.

Cook's Tip

Curry making becomes easy if, before starting to cook, you assemble the required ingredients: measure out spices and seasonings and put them in separate piles; chop or slice the other foodstuffs before starting.

155 | Kiwi Lamb Chops

Preparation time
5 minutes

Cooking time
20 minutes

Serves 4–6

Calories
431 per portion

You will need
4–6 lamb chump chops, about
175 g / 6 oz each, cut in half
1 kiwi fruit, sliced, to garnish

For the sauce
3–4 kiwi fruit, sliced
sugar to taste

Grill the lamb chops under a preheated moderate grill for 10 minutes on each side.

Stew the kiwi fruit in a little water until it can be mashed with a fork, then add sugar to taste, keeping the sauce sharp.

Arrange the lamb on a warmed serving dish and garnish with kiwi fruit slices. Serve immediately with the sauce spooned over.

156 | Lamb Chops in Red Wine Sauce

Preparation time
15 minutes

Cooking time
30 minutes

Oven temperature
190C, 375F, Gas 5

Serves 4

Calories
350 per portion

You will need
4 loin of lamb chops, about 100g /
4 oz each, well trimmed
1 garlic clove, peeled and finely
chopped
25 g / 1 oz butter
2 small courgettes, sliced
175 g / 6 oz button mushrooms,
sliced
4 large tomatoes, skinned and
sliced
1 tablespoon clear honey
150 ml / ¼ pint dry red wine
1 tablespoon chopped fresh
marjoram, or 1 teaspoon dried
salt and pepper
1 tablespoon chopped fresh
parsley to garnish

Fry the chops with the garlic over moderate heat for 3 minutes on each side. Transfer the chops to a casserole, discarding any fat remaining in the pan.

Melt the butter and fry the courgettes and mushrooms, stirring once or twice, for 2 minutes. Add to the chops with the tomatoes, honey, wine, marjoram and salt and pepper to taste.

Cover the casserole and cook in a preheated oven for 15–20 minutes until the chops are cooked to your liking.

Serve garnished with parsley.

Cook's Tip

For extra tender chops, gently rub all sides with a kiwi fruit and set aside for 30 minutes before grilling. The kiwi fruit contains an enzyme which is a natural meat tenderizer.

Cook's Tip

The casserole can be made a day ahead. Set aside to cool completely, then cover and store in the refrigerator. Reheat thoroughly before serving.

157 | Lamb Korma

Preparation time
15 minutes

Cooking time
about 1½ hours

Serves 4

Calories
500 per portion

You will need
5 tablespoons oil
6 cardamoms
6 cloves
6 peppercorns
2.5 cm/1inch cinnamon stick
675 g/1½ lb boned leg of lamb,
   cubed
6 small onions, chopped
2 garlic cloves, chopped
5 cm/2 inch piece root ginger,
   chopped
2 tablespoons ground coriander
2 teaspoons ground cumin
1 teaspoon chilli powder
salt
150 g/5 oz natural yogurt
1 teaspoon garam masala

Heat 4 tablespoons of the oil in a pan, add the carda-moms, cloves, peppercorns and cinnamon and fry for 1 minute. Add the lamb, a few pieces at a time, and fry until browned on all sides; transfer to a dish. Remove the whole spices and discard.

Add the remaining oil to the pan and fry the onions, gar-lic and ginger for 5 minutes, then add the coriander, cumin, chilli powder and salt to taste and cook for 5 minutes, stirring frequently. Gradually stir in the yogurt. Return the meat and any juices and sufficient water to just cover the meat. Bring to simmering point, cover and cook for about 1 hour until tender.

Sprinkle on the garam masala and cook for 1 minute. Serve at once.

Cook's Tip

Lamb Korma is one of the mildest of curries, using a subtle blend of spices with yogurt. Serve with a lentil and spinach dish such as Dhal Sag (recipe 26) and boiled rice.

158 | Roghan Ghosht

Preparation time
20 minutes

Cooking time
about 1¼ hours

Serves 4

Calories
650 per portion

You will need
4 tablespoons oil
2 onions, finely chopped
675 g/1½ lb boned leg of lamb,
   cubed
300 g/10 oz natural yogurt
2 garlic cloves
2.5 cm/1 inch piece root ginger,
   chopped
2 green chillies
1 tablespoon coriander seeds
1 teaspoon cumin seeds
1 teaspoon chopped fresh mint
   leaves
1 teaspoon chopped coriander
   leaves
6 cardamoms
6 cloves
2.5 cm/1 inch cinnamon stick
100 g/4 oz flaked almonds

Heat 2 tablespoons of the oil in a pan, add 1 onion and fry until golden. Add the lamb and 175 g/6 oz of the yogurt; stir well, cover and simmer for 20 minutes.

Place the garlic, ginger, chillies, coriander seeds, cumin, mint, coriander and 2–3 tablespoons of the yogurt in a liquidizer or food processor and work to a paste.

Heat the remaining oil in a large pan, add the carda-moms, cloves and cinnamon and fry for 1 minute. Add the second onion, prepared paste and fry for 5 minutes, stirring constantly. Add the lamb and yogurt mixture and salt to taste. Bring to simmering point, cover and cook for 30 minutes. Add the almonds and cook for a further 15 minutes. Serve hot.

Cook's Tip

If liked, serve the curry sprinkled with chopped fresh mint and garnished with fresh mint leaves. Serve with boiled rice and selection of chutneys and relishes.

159 | Steamed Stuffed Aubergines

Preparation time
15 minutes

Cooking time
about 1 hour

Serves 4–6

Calories
190–130 per portion

You will need
1 tablespoon oil
2 garlic cloves, crushed
2.5 cm/1 inch piece root ginger, chopped
4 spring onions, chopped
2 red or green chillies, seeded and chopped
225 g/8 oz minced pork
2 tablespoons soy sauce
2 tablespoons dry sherry
4 medium aubergines
50 g/2 oz peeled prawns

Heat the oil in a wok or deep frying pan, add the garlic, ginger and spring onions and stir-fry for 1 minute. Increase the heat, add the chillies and pork and cook for 2 minutes. Stir in the soy sauce and sherry and cook for 10 minutes.

Meanwhile, halve the aubergines lengthways, carefully scoop out the flesh and chop finely. Add the flesh to the pan and cook for 10 minutes. Stir in the prawns and cook for 1 minute.

Blanch the aubergine shells in boiling water for 1 minute. Drain and stuff with the meat mixture. Place in a dish in a steamer and steam for 25–30 minutes, then serve at once.

160 | Crispy Barbecued Pork

Preparation time
10 minutes, plus 1¾ hours standing time

Cooking time
about 1¼ hours

Oven temperature
230 C, 450 F, gas 8
then
200 C, 400 F, gas 6

Serves 6–8

Calories
650–500 per portion

You will need
1.5 kg/3 lb lean belly of pork, in one piece
salt
1 tablespoon soy sauce
1 teaspoon Chinese 5-spice powder

Pour a kettleful of boiling water over the skin of the pork; drain and dry. Rub the pork with salt and leave to dry for 45 minutes.

Score the skin of the pork in a diamond pattern. Pierce the meat with a skewer in several places. Rub the soy sauce and 5-spice powder into the pork. Cover and leave to stand for 1 hour.

Place the pork, skin side up, in a roasting tin and roast at the higher temperature for 20 minutes. Lower the heat and continue to roast for 50–55 minutes, or until the pork is tender and the skin is crisp. Slice to serve.

Cook's Tip

Make sure that the cooking dish for the aubergines is heatproof or ovenproof for steaming the aubergines.

Cook's Tip

Serve the pork garnished with a radish rose, turnip flowers and coriander leaves if liked.

Should the skin still not be crisp enough at the end of the cooking time then place under a preheated hot grill for 1–2 minutes to crisp.

161 | Cassoulet

Preparation time
10 minutes, plus
overnight soaking

Cooking time
2½ hours

Oven temperature
160 C, 325 F, gas 3

Serves 4

Calories
605 per portion

You will need
350 g / 12 oz haricot beans
2 onions, chopped
100 g / 4 oz rindless streaky
  bacon, chopped
100 g / 4 oz cervelat sausage,
  sliced
4 chicken drumsticks
225 g / 8 oz tomatoes, peeled and
  quartered
3 tablespoons tomato purée
900 ml / 1½ pints chicken stock
bouquet garni
salt and pepper
1 teaspoon chopped parsley to
  garnish

Soak the haricot beans in cold water overnight, then drain well. Mix the beans, onion, bacon, sausage, chicken and tomatoes in a casserole. Add the tomato purée, chicken stock, bouquet garni, season well and mix together.

Cover the casserole with a lid and cook in a moderate oven for about 2½ hours until the haricot beans are cooked.

Serve immediately, garnished with chopped parsley.

162 | Sweet 'n' Sour Pork Casserole

Preparation time
20 minutes

Cooking time
1 hour 45 minutes

Oven temperature
160 C, 325 F, gas 3

Serves 4

Calories
435 per portion

You will need
25 g / 1 oz plain flour
1 teaspoon ground ginger
salt and pepper
575 g / 1¼ lb lean pork, cut into
  2.5-cm / 1-in cubes
1 onion, finely chopped
1 green pepper, deseeded and
  sliced
2 tablespoons oil
150 ml / ¼ pint chicken stock
1 (454-g / l-lb) can pineapple
  chunks
2 tablespoons soy sauce
3 tablespoons vinegar
50 g / 2 oz no-need-to-soak dried
  apricots

Garnish
tomato rose
cucumber leaves

Mix the flour, ground ginger, salt and pepper together and toss the pork in the mixture. Fry the onion and pepper in the oil for 2–3 minutes. Transfer to a casserole.

Brown the pork cubes in the oil, then add to the casserole. Stir any remaining flour into the pan, blend in the stock and the juice from the pineapple. Bring to the boil, then add to the casserole with the remaining ingredients. Cover and cook in a moderate oven for 1½ hours. Serve with boiled rice, garnished as shown.

Cook's Tip

Cervelat is a smoked, moist sausage, usually containing finely minced beef and pork. It is made in various European countries, including France and Germany. Cervelat is matured for a shorter time than the Italian salami sausage, and as a result is more pliable. It is also less highly seasoned. Select from a delicatessen.

Microwave Tip

Lean pork microwaves well. Mix all the ingredients, coating meat in flour and omitting oil. Microwave on full power for 15–20 minutes.

163 | Twice-Cooked Pork with Chilli Bean Sauce

Preparation time
15 minutes

Cooking time
about 35–40 minutes

Serves 3–4

Calories
550–400 per portion

You will need
350 g/12 oz belly pork in one piece, not too lean
100 g/4 oz bamboo shoots
100 g/4 oz celery sticks
3 tablespoons oil
2 spring onions, chopped
1 garlic clove, chopped
2 tablespoons sake or dry sherry
1 tablespoon soy sauce
1 tablespoon chilli bean paste

Place the whole piece of pork in a pan of boiling water and cook for 25–30 minutes. Remove and leave to cool.

Cut across the grain of the meat into thin slices, about 5×2.5 cm/2×1 inch in size. Cut the bamboo shoots and celery into chunks roughly the same size.

Heat the oil in a wok or deep frying pan until smoking, add the spring onions and garlic to flavour the oil, then add the vegetables and stir a few times. Add the pork, followed by the sake or sherry, soy and chilli bean sauces. Stir-fry for about 1–2 minutes. Serve hot.

164 | Grilled Ginger Pork

Preparation time
10 minutes, plus 30 minutes marinating time

Cooking time
about 35 minutes

Serves 4

Calories
150 per portion

You will need
2 pork fillets, each weighing 175–225 g/6–6 oz
5 cm/2 inch piece root ginger, grated
4 tablespoons soy sauce

Put the pork fillets in a shallow dish, add the ginger and soy sauce and leave to marinate for at least 30 minutes.

Wrap each fillet in foil, reserving the marinade. Place under a preheated hot grill for 5 minutes, then turn the grill down to low and cook for a further 20–25 minutes or until thoroughly cooked.

Unwrap the pork and cut each fillet into 1-cm/½-inch slices. Place on warmed individual plates. Pour the meat juices from the foil into a pan and add the reserved marinade. If there is not enough sauce add a few spoonfuls of water and soy sauce to taste. Bring to the boil and simmer for 5 minutes. Pour over the meat and serve at once.

Cook's Tip

To be authentic, the cut of meat usually used in this dish is belly of pork, known as 'five-flower' pork in China because the alternate layers of fat and meat form a pretty pink and white pattern when viewed in cross-section.

Cook's Tip

This is an easy, economical Japanese dish, which nonetheless is delicious enough to be served at dinner parties. Serve with French beans and plain boiled rice if wished. Garnish with grated daikon (Japanese radish).

165 | Pork Fillet in Egg and Lemon Sauce

Preparation time
15 minutes

Cooking time
20 minutes

Serves 4

Calories
521 per portion

You will need
2 pork fillets, about 350 g / 12 oz
   each, trimmed
1 tablespoon oil
75 g / 3 oz butter
100 g / 4 oz button mushrooms,
   wiped and thinly sliced
2 tablespoons plain flour
300 ml / ½ pint chicken stock
2 eggs
2 tablespoons lemon juice
1 tablespoon water
1 tablespoon chopped fresh
   parsley to garnish

Cut the pork into 2 cm / ¾ inch thick slices. Heat the oil with 25 g / 1 oz of the butter and fry the pork over moderate heat for 4 minutes on each side. Add half the remaining butter and the mushrooms and cook for a further 4 minutes, turning the meat once. Remove the meat and mushrooms and keep them warm.

To make the sauce, melt the remaining butter, stir in the flour and cook for 2 minutes. Gradually stir in the stock, until the sauce boils. Beat the eggs until they are frothy, then beat in the lemon juice and add the water. Reduce the heat.

Add 5 tablespoons of the hot stock to the egg mixture, then pour it into the sauce remaining in the pan. Stir until the sauce thickens, and add salt and pepper to taste.

Add the pork and mushrooms to the sauce and serve at once, garnished with parsley.

Cook's Tip

After adding the eggs to the sauce, do not boil or the eggs will scramble.

166 | Pork and Mango Curry

Preparation time
15 minutes

Cooking time
30 minutes

Serves 4–6

Calories
601 per portion

You will need
750 g / 1½ lb pork fillet, cut into
   2.5 cm / 1 inch cubes
25 g / 1 oz plain flour
2 tablespoons oil
1 Spanish onion, peeled and sliced
2 small green or red peppers,
   cored, seeded and sliced
1 teaspoon tumeric
2 teaspoons salt
1 tablespoon curry powder
1 teaspoon ground cumin
1 teaspoon ground ginger
½ teaspoon chilli seasoning
5 tomatoes, peeled and chopped
2 teaspoons tomato purée
450 ml / ¾ pint light meat stock
750 g / 1½ lb small new potatoes,
   scrubbed or peeled
2 large mangos, peeled, stoned
   and sliced

Toss the pork in the flour to coat. Heat the oil and fry the pork for 5 minutes until golden. Add the onion and peppers and cook for a further 3 minutes. Add the tumeric, salt, curry powder, cumin, ginger and chilli seasoning and cook for 1 minute, stirring constantly.

Add the tomatoes, tomato purée and stock, blending well. Add the potatoes, cover and cook for 15 minutes over a gentle heat, stirring occasionally. Add the mango slices and cook for a further 5 minutes until the potatoes are tender. Serve at once.

Cook's Tip

Some ideal accompaniments to serve with the spicy curry are boiled rice, banana slices tossed in lemon juice, mango chutney and chopped cucumber in plain unsweetened yogurt.

167 | Prune-Stuffed Fillet of Pork

Preparation time
15 minutes

Cooking time
30 minutes

Serves 4

Calories
300 per portion

You will need
2 pork fillets or tenderloin, about
  350 g / 12 oz each, well
  trimmed
8 prunes, halved and stoned
2 tablespoons seedless raisins
3 tablespoons clear honey
1 tablespoon butter
1 teaspoon plain flour
150 ml / ¼ pint sweet cider
salt and pepper

Cut the pork fillets lengthways without cutting them right through.

Arrange the prune halves along one side of each fillet, cover the prunes with 1 tablespoon of the raisins and with 1 tablespoon of the honey. Close up the fillets again, enclosing the fruit, and tie with thin string.

Melt the butter and fry the pork fillets until brown on both sides.

Stir in the flour, pour on the cider and bring to the boil. Add salt and pepper to taste, and the remaining raisins. Simmer, covered, turning the pork once, for 25 minutes until cooked through.

Remove the string and spread the remaining honey along the fillets of pork. Glaze under a preheated hot grill for 2 minutes.

168 | Pork Fillet with Orange and Ginger

Preparation time
15 minutes

Cooking time
10–12 minutes

Serves 4

Calories
221 per portion

You will need
25 g / 1 oz butter
450 g / l lb pork fillet or tenderloin,
  sliced into 5 mm / ¼ inch
  rounds or medallions
salt and pepper
1 tablespoon ginger marmalade
1 tablespoon brown sugar
1 tablespoon orange juice
1 tablespoon cider vinegar
4 spring onions, finely shredded

For the garnish
matchstick strips of orange rind
mint sprigs

Melt the butter and quickly brown the pork on all sides for 6–8 minutes until golden and tender. Season with salt and pepper to taste. Remove with a slotted spoon and arrange decoratively on a warmed serving plate. Keep warm.

Add the marmalade, sugar, orange juice, cider vinegar and spring onions to the pan juices and heat until the mixture forms a syrupy glaze. Spoon over the meat.

Garnish with orange rind and mint.

Cook's Tip

Orange juice is a good alternative to the cider in this recipe. You can also add the finely grated rind of 1 orange.

Cook's Tip

For a dinner party, serve this quick but impressive looking dish with boiled rice and a green vegetable such as French beans. Because the sauce is so rich and flavourful the accompanying vegetables should be kept simple.

169 | Pork Chops with Orange and Cashew Nut Stuffing

Preparation time
15 minutes

Cooking time
16–20 minutes

Serves 4

Calories
370 per portion

You will need
4 loin pork chops
salt and pepper

For the stuffing
1 onion, grated
grated rind of 1 orange
50 g/2 oz cashew nuts, chopped
½ teaspoon sage
1 teaspoon Dijon mustard
50 g/2 oz fresh brown
   breadcrumbs
salt and pepper
1 egg, lightly beaten
1–2 tablespoons oil

Garnish
orange slices
parsley sprigs

Cut the rind and excess fat off the chops and season the chops with salt and pepper. Carefully cut each chop horizontally, leaving joined at the bone.

Mix together the onion, orange rind, cashew nuts, sage, mustard, breadcrumbs, seasoning and bind with the egg. Place the stuffing inside the chops. Brush with the oil and cook under a medium grill for 8–10 minutes on each side or until the chops are golden and the stuffing is cooked. Serve garnished with orange slices and parsley sprigs.

Cook's Tip

For a change, substitute **lemon rind and almonds for the orange rind and cashew nuts in this stuffing.**

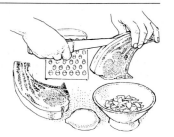

170 | Spiced Glazed Ham

Preparation time
10 minutes, plus
overnight soaking

Oven temperature
220 C, 425 F, gas 7

Calories
165 per 100 g/4 oz
portion lean cooked
gammon

You will need
1 joint middle or corner of
   gammon
1.15 litres/2 pints water
1 onion
1 bay leaf
salt and pepper
100 g/4 oz soft brown sugar
grated rind of 1 orange
½ teaspoon grated nutmeg
½ teaspoon ground cinnamon

To serve
3 dessert apples
cloves
zested orange rind
orange slices to garnish

Weigh the gammon and calculate the cooking time, allowing 30 minutes per 450 g/1 lb. Soak the gammon in cold water overnight. Drain.

Put the gammon in a saucepan with the water, onion, bay leaf and seasoning. Cover, bring to the boil, then reduce the heat and simmer for 1½ hours. Drain the gammon and peel off the skin, marking the fat into diamond shapes with a sharp knife. Mix together the sugar, orange rind, nutmeg and cinnamon for the glaze and rub into the gammon fat. Place joint in a roasting tin.

Bake the gammon in a hot oven for the remainder of the calculated cooking time, or until the fat is crisp and golden. Stick the cloves in the apples and place them in the roasting tin for the final 15 minutes cooking time, basting with any meat juices. Garnish with orange slices.

Cook's Tip

For a delicious sauce with the gammon, pour a small bottle of ginger ale around the joint before roasting and if liked substitute ground ginger for the spices.

171 | *Fried Pork with Baby Corn*

Preparation time
5 minutes

Cooking time
about 5 minutes

Serves 4

Calories
260 per portion

You will need
1 tablespoon dry sherry
1 tablespoon soy sauce
1½ teaspoons cornflour
450 g/1 lb pork fillet, sliced as
   thinly as possible
1 tablespoon oil
50 g/2 oz mangetout
1 teaspoon salt
1 (425-g/15-oz) can baby corn
   drained
1 (425-g/15-oz) can straw
   mushrooms, drained
2 teaspoons sugar

Mix the sherry and soy sauce with 1 teaspoon of the cornflour. Add the pork and toss to coat well. Heat the oil in a pan, add the pork and stir-fry until lightly browned. Add the mangetout and salt and stir-fry for 30 seconds. Add the baby corn and mushrooms and stir-fry for 1 minute. Sprinkle in the sugar.

Mix the remaining cornflour with 2 teaspoons water and stir into the pan. Cook, stirring continuously until thickened. Serve at once.

172 | *Stir-Fried Liver with Spinach*

Preparation time
10 minutes

Cooking time
about 3–4 minutes

Serves 4

Calories
300 per portion

You will need
350 g/12 oz pig's liver, cut into
   thin triangular slices
2 tablespoons cornflour
4 tablespoons oil
450 g/1 lb spinach leaves, rinsed
1 teaspoon salt
2 thin slices root ginger
1 tablespoon soy sauce
1 tablespoon rice wine or sherry
   (see Cook's Tip)
shredded spring onion to garnish

Blanch the liver for a few seconds in boiling water, then drain and coat with cornflour.

Heat 2 tablespoons of the oil in a wok or frying pan. Add the spinach and salt and stir-fry for 2 minutes. Remove from the pan and arrange around the edge of a warmed serving dish. Keep hot.

Heat the remaining oil in a pan until it is very hot. Add the ginger, liver, soy sauce and wine or sherry. Stir well, then pour over the spinach. Avoid overcooking the liver or it will become tough. Stir well and pour over the spinach.

Serve at once, garnished with chopped spring onions.

Cook's Tip

This is a recipe from the Canton region of southern China. This dish illustrates the quick stir-fry method of cooking that is so typical of Cantonese cooking – a way of cooking that helps to retain nutrients, colour and flavour of foods. It is a colourful and aromatic way to cook food which has done much to spread the popularity of Chinese cooking all over the world.

Cook's Tip

The two most popular wines in China are the white and yellow wines made from rice. The ordinary yellow rice wine called shaosing is used for cooking.

173 | Pork Chops with Spicy Mustard Cream

Preparation time
5 minutes

Cooking time
35–40 minutes

Serves 4

Calories
353 per portion

You will need
1 tablespoon oil
4 pork chops, about 175 g / 6 oz each
4 tablespoons whole grain mustard
1 teaspoon grated nutmeg
300 ml / ½ pint dry white wine
salt and pepper
150 ml / ¼ pint double cream
1 tablespoon chopped fresh parsley to garnish

Heat the oil in a deep frying pan with a lid. Score the fat on the pork chops, and brown them quickly on either side. Remove and keep warm.

Add the mustard, nutmeg, wine and salt and pepper to taste, blending well. Return the chops to the pan, cover and simmer gently for 20 minutes until the chops are cooked through.

Add the cream and cook gently until the sauce reduces and thickens. Garnish with chopped parsley. Serve with freshly cooked green noodles and a crisp salad.

174 | Pork with Prune Sauce

Preparation time
8 minutes

Cooking time
20 minutes

Serves 4–6

Calories
339 per portion

You will need
4–6 pork loin chops, about 150 g / 5 oz each
1 tablespoon oil
1 small onion, peeled and thinly sliced
1 garlic clove, peeled and crushed
1 × 425-g / 15-oz can unsweetened prunes
2 teaspoons cornflour
1 tablespoon soy sauce
2 teaspoons wine vinegar
brown sugar
watercress sprigs to garnish

Cook the pork chops under a preheated moderate grill for 10 minutes on each side or until cooked through.

Meanwhile, heat the oil and fry the onion for 2 minutes, stirring. Stir in the garlic and set aside.

Drain the prunes, reserving the juice. Remove and discard the stones. Set aside 4–6 for garnishing and place the remaining prunes and the juice in a liquidizer or food processor with the cornflour, soy sauce, vinegar and onion mixture and purée. Pour into the pan and cook, stirring, until thick and shiny. Stir in sugar to taste.

Divide the sauce between individual warmed serving plates and top each with a pork chop. Serve at once, garnished with the reserved prunes and watercress sprigs.

Cook's Tip

Instead of using dry white wine, the pork chops can be cooked in a sauce made with chicken stock. If you use a stock cube, do not add too much salt to the sauce because the cubes are very salty.

Cook's Tip

Grilling is one of the healthiest ways to cook pork because it allows the excess fat to drip off. For successful grilling, preheat the grill so it is hot, and have the meat at room temperature.

175 | Bacon Steaks with Cucumber Sauce

Preparation time
5 minutes

Cooking time
8–9 minutes

Serves 4

Calories
269 per portion

You will need
4 bacon steaks, about 100 g / 4 oz each, fat snipped
1 teaspoon oil
cucumber slices to garnish

For the sauce
1 cucumber, peeled and sliced
salt
20 g / ¾ oz butter
20 g / ¾ oz plain flour
300 ml / ½ pint milk
2 tablespoons double cream
1 tablespoon chopped chives
pepper
pinch cayenne pepper

Brush the bacon steaks with oil and cook them under a preheated moderate grill for 4–5 minutes on each side.

Meanwhile, to make the sauce, cook the cucumber in boiling, salted water for 3 minutes, then drain thoroughly and dry. Melt the butter, stir in the flour and stir over moderate heat for 30 seconds. Gradually pour on the milk, stirring constantly, until boiling, then simmer for 3 minutes. Stir the cucumber, cream and chives into the sauce, and add salt, pepper and cayenne to taste.

Spoon a little of the sauce on to the bacon steaks and serve the rest separately. Garnish with cucumber slices.

176 | Grilled Gammon with Orange Butter

Preparation time
10 minutes, plus chilling

Cooking time
10 minutes

Serves 4

Calories
856 per portion

You will need
4 gammon steaks, about 150 g / 6 oz each
65 g / 2½ oz butter, melted
fresh parsley springs to garnish

For the seasoned butter
2 oranges
100 g / 4 oz butter
2 teaspoons finely chopped parsley

To make the seasoned butter, finely grate the rind from the oranges. Mix this with the butter, then form into a neat, long log. Roll in the parsley, then wrap in cling film and chill until ready to serve.

Snip the fat on the steaks at 2.5 cm / 1 inch intervals. Cook under a preheated grill, brushing with the butter, for 5 minutes on each side.

Meanwhile, peel the oranges and thinly slice. Cut the butter into four portions.

Serve the gammon steaks, topped with the butter and garnished with the orange slices.

Cook's Tip

Snipping the fat around the bacon steaks at 2.5 cm / 1 inch intervals prevents the edges from curling up during cooking.

Cook's Tip

Flavoured butters are ideal to serve with most grilled meats. They freeze well, so it's easy to have a selection on hand. Try finely chopped mixed herbs with steaks and mint with lamb chops.

177 | Chicken Livers with Sage and Wine

Preparation time
10 minutes

Cooking time
15–18 minutes

Serves 4

Calories
196 per portion

You will need
750 g / 24 oz chicken livers, thawed if frozen, and trimmed
50 g / 2 oz butter
2 small onions, peeled and finely chopped
12 whole sage leaves, or 2 teaspoons dried
salt and pepper
300 ml / ½ pint dry white wine
sage leaves and orange slices to garnish

Pat the chicken livers dry with paper towels.

Melt the butter and fry the onion for 5–6 minutes until softened. Add the chicken livers and sage and fry for 3–4 minutes, stirring until the chicken livers have changed colour.

Sprinkle with salt and pepper to taste and pour in the wine. Bring to the boil, then simmer for 6–8 minutes until the chicken livers are tender.

Serve at once, garnished with sage and orange slices.

178 | Chicken Liver Ring

Preparation time
15 minutes, plus chilling and setting

Serves 4

Calories
161 per portion

You will need
1 × 25-g / 1-oz packet aspic jelly powder
600 ml / 1 pint water
2 tablespoons dry or medium sherry
25 g / 1 oz butter
225 g / 8 oz chicken livers, trimmed and roughly chopped
2 spring onions, thinly sliced
1 carton mustard and cress to garnish

Make up the aspic jelly with the water according to the packet instructions. Leave to cool until beginning to thicken but not set. Stir in the sherry.

Melt the butter and fry the chicken livers for 3 minutes, turning frequently, until cooked through. Drain on paper towels and allow to cool.

Pour 150 ml / ¼ pint of the aspic jelly into the base of a 900 ml / 1½ pint ring mould. Place in the refrigerator or freezer to set.

Sprinkle the spring onions on top of the set aspic jelly. Distribute the chicken livers in the ring mould, then pour in the remaining aspic jelly to fill up the mould. Place in the refigerator until set.

To serve, turn out and surround with a garnish of mustard and cress.

Cook's Tip

Thaw tubs of frozen chicken livers in the microwave oven without removing from the tub. Alternatively, place the frozen tub in a bowl of water at room temperature. Do not place in hot water; this would encourage bacterial growth.

Cook's Tip

When trimming the chicken livers, carefully remove any sections with a slight green tinge. If left on, the livers will taste very bitter.

179 | Calves' Liver with Sage Sauce

Preparation time
20 minutes

Cooking time
20 minutes

Serves 6

Calories
340 per portion

You will need
75 g / 3 oz butter
1 tablespoon oil
6 slices calves' liver, 90–100g /
    3½–4 oz each
1 onion, peeled and chopped
75 g / 3 oz button mushrooms,
    wiped and sliced
1 tablespoon plain flour
300 ml / ½ pint beef stock
150 ml / ¼ pint dry red wine
1 tablespoon chopped fresh sage
    or 1 teaspoon dried
salt and pepper
sprigs of fresh sage leaves to
    garnish (optional)

Melt the butter and oil and fry the liver quickly on either side until it is light golden brown. Remove from the pan and keep warm.

Fry the onion in the pan juices for 3–4 minutes, then add the mushrooms and cook for a further 3–4 minutes. Remove the pan from the heat.

Sprinkle in the flour and mix gently, taking care not to break up the mushrooms. Return the pan to the heat and gradually add the stock and wine with the sage and salt and pepper to taste.

Return the liver to the pan and coat with the sauce. Simmer gently for 8–10 minutes. Arrange the liver slices overlapping on a serving dish, pour over the sauce and garnish with the fresh sage leaves if liked.

Cook's Tip

Ask your butcher to slice the liver as thinly as possible. That way it cooks quickly and remains very tender.

180 | Japanese-style Kidneys

Preparation time
25 minutes, plus
marinating

Cooking time
10–12 minutes

Serves 4

Calories
415 per portion

You will need
4 tablespoons soy sauce
3 tablespoons dry sherry
2 tablespoons clear honey
300-ml / ½-pint beef consommé
1 garlic clove, peeled and crushed
pinch five spice powder
12 lamb's kidneys, halved and
    cored
25 g / 1 oz seasoned plain flour
40 g / 1½ oz butter
1 tablespoon cornflour
salt and pepper
spring onion curls and carrot
    shapes to garnish

Mix the soy sauce, sherry, honey, beef consommé, garlic and five spice powder in a bowl. Add the kidneys, tossing well to coat, cover and marinate for 30 minutes.

Remove the kidneys and pat dry with paper towels. Toss in seasoned flour to coat. Melt the butter and fry the kidneys over a moderate heat for 5 minutes, turning occasionally. Remove with a slotted spoon and reserve.

Add the marinade to the pan and bring to the boil. Blend the cornflour with a little water and pour into the sauce, stirring constantly, until lightly thickened.

Add the kidneys to the sauce with salt and pepper to taste. Cook for 1–2 minutes or until the kidneys are heated through and cooked but still tender. Garnish with spring onion curls and carrot scrolls or decorative shapes and serve with hot rice if liked.

Cook's Tip

To make carrot and other vegetable shapes, slice a peeled carrot, swede or turnip crossways and cut out shapes with a canapé cutter or knife. Traditional shapes include hearts, fish, moons and flowers.

181 | Pork and Dumplings

Preparation time
20 minutes

Cooking time
2 hours 45 minutes

Oven temperature
180 C, 350 F, gas 4

Serves 4

Calories
570 per portion

You will need
575 g/ 1¼ lb lean boneless pork, cut
   into cubes
25 g/ 1 oz butter or margarine
2 onions, chopped
100 g/ 4 oz no-need-to-soak
   dried apricots
25 g/ 1 oz plain flour
600 ml/ 1 pint chicken stock
300 ml/½ pint dry cider
salt and pepper
100 g/ 4 oz self-raising flour
1 tablespoon chopped parsley
50 g/ 2 oz suet
2 tablespoons water

Garnish
halved orange slices
rosemary sprigs

Cook the pork cubes in the butter or margarine until golden, then transfer to a casserole. Cook the onion in the remaining fat until soft and add to the casserole with the apricots. Stir the flour into the fat in the pan and pour in the stock. Bring to the boil and add to the casserole with the cider. Mix all the ingredients together, season, cover, and cook in a moderate oven for 2 hours.

    Sift the flour and a pinch of salt into a bowl, add the parsley and suet and mix well. Stir in the water and blend to make a soft dough. Divide and roll into small balls on a lightly floured surface. Add the dumplings to the casserole and cook for a further 30 minutes, or until the dumplings are cooked. Garnish as shown.

182 | Coq au Vin

Preparation time
10 minutes

Cooking time
1 hour 15 minutes

Oven temperature
180 C, 350 F, gas 4

Serves 4

Calories
345 per portion

You will need
2 cloves garlic, crushed
½ teaspoon salt
4 chicken joints
25 g/ 1 oz butter or margarine
2 tablespoons oil
12 button onions
100 g/ 4 oz button mushrooms
25 g/ 1 oz plain flour
300 ml/½ pint dry red wine
150 ml/¼ pint chicken stock
bouquet garni
1 teaspoon brown sugar
salt and pepper
chopped parsley to garnish

Rub the crushed garlic and salt into each chicken joint. Heat the butter or margarine and oil in a frying pan and cook the chicken joints until golden on all sides. Transfer the joints to a casserole.

    Fry the onions and mushrooms in the remaining fat until golden and add to the casserole.

    Stir the flour into the pan, add the wine and bring to the boil. Pour over the chicken joints. Add the stock, bouquet garni and sugar to the casserole, then season well. Cover the casserole with a lid or foil and cook in a moderate oven for about 1 hour. Remove the bouquet garni.

    Serve garnished with chopped parsley.

Cook's Tip

A flameproof casserole is useful for this type of dish. The ingredients can be browned and casseroled in the one pan.

Cook's Tip

For an excellent flavour, marinate the chicken joints in the wine overnight. Drain, reserving the wine and cook as above.

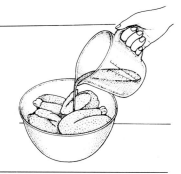

183 | *Chop Suey*

Preparation time
8 minutes

Cooking time
8 minutes

Serves 4

Calories
230 per portion

You will need
2 tablespoons oil
5 spring onions, chopped
2.5 cm/1 inch piece root ginger,
    peeled and chopped
2 garlic cloves, crushed
175 g/6 oz chicken breast,
    skinned and cut into thin strips
1 tablespoon tomato purée
2 tablespoons dry sherry
2 tablespoons soy sauce
1 teaspoon sugar
8 tablespoons water
275 g/10 oz beansprouts
3 eggs, beaten with 2 tablespoons
    water

Heat 1 tablespoon of the oil, add the spring onions and ginger and stir-fry for 1 minute. Add the garlic and chicken and stir-fry for 2 minutes. Lower the heat, add the tomato purée, sherry, soy sauce, sugar and 5 tablespoons of the water. Heat through gently, then transfer to a warmed serving dish.

Heat 2 teaspoons of the oil in the pan, add the beansprouts and remaining water and stir-fry for 3 minutes. Add to the serving dish and keep warm.

Wipe out the pan and heat the remaining oil. Pour in the beaten eggs and cook until set and crisp. Place on top of the beansprout mixture and serve at once.

184 | *Chicken Wings with Oyster Sauce*

Preparation time
10 minutes, plus 15
minutes marinating
time

Cooking time
about 20 minutes

Serves 4–6

Calories
200–140 per portion

You will need
450 g/1 lb chicken wings
2 tablespoons oil
2 leeks, sliced
3 tablespoons oyster sauce

For the marinade
4 spring onions, chopped
1 cm/½ inch piece root ginger,
    peeled and shredded
1 garlic clove, sliced
1 tablespoon soy sauce
2 tablespoons dry sherry

Trim the tips off the chicken wings, then cut the wings in half at the joints.

To make the marinade, mix the spring onions with the ginger, garlic, soy sauce and sherry. Add the chicken wings, stir well and leave to marinate for 15 minutes.

Heat the oil in a wok or frying pan, add the chicken and marinade and stir-fry for 15 minutes. Add the leeks and oyster sauce and cook for a further 3–4 minutes.

Serve at once, garnished with radish roses and cucumber slices if liked.

Cook's Tip

You can grow your own beansprouts by placing some beans in a jam jar. Cover with a piece of muslin and secure with an elastic band. Rinse the beans every day until the sprouts are long enough.

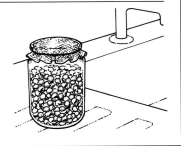

Cook's Tip

Oyster sauce is a light sauce made from oysters and soy sauce. It is often used for flavouring meat, poultry and vegetables in Chinese-style dishes.

185 | Easy Chicken Kiev

Preparation time
20 minutes, plus 30
minutes to freeze

Cooking time
30–40 minutes

Oven temperature
190 C, 375 F, gas 5

Serves 4

Calories
435 per portion

You will need
4 boneless breasts of chicken
2 cloves garlic, crushed
grated rind of 1 lemon
100 g / 4 oz butter
1 tablespoon chopped parsley
salt and pepper
25 g / 1 oz plain flour
1 egg, lightly beaten
100 g / 4 oz fresh white
breadcrumbs

Beat the chicken breasts flat with a meat mallet or a
rolling pin. Mix together the garlic, lemon rind, butter,
parsley and seasoning to form a paste. Divide the butter
evenly between the chicken breasts and carefully roll up.
Secure with string.

Freeze for 15 minutes, or until the butter is firm. Coat
the chicken in the flour, dip in the beaten egg and coat in
the breadcrumbs, pressing firmly to make sure they stick.
Return to the freezer for a further 15 minutes.

Bake the chicken Kiev in a moderately hot oven for 30–
40 minutes or until the outside is golden and crisp.

Serve with boiled vegetables.

186 | Tandoori Chicken

Preparation time
15 minutes, plus
overnight marinating

Cooking time
25–30 minutes

Serves 4

Calories
240 per portion

You will need
4 chicken joints
1 teaspoon chilli powder
1 teaspoon ground coriander
1 teaspoon ground cumin
2 teaspoons garam masala
$\frac{1}{2}$ teaspoon ground ginger
2 cloves garlic, crushed
juice of 1 lemon
2 tablespoons tomato purée
salt and pepper
150 ml / $\frac{1}{4}$ pint natural yogurt
50 g / 2 oz butter or margarine

Remove the skin from the chicken joints. Place the
chicken in a glass or earthenware dish. Mix together the
remaining ingredients, except for the butter or margarine.
Pour the marinade over the chicken, cover and chill
overnight.

Remove the chicken from the marinade and dot with
the butter or margarine. Grill the chicken, turning and
basting with the marinade frequently, for 25–30 minutes
or until the chicken juices run clear when the joints are
pierced with the point of a sharp knife.

Serve immediately with boiled rice, garnished with
lemon wedges and a parsley sprig, and a mixed salad.

Cook's Tip

Use a pastry brush to
remove grated lemon rind
from grater.

Cook's Tip

Line the base of the grill
pan with kitchen foil before
putting the chicken on the
rack for easy cleaning of
grill.

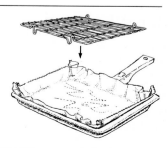

187 | *Chicken in Sesame Sauce*

Preparation time
15 minutes, plus 30 minutes marinating time

Cooking time
3–5 minutes

Serves 4–6

Calories
500–340 per portion

You will need
450 g/1 lb boneless chicken breasts, cut into cubes
1 tablespoon oil
100 g/4 oz unsalted cashew nuts
75 g/3 oz canned straw mushrooms, drained and halved

For the marinade
3 spring onions, chopped
3 tablespoons soy sauce
2 tablespoons hot pepper oil
2 tablespoons sesame oil
1 tablespoon sesame seed paste or tahini
1 teaspoon ground Szechuan peppercorns

Put the marinade ingredients into a bowl. Add the chicken cubes, turning to coat thoroughly. Leave to marinate for 30 minutes.

Meanwhile, heat the oil in a wok or frying pan, add the cashew nuts and fry until golden. Drain on absorbent kitchen paper.

Add the chicken and marinade to the pan and stir-fry for 2 minutes. Add the mushrooms and cook for a further 1 minute. Pile the mixture into a warmed serving dish and sprinkle with the nuts. Serve at once.

Cook's Tip

Szechuan peppercorns are reddish-brown Chinese peppercorns with a specially pungent flavour. They are usually dry roasted in a frying pan before cooking to develop the full flavour.

188 | *Rice Cooked with Chicken*

Preparation time
30 minutes

Cooking time
about 3–3¼ hours

Serves 6

Calories
880 per portion

You will need
4 small onions, halved
2 bay leaves
1 litre/1¾ pints water
1.75 kg/4 lb boiling chicken
½ teaspoon saffron threads
675 g/1½ lb Basmati rice
100 g/4 oz ghee
5 garlic cloves, sliced
10 cloves
10 cardamoms
2 (7.5-cm/3-inch) cinnamon sticks
50 g/2 oz blanched almonds
100 g/4 oz sultanas

For the garnish
hard-boiled egg quarters
fried onion rings

Place the onion halves, bay leaves, 1 litre/1¾ pints water in a pan and bring to the boil. Add the chicken, cover and simmer for 1½–2 hours until tender. Remove the flesh from the chicken and cut into pieces; reserve the cooking liquid and onions. Put the saffron in a cup and pour over a little boiling water; leave for 20 minutes. Wash the rice well.

Heat the ghee in a pan, add the reserved onions, garlic, cloves, cardamoms and cinnamon and fry for 5 minutes. Add the rice and enough cooking liquid to cover the rice, then the strained saffron water. Cook, uncovered, for 10–15 minutes, then cover to cook until tender. Mix with the chicken, almonds and sultanas. Garnish and serve.

Cook's Tip

To prevent black rings forming around the yolks of hard-boiled eggs, after cooking drain and leave in a saucepan under a running cold tap for about 2 minutes.

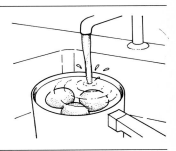

189 | Pineapple Chicken Curry

Preparation time
1 hour, including
soaking time

Cooking time
45 minutes

Serves 4

Calories
620 per portion

You will need
2 onions, quartered
2 garlic cloves, peeled
3.5 cm/1½ inch piece root ginger,
   peeled and chopped
1 teaspoon turmeric
1 tablespoon ground coriander
1–2 teaspoons chilli powder
2 tablespoons paprika
1 teaspoon sugar
1 teaspoon salt
2 tablespoons oil
8 chicken thighs, skinned
300 ml/½ pint water
100 g/4 oz cashew nuts, soaked
   in boiling water for 1 hour
6 curry leaves
4 green chillies, slit
1 medium pineapple, cubed
juice of ½–1 lemon

Place the first 9 ingredients in a liquidizer or food processor and work until smooth.

Heat the oil, add the spice paste and fry for 10 minutes. Add the chicken pieces and fry for 5 minutes. Pour in the water and bring to simmering point. Add the drained nuts, curry leaves and chillies, cover and simmer for 25 minutes. Add the pineapple and lemon juice to taste and simmer for a further 10 minutes. Serve hot.

190 | Indonesian Spicy Chicken

Preparation time
35 minutes, including
marinating time

Cooking time
45 minutes

Serves 4

Calories
400 per portion

You will need
8 chicken pieces, skinned
juice of 1 lemon
4 tablespoons desiccated
   coconut, soaked in 4
   tablespoons hot water
2–4 red chillies, chopped
4 small onions, quartered
2 garlic cloves, peeled
4 Brazil nuts, shelled
1 cm/½ inch piece root ginger,
   peeled
1 teaspoon grated lemon rind
1 teaspoon shrimp paste
1 teaspoon sugar
1 teaspoon salt
3 tablespoons oil
300 ml/½ pint water

Rub the chicken pieces with the lemon juice and leave to stand for 20 minutes.

Put all the remaining ingredients except the oil and water in a liquidizer or food processor and work to a smooth paste. Heat the oil in a large pan and fry the paste, stirring, for 5 minutes.

Add the chicken and fry for 5 minutes. Stir in the water and cook, uncovered, for 30 minutes or until the chicken is tender and the sauce is thick. Serve hot.

Cook's Tip

Pineapple is the ideal fruit for a curry, combining acidity with sweetness and, when fresh, crispness. Canned pineapple chunks may be used, but they tend to be too sweet and bland.

Cook's Tip

Serve Indonesian Spicy Chicken with krupuk or prawn crisps, fried bananas and a selection of sambals.

191 | Chicken with Piquant Green Sauce

Preparation time
10 minutes

Serves 4

Calories
261 per portion

You will need
4 cooked chicken breasts, about
150 g / 5 oz each, skinned
lemon wedges to garnish

For the sauce
2 garlic cloves, peeled and
crushed
2 tablespoons capers, drained and
finely chopped
50 g / 2 oz fresh parsley, finely
chopped
2 tablespoons wine vinegar
1 teaspoon Dijon mustard
75 ml / 3 fl oz olive oil
salt and pepper

To make the sauce, mix together the garlic, capers, parsley, vinegar and mustard. Gradually stir in the oil, then add salt and pepper to taste. Cover and chill until ready to serve.

Slice the chicken breasts thinly and arrange on a serving dish. Pour a little sauce over each slice and serve any remaining separately. Garnish with lemon wedges.

192 | Chicken Salad Véronique

Preparation time
20 minutes

Cooking time
10 minutes

Serves 4

Calories
357 per portion

You will need
4 tablespoons cooking oil
1 garlic clove, peeled
4 boned chicken breasts
50 g / 2 oz split or flaked almonds
1 head endive to serve
225 g / 8 oz green grapes, halved,
pips removed, or whole
seedless grapes to garnish

For the dressing
150 ml / 5 fl oz soured cream
1 tablespoon white vermouth or
dry white wine
salt and pepper

Heat the oil in a frying pan with the garlic. Fry the chicken on both sides for 5–10 minutes until golden brown and cooked through.

Remove the chicken and drain on paper towels. Add the almonds to the pan and fry gently, stirring constantly, until lightly browned. Remove from the pan and drain. Cool the chicken and almonds. Reserve the cooking oil and cool, discarding the garlic.

Spoon the soured cream into a bowl and beat in the cold cooking oil, vermouth or white wine, and salt and pepper to taste. Add a little more vermouth or white wine if a sharper dressing is preferred.

Arrange a bed of endive on a serving dish and place the cold chicken breasts on top. Spoon the dressing over the chicken and scatter with almonds and grapes.

Cook's Tip

Serve this chilled chicken dish as part of a summer buffet. It goes well with a selection of lettuce salads and slices of wholemeal bread with unsalted butter.

Cook's Tip

When recipe titles include the word 'Véronique' it means they are garnished with green grapes. The best-known example is Sole Véronique, a French dish of sole fillets in a creamy white wine sauce with green grapes that is served hot. This cold dish is an excellent choice for a light lunch main course or as part of a buffet. The chicken and dressing can each be prepared in advance but the salad should be assembled just before serving.

193 | Diced Chicken with Chillies

Preparation time
10 minutes

Cooking time
4 minutes

Serves 4

Calories
200 per portion

You will need
2 tablespoons oil
1 garlic clove, sliced
350 g/12 oz boneless chicken breast, diced
1 red pepper, cored, seeded and diced
2 green chillies, seeded and sliced
50 g/2 oz beansprouts
2 tablespoons soy sauce
2 tablespoons chilli sauce
fresh coriander leaves to garnish

Heat the oil in a wok or frying pan, add the garlic and fry for 1 minute. Add the chicken and stir-fry for 1 minute. Add the pepper and chillies and cook for a further 1 minute. Stir in the beansprouts, soy sauce and chilli sauce and cook for 2 minutes.

Turn into a warm serving dish, garnish with coriander and serve at once.

Cook's Tip

Chilli sauce is a very hot sauce made from chillies, vinegar and salt. Tabasco sauce can be used as a substitute.

194 | Stir-Fried Chicken with Ginger

Preparation time
10 minutes

Cooking time
12–15 minutes

Serves 4

Calories
300 per portion

You will need
2.5 cm/1 inch piece root ginger, peeled and shredded
salt
2 tablespoons oil
2 garlic cloves, chopped
6 chicken thighs, chopped into 2.5-cm/1-inch squares
1 tablespoon fish sauce
1 teaspoon sugar
1 tablespoon water
2 spring onions, cut into 5-cm/2-inch pieces
parsley sprigs to garnish

Sprinkle the ginger with salt, leave to stand a few minutes then squeeze and discard the liquid. Rinse and squeeze out again.

Heat the oil, add the garlic and stir-fry for 1–2 minutes. Add the ginger and stir-fry for 1 minute. Add the chicken and remaining ingredients, except the spring onions and parsley, then cover and cook over a moderate heat for 10 minutes, or until the chicken is cooked.

Stir in the spring onions and serve at once, garnished with parsley sprigs.

Cook's Tip

Fresh root ginger may be stored in a plastic bag in the refrigerator for several weeks, but check to make sure that any cut ends do not develop a mould.

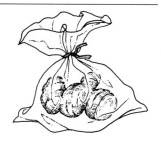

195 | Ginger Chicken

Preparation time
10 minutes, plus 20–30 minutes standing time

Cooking time
about 10 minutes

Serves 4

Calories
370 per portion

You will need
675 g/1½ lb chicken breasts, cut into finger-sized pieces
1 teaspoon sugar
salt and pepper
4 tablespoons sesame oil
10 cm/4 inch piece root ginger, peeled and finely sliced
75–100 ml/3–4 fl oz water
100 g/4 oz button mushrooms
2 tablespoons brandy
2 teaspoons cornflour, blended with 3 tablespoons water
1 teaspoon soy sauce

Sprinkle the chicken with the sugar and leave to stand for 20–30 minutes. Season with salt and pepper.

Heat the oil and fry the ginger for 1 minute. Add the chicken pieces and cook for 3 minutes. Stir in the water and mushrooms. Cover and cook for a further 5 minutes, or until the chicken is tender.

Add the brandy, cornflour mixture and soy sauce. Bring to the boil, stirring, until thickened. Serve at once.

196 | Braised Chicken Wings

Preparation time
15 minutes

Cooking time
about 10 minutes

Serves 4

Calories
400 per portion

You will need
12 chicken wings
4 dried Chinese mushrooms, soaked in warm water for 20–30 minutes
2 tablespoons oil
2 spring onions, finely chopped
2 slices root ginger, chopped
2 tablespoons soy sauce
2 tablespoons sake or sherry
1 tablespoon sugar
½ teaspoon 5-spice powder
350 ml/12 fl oz water
175 g/6 oz bamboo shoots, cubed
2 teaspoons cornflour, mixed with 1 tablespoon water

Remove and discard the tips of the chicken wings, then cut each wing into 2 pieces by breaking the joint.

Squeeze the mushrooms dry, discard the stalks and slice the caps.

Heat the oil until smoking, add the spring onions and ginger, then the chicken wings. Stir-fry until the chicken changes colour, then add the soy sauce, sake, sugar, 5-spice powder and water. Lower the heat and cook until the liquid is reduced by about half. Add the mushrooms and bamboo shoots and continue to cook until nearly all the juices have evaporated. Remove the bamboo chunks, wash and place around a serving dish.

Add the cornflour to the chicken and stir until any juices are thickened. Place in a serving dish and serve at once.

Cook's Tip

Never dip mushrooms into water when cleaning them; they will absorb too much water and will be difficult to fry. Just wipe them over with a damp cloth.

Cook's Tip

Chinese 5-spice powder is an aromatic seasoning made from a selection of 5 ground spices: star anise, fennel, cloves, cinnamon and szechuan pepper. It is used sparingly since it has an intense flavour.

197 | Cashew Chicken

Preparation time
5 minutes

Cooking time
3 minutes

Serves 4

Calories
420 per portion

You will need
350 g/12 oz boneless chicken
1 egg white
4 tablespoons dry sherry
2 teaspoons cornflour
3 tablespoons oil
4 spring onions, chopped
2 garlic cloves, chopped
2.5 cm/1 inch piece root ginger,
  peeled and finely chopped
1 tablespoon light soy sauce
100 g/4 oz unsalted cashew nuts

Cut the chicken into 1-cm/½-inch cubes. Mix the egg white, half the sherry and the cornflour together, add the chicken and toss until evenly coated.

Heat the oil, add the spring onions, garlic and ginger and stir-fry for 30 seconds. Add the chicken and cook for 2 minutes. Pour in the remaining sherry and the soy sauce and stir well. Add the cashew nuts and cook for a further 30 seconds. Serve at once.

198 | Chicken and Leeks

Preparation time
25 minutes

Cooking time
2½ minutes

Serves 4

Calories
190 per portion

You will need
½ cucumber
salt
350 g/12 oz boneless chicken
  breasts, skinned
2 tablespoons oil
3 leeks, thinly sliced diagonally
4 garlic cloves, sliced
1 tablespoon light soy sauce
1 tablespoon dry sherry
1 dried red chilli, crumbled
1 tablespoon chopped fresh
  coriander leaves
coriander leaves to garnish

Peel the cucumber, cut in half and remove the seeds. Cut into 2.5-cm/1-inch cubes, place in a colander, sprinkle with salt and leave for 20 minutes. Cube the chicken.

Heat the oil, add the leeks and garlic and cook for 30 seconds. Add the chicken and brown for 1 minute. Add the soy sauce, sherry and chilli and cook for a further 30 seconds. Stir in the cucumber and cook for 30 seconds.

Serve hot sprinkled with chopped coriander and garnished with coriander leaves.

Cook's Tip

This chicken recipe originates from the southern region of China, and exemplifies the Chinese taste for contrasting textures. It also uses some of the best Chinese cooking principles: stir-frying to keep in the juices of the chicken, *then stir-frying again with other ingredients to flavour it.*

Cook's Tip

When cutting the chicken for this dish, and for most stir-fried dishes, always cut across the grain; this ensures tenderness and succulence after cooking.

199 | Turkey with Peaches

Preparation time
15 minutes

Cooking time
30 minutes

Serves 4

Calories
315 per portion

You will need
25 g/1 oz plain flour
½ teaspoon grated nutmeg
salt and pepper
4 turkey fillets, cut into fine strips
2 tablespoons oil
1 onion, thinly sliced
1 (227-g/8-oz) can peach slices, drained
300 ml/½ pint chicken or turkey stock
150 ml/¼ pint soured cream

Garnish
chopped parsley
peach slices
bay leaves

Mix together the flour, nutmeg, salt and pepper and toss the turkey strips in the seasoned flour. Heat the oil in a frying pan and brown the turkey strips all over. Add the onion and cook for a further 2–3 minutes until soft. Add the peach slices, reserving a few for garnish, and chicken stock to the pan and bring to the boil. Reduce the heat and simmer gently for 20 minutes.

Remove the pan from the heat and add the soured cream. Reheat without boiling. Garnish with chopped parsley, reserved peach slices and bay leaves, and serve with a mixed salad.

200 | Chicken Fricassee

Preparation time
15 minutes

Cooking time
30 minutes

Serves 4

Calories
335 per portion

You will need
4 boneless breasts of chicken, cut into 1-cm/½-in wide strips
25 g/1 oz plain flour
50 g/2 oz butter or margarine
1 onion, chopped
100 g/4 oz mushrooms, sliced
½ teaspoon dried thyme
salt and pepper
150 ml/¼ pint chicken stock
150 ml/¼ pint dry white wine
150 ml/¼ pint soured cream
zested lemon rind to garnish

Toss the chicken strips in the flour. Heat the butter or margarine in a frying pan and cook the chopped onion until soft. Add the mushrooms and cook for another 2 minutes. Add the chicken strips and cook until they are golden all over. Sprinkle over the thyme, and season to taste.

Mix in the stock and wine and bring to the boil, then reduce the heat and simmer gently for 20 minutes. Reduce the heat further, stir in the soured cream and cook until the sauce is warmed through, but do not allow the sauce to boil.

Garnish with lemon rind and serve the chicken with parslied boiled rice and buttered carrots.

Cook's Tip

Serve fresh spinach noodles with this dish. Cook fresh pasta in boiling salted water for about 5 minutes. Drain, butter and serve.

Cook's Tip

If your eyes run very badly when peeling onions, then hold the onions under a slow running cold tap.

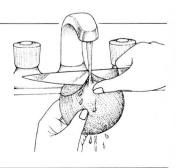

201 | Chicken with Sesame Seeds

Preparation time
20 minutes, including marinating time

Cooking time
4 minutes

Serves 4

Calories
230 per portion

You will need
350 g/12 oz boneless chicken
1 egg white
½ teaspoon salt
2 teaspoons cornflour
2 tablespoons white sesame seeds
2 tablespoons oil
1 tablespoon dark soy sauce
1 tablespoon wine vinegar
½ teaspoon chilli bean sauce
½ teaspoon sesame oil
1 tablespoon dry sherry
½ teaspoon roasted Szechuan peppercorns
4 spring onions, chopped

Cut the chicken into 7.5-cm/3-inch long shreds. Mix the egg white, salt and cornflour, toss in the chicken and mix well. Leave to stand for 15 minutes.

Fry the sesame seeds until golden in a pan or wok. Remove and set aside.

Heat the oil, add the chicken and stir-fry for 1 minute. Remove with a slotted spoon. Add the soy sauce, vinegar, chilli bean sauce, sesame oil, sherry and peppercorns and bring to the boil. Add the chicken and spring onions and cook for 2 minutes. Sprinkle with the sesame seeds and serve at once.

202 | Chicken Curry

Preparation time
15 minutes, plus 4 hours marinating time

Cooking time
about 35 minutes

Serves 4

Calories
350 per portion

You will need
2 garlic cloves, chopped
5 cm/2 inch piece root ginger, peeled and chopped
1 teaspoon turmeric
2 teaspoons cumin seeds, ground
1 teaspoon chilli powder
1 teaspoon pepper
3 tablespoons finely chopped fresh coriander leaves
450 g/1 lb natural yogurt
salt
1 kg/2 lb chicken pieces, skinned
4 tablespoons oil
2 onions, chopped

Put the garlic, ginger, turmeric, cumin, chilli, pepper, coriander, yogurt and salt to taste into a large bowl. Mix well, add the chicken and leave for 4 hours, turning the chicken occasionally.

Heat the oil in a pan, add the onions and fry until golden. Add the chicken and the marinade. Bring to simmering point, cover and cook for about 30 minutes, until the chicken is tender.

Cook's Tip

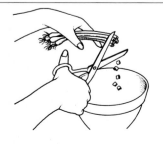

You can 'chop' spring onions very simply by first washing them, then holding them over a bowl. Snip them up from the green end towards the root with a pair of scissors.

Cook's Tip

It is difficult to grind just a teaspoon or two of spices in a blender or food processor – this is best done in a pestle and mortar, coffee grinder or small herb mill.

203 | Turkey Escalopes with Anchovies

Preparation time
15 minutes, plus marinating

Cooking time
10 minutes

Serves 4

Calories
304 per portion

You will need
juice and grated rind of 1 lemon
2 tablespoons olive oil
1 teaspoon dried oregano
salt and pepper
450 g / 1 lb turkey breast slices
2 tablespoons plain flour
75 g / 3 oz fresh breadcrumbs
2 tablespoons chopped fresh mint
1 egg
1 tablespoon milk
1 tablespoon oil for frying

For the garnish
1 × 50-g / 2-oz can anchovy fillets, drained
8 stuffed olives
2 hard-boiled eggs, sliced

To make the marinade, mix together the lemon juice, olive oil, oregano and salt and pepper. Pour into a shallow dish and add the turkey breast slices. Cover and marinate for 1 hour, or overnight in the refrigerator, turning once.

Drain the meat and pat it dry. Season the flour with salt and pepper and put on a plate. Mix the breadcrumbs, lemon rind and mint together in a bowl. Beat the egg and milk together. Coat the turkey with the seasoned flour, then dip in the egg and roll in the breadcrumb mixture.

Heat the oil and fry the turkey slices for 3–4 minutes on each side until evenly browned. Arrange on a heated serving dish. Garnish with the anchovy fillets, each one rolled around an olive, and with egg slices.

Cook's Tip

If you have time, chill the coated turkey pieces for 30 minutes before frying. This helps to set the coating, so it is less likely to fall off during cooking.

204 | Turkey with Walnuts

Preparation time
10 minutes

Cooking time
6 minutes

Serves 4

Calories
115 per portion

You will need
1 tablespoon oil
1 onion, peeled and finely chopped
1 garlic clove, peeled and crushed
1 turkey breast, skinned, sliced and cut into small slivers
grated rind and juice of 1 orange
25 g / 1 oz walnut halves, chopped
1 tablespoon soy sauce
2 teaspoons cornflour, blended with 4 tablespoons water
1 teaspoon soft brown sugar
1 tablespoon finely chopped fresh parsley
salt and pepper
shredded orange rind to garnish

Heat the oil and fry the onion, stirring, for 2 minutes. Stir in the garlic and push the mixture to one side of the pan. Tilt the pan to let the juices run out over the base.

Add the turkey and stir-fry for 2 minutes. Remove with a slotted spoon, transfer to a serving dish and keep warm.

Add the orange rind and juice, walnuts, soy sauce, blended cornflour, sugar and parsley to the pan. Bring to the boil, stirring, then simmer until thickened. Stir in salt and pepper to taste and pour over the turkey. Serve hot, garnished with shredded orange rind.

Cook's Tip

This is a good dish to use up leftover turkey meat. If you do use cooked meat, make sure the skin and any small bones are removed. Stir-fry the onion and garlic for 3 minutes before adding the meat.

205 | *Turkey Parcels*

Preparation time
35 minutes, including
marinating time

Cooking time
5 minutes

Serves 4

Calories
300 per portion

You will need
1 tablespoon soy sauce
1 tablespoon dry sherry
1 tablespoon sesame oil
450 g/1 lb turkey breast, cut into
  16 pieces
4 spring onions, each cut into 4
  pieces
5 cm/2 inch piece root ginger,
  peeled and shredded
½ red pepper, cored, seeded and
  shredded
1 celery stick, shredded
4 tablespoons oil

Mix the soy sauce, sherry and sesame oil together, add
the turkey and toss well to coat. Leave to marinate for
15–20 minutes.

Cut out 16 pieces of foil large enough to enclose the
pieces of turkey generously. Brush the foil with oil, place
a piece of turkey in the centre of each and top with a
piece of spring onion, a little ginger, pepper and celery.
Fold the foil over to enclose and seal the edges well.

Heat the oil in a wok, add the foil parcels and fry for 2
minutes on each side. Remove and leave to drain.

Reheat the oil to very hot and return the turkey parcels
to the wok for 1 minute. Drain and serve.

Cook's Tip

**Turkey Parcels are a variation
of the traditional paper-
wrapped chicken, where the
food is wrapped in
greaseproof paper and fried or
steamed. Diners should
unwrap their own parcels
with their chopsticks.**

206 | *Soy-Braised Duck*

Preparation time
15 minutes, plus 1 hour
marinating time

Cooking time
about 1½ hours

Oven temperature
220 C, 425 F, gas 7
then
190 C, 375 F, gas 5

Serves 4–6

Calories
880–590 per portion

You will need
1.75 kg/4 lb duck
4 (1-cm/½-inch) pieces root
  ginger, finely chopped
1 large onion, finely chopped
1 teaspoon salt
6 tablespoons soy sauce
3 tablespoons malt vinegar
1 tablespoon oil
4 spring onions, chopped
150 ml/¼ pint chicken stock
1 tablespoon cornflour
2 tablespoons water
1 (227-g/8-oz) can pineapple
  slices, halved, with juice
3 tablespoons dry sherry

Prick the duck skin. Mix the ginger with the onion and salt
and rub inside the duck. Put in a large bowl, add the soy
sauce and vinegar and leave to marinate for 1 hour, basting occasionally. Transfer to a roasting tin and roast at the
higher temperature for 30 minutes.

Heat the oil in a pan, add the spring onions and fry until
lightly browned. Remove and set aside. Pour off any excess fat from the duck, sprinkle with the spring onions,
remaining marinade and stock. Cover and cook at the
lower oven temperature for 1 hour, basting occasionally.

Remove the duck and cut into 16 pieces. Place on a
warmed serving dish. Blend the cornflour with the water,
then the pineapple juice. Place in a pan with the pineapple and duck juices. Cook for 2 minutes, stirring then
serve with the duck. Garnish as shown.

Cook's Tip

**Duck is a very fatty meat, so
the skin is pricked before
cooking to help release any
excess – this is discarded after
the first stage of cooking.**

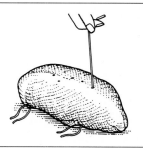

207 | Diced Turkey with Celery

Preparation time
20 minutes, including soaking time

Cooking time
3 minutes

Serves 4

Calories
300 per portion

You will need
4 Chinese dried mushrooms
350 g/12 oz turkey breast, diced
salt
1 egg white
1 tablespoon cornflour
4 tablespoons oil
2 garlic cloves, sliced
2 slices root ginger, chopped
2 leeks, diagonally sliced
1 small head celery, diagonally sliced
1 red pepper, cored, seeded and sliced
3 tablespoons light soy sauce
2 tablespoons dry sherry
celery leaves to garnish

Soak the mushrooms in warm water for 15 minutes, squeeze dry, discard the stalks and slice the caps.

Season the turkey with salt, dip in egg white, then coat with cornflour. Heat the oil, add the turkey and stir-fry for 1 minute, until golden. Remove with a slotted spoon and set aside.

Increase the heat, add the garlic, ginger, leeks and celery and stir-fry for 1 minute. Add the turkey and red pepper and cook for 30 seconds. Stir in the soy sauce and sherry and cook for a further 30 seconds.

Spoon into a warmed serving dish and garnish with celery leaves.

208 | Sweet and Sour Turkey

Preparation time
6 minutes

Cooking time
6 minutes

Serves 4

Calories
120 per portion

You will need
1 tablespoon oil
1 onion, finely chopped
1 turkey breast, skinned and cubed
½ yellow or red pepper, cored, seeded and sliced
3 mushrooms, sliced

For the sauce
1½ tablespoons soy sauce
1 heaped tablespoon tomato purée
2 teaspoons cornflour
300 ml/½ pint water
3 tablespoons unsweetened pineapple juice
2 tablespoons wine vinegar
1 heaped teaspoon brown sugar
spring onion fan to garnish

To make the sauce, place all the ingredients in a small pan and mix well. Bring to the boil, then simmer, stirring until thickened. Keep warm.

Heat the oil, add the onion and stir-fry for 2 minutes. Add the turkey and stir-fry for 2–3 minutes. Add the pepper and mushrooms and cook for 2–3 minutes.

Transfer to a serving dish and pour over the sauce to serve. Garnish with a spring onion fan if liked.

Cook's Tip

This stir-fried dish is ideally cooked in a wok. If you wish to buy a wok, buy one that is made from carbon steel rather than stainless steel or aluminium which tends to scorch.

Cook's Tip

Serve this speedy stir-fry recipe with boiled rice and a green vegetable such as French beans or mangetout.

VEGETABLES AND SALADS

There is nothing to compare with fresh vegetables in season to bring a meal to life. Use vegetables as a refreshing contrast to meat or fish, and make sure they are just cooked, not only to preserve maximum colour and crisp texture, but vitamin content too. Lemon Cabbage with Poppy Seeds and Braised Chinese Leaves with Mushrooms show how green-leaved vegetables (high in vitamin C) can be served as the perfect accompaniment to pork or fish dishes. Aubergine and Onion Gratin or Leeks in Sauce go splendidly with lamb, while Ratatouille and Celery with Walnuts make good partners for grilled steak.

Complement the range and texture of fresh vegetables by including pulses in your diet too: dishes like Spanish Chick Peas and Masoor Dhal are delectably spicy, warm and filling. Dishes like these make a complete meal with a side salad and fruit to follow. For a substantial vegetable accompaniment to a main meal, or as a light supper dish, Stuffed Cabbage Leaves, Stuffed Marrow Rings or Chilli-Stuffed Peppers are excellent.

In recent years, salads have become increasingly popular with many imaginative ideas for new combinations. Simple fresh vegetables in a tangy dressing like Carrot Salad or Chicory and Orange Salad refresh the palate served with roast meats. More complex mixtures can be served alone as a delicious summer lunch. Modern dinner parties are not complete without a beautiful arrangement such as Tuscan Nectarine and Avocado Salad as a starter or to accompany the cheese. Whatever the occasion, salads and vegetables add the essential finishing touch.

209 | Russian-style Potatoes

Preparation time
5 minutes

Cooking time
20 minutes

Serves 3

Calories
164 per portion

You will need
1 tablespoon butter
1 tablespoon oil
450 g / 1 lb small potatoes,
    unpeeled and thickly sliced
salt and pepper
2 spring onions, chopped

Heat the butter and oil until sizzling. Add the potatoes and fry quickly until golden brown but not cooked through.

Turn the slices and sprinkle generously with salt and pepper. Cover the pan, lower the heat and continue to fry/steam the slices for 20 minutes, shaking the pan occasionally to prevent them sticking, until tender.

Take the lid off the pan and turn up the heat again for a minute or two. Serve immediately, sprinkled with the spring onions.

Cook's Tip

Also known as kartoshki, this traditional Russian dish produces potatoes that taste as if they have been roasted without having to use the oven. This is a good side dish to serve with meat. Use the largest frying pan you have.

210 | Celeriac Sticks with Mustard

Preparation time
10 minutes

Cooking time
20–25 minutes

Serves 4

Calories
70 per portion

You will need
750 g / 1½ celeriac, peeled
salt
1 tablespoon lemon juice

For the sauce
150 ml / ¼ pint double or whipping
    cream, or plain yogurt
pepper
1 tablespoon whole grain mustard
lemon slices and parsley sprigs to
    garnish

Carefully cut the celeriac into chips about 1 × 7.5 cm / ½ × 3 inches.

Put the chips into a pan with a pinch of salt and the lemon juice and cover with water. Bring to the boil, cover and simmer for 15–20 minutes until the celeriac is tender but still firm. Drain and keep warm in a serving dish.

Pour the cream into the rinsed-out pan and stir in the salt and pepper to taste and mustard. Heat very gently until hot *but do not boil.*

Pour the sauce over the celeriac. Serve at once, garnished with lemon slices and parsley.

Cook's Tip

Celeriac looks like a knobbly swede with a turnip-like texture. As its name implies, it tastes like celery. If the cut flesh isn't coated with lemon juice, it will turn brown.

211 | Leeks in Sauce

Preparation time
10 minutes

Cooking time
20 minutes

Serves 4

Calories
215 per portion

You will need
8 medium leeks
salt

For the cheese sauce
25 g / 1 oz butter or margarine
25 g / 1 oz plain flour
150 ml / ¼ pint milk
75 g / 3 oz Cheddar cheese,
   grated
salt and pepper
pinch of mustard powder

Trim, wash and slice the leeks in half lengthways. Put the leeks in a large saucepan, add a little salt, then pour in enough water to just cover the vegetables. Bring to the boil, then simmer for 10 minutes. Drain the leeks well and reserve 150 ml / ¼ pint of the cooking water for the sauce. Place in a serving dish and keep hot.

To make the sauce, melt the butter or margarine over a gentle heat, then stir in the flour and cook for 2 minutes. Gradually add the milk and leek water, stirring the mixture all the time. Bring the sauce to the boil and simmer gently for a few minutes. Remove from the heat, stir in the Cheddar, seasoning and mustard. Mix until smooth and pour the sauce over the leeks. Serve at once.

212 | Celery with Walnuts

Preparation time
5–10 minutes

Cooking time
25–30 minutes

Serves 4

Calories
195 per portion

You will need
1 large head of celery
1 large onion, chopped
50 g / 2 oz butter or margarine
50 g / 2 oz walnut halves
300 ml / ½ pint chicken stock
few drops of soy sauce

Trim and wash the celery. Cut the sticks in 5-cm / 2-in lengths.

Fry the onion in the butter or margarine in a large pan. Add the celery and walnuts. Cook for a few minutes, then pour in the stock. Simmer uncovered for 25–30 minutes until softened. Season with soy sauce. Serve immediately.

Cook's Tip

Substitute dry white wine for cooking water and use half the quantity of cheese to make a wine sauce. Or use all milk to make a creamy sauce.

Cook's Tips

To keep a head of celery fresh, store it on a cool windowsill with root end in a jug of water.

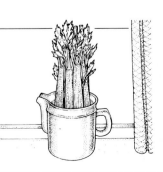

213 | *Creamed Chicory and Mushrooms*

Preparation time
15 minutes

Cooking time
10 minutes

Serves 4

Calories
200 per portion

You will need
50 g / 2 oz onion, chopped
40 g / 1½ oz butter
275 g / 10 oz chicory, sliced in half
100 g / 4 oz button mushrooms, sliced
120 ml / 4 fl oz vegetable stock
120 ml / 4 fl oz double cream
salt and freshly ground black pepper
chopped parsley to garnish

Soften the onion in the butter over a gentle heat, without browning. Add the chicory and mushrooms and cook for a few minutes. Pour in the stock and simmer, covered, for 5 minutes. Remove from the heat, add the cream, season well and reheat for a few minutes without boiling. Transfer to a warmed dish and sprinkle with chopped parsley.

214 | *Mushroom Fondue*

Preparation time
15 minutes

Cooking time
10–15 minutes

Serves 4

Calories
665 per portion

You will need
½ clove garlic
150 ml / ¼ pint medium dry cider
1 teaspoon lemon juice
400 g / 14 oz Gouda cheese, grated
1 tablespoon cornflour
1½ tablespoons gin
100 g / 4 oz button mushrooms, chopped
freshly ground black pepper
pinch of grated nutmeg

To serve
1 stick French bread, cut into cubes
100 g / 4 oz button mushrooms

Rub the inside of a fondue pot or flameproof casserole with the cut garlic, and place a little finely chopped garlic in the pot. Pour in the cider and lemon juice and heat slowly until nearly boiling. Gradually add the grated cheese, a little at a time, stirring continuously with a fork until all the cheese has melted. When the mixture is bubbling, blend the cornflour with the gin until smooth and add to the fondue, stirring well. Add the chopped mushrooms, pepper and nutmeg.

Serve the cheese fondue in the cooking pot at the table. There should be a fondue fork for each person, and the cubes of French bread and whole button mushrooms are speared with the fork and dipped into the fondue. This is delicious accompanied by an orange and cucumber salad.

Cook's Tip

Frozen double cream is a useful item to keep in the freezer. Packed in neat sticks, just remove the number required for the dish and defrost at room temperature.

Cook's Tip

If gin is not to your taste, substitute an equal amount of any of the following: Kirsch, whisky, brandy or dry sherry.

215 | Chicory in Mustard Sauce

Preparation time
5 minutes

Cooking time
18 minutes

Serves 4

Calories
85 per portion

You will need
8 small heads chicory
150 ml/¼ pint salted water
juice of 1 lemon
15 g/½ oz butter
scant 1 tablespoon plain flour
150 ml/¼ pint vegetable stock
2–3 tablespoons single cream
scant 2 tablespoons prepared mild
    mustard
1 teaspoon sugar
1 tablespoon chopped dill to
    garnish

Rinse and drain the chicory and remove the thick stems. Bring the water and lemon juice to the boil. Add the chicory heads, lower the heat and cook for about 10 minutes. Drain and keep hot. Reserve cooking liquid.

Melt the butter in a small pan, stir in the flour and cook for 2–3 minutes. Gradually add the reserved cooking liquid and stock, stirring constantly.

Add the cream, mustard and sugar and bring to the boil, stirring constantly. Cook for 3 minutes, stirring. Arrange the chicory heads on a warmed serving dish, pour over the sauce. Sprinkle with the chopped dill. Serve immediately.

Cook's Tip

Look out for different mustards in delicatessens and health food shops. Try wholegrain varieties, those flavoured with herbs and continental types, such as Swedish mustard which can be slightly sweet and very mild.

216 | Spinach with Flaked Almonds

Preparation time
10 minutes

Cooking time
20 minutes

Serves 4

Calories
200 per portion

You will need
1 kg/2¼ lb leaf spinach
50 g/2 oz butter
½ onion, finely chopped
salt
grated nutmeg
4 tablespoons natural yogurt
50 g/2 oz flaked almonds

Place the spinach in a sieve, rinse and drain thoroughly. Tear the leaves into manageable pieces. Melt half the butter in a large saucepan, add the onion and cook for 2–3 minutes until softened. Add the spinach, a little at a time, turning it in the butter to coat. Season with salt and nutmeg to taste. Cook over a low heat for 10–15 minutes until tender, depending upon the thickness of the spinach leaves.

Stir the natural yogurt into the spinach mixture. Remove the spinach from the heat and transfer to a warmed serving bowl. Fry the almonds in the remaining butter, stirring, until golden. Fold the almonds into the spinach and serve immediately.

Cook's Tip

Freshly grated nutmeg gives the best flavour. Keep whole nutmegs in an airtight jar, then grate them as required on a special miniature, very fine grater.

217 | Stuffed Marrow Rings

Preparation time
5–10 minutes

Cooking time
55 minutes

Oven temperature
190 C, 375 F, gas 5

Serves 4

Calories
440 per portion

You will need
1 onion, chopped
1 tablespoon oil
450 g/1 lb minced beef
1 (400-g/14-oz) can chopped
    tomatoes
50 g/2 oz flaked almonds
50 g/2 oz sultanas
1 teaspoon ground cinnamon
1 teaspoon grated nutmeg
salt and pepper
4 (5-cm/2-in) thick slices
    marrow, peeled
parsley sprig to garnish

Fry the onion in the oil until softened and transparent. Add the minced beef and cook until browned, stirring briskly. Add the remaining ingredients, except the marrow slices, bring the mixture to the boil and simmer until thickened, about 15 minutes.

Meanwhile, scoop out the seeds from the marrow slices, leaving a hole in the centre of each slice. Arrange the rings in a baking dish.

Pour the meat mixture into the centre of each marrow slice and pile the remainder on top. Cover the dish with foil and bake in a moderately hot oven for 30 minutes or until the marrow is tender.

Transfer to a serving plate, garnish with a sprig of parsley, and serve immediately with baked potatoes.

218 | Hot Spring Salad

Preparation time
10 minutes

Cooking time
15 minutes

Serves 4

Calories
370 per portion

You will need
675 g/1½ lb fresh spinach
4 slices bread, crusts removed,
    cut into cubes
50 g/2 oz butter, or 15 g/½ oz
    butter and 2 tablespoons oil
8 rashers rindless streaky bacon,
    diced
100 g/4 oz button mushrooms,
    whole
3 tablespoons oil
2 cloves garlic, crushed
1 tablespoon wine vinegar
¼ teaspoon mustard powder
salt and pepper

Wash and shred the spinach. Place in a large salad bowl. Fry the bread cubes in the butter, or butter and oil mixture, until golden. Remove, drain on absorbent kitchen paper, then sprinkle the cubes over the spinach. Fry the bacon in any remaining fat until really crispy. Add the mushrooms and continue cooking for a few minutes.

Mix the remaining ingredients together and pour over the mushrooms and bacon. Bring the mixture quickly to the boil, pour over the spinach and toss gently. Serve at once.

Cook's Tip

Use the meat mixture to stuff courgettes. Cut 4 large courgettes in half lengthways. Scoop out the middle and fill with the mixture. Bake as above.

Cook's Tip

Prepare flavoured vinegars for use in salads. Put herb sprigs – tarragon, thyme, basil, rosemary – into bottles of white wine vinegar and leave for 1 month before use.

219 | Dhai Aloo

Preparation time
15 minutes

Cooking time
about 25–30 minutes

Serves 4—6

Calories
400–270 per portion

You will need
4 tablespoons oil
1 onion, chopped
2.5 cm/1 inch piece root ginger,
  peeled and finely chopped
1 tablespoon ground coriander
2 green chillies, finely chopped
675 g/1½ lb small new potatoes
1 (227-g/8-oz) can tomatoes
100 g/4 oz raisins
salt
300 ml/½ pint natural yogurt
2 tablespoons chopped fresh
  coriander leaves to garnish

Heat the oil in a large pan, add the onion and ginger and fry until soft. Stir in the ground coriander and chillies and fry for 2 minutes. Add the potatoes, stir well, cover and cook very gently for 5 minutes, stirring occasionally so they colour evenly.

Add the tomatoes with their juice, raisins and salt to taste and stir well. Increase the heat a little and cook, uncovered. As the liquid evaporates, add half the yogurt, a tablespoon at a time. When the potatoes have cooked for 20 minutes and are just about ready, add the remaining yogurt, a tablespoon at a time, lower the heat and cook for 2 minutes.

Sprinkle with the coriander leaves to serve.

220 | Braised Chinese Leaves and Mushrooms

Preparation time
20 minutes

Cooking time
about 5–10 minutes

Serves 4

Calories
180 per portion

You will need
450 g/1 lb Chinese leaves
350 g/12 oz canned straw
  mushrooms or 225 g/8 oz fresh
  straw or button mushrooms
4 tablespoons vegetable oil
2 teaspoons salt
1 teaspoon sugar
1 tablespoon cornflour
3 tablespoons water
50 ml/2 fl oz milk

Separate and wash the Chinese leaves, then cut each leaf in half lengthways. Drain the canned mushrooms; if using fresh, do not peel, simply wash or wipe and then trim off the stalk ends.

Heat about half of the oil in a wok, add the Chinese leaves and stir-fry for 1 minute. Add 1½ teaspoons of the salt and the sugar and stir-fry for a further 1 minute. Remove the Chinese leaves and arrange neatly on a warmed serving dish. Keep hot.

Mix the cornflour to a smooth paste with 3 tablespoons cold water. Heat the remaining oil in the wok until hot, add the mushrooms and remaining salt and stir-fry for 1 minute. Add the cornflour paste and the milk and stir constantly until the sauce is smooth, white and thickened. Pour evenly over the Chinese leaves and serve at once.

Cook's Tip

Ground coriander, not to be confused with green coriander leaves, is a spice with a flavour something like a mixture of sage and lemon peel. It is used extensively in curries and Indian dishes and to give a lift to rice dishes.

Cook's Tip

Chinese straw mushrooms are available both canned and fresh from Chinese supermarkets or stores. Should you have difficulty obtaining them, use small button mushrooms instead.

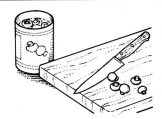

221 | Cauliflower with Peanut Sauce

Preparation time
25 minutes

Cooking time
15 minutes

Serves 4

Calories
227 per portion

You will need
1 cauliflower, about 500 g / 1¼ lb, cut into florets
salt
2 tablespoons chopped salted peanuts to garnish

For the sauce
1 tablespoon butter
1 tablespoon plain flour
150 ml / ¼ pint milk
150 ml / ¼ pint vegetable stock
4 tablespoons crunchy peanut butter
½ teaspoon yeast extract
pepper

Cook the cauliflower in boiling salted water for 6–8 minutes, until tender but still crisp. Drain and keep warm in a serving dish.

Meanwhile, to make the sauce, melt the butter, add the flour and cook for 3 minutes, stirring constantly. Pour in the milk and vegetable stock and bring to the boil, stirring. Simmer for 2–3 minutes, then stir in the peanut butter, a spoonful at a time. The peanut butter will thicken the sauce. Add the yeast extract, a little salt if necessary (there is probably enough in the peanut butter) and pepper to taste.

Pour the sauce over the cauliflower and sprinkle with the chopped peanuts. Serve hot.

222 | Lemon Cabbage with Poppy Seeds

Preparation time
5 minutes

Cooking time
10–15 minutes

Serves 4

Calories
123 per portion

You will need
150 ml / ¼ pint water
½ teaspoon salt
350 g / 12 oz white cabbage, shredded
350 g / 12 oz spring greens or green cabbage, shredded
25 g / 1 oz butter, diced
grated rind of 1 lemon
1½ teaspoons poppy seeds
pepper
2–3 tablespoons soured cream to serve (optional)

Boil the water and salt. Add both white and green cabbages, cover and simmer steadily for 7–10 minutes until tender but still crisp and most of the water absorbed.

Uncover and boil quickly to reduce any remaining liquid. Add the butter, lemon rind, poppy seeds and lots of black pepper. Stir briefly until the butter is melted and the cabbage well coated.

Spoon the hot cabbage into a warm dish and serve with soured cream spooned over the top if liked.

Cook's Tip

Available all year round, cauliflowers should be eaten within a day of purchase. Buy firm heads, as any rubberiness indicates they are not fresh. Wrap in cling film or foil and store in the salad drawer of the refrigerator. For this recipe the florets can also be steamed rather than boiled.

Cook's Tip

Use a pastry brush to get all the grated lemon rind off the back of the grater.

223 | Ratatouille

Preparation time
15 minutes

Cooking time
20–25 minutes

Serves 4

Calories
235 per portion

You will need
1 aubergine
salt and pepper
2 medium onions
2 courgettes
1 red pepper
1 green pepper
675 g/ 1½ lb tomatoes
4–6 tablespoons oil
2 cloves garlic, crushed
¼ teaspoon dried mixed herbs

Thinly slice the aubergine, place in a colander and sprinkle generously with salt to remove the bitter flavour. Leave to drain while preparing the other vegetables. Thinly slice the onions and courgettes. Core, deseed and slice the peppers. Peel, quarter and deseed the tomatoes.

Heat the oil in a large saucepan. Cook the onion with the garlic until softened. Rinse and dry the aubergine slices and add to the pan with the remaining vegetables, herbs and seasoning. Bring the mixture to the boil, reduce the heat and simmer gently, covered, for 15–20 minutes. Stir the vegetables from time to time during cooking to ensure that the juices are evenly mixed.

224 | Chilli-Stuffed Peppers

Preparation time
15 minutes

Cooking time
50 minutes

Oven temperature
180 C, 350 F, gas 4

Serves 4

Calories
375 per portion

You will need
4 green peppers, tops reserved
  and deseeded

For the filling
1 onion, chopped
1 clove garlic, crushed
350 g/ 12 oz minced beef
1 tablespoon oil
100 g/ 4 oz mushrooms, sliced
2 teaspoons chilli powder
1 tablespoon tomato purée
150 ml/ ¼ pint beef stock
salt and pepper
1 (425-g/ 15-oz) can kidney
  beans

Blanch the peppers in boiling salted water for 1–2 minutes and drain. Place in an ovenproof dish.

Fry the onion, garlic and minced beef in the oil until browned. Stir in the mushrooms, chilli powder, tomato purée, stock and seasoning and simmer gently for 10 minutes. Drain the kidney beans and add to the meat.

Fill the peppers with the chilli mixture, cover the dish and bake in a moderate oven for 30 minutes.

Cook's Tip

Ratatouille makes a refreshing starter – cut the vegetables into chunks instead of slices. Cook and cool, then chill and serve with warm French bread.

Cook's Tip

If you find a whole pepper too much for 1 serving, then cut 2 peppers in half lengthways to make boat shapes. Place in a baking dish and pile the filling in. Cook as above.

225 | Aubergines Bonne Femme

Preparation time
20 minutes

Cooking time
30 minutes

Oven temperature
200 C, 400 F, gas 6

Serves 4—6

Calories
295 200 per portion

You will need
5 tablespoons olive oil
3 medium aubergines, cut in
   quarters lengthways, then in
   2 cm/ $\frac{3}{4}$ in slices
1 large onion, coarsely chopped
2 cloves garlic, halved
250 g/9 oz tomatoes, roughly
   chopped
salt and pepper
1 teaspoon chopped fresh oregano
1 parsley sprig, chopped
50 g/2 oz Parmesan cheese,
   grated
1 tablespoon butter

Heat the oil in a saucepan, add the aubergines, onion and garlic and fry for 7–8 minutes. Remove and discard the garlic.

Add the tomatoes to the pan and season with salt and pepper to taste. Stir in the oregano and parsley. Cook for a few minutes then transfer the mixture to a shallow ovenproof dish. Sprinkle with the Parmesan cheese and dot with the butter. Cook in a moderately hot oven for about 20 minutes. Serve immediately.

226 | Aubergine and Onion Gratin

Preparation time
20 minutes, plus 1 hour
to prepare aubergine

Cooking time
50 minutes 1 hour

Oven temperature
200 C, 400 F, gas 6

Serves 4

Calories
350 per portion

You will need
4 medium aubergines
salt and pepper
2 3 tablespoons oil
225 g/8 oz onions, sliced
225 g/8 oz Cheddar cheese, grated
chopped parsley to garnish

Slice the aubergines and layer in a colander, sprinkling each layer with salt. Set aside for 1 hour.

Rinse the aubergine slices under cold running water, then pat dry. Heat the oil in a frying pan and fry the aubergine slices, a few at a time, for 2–3 minutes on each side. Drain on absorbent kitchen paper. Fry the onions in the pan until soft.

Arrange the aubergine and onion slices in layers in a greased ovenproof dish, seasoning each layer. Sprinkle with the cheese. Cook in a moderately hot oven for 40 minutes. Garnish with parsley and serve.

Cook's Tip

Serve this delicious dish accompanied by salad, French bread and a French red wine.

Cook's Tip

If preferred, courgettes can be used in place of the aubergines in this recipe. Courgettes do not need to be salted prior to cooking but you will need the equivalent weight of the aubergines.

227 | Beetroot with Soured Cream and Cumin

Preparation time
5 minutes

Cooking time
5 minutes

Serves 4

Calories
119 per portion

You will need
25 g / 1 oz butter
2 teaspoons ground cumin
150 ml / ¼ pint soured cream
450 g / 1 lb beetroot, peeled and diced
salt and pepper

Melt the butter, sprinkle in the cumin and cook for 1–2 minutes, stirring.

Add the soured cream, beetroot and salt and pepper to taste. Cook until the beetroot is heated through, stirring gently. Transfer to a warmed serving dish and serve at once.

228 | Mixed Winter Vegetables

Preparation time
10 minutes

Cooking time
1 hour

Oven temperature
190C, 375F, Gas 5

Serves 4

Calories
50 per portion

You will need
500 g / 1¼ lb peeled mixed winter root vegetables, diced
salt and pepper
1 tablespoon butter or margarine
2–3 tomatoes, sliced
watercress sprigs to garnish

Put the vegetables into a casserole with water to cover, salt and pepper to taste and the butter. Cover and cook for 1 hour until very tender.

Strain the vegetables and place in individual serving dishes. Add the tomato slices, garnish with watercress and serve at once.

Cook's Tip

The ground cumin can be replaced with dried dill weed or 1 tablespoon chopped fresh dill. Grated orange rind also adds extra flavour.

Cook's Tip

Try to dice the vegetables to the same size so they cook in the same time. Use potatoes, carrots, swedes, parsnips and turnips. For added fibre, do not peel the potatoes and carrots.

229 | Fantail Potatoes

Preparation time
15 minutes, plus 2
hours for soaking

Cooking time
1 hour

Oven temperature
190 C, 375 F, gas 5

Serves 4

Calories
280 per portion

You will need
4 medium potatoes
2 tablespoons lemon juice
50 g/ 2 oz butter or margarine,
  melted
1 onion, finely chopped
1 clove garlic, crushed (optional)
salt and pepper
50 g/ 2 oz Cheddar cheese, finely
  grated
parsley sprig to garnish

Peel the potatoes and slice thinly into vertical slices, leaving them attached at the base. Soak the potatoes in a bowl of water with the lemon juice for 2 hours or until the potatoes have fanned out. Drain.

Mix together the melted butter or margarine, the onion, garlic, if using, and seasoning. Place the potatoes in a baking tin, pour over the butter mixture and bake in a moderately hot oven for 50 minutes, basting occasionally. Sprinkle the Cheddar on each potato and bake for a further 10–15 minutes or until the potatoes are crisp and golden. Serve immediately, garnished with a sprig of parsley.

230 | Lyonnaise Potatoes

Preparation time
15 minutes

Cooking time
25 minutes

Serves 4

Calories
235 per portion

You will need
675 g/ 1½ lb potatoes
salt
50 g/ 2 oz butter or margarine
2–3 small onions, sliced into
  rings
chopped parsley to garnish

Peel and cook the potatoes whole in plenty of boiling salted water for 15 minutes. Drain and cool. Slice the potatoes evenly. Fry the potato slices in the butter or margarine until crisp and golden. When two-thirds cooked, add the onion rings and continue cooking until they are softened.

Garnish with chopped parsley and serve immediately.

Microwave Tip

Microwave these for about 10–12 minutes on full power. Cook the butter, onion and garlic separately for 5 minutes, pour over potatoes, sprinkle with cheese and grill to brown.

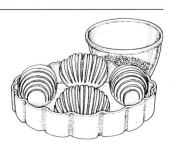

Microwave Tip

This recipe can be microwaved. Put the raw sliced potatoes in a serving dish with the onions. Cover with cling film. Cook on high for about 30 minutes, stirring several times.

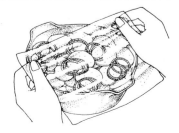

231 | Sunflower Okra with Mushrooms

Preparation time
10 minutes

Cooking time
18–20 minutes

Serves 4

Calories
130 per portion

You will need
2 teaspoons vegetable oil
2 tablespoons sunflower seeds
350 g/12 oz okra, topped and tailed
25 g/1 oz butter
100 g/4 oz button mushrooms,
    halved
salt and pepper

Heat the oil in a small pan and cook the sunflower seeds for 1–2 minutes until brown. Drain on absorbent kitchen paper and set aside.

It is best to cook the okra whole but, if any are too large, cut them in half lengthways.

Melt the butter in a frying pan or wok and stir-fry the okra quickly for 3–4 minutes. Add the mushrooms and cook for a further 3–4 minutes. Sprinkle with salt and pepper, cover the pan and leave to cook for about 10 minutes until the mushrooms are soft and the okra crisply tender.

Remove the lid and cook quickly for 1–2 minutes to reduce the liquid in the pan. Spoon into a hot dish and sprinkle with the sunflower seeds.

232 | Leeks au Gratin

Preparation time
10 minutes

Cooking time
45 minutes

Oven temperature
180 C, 350 F, gas 4
then
200 C, 400 F, gas 6

Serves 6

Calories
280 per portion

You will need
1 kg/2 lb leeks, trimmed and cut
    into 2 cm/¾ in thick rings
15 g/½ oz butter
1 clove garlic, halved
300 ml/½ pint milk
pinch of grated nutmeg
½ teaspoon dried tarragon
salt and pepper
150 ml/¼ pint double cream
100 g/4 oz Emmental cheese,
    grated

Rinse the leeks and drain thoroughly. Place in a large ovenproof dish.

Heat the butter in a small saucepan and fry the garlic for a few minutes until golden. Remove the pieces of garlic from the pan with a slotted spoon and discard. Pour the butter over the leeks.

Heat the milk with the nutmeg, tarragon and salt and pepper to taste, until almost boiling. Stir in the cream and pour over the leeks. Cover the dish tightly with greased foil and cook in a moderate oven for 20 minutes. Remove the foil and sprinkle with the cheese. Increase the oven temperature to moderately hot and bake for a further 15–20 minutes until the cheese is golden and bubbling. Serve immediately.

Cook's Tip

Make sure the okra you buy are fresh, with no damaged ridges or brown patches.

Cook's Tip

This dish can make a filling main course when served with jacket potatoes.

233 | *Masoor Dhal*

Preparation time
15 minutes

Cooking time
about 35 minutes

Serves 4

Calories
350 per portion

You will need
4 tablespoons oil
6 cloves
6 cardamoms
2.5 cm/1 inch cinnamon stick
1 onion, chopped
2.5 cm/1 inch piece ginger,
    chopped
1 green chilli, finely chopped
1 garlic clove, chopped
½ teaspoon garam masala (see
    Cook's Tip)
225 g/8 oz masoor dhal or orange
    lentils
salt
juice of 1 lemon

Heat the oil in a pan, add the cloves, cardamoms and cinnamon and fry until they start to swell. Add the onion and fry until softened. Add the ginger, chilli, garlic and garam masala and cook for about 5 minutes.

Add the lentils, stir thoroughly and fry for 1 minute. Add salt to taste and enough water to come about 3 cm/1¼ inches above the level of the lentils. Bring to the boil, cover and simmer for about 20 minutes, until really thick and tender.

Sprinkle with the lemon juice, stir and serve at once.

234 | *Spicy Vegetables*

Preparation time
30 minutes, including
soaking time

Cooking time
about 15 minutes

Serves 4

Calories
360 per portion

You will need
1.2 litres/2 pints water
200 g/7 oz bean threads
3 tablespoons vegetable oil
225 g/8 oz Chinese cabbage,
    shredded
salt
1 large carrot, thinly sliced
100 g/4 oz fresh spinach leaves,
    cooked and chopped
8 medium dried Chinese
    mushrooms, soaked in warm
    water for 20 minutes then
    drained

For the sauce
1 tablespoon sesame oil
1 tablespoon soy sauce
2 teaspoons sugar
2 teaspoons sesame seeds
½ teaspoon salt

Bring the water to the boil in a pan, add the bean threads and boil for 3 minutes. Drain and set aside.

Heat 2 tablespoons of the oil in a pan, add the cabbage and salt to taste and fry for 2 minutes. Remove and set aside. Heat the remaining oil in the pan, add the carrot and fry for 1 minute. Return the cabbage to the pan, add the spinach and mushrooms and cook for 2 minutes, stirring constantly.

To make the sauce, put all the ingredients in a pan and stir well. Bring to the boil then mix into the vegetable mixture with the bean threads. Heat through to serve.

Cook's Tip

Garam masala is a ground spice mixture used in many Indian recipes. You can buy it or prepare your own: the flavour is better when it is freshly ground. To make it, place 2 tablespoons black peppercorns, 1 tablespoon black cumin seeds, 1 small cinnamon stick, 1 teaspoon cloves, ¼ nutmeg, 2 teaspoons cardamom seeds and 2 tablespoons coriander seeds in a coffee grinder or pestle and mortar and grind to a powder. Store in a jar.

Cook's Tip

Bean threads are also known as cellophane noodles. They are very fine dried noodles made from moong bean flour and are sold in packets. Soak in water for about 10 minutes before using.

235 | Spanish Chick Peas

Preparation time
20 minutes, plus
overnight to soak

Cooking time
1½–2 hours

Serves 4

Calories
320 per portion

You will need
175 g/6 oz chick peas
900 ml/1½ pints cold water
1 tablespoon oil
1 teaspoon salt
25 g/1 oz butter
1 onion, chopped
1 clove garlic, crushed
1 green pepper, deseeded and
   chopped
1 (397-g/14-oz) can chopped
   tomatoes
1 (340-g/12-oz) can sweetcorn,
   drained
2 green chillies, deseeded and
   chopped
¼ teaspoon oregano
generous pinch of ground cumin

Soak the chick peas overnight in water to cover. Drain, discarding peas that have not absorbed any water. Place in a medium saucepan, add measured cold water, and oil and bring to the boil. Reduce the heat, cover the pan and simmer for 1–1½ hours, until the chick peas are tender, adding the salt towards the end of cooking. Drain and return the peas to the saucepan.

Melt the butter in a heavy-based frying pan and sauté the onion, garlic and green pepper until the onion is soft. Stir in the tomatoes, sweetcorn, chillies, oregano and cumin.

Add the sautéed onion mixture to the chick peas. Cover and cook gently, stirring frequently, for 20 minutes. Serve hot.

Cook's Tip

Canned chick peas can be used instead of the dried variety. They should be drained and mixed with the sautéed mixture, then cooked as above.

236 | Creamed Lentils

Preparation time
10 minutes

Cooking time
30–35 minutes

Serves 4

Calories
470 per portion

You will need
25 g/1 oz butter
1 small onion, chopped
1 clove garlic, crushed
1 leek, sliced and washed
2 medium carrots, chopped
350 g/12 oz green lentils
1 litre/1¾ pints water
2 cloves
1 bay leaf
3 white peppercorns
3 tablespoons snipped chives
300 ml/½ pint soured cream
salt and pepper

Melt the butter in a saucepan and cook the onion, garlic, leek and carrots for 3 minutes, stirring frequently. Add the lentils and cook for 1 minute, stirring. Add the water, cloves, bay leaf and peppercorns, bring to the boil, cover, and cook very gently for 25–30 minutes or until the lentils are tender but still have some bite. Check that the mixture doesn't become too dry. Remove the cloves and bay leaf. Turn into a warmed serving dish. Stir half the chives into half the soured cream and swirl through the lentils.

Swirl over the remaining soured cream and sprinkle with the remaining chives. Serve with wholewheat pasta or brown rice.

Cook's Tip

Dried flower buds of the Asian clove tree, cloves have a wonderful spicy fragrance. They are used in sweet and savoury dishes but extracted before serving to avoid the rather over powering effect of biting on them.

237 | Crispy Pea Croquettes

Preparation time
20 minutes

Cooking time
8–10 minutes

Serves 4

Calories
320 per portion

You will need
450 g/1 lb cooked peas
100 g/4 oz cream cheese with
  herbs and garlic
100 g/4 oz fresh wholewheat
  breadcrumbs
2 eggs
1 teaspoon ground coriander
1 teaspoon chopped mixed herbs
salt and pepper
75 g/3 oz dry breadcrumbs
oil for deep-frying
dill sprig to garnish (optional)

For the garnish
1 tomato, quartered
chopped parsley
watercress sprigs

Mash the cooked peas to a purée with the cream cheese. Mix in the breadcrumbs, 1 egg, coriander, herbs and salt and pepper to taste to make a fairly stiff paste.

Shape into croquettes, about 2.5 cm/1 in in diameter and 7.5 cm/3 in long. Beat the remaining egg and dip the croquettes first into beaten egg, then into the breadcrumbs.

Heat the oil for deep-frying to 190 C, 375 F, and fry the croquettes quickly, in 2–3 batches, until crisp and golden. Serve hot or cold, garnished as shown.

Cook's Tip

For a light lunch party, serve these crisp croquettes with Creamed Lentils (Recipe 64) and ratatouille.

238 | Provençal Beans

Preparation time
15 minutes, plus
overnight to soak

Cooking time
2 hours 15 minutes

Serves 4

Calories
355 per portion

You will need
350 g/12 oz haricot beans or pinto
  beans, soaked overnight
salt and pepper
2 tablespoons olive oil
2 onions, sliced
1 red pepper, deseeded and sliced
1 green pepper, deseeded and
  sliced
2 cloves garlic, crushed
1 (397-g/14-oz) can chopped
  tomatoes
2 tablespoons tomato purée
1 teaspoon chopped marjoram
1 bouquet garni
50 g/2 oz black olives, halved and
  stoned
2 tablespoons chopped parsley

Drain the beans, place in a medium saucepan and cover with cold water. Bring to the boil, boil rapidly for 10 minutes, then cover and simmer for 1–1¼ hours, until almost tender, adding a pinch of salt towards the end of cooking. Drain, reserving 300 ml/½ pint of the liquid.

Heat the oil in a medium saucepan, add the onions and fry until softened. Add the peppers and garlic and fry gently for 10 minutes. Add the tomatoes with their juice, tomato purée, herbs, beans, reserved liquid, and salt and pepper to taste. Cover and simmer for 45 minutes, adding the olives and parsley 5 minutes before the end of the cooking time. Remove the bouquet garni and serve.

Cook's Tip

It is a good idea to make a fresh bouquet garni – tie a bay leaf, parsley sprig, thyme sprig, rosemary sprig and a few chives together. Vary the herbs according to taste and season. Make a few and freeze them for future use if you like.

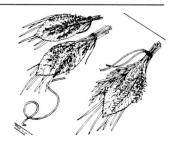

239 | Coriander Tomatoes

Preparation time
10 minutes

Cooking time
about 15 minutes

Serves 4

Calories
160 per portion

You will need
3 tablespoons oil
2 onions, finely chopped
1 teaspoon ground coriander
seeds
1 teaspoon ground cumin seeds
½ teaspoon chilli powder
2 teaspoons finely chopped root
ginger
1–2 garlic cloves, crushed
1 kg/2 lb tomatoes, sliced
2 green chillies, finely chopped
½–1 teaspoon salt
1–2 tablespoons chopped fresh
coriander leaves
coriander leaves to garnish

Heat the oil in a wok or large deep frying pan, add the onions and cook for 5 minutes until golden.

Lower the heat, stir in the spices and cook for 2 minutes, stirring. Add the ginger, garlic, tomatoes and chillies and stir well. Cook for 5-7 minutes until fairly thick. Season with salt to taste and cook for 1 minute.

Spoon into a warmed serving dish and sprinkle with the chopped coriander. Garnish with coriander leaves.

240 | Stir-Fried Ginger Broccoli

Preparation time
3–4 minutes

Cooking time
about 3 minutes

Serves 4

Calories
90 per portion

You will need
450 g/1 lb broccoli
salt
2 tablespoons oil
1 garlic clove, thinly sliced
(optional)
2.5 cm/1 inch piece root ginger,
peeled and finely shredded
½–1 teaspoon sesame oil

Separate the broccoli heads into small florets and peel and diagonally slice the stems. Blanch in boiling salted water for 30 seconds, drain well and cool rapidly under cold running water; drain thoroughly.

Heat the oil in a large wok or frying pan, add the garlic and ginger and stir-fry for 2–3 seconds. Add the broccoli and cook for 2 minutes. Sprinkle over the sesame oil and stir-fry for a further 30 seconds. Spoon into a serving dish and serve at once.

Cook's Tip

Coriander seeds are small round balls with a mild, slightly bitter taste. Cumin seeds are small half-crescent shaped seeds with a pungent taste. Both give a wonderful aromatic flavour to the tomatoes in the recipe above.

Cook's Tip

To ring the changes use purple sprouting broccoli for the above recipe instead of broccoli spears.

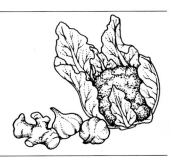

241 | *Vegetable Curry*

Preparation time
15 minutes

Cooking time
20–25 minutes

Serves 4

Calories
100 per portion

You will need
25–40 g/1–1½ oz ghee or 2–3
   tablespoons oil
1 small onion, chopped
450 g/1 lb diced mixed vegetables
   (potatoes, carrots, swede,
   peas, beans or cauliflower, for
   example)
about 1 teaspoon chilli powder
2 teaspoons ground coriander
½ teaspoon turmeric
salt
2–3 tomatoes, skinned and
   chopped

Heat the ghee or oil in a pan and gently fry the onion until light brown. Add the diced vegetables and stir in the chilli powder, coriander, turmeric and salt to taste. Fry for 2–3 minutes.

Add the tomatoes, stir well and add 1–2 tablespoons water, then cover and cook gently for 10–12 minutes until the mixture is dry.

Serve as a side dish or as a main dish with rice or naan bread (see recipe 219).

242 | *Pumpkin Curry*

Preparation time
25 minutes

Cooking time
about 30 minutes

Serves 4

Calories
220 per portion

You will need
450 g/1 lb pumpkin
20 g/¾ oz tamarind pods
40 g/1½ oz ghee or 3 tablespoons
   oil
¼ teaspoon cumin seeds
¼ teaspoon mustard seeds
¼ teaspoon fenugreek seeds
¼ teaspoon onion seeds
¼ teaspoon aniseed
3 medium potatoes, peeled and
   cut into chunks
about 1 teaspoon chilli powder
½ teaspoon ground turmeric
1 teaspoon ground coriander
salt
1 teaspoon sugar

Peel the pumpkin in alternate strips so as to keep the flesh intact during cooking and cut into cubes. Wash and drain well.

Soak the tamarind pods in a cup of hot water for 10–15 minutes and extract the pulp. Repeat the process to extract any remaining pulp.

Heat the ghee or oil in a pan and fry the cumin, mustard seeds, fenugreek, onion seeds and aniseed for 30 seconds, then add the potatoes and fry for 2–3 minutes. Add the pumpkin cubes, stir well and fry for 4–5 minutes.

Stir in the chilli, turmeric, coriander, salt to taste and sugar, and continue frying for 5–6 minutes. Add the tamarind pulp, cover and cook until the potatoes are tender. Serve hot.

Cook's Tip

This is the dry method for cooking a curried mixture – just a little water being added to prevent the vegetables from sticking to the pan. If a moister curry is preferred then 30 ml/½ pint water may be added with the tomatoes and simmered for 5–6 minutes until tender.

Cook's Tip

Pumpkins shouldn't be reserved for Halloween lanterns. A nutritious vegetable, high in vitamin A, it is delicious roasted in the oven or boiled and masked with lots of black pepper and nutmeg.

243 | *Kohlrabi with Walnuts*

Preparation time
15 minutes

Cooking time
18 20 minutes

Serves 4

Calories
345 per portion

You will need
1 kg/2 lb young, tender kohlrabi
1 tablespoon vegetable oil
2 shallots, peeled and finely
    chopped
salt and pepper
grated nutmeg
120 ml/4 fl oz double cream
2 tablespoons chopped basil or
    marjoram
100 g/4 oz walnuts, coarsely
    chopped

Trim the kohlrabi, cutting off the feathery leaves and reserving for garnish. Peel the kohlrabi, cut out any tough parts, wash and halve. Cut the halves first into 1-cm/½-in slices and then into sticks.

Heat the oil in a frying pan and fry the shallots over a moderate heat until transparent, stirring continuously. Add the kohlrabi and stir until completely coated in oil.

Season with salt, pepper and nutmeg to taste. Add the cream, reduce the heat, cover and cook over low heat for 5–8 minutes until the kohlrabi is tender but still firm to the bite.

Rinse the kohlrabi leaves, pat dry and finely chop. Stir the basil into the kohlrabi mixture and transfer to a warmed serving dish. Sprinkle with the kohlrabi leaves and walnuts. Accompany with jacket-boiled new potatoes or brown rice.

244 | *Walnut-filled Fennel*

Preparation time
15 20 minutes

Cooking time
1½ hours

Oven temperature
180 C, 350 F, gas 4

Serves 2–4

Calories
630 315 per portion

You will need
4 large heads fennel
50 g/2 oz fresh breadcrumbs
75 g/3 oz walnuts, chopped
2 tablespoons clear honey
1 tablespoon snipped chives
1 tablespoon milk
salt and pepper
50 g/2 oz butter

For the garnish
tomato wedges
parsley sprigs

Cut out the hard core of the fennel and discard. Remove and chop up a little more fennel, ensuring there is a reasonably large cavity to fill with stuffing.

Mix the chopped fennel, breadcrumbs, walnuts, honey, chives and milk, and season well with salt and pepper. Press this stuffing into the fennel cavities and place in an ovenproof dish.

Dot the surface with butter, cover tightly with foil and bake in a moderate oven for about 1½ hours, until the fennel is tender. Garnish with tomato and parsley.

Cook's Tip

Kohlrabi looks like a large green turnip but is actually a member of the cabbage family. It is high in vitamins and low in calories.

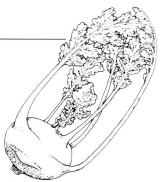

Cook's Tip

Serve this dish as an interesting light main course. Alternatively, it can be offered as an accompaniment or an appetising starter.

245 | Stuffed Cabbage Leaves

Preparation time
20 minutes

Cooking time
35 minutes

Serves 4—6

Calories
510—340 per portion

You will need
1 cabbage
5 tablespoons oil
1 onion, chopped
1 cm/½ inch piece root ginger, peeled and chopped
1 teaspoon turmeric
450 g/1 lb lean minced lamb
75 g/3 oz long-grain rice
2 tomatoes, skinned and chopped
grated rind and juice of 2 lemons
2 teaspoons sugar
salt and pepper
150 ml/¼ pint water

Hollow out the stem end of the cabbage and discard. Place the cabbage in a large pan, cover with water and bring to the boil. Remove from the heat, cover and leave for 15 minutes; drain.

Fry the onion in 2 tablespoons of the oil until soft. Add the ginger and turmeric and fry for 1 minute. Add the lamb and fry briefly until brown. Cool slightly, then mix with the remaining ingredients, minus the water.

Carefully remove 12 inner leaves of the cabbage. Divide the meat mixture between these, gently squeezing out and reserving any liquid. Shape each leaf into a packet. Heat the remaining oil in a large frying pan, add the cabbage rolls in one layer and heat through. Pour over the reserved liquid and water. Cover and simmer for about 30 minutes, uncover, turn over and cook for a further 5 minutes. Serve hot.

Cook's Tip

Most of the liquid should have evaporated from the dish towards the end of cooking – if it hasn't then increase the heat and cook uncovered for a few minutes longer.

246 | Spicy Turnips

Preparation time
20 minutes

Cooking time
about 20 minutes

Serves 4—6

Calories
260—180 per portion

You will need
about 3 tablespoons ghee or concentrated butter
1 kg/2 lb turnips, peeled and quartered
2 garlic cloves, peeled
2 green chillies
2.5 cm/1 inch piece root ginger, peeled
1 teaspoon cumin seeds
2 teaspoons coriander seeds
2 tablespoons natural yogurt
1 teaspoon salt
150 ml/¼ pint water
1 teaspoon sugar
1 teaspoon garam masala (see Cook's Tip recipe 67)

Heat the ghee in a pan, add the turnips and fry lightly then set aside.

Put the garlic, chillies, ginger, cumin, coriander and yogurt into a liquidizer or food processor and work to a paste. Add to the pan and fry for 2 minutes.

Return the turnips to the pan, add the salt and stir well. Add the water and simmer, covered, for about 10 minutes, until almost tender. Uncover the pan, add the sugar and garam masala and cook briskly, stirring until most of the liquid has evaporated.

Cook's Tip

This is a deliciously spicy vegetable side dish to serve with a meat or poultry main course. You could of course use swede instead of the turnips if liked.

247 | Crispy Vegetables

Preparation time
15 minutes

Cooking time
20 minutes

Serves 6

Calories
230 per portion

You will need
100 g/4 oz plain flour
pinch of salt
1 tablespoon oil
150 ml/¼ pint water
2 egg whites, stiffly whisked
450 g/1 lb mixed vegetables
(cauliflower florets, beans,
whole mushrooms, mangetout,
pepper strips, aubergine cubes
are all suitable)
oil for deep frying

Sift the flour and salt into a bowl, gradually beat in the oil and water, then fold in the egg white.

Heat the oil in a wok or frying pan, dip the vegetables into the batter, then deep-fry, in batches, for 2–3 minutes until golden.

Drain and serve with a dip (see Cook's Tip).

248 | Potato and Courgette

Preparation time
15 minutes

Cooking time
25 minutes

Serves 4

Calories
160 per portion

You will need
3 tablespoons oil
1 large garlic clove, crushed
½ teaspoon chilli powder
2 teaspoons ground coriander
1 teaspoon ground cumin
1 teaspoon salt
2 tablespoons water
450 g/1 lb courgettes, sliced
225 g/8 oz new potatoes, halved
1 tablespoon finely sliced red
pepper to garnish

Heat the oil in a pan and fry the garlic for 30 seconds. Add the spices, salt and water, stir well and fry gently for 2 minutes. Add the vegetables, stir thoroughly, cover the pan and cook gently for 20 minutes or until the vegetables are cooked, stirring occasionally.

Garnish with the red pepper to serve.

Cook's Tip

To make a tasty dip for this recipe put 1–2 chopped garlic cloves, 4 tomatoes, skinned, seeded and chopped, 1 teaspoon chilli powder, 2 avocado pears, peeled and stoned, 1 tablespoon chopped fresh coriander and a pinch of ground coriander in a blender and work until smooth. Spoon into a serving dish and chill.

Cook's Tip

To crush garlic without a crusher, place a peeled garlic clove on a chopping board and sprinkle with a little salt. Then crush with the flat, wide blade of a knife, pressing hard with the palm of your hand.

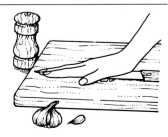

249 | Tabbouleh

Preparation time
10 minutes, plus
soaking

Serves 8

Calories
324 per portion

You will need
350 g / 12 oz bulghar (cracked
  wheat)
2 bunches spring onions, finely
  chopped
1 large bunch fresh parsley,
  chopped
1 large bunch fresh mint, chopped
juice of 2 lemons
150 ml / ¼ pint olive oil
salt and pepper

Place the bulghar in a large bowl and cover with plenty of cold water. Soak for 1 hour. Strain well, pressing out as much water as possible.

Put the bulghar back into the bowl and add the spring onions, parsley, mint, lemon juice, olive oil, salt and pepper. Mix well. Cover and chill until ready to serve.

250 | Lentil and Tomato Salad

Preparation time
15 minutes

Cooking time
30 minutes

Serves 4

Calories
322 per portion

You will need
225 g/ 8 oz green lentils
1 small onion, peeled and finely
  chopped
900 ml / 1½ pints water
1 bay leaf
salt
6 tablespoons vinaigrette
225 g / 8 oz tomatoes, chopped
1 small green pepper, cored,
  seeded and diced
4 spring onions, chopped
8 black olives, stoned and
  chopped
1 tablespoon chopped fresh
  parsley

Place the lentils and chopped onion in a saucepan with the water, bay leaf and some salt. Bring to the boil. Cover and simmer for 30 minutes until the lentils are tender but not mushy.

Drain the lentils and place in a salad bowl. Stir in the vinaigrette while they are still warm and leave to cool.

Stir in the tomatoes, green pepper, spring onions and black olives. Sprinkle with the parsley and serve.

Cook's Tip

Bulghar, or cracked wheat, is grain which has been steamed and toasted. Consequently it has a slightly nutty taste. It is the traditional ingredient of this Lebanese salad.

Cook's Tip

French dressing or vinaigrette is a classic combination of oil, vinegar and flavourings. It is widely available , but you can make your own. Combine 2 tablespoons white wine vinegar or lemon juice and 6 tablespoons oil in a screw-top jar with a pinch of mustard powder and salt and pepper to taste. Shake well. Alternatively, whisk all the ingredients together in a small bowl. The dressing will keep for at least one week in the refrigerator.

251 | Cheese and Fruit Salad

Preparation time
15 minutes, plus time
to chill

Serves 4

Calories
290 per portion

You will need
small head of Chinese leaves,
  shredded
1 (227-g/8-oz) can pineapple
  chunks
100 g/4 oz cottage cheese
100 g/4 oz Cheddar cheese,
  diced
100 g/4 oz cooked ham, diced
salt and pepper
1 avocado
1 tablespoon lemon juice

Arrange the Chinese leaves in the bottom of a serving
dish. Drain the pineapple chunks. Mix with the cottage
cheese, Cheddar and ham. Season well and spoon the
mixture on top of the leaves.

Halve the avocado. Scoop out the stone, then peel and
thinly slice. Sprinkle with lemon juice and arrange the
slices on top of the cheese mixture. Chill before serving.

252 | Smoked Mackerel and Egg Salad

Preparation time
15 minutes

Serves 4

Calories
335 per portion

You will need
1 lettuce, shredded
2 smoked mackerel fillets
4 hard-boiled eggs
4 tomatoes, peeled and quartered

For the dressing
1 tablespoon wine vinegar
2 tablespoons oil
1 teaspoon prepared French
  mustard
salt and pepper
1 tablespoon chopped parsley

Put the lettuce in a serving bowl. Skin and flake the
mackerel. Roughly chop the hard-boiled eggs. Mix
together the mackerel, eggs and tomatoes and arrange
on top of the lettuce.

Combine the ingredients for the dressing and pour
over the fish. Serve immediately.

Cook's Tip

If you're counting the
calories, omit the avocado.
Use fruit canned in
unsweetened juice, low-fat
Cheddar and lean ham.

Cook's Tip

In Spring thin out young
lettuce plants to use in this
salad. Use horseradish
sauce instead of the
mustard to pep up the
salad.

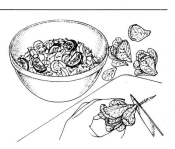

253 | Kidney Bean Coleslaw

Preparation time
30 minutes

Serves 4—6

Calories
210 140 per portion

You will need
225 g/8 oz white cabbage, shredded
175 g/6 oz carrots, grated
½ small onion, chopped
1 dessert apple, cored and grated
1 (415-g/14½-oz) can red kidney beans, drained
4 spring onions, chopped
2 tablespoons chopped parsley
salt and pepper
50 g/2 oz low-fat soft cheese (for example Shape cheese)
1 tablespoon lemon juice
2 tablespoons sunflower oil
2 tablespoons natural yogurt
watercress sprigs to garnish (optional)

Mix the cabbage, carrots, onion and apple. Add the beans, spring onions and parsley then season to taste.

Mix the low-fat cheese with the lemon juice, oil and yogurt. Toss this dressing with the salad before serving.

A watercress garnish may be added, if liked.

254 | Colourful Bean Salad

Preparation time
15 20 minutes

Cooking time
15 minutes

Serves 4—6

Calories
275 185 per portion

You will need
450 g/1 lb green beans, topped and tailed
salt and pepper
pinch of grated nutmeg
3 4 tomatoes, quartered
575 g/1¼ lb new potatoes, scrubbed and cooked
1 onion, chopped
1 small bunch herbs, (e.g. chives, parsley, thyme) chopped
2 tablespoons mayonnaise
6 tablespoons double or soured cream

Bring a large saucepan of water to the boil, add the beans with a little salt and the nutmeg. Bring back to the boil, then reduce heat and cook gently for 10–12 minutes until tender. Drain, rinse under cold water, drain again and place in a serving bowl. Add the tomatoes and potatoes and toss well. Scatter the onion and herbs on top.

To make the dressing, blend the mayonnaise with the cream and salt and pepper to taste. Pour over the bean salad and toss well to mix.

Cook's Tip

Sunflower oil is a polyunsaturated fat – a good choice for the health-conscious eater. Avoid blended oils, which may contain coconut or palm oil, both high in saturated fatty acids.

Cook's Tip

Counting calories? Use low-fat yogurt in place of the double cream – you may need slightly less than the 6 tablespoons suggested above.

255 | Crunchy Green Salad

Preparation time
25 minutes

Serves 4

Calories
212 per portion

You will need
100 g / 4 oz green cabbage
100 g / 4 oz broccoli
100 g / 4 oz courgettes
1 small green pepper
1 stick celery, thinly sliced

For the dressing
150 ml / ¼ pint plain yogurt or
   soured cream
1 tablespoon white wine vinegar
salt and black pepper
2 tablespoons crumbled blue
   cheese, such as Danish blue,
   Stilton or Roquefort

Slice the green cabbage very thinly, discarding any core. Wash, drain and place in a bowl.

Divide the broccoli into florets, cutting away the coarse central stalks and slicing down the thin stalks and heads. Wash, drain and add to the bowl.

Top and tail the courgettes and slice as thinly as possible. Add to the bowl.

Cut the pepper into halves or quarters, remove the core and seeds, and slice very thinly. Add to the bowl with the celery.

To make the dressing, blend the yogurt or soured cream, vinegar and salt and pepper in a liquidizer or food processor. Stir in the cheese. Pour over the vegetables and toss well. Marinate for 1 hour before serving.

256 | Red Cabbage Salad

Preparation time
15 minutes

Serves 4

Calories
263 per portion

You will need
350 g / 12 oz red cabbage
1 large Cox's apple
2 sticks celery, chopped
50 g / 2 oz seedless raisins
50 g / 2 oz walnut halves chopped

For the dressing
3 tablespoons mayonnaise
1 tablespoon white wine vinegar
1 tablespoon oil
1 garlic clove, peeled and crushed
1 teaspoon clear honey
1 teaspoon whole grain mustard
salt and pepper

Cut away the cabbage's core, then finely shred, using a sharp knife or food processor. Quarter and core the apple, then cut into small pieces.

Mix together the cabbage, apple, celery, raisins and walnuts.

To make the dressing, mix all the ingredients together. Pour over the salad and mix thoroughly. Serve at once or cover and chill.

Cook's Tip

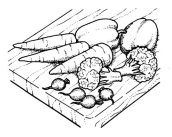

Another colourful combination of vegetables that goes well with this piquant cheese dressing is thinly sliced carrots, diced red and yellow peppers, thinly sliced radishes and small cauliflower florets.

Cook's Tip

This salad remains crisp even if made a day ahead. Make sure the apples are well coated with the dressing so they don't discolour.

257 | Pear Waldorf Salad

Preparation time
25 minutes

Serves 4

Calories
171 per portion

You will need
1 lettuce, shredded
2 sticks celery, chopped
1 red pepper, cored and sliced
25 g / 1 oz walnut halves
75 g / 3 oz green grapes, peeled, halved and seeded
1 dessert pear, peeled, cored and sliced
225 g / 8 oz smoked chicken, skinned and boned

For the dressing
2 tablespoons plain yogurt
2 tablespoons mayonnaise
2 tablespoons grated cucumber
1 teaspoon grated onion
½ teaspoon chopped fresh tarragon

For the garnish
1 dessert pear, cored and sliced
few sprigs fresh tarragon

Mix the lettuce with the celery, red pepper, walnuts, grapes, pear and smoked chicken.

To make the dressing, mix the yogurt with the mayonnaise, add the remaining ingredients and blend well.

Just before serving, spoon the dressing over the salad and toss well to mix. Garnish with slices of pear and a few sprigs of fresh tarragon.

Cook's Tip

This is a variation on a classic Waldorf salad, which is made with apples. The dressing can be made up to three days in advance, then tossed with the salad ingredients just before serving.

258 | Tuscan Nectarine and Avocado Salad

Preparation time
10 minutes

Serves 4
as a starter

Calories
253 per portion

You will need
2 fresh nectarines, blanched and peeled
1 avocado, halved and stoned
225 g / 8 oz mixed salad leaves
8–12 small cherry tomatoes

For the dressing
5 tablespoons olive oil
5 teaspoons tarragon vinegar
1 garlic clove, peeled and crushed
1 teaspoon whole grain mustard
1 teaspoon chopped fresh tarragon
1 teaspoon chopped fresh chives
salt and pepper

Slice the nectarines thinly and place in a large salad bowl. Cut the avocado into small balls using a melon baller or teaspoon and add to the nectarines. Add the mixed salad leaves and tomatoes, tossing gently to blend, taking care not to break up the avocado balls.

To make the dressing, beat the oil and vinegar together until well blended and lightly thickened. Add the garlic, mustard, tarragon, chives and salt and pepper to taste, blending well. Spoon over the salad and toss lightly to mix. Serve at once with chunks of wholemeal or granary bread.

Cook's Tip

Curly endive, lamb's lettuce, radicchio and chicory leaves are all suitable for using in this salad. Supermarkets now stock a greater variety of salad greens.

259 | *Potato and Mortadella Salad*

Preparation time
20 minutes

Cooking time
15 minutes

Serves 4

Calories
443 per portion

You will need
450 g / 1 lb small potatoes, washed
salt and pepper
6–8 spring onions, thinly sliced
2 tablespoons chopped fresh chives
1 tablespoon chopped fresh chervil or parsley
125 ml / 4 fl oz soured cream
1 tablespoon white wine vinegar
175 g / 6 oz mortadella, in one piece, skinned

Cook the potatoes in boiling salted water until just tender. Drain and, when cool enough to handle, rub off the skins. Slice the potatoes thickly or cut in quarters.

Stir the onions and herbs into the soured cream, then stir in the vinegar and season well with pepper. Toss the potatoes in this mixture.

Cut four thin slices of sausage to garnish. Cube the remainder.

Cut from the edge to the centre of each slice of mortadella and wrap it into a cone. Just before serving, stir the cubed mortadella carefully into the potato salad. Spoon it into a dish and garnish with the four cones.

260 | *Hot Potato Salad*

Preparation time
10 minutes

Cooking time
10–15 minutes

Serves 4

Calories
311 per portion

You will need
450 g / 1 lb waxy potatoes
1 onion, peeled and chopped
1 tablespoon boiling water
1 tablespoon white wine vinegar
3 tablespoons mayonnaise
2 tablespoons single cream
salt and pepper
1 tablespoon chopped fresh parsley

Peel and cut the potatoes into 1 cm / ½ inch cubes. Boil in salted water until just cooked and still holding their shapes.

Meanwhile, place the onion in a large bowl, with the boiling water and vinegar. Strain the potatoes and add to the onion with the mayonnaise, cream and add salt and pepper to taste. Reheat gently if necessary.

Transfer to a warm serving bowl. Sprinkle with parsley and serve at once.

Cook's Tip

Mortadella is a variety of pork sausage that has been made in Italy for centuries. It has a smooth texture and is best served thinly sliced.

Cook's Tip

Serve this German-style potato salad as an accompaniment to roast chicken or meatloaf.

261 | Mushroom and Mange Tout Salad

Preparation time
10 minutes, plus 20 minutes to cool

Cooking time
4–5 minutes

Serves 4

Calories
55 per portion

You will need
175 g/6 oz mange tout
225 g/8 oz small button mushrooms, sliced
6 spring onions, chopped
150 ml/¼ pint natural yogurt
salt and pepper
snipped chives to garnish

Cook the mange tout in boiling salted water for 4–5 minutes until just tender. Drain and cool. Combine the mushrooms, spring onions and yogurt with seasoning to taste.

Arrange the mange tout on a plate and top with the mushrooms. Sprinkle with chives and serve.

262 | Broad Bean Salad

Preparation time
15 minutes

Cooking time
10 minutes

Serves 4–6

Calories
420–280 per portion

You will need
350 g/12 oz fresh or frozen broad beans
salt
tarragon or parsley sprigs to garnish

For the hollandaise sauce
3 egg yolks
2 tablespoons lemon juice
175 g/6 oz unsalted butter, melted
salt and pepper

Cook the beans in boiling salted water for 5–10 minutes or until tender. Drain the beans, cool and pop the beans out of their outer skins, if liked (with young beans this will not be necessary). Put the beans into a serving bowl.

To make the hollandaise sauce, blend the egg yolks and lemon juice together in a food processor for 30 seconds. Slowly pour in the hot melted butter to make a creamy sauce. Add salt and pepper to taste. Pour over the beans immediately and garnish with the tarragon or parsley. Serve warm or cool.

Cook's Tip

The best way of preparing chives is to hold the washed bunch firmly and use a pair of scissors to snip them into a small basin.

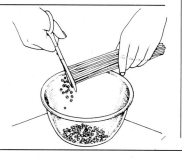

Cook's Tip

If using fresh broad beans, do not remove from the furry lined pods until just before cooking. There is no need to shell young, tender broad beans; top, tail, cut them up, then cook and serve in the pods.

263 | Broad Bean and Bacon Salad

Preparation time
10 minutes

Cooking time
5–10 minutes

Serves 6

Calories
136 per portion

You will need
450 g / 1 lb shelled broad beans
salt
4 rashers streaky bacon, rinded, to
    garnish

For the dressing
2 tablespoons chopped fresh
    parsley
150 ml / 5 fl oz plain yogurt
pepper

Put the broad beans into a pan with a little salt. Pour over just enough boiling water to cover and simmer for 5 minutes until tender. Drain and rinse under cold water to cool quickly.

Grill the bacon until crispy. Drain and cool.

To make the dressing, stir the parsley into the yogurt and add salt and pepper to taste.

Stir the dressing into the beans. Turn the bean salad into a serving dish and crumble the crispy bacon over the top. This is an especially good accompaniment to cold roast lamb.

Cook's Tip

Broad beans are in season from late May to early September. Very young ones have tender skins that can be eaten with the beans but older beans have tough outer skins; these may be difficult to remove. If necessary, drop **the podded bean in boiling water for a few minutes, then drain and rub off the skin with a tea towel. Broad beans are also available tinned and frozen.**

264 | Gado Gado

Preparation time
15 minutes

Cooking time
15–20 minutes

Serves 6

Calories
147 per portion

You will need
100 g / 4 oz cabbage, shredded
100 g / 4 oz French beans, cut into
    4 cm / 1½ inch lengths
100 g / 4 oz carrots, sliced
100 g / 4 oz cauliflower, divided
    into small florets
salt
50 g / 2 oz bean-sprouts
2 hard-boiled eggs, shelled and
    sliced (optional)
50 g / 2 oz salted peanuts to
    garnish

For the sauce
4 tablespoons crunchy peanut
    butter
juice of 1 lemon
4 tablespoons water
few drops Tabasco sauce
pepper

Simmer the cabbage, beans, carrots and cauliflower separately in boiling salted water for a few minutes until just tender. Rinse under cold water to cool quickly.

To make the sauce, place the peanut butter in a bowl. Blend in the lemon juice and then the water until well mixed. Stir in enough Tabasco sauce to make a spicy sauce, and then add salt and pepper.

Combine the vegetables and the bean-sprouts and arrange in a shallow serving dish. Lay the slices of hard-boiled egg over the top, if liked, and pour the peanut sauce over the centre of the salad. Sprinkle with the salted peanuts.

Cook's Tip

This crunchy vegetable salad is Indonesian. For a more authentic flavour, add grated fresh coconut or desiccated coconut to the sauce.

265 | Mushroom and Cucumber Side Salad

Preparation time
15 minutes

Serves 4

Calories
65 per portion

You will need
¼ Webbs lettuce, finely shredded
100 g/4 oz button mushrooms,
  wiped and quartered
½ cucumber, diced
4 tablespoons low-calorie
  mayonnaise
2 teaspoons tomato ketchup
½ teaspoon lemon juice
paprika to sprinkle

Arrange the shredded lettuce in the base of four salad bowls. Mix together the mushrooms and cucumber and place over the lettuce. Combine the mayonnaise with the tomato ketchup and lemon juice and spoon over the salad. Sprinkle with a little paprika and serve at once.

266 | Mushroom and Celeriac Salad

Preparation time
25 minutes, plus about
1 hour to chill

Serves 6

Calories
315 per portion

You will need
225 g/8 oz button mushrooms,
  halved if large
½ large celeriac root, coarsely
  grated
225 g/8 oz carrots, coarsely grated
chopped parsley to garnish

For the dressing
1 egg yolk
150 ml/¼ pint olive oil
2 tablespoons white wine vinegar
150 ml/¼ pint soured cream
salt and pepper

First make the dressing. Place the egg yolk in a small bowl and beat with 2–3 drops of the olive oil. Gradually whisk in the remaining olive oil, drop by drop, until pale and thick. Whisk in the vinegar, soured cream and seasoning to taste. Fold half the dressing into the mushrooms. Fold the rest of the dressing into the celeriac. Turn the celeriac on to a serving dish, top with the carrot and mushrooms, then sprinkle with parsley. Chill before serving.

Cook's Tip

Choose lettuces with care, avoiding any with rust spots, wilted leaves or yellowing tips. Wash the leaves carefully and quickly (do not soak), dry between sheets of absorbent kitchen paper. Store in plastic bags in the refrigerator.

Cook's Tip

For a substantial lunch or supper, serve this salad with a generous slice of quiche or flan.

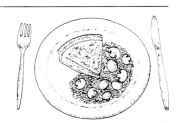

267 | Leek, Orange and Hazelnut Salad

Preparation time
10 minutes, plus
marinating

Serves 4

Calories
276 per portion

You will need
450 g / 1 lb leeks
50 g / 2 oz shelled hazelnuts,
    toasted and chopped

For the dressing
2 medium oranges
4 tablespoons olive oil
salt and pepper

Slice the leeks into rounds as thinly as possible. Wash well, then separate into rings and drain.

To make the dressing, cut the orange rinds into long thin strips and place in a large bowl. Add the juice from the oranges, the olive oil and salt and pepper to taste.

Whisk the dressing together and then add the leeks to the bowl. Toss until all the leeks are coated in dressing.

Marinate for at least 1 hour to soften the leeks. Stir in the hazelnuts just before serving. This salad goes particularly well with chicken and lamb.

Cook's Tip

This is a good winter salad.
If the leeks are very strong tasting, blanching them for 1 minute will give them a milder flavour. Drain well before adding to the dressing.

268 | Chicory and Orange Salad

Preparation time
15 minutes

Serves 4

Calories
118 per portion

You will need
3 large or 4 small heads chicory
3 medium oranges
1 shallot or small onion, peeled
    and cut in rings
4 tablespoons French dressing
6 large or 8 small stuffed olives to
    garnish

Cut the chicory crosswise into slices and place in a salad bowl.

Cut away the peel and pith from the oranges. Cut the flesh into segments and add to the chicory, squeezing in any juice as well.

Pour the French dressing over and toss well. Scatter the stuffed olives on top. This is a good accompaniment to salamis and cold meats.

Cook's Tip

The sharp, bitter taste of chicory is off-set by the fresh-tasting, juicy oranges in this salad. Store chicory leaves in a polythene bag in the salad drawer of your refrigerator; they should keep for about a week.

269 | Crunchy Beansprout and Cheese Salad

Preparation time
10 minutes

Serves 4

Calories
305 per portion

You will need
4 tablespoons natural wholenut
    peanut butter
4 tablespoons lemon juice
1 red pepper, deseeded and cut
    into thin strips
175 g/6 oz beansprouts
175 g/6 oz Double Gloucester
    cheese, cubed
½ crisp lettuce, shredded

Stir the peanut butter and lemon juice together until well mixed. Combine the remaining ingredients in a salad bowl then stir in the peanut butter dressing just before serving.

270 | Two-Cheese Salad

Preparation time
20 minutes

Serves 4

Calories
485 per portion

You will need
1 green pepper, deseeded and cut
    into thin strips
1 red pepper, deseeded and cut
    into thin strips
4 tomatoes, sliced
175 g/6 oz blue cheese, cubed
175 g/6 oz Edam or Gouda cheese,
    cubed
12 stuffed green olives
2 tablespoons olive oil
1 tablespoon lemon juice
1 cos lettuce

For the sauce
300 ml/½ pint natural yogurt
salt and pepper
1 small avocado

Place the peppers, tomatoes, cheeses and olives in a bowl. Whisk the oil and lemon juice together until well blended, pour over salad and toss lightly, to coat. Wash and prepare the lettuce and arrange it on a serving platter. Pile the cheese salad in the centre.

    To make the sauce, mix yogurt with plenty of seasoning. Peel and finely chop the avocado, then fold it lightly into the yogurt. Serve separately.

Cook's Tip

If you have a grinder, making your own peanut butter is easy. Grind 100 g/4 oz roasted peanuts finely and mash them to a paste in a bowl, adding a little vegetable oil if necessary. Hazelnuts, cashews and walnuts may also be used.

Cook's Tip

Vary the choice of cheese to suit your palate. For example try smoked cheese with Cheshire cheese or Sage Derby cheese with Edam. Strict vegetarians may prefer to make a selection from the rennet-free varieties.

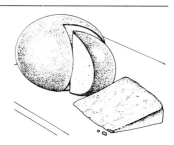

271 | Celery Salad Flavia

Preparation time
15 minutes, plus 30
minutes to chill

Serves 4

Calories
140 per portion

You will need
1 clove garlic, peeled and
   halved
1 head celery, cut into small strips
1 (200-g/7-oz) can artichoke hearts
   in brine, drained and halved
1 tablespoon black olives, stoned
1 tablespoon chopped parsley
3 tablespoons olive oil
1 tablespoon lemon juice
dash of Tabasco sauce
½ teaspoon prepared mustard
pinch of dried oregano
salt
few celery leaves to garnish

Using the cut side of the garlic, vigorously rub the inside
of a salad bowl, then discard. Add the celery, artichoke
hearts, olives and parsley to the bowl.

To make the dressing, beat the olive oil with the
lemon juice, Tabasco sauce, mustard, oregano and salt
to taste.

Pour the dressing over the salad and toss well. Cover
and chill for 30 minutes to allow the flavours to develop
well.

Toss the salad again before serving and garnish with
the celery leaves.

272 | Winter Radish Salad

Preparation time
5 minutes, plus 10
minutes to stand

Serves 4

Calories
90 per portion

You will need
1 large winter radish
salt
150 ml/¼ pint soured cream
1 tablespoon snipped chives to
   garnish

Scrub or thinly peel the radish. Grate or cut into very thin
slices. Place in a bowl and sprinkle generously with salt.
Leave to stand for 10–12 minutes. Rinse thoroughly and
place in a salad bowl. Spoon over the soured cream,
toss well and garnish with the chives.

Cook's Tip

**To make this salad more
filling, garnish with a ring of
hard-boiled egg slices and
tomato wedges.**

Cook's Tip

**It is important to rinse the
radish slices thoroughly to
remove all the salt. Dry
thoroughly between sheets of
absorbent kitchen paper
before mixing with the soured
cream.**

273 | *Carrot Salad*

Preparation time
10 minutes, plus 1–2
hours chilling time

Serves 4

Calories
10 per portion

You will need
100 g/4 oz carrots, peeled and
    grated
25 g/1 oz grated onion
½ tablespoon grated root ginger
1 tablespoon finely chopped mint
½ teaspoon salt
½ teaspoon sugar
1 tablespoon lemon juice

Mix all the ingredients together in a bowl, cover and chill
for 1–2 hours before serving.

274 | *Pickled Salad*

Preparation time
15 minutes, plus 5
hours standing time

Serves 4–6

Calories
100–65 per portion

You will need
450 g/1 lb cucumber, peeled
450 g/1 lb cabbage, cored and
    chopped
2 teaspoons salt
1 teaspoon crushed garlic
1 teaspoon ground Szechuan or
    black peppercorns
1 teaspoon sugar
1 tablespoon soy sauce
2 tablespoons sesame oil
1 tablespoon red wine vinegar

Crush the cucumbers until cracks appear on the surface.
Quarter lengthways, then cut into pieces. Place in a bowl
with the cabbage, sprinkle with salt and leave for 2 hours.
   Rinse the vegetables and drain on absorbent kitchen
paper. Mix together the garlic, pepper, sugar, soy sauce,
oil and vinegar. Pour over the vegetables, mix well and
allow to stand for at least 3 hours before serving. Serve
on a cabbage-lined plate if liked.

Cook's Tip

*Indian salads are invariably
chopped and mixed with
various spices – this recipe is
something of an exception
since the flavourings are mild
and feature herbs. You can of
course try using grated
celeriac instead of the carrots*
*or vary the herbs – try
coriander, chervil or parsley
instead of the mint.*

Cook's Tip

*Szechuan pepper, also sold as
anise pepper, is one of the 5
spices used in Chinese 5-spice
powder. It can be bought from
specialist shops. If you have
difficulty obtaining it then use
ordinary black pepper instead.*

275 | Pasta Slaw

Preparation time
15 minutes, plus 30 minutes to cool

Cooking time
13–15 minutes

Serves 4

Calories
225 per portion

You will need
75 g/3 oz pasta spirals
1 (283-g/10-oz) packet frozen whole French beans
75 g/3 oz white cabbage, finely chopped
½ green pepper, deseeded and finely chopped
1 carrot, grated
4 spring onions, finely chopped
salt and freshly ground pepper
parsley sprigs to garnish (optional)

For the dressing
4 tablespoons mayonnaise
2 tablespoons milk or cream
1 tablespoon wine vinegar
2 teaspoons sugar
salt and freshly ground pepper

Cook the pasta in a large saucepan of boiling salted water for 10–12 minutes, until just tender. Cook the French beans in boiling salted water for 3–5 minutes. Refresh both under cold water, drain and allow to cool.

Meanwhile, mix together the remaining salad ingredients in a bowl. Combine the ingredients for the dressing and add to the salad bowl with the pasta and chopped French beans. Season to taste and garnish with sprigs of parsley to serve.

Cook's Tip

For additional fibre and B vitamins, use wholemeal pasta in this recipe.

276 | Fruit Coleslaw

Preparation time
25 minutes

Serves 4

Calories
280 per portion

You will need
½ medium white cabbage, finely shredded
4 celery sticks, cut into matchstick strips
2 red dessert apples. cored and chopped
50 g/2 oz raisins
50 g/2 oz walnuts, chopped
100 g/4 oz grapes, halved and seeded
1 tablespoon chopped chives

For the dressing
4 tablespoons oil
1 tablespoon wine vinegar
pinch of mustard powder
1 teaspoon sugar
salt and pepper

To make the dressing, combine the ingredients in a screw-topped jar and shake well to blend. Place the cabbage in a large salad bowl and stir in sufficient dressing to just moisten. Add the celery, apples, raisins, walnuts, grapes and chives and toss all well together.

Cook's Tip

To shred cabbage finely, choose a long-bladed, sharp knife, secure the cabbage with your fingers, moving them back as you shred.

277 | Japanese Salad

Preparation time
30 minutes

Cooking time
12 minutes

Serves 4

Calories
140 per portion

You will need
½ medium carrot, peeled
1 cucumber
½ bunch spring onions
100 g/4 oz boneless chicken
1 tablespoon sake (rice wine)
15 g/½ oz dried young seaweed
shiso or lettuce leaves to serve

For the Gomadare dressing
4 tablespoons seasame seeds, toasted
1 small garlic clove, grated
5 tablespoons rice vinegar
3 tablespoons Dashi/soup stock (see Cook's Tip)
1 tablespoon soy sauce
1 tablespoon mayonnaise
pinch of chilli powder
1 teaspoon salt

To make the dressing, mix all the ingredients together in a bowl. Set aside.

To make the salad, finely shred the carrot, cucumber and spring onions and place in ice cold water to crisp.

Skin the chicken, place on a plate, sprinkle with the sake and a little salt then steam for 12 minutes until tender. Cool, then shred with the fingers.

Put the seaweed in a bowl and cover with cold water. Leave to soak for 5–10 minutes. Drain, rinse in boiling water then under cold running water. Squeeze out excess water and cut into 2.5-cm/1-inch lengths.

To serve, line a large plate with the shiso or lettuce leaves and serve as shown.

Cook's Tip

To make Dashi or soup stock place 25 g/1 oz kombu (dried kelp) in a pan, add 1 litre/1¾ pints cold water and leave to soak for 10 minutes. Bring slowly to boiling point but remove before it boils. Immediately add 25 g/1 oz katsuobushi (dried bonito flakes) and bring to a rapid boil. Boil for a few seconds only, then remove from the heat. Leave to stand for 1 minute, or until the bonito flakes sink, then strain through a tea-towel into a bowl.

278 | Serundeng

Preparation time
10 minutes

Cooking time
40 minutes

Serves 4

Calories
470 per portion

You will need
oil (see method)
175 g/6 oz unsalted peanuts
1 small onion, quartered
2 garlic cloves
1 cm/½ inch piece root ginger
½ teaspoon ground cumin
1 teaspoon ground coriander
1 tablespoon lemon juice
75 g/3 oz desiccated coconut
1 teaspoon salt
1 teaspoon sugar

Coat the base of a non-stick frying pan with oil. Heat the pan and put in the peanuts. Stir-fry the nuts until lightly browned, remove to a plate and leave to cool.

Put the onion, garlic, ginger, cumin, coriander and lemon juice in a food processor or liquidizer and work until smooth.

Put 2 tablespoons oil in the frying pan and fry the spice paste for 1 minute. Add the coconut, salt and sugar and fry over a low heat, stirring for 20–30 minutes or until crisp and golden. Transfer to small dish and leave to cool.

Mix in the peanuts and serve.

Cook's Tip

Serundeng is a relish from Indonesia and should be served in tiny portions.

279 | Orchard Salad

Preparation time
15 minutes

Serves 4

Calories
175 per portion

You will need
grated rind and juice of 2 small
  oranges
1 tablespoon chopped fresh mint
  or parsley
salt and pepper
350 g / 12 oz firm pears
350 g / 12 oz dessert apples, such
  as Cox's or Worcesters
100 g / 4 oz blackberries
50 g / 2 oz shelled hazelnuts with
  skins, roughly chopped

Place the orange rind and juice in a bowl. Stir in the herbs and salt and pepper to taste.

Quarter and core the pears and apples. Cut each quarter crosswise into wedge-shaped slices. Add to the orange juice and toss well.

Add the blackberries and hazelnuts to the other fruit and toss all together. This salad goes well with rich meats such as pork and duck.

280 | Orange Winter Salad

Preparation time
15 minutes

Serves 4

Calories
327 per portion

You will need
4 large oranges
1 × 400-g / 14-oz can red kidney
  beans, drained and rinsed
275 g / 10 oz bean-sprouts
4 sticks celery, thinly sliced
watercress sprigs to garnish

For the dressing
5 tablespoons olive oil
2 tablespoons lemon juice
¼ teaspoon sugar
¼ teaspoon English mustard
salt and pepper

Peel the oranges, removing all the pith, then segment, cutting down either side of each membrane. Put in a bowl with any juice that runs out while cutting.

Add the beans, bean-sprouts and celery and toss gently together.

To make the dressing, put the oil, lemon juice, sugar, mustard and salt and pepper to taste, into a screw-top jar and shake until blended.

Just before serving the salad, spoon the dressing over and garnish with watercress.

Cook's Tip

Adding the cut apples and pears to the orange juice prevents the fruits' flesh from turning brown.

Assemble this salad at the last minute so the fruits retain their textures and the hazelnuts do not become soft.

Cook's Tip

Dried kidney beans can be used instead of the canned variety. Soak the beans overnight in water to cover, then drain and cover again with fresh water. Boil for 10 minutes, then simmer for 35–40 minutes until tender.

RICE AND PASTA

The classic recipes for rice come from Asia (and Italy); the best pasta dishes from Italy (and Asia). This cross fertilization of culinary ideas is a legacy of the time when European explorers such as Marco Polo travelled East, and brought home new foods and ideas. Rice may be a staple food in Asia, but there is still a host of ideas for adding colour and interest to the basic dishes. Kedgeree is rightly one of the world's most popular one-dish meals, and a fluffy Vegetable Pilaff makes a perfect supper dish. The most vivid rice dish is certainly Paella from Spain, beautiful to look at and full of good things.

Recent research shows that rice, like fish, is a positively healthy component of the diet: Fish and Vegetable Rice or Risotto with Spinach and Herbs are particularly delicious ways to keep fit! Rice and Beans is a tasty family dish full of protein and particularly suitable for vegetarians.

Pasta, like rice, is a perfect foil for sauces, and while there are dozens of different pastas, there are probably hundreds of different accompaniments. The classics, such as Spaghetti with Tomato Sauce and Tagliatelle alla Carbonara, are included here, but there are some innovations too. Spaghetti with Watercress and Walnut Sauce and Courgette and Cauliflower Macaroni are sure to become new family favourites.

In northern China and Japan noodle dishes are just as important as rice. Standard Oriental recipes like Nasi Goreng and Pork Chow Mein are already popular, but Szechuan Noodles are equally delicious and easy to prepare.

281 | Plain Boiled Rice

Preparation time
35 minutes, including
soaking time

Cooking time
20–25 minutes

Serves 4

Calories
300 per portion

You will need
350 g/12 oz long-grain rice
450 g/¾ pint water
salt

Wash the rice thoroughly under cold running water, then soak in cold water for 30 minutes; drain.

Place the rice in a pan with the water and salt to taste, bring to the boil, cover and simmer very gently for 20–25 minutes, until the rice is tender and the liquid absorbed. If cooking on an electric hob, the heat can be turned off once the rice has come to the boil.

Transfer the rice to a warmed serving dish. Serve as an accompaniment to curries and other spicy dishes.

282 | Tomato Rice

Preparation time
35 minutes, including
soaking time

Cooking time
20–25 minutes

Serves 4

Calories
320 per portion

You will need
225 g/8 oz long-grain rice
3 tablespoons oil
1 onion, sliced
1 garlic clove, crushed
2.5 cm/1 inch piece root ginger,
    peeled and chopped
1 (539-g/1 lb 3-oz) can tomatoes
salt
2 tablespoons finely chopped
    fresh coriander leaves

Wash the rice thoroughly under cold running water, then soak in cold water for 30 minutes; drain.

Heat the oil in a large pan, add the onion and fry until golden. Add the garlic and ginger and fry for 2 minutes. Add the rice, stir well and fry for 2 minutes.

Break up the tomatoes in their juice and add to the rice with salt to taste. Bring to the boil, then cover and simmer for 15–20 minutes, until tender.

Transfer to a warmed serving dish and sprinkle with the coriander.

Cook's Tip

Successful rice cooking is essential for ethnic meals. The best rice for Indian meals is undoubtedly Basmati, although Patna rice can also be used. There are many different methods for cooking rice, but one of the most **important things to remember is to wash the rice thoroughly before cooking. This helps to prevent the grains of rice from sticking together during cooking.**

Cook's Tip

It is now possible to buy tomatoes flavoured with herbs or spices – they may be used instead of the plain canned tomatoes in this recipe.

283 | Basic Rice

Serves 2

Calories
180 per portion of
white, brown, or
Basmati rice

You will need
For white rice
100 g / 4 oz long-grain rice
300 ml / ½ pint water
salt

For brown rice
100 g / 4 oz long-grain rice
350 ml / 12 fl oz water
salt

For Basmati rice
100 g / 4 oz Basmati rice
scant 300 ml / ½ pint water
salt

The method is the same for white and brown rice. Easy-cook varieties do not need washing, but other types of rice should be placed in a sieve and thoroughly rinsed. Put the rice in a saucepan and pour in the water. Add a little salt, then bring to the boil. Reduce the heat so that the liquid barely simmers. Give a light stir to make sure the grains are not stuck together and cover the pan.

Simmer very gently, allowing about 15–20 minutes for white rice and about 30–40 minutes for brown rice. At the end of cooking all the liquid should have been absorbed. Fork up the grains and serve.

Basmati rice has a unique and delicate flavour. The grains are quite fragile and starchy. To wash the rice, put it in a basin and pour in cold water to cover. Gently swirl the water with your fingertips, then drain it off. Repeat once or twice until the water runs clear. Cook as white and brown rice, allowing about 25 minutes cooking time.

Cook's Tip

To keep rice hot for up to
30 minutes, place in a metal
colander over an open pan
of simmering water. Cover
with a tea towel and lid.

284 | Pilau Rice

Preparation time
10 minutes

Cooking time
25–30 minutes

Serves 4

Calories
390 per portion

You will need
225 g / 8 oz Basmati rice
1 onion, chopped
50 g / 2 oz butter or margarine
3 cloves
5-cm / 2-in piece cinnamon stick
1 bay leaf
50 g / 2 oz flaked almonds
25 g / 1 oz raisins
600 ml / 1 pint water
salt and pepper

Wash and drain the Basmati rice and set aside. Cook the onion in the butter or margarine in a saucepan until soft. Add the remaining ingredients and bring to the boil. Reduce the heat, cover the pan tightly and simmer gently for 20–25 minutes, or until all the water has been absorbed. Fluff up the rice with a fork and serve immediately.

This is the traditional accompaniment to curry and chicken dishes.

Cook's Tip

Add a little chopped cooked
meat, chicken or fish to the
pilau for a light lunch or
supper dish.

285 | Rice Cakes

Preparation time
10–15 minutes

Cooking time
25 minutes

Makes 8 cakes

Calories
370 per portion

You will need
225 g/8 oz long-grain rice
300 ml/½ pint water
salt and pepper
350 g/12 oz smoked haddock,
    cod or coley
3 tablespoons oil
1 onion, chopped
grated rind and juice of 1 lemon
2 tablespoons tomato ketchup
2 tablespoons chopped parsley
1 egg

Put the rice in a saucepan and pour in the water. Add a little salt, then bring to the boil. Reduce the heat so that the liquid barely simmers. Give the rice a light stir to make sure the grains are not stuck together and cover the pan tightly.

Simmer very gently, allowing about 15–20 minutes for white rice and about 30–40 minutes for brown rice. At the end of cooking all the liquid should have been absorbed.

Place the fish in a frying pan, cover with water and poach for 10 minutes or until the fish is cooked. Skin the fish and remove any bones, then flake the fish.

Heat 1 tablespoon of the oil and cook the onion for a few minutes, then add the rice, fish and remaining ingredients. Mash together well, remove from the heat and form the mixture into cakes. Fry the cakes in the remaining oil until brown, and serve immediately.

286 | Kedgeree

Preparation time
10 minutes

Cooking time
30 minutes

Serves 4

Calories
430 per portion

You will need
1 onion, chopped
2 tablespoons oil or 25 g/1 oz
    butter
175 g/6 oz long-grain rice
¼ teaspoon turmeric
450 ml/¾ pint water
225 g/8 oz smoked haddock
50 g/2 oz raisins
50 g/2 oz salted peanuts
3 hard-boiled eggs, roughly
    chopped
1 tablespoon lemon juice
salt and pepper
1 tablespoon chopped parsley

Cook the onion in the oil or butter until soft but not browned. Add the rice and turmeric, cook for a minute, then pour in the water. Bring to the boil, reduce the heat and cover the pan. Simmer for 15 minutes until the water is absorbed.

Meanwhile, put the smoked haddock in a pan, cover with water and bring to the boil. Reduce the heat and simmer for 5 minutes, or until the fish flakes easily with the point of a knife. Drain and coarsely flake the fish, discarding the skin and any bones.

Add the fish, raisins, peanuts, eggs, lemon juice, seasoning and parsley to the rice. Fork together gently.

Serve the kedgeree immediately.

Cook's Tip

For a quick supper substitute canned pilchards or tuna fish for the smoked fish.

Cook's Tip

For a more spicy kedgeree omit raisins and peanuts and add ¼ teaspoon freshly grated nutmeg.

287 | *Stuffed Tomatoes*

Preparation time
20 minutes

Cooking time
20 minutes

Oven temperature
180C, 350F, Gas 4

Serves 2

Calories
371 per portion

You will need
2 large Mediterranean tomatoes
salt

For the stuffing
2 tablespoons oil
75 g / 3 oz button mushrooms,
    wiped and finely chopped
65 g / 2½ oz brown rice, cooked
25 g / 1 oz brazil nuts, roughly
    chopped
25 g / 1 oz currants
1 teaspoon chopped fresh basil, or
    ½ teaspoon dried
pepper
4 tablespoons soured cream and
    watercress sprigs to garnish

Cut the tomatoes in half and scoop out the insides. Sprinkle the shells with salt and place in a baking dish.

To make the stuffing, heat the oil and gently fry the mushrooms for 5 minutes. Stir in the cooked rice, nuts, currants and basil. Add a little salt and plenty of pepper. Spoon the stuffing into the tomato halves.

Cover the dish with foil to keep the stuffing moist and cook for 20 minutes in a preheated oven.

Remove from the oven, top each stuffed tomato with a spoonful of soured cream and garnish with watercress. Serve piping hot.

Cook's Tip

For finger food to serve at a drinks party, use this filling to stuff hollowed-out cherry tomatoes. Serve on a tray lined with lettuce leaves.

288 | *Vegetable Pilaf*

Preparation time
10 minutes

Cooking time
15 minutes

Serves 4

Calories
309 per portion

You will need
50 g / 2 oz margarine
2 onions, peeled and finely
    chopped
175 g / 6 oz long-grain rice
450–600 ml / ¾–1 pint chicken
    stock
2 carrots, roughly grated
1 cucumber, diced
4 radishes, thinly sliced
1 red or green pepper, cored,
    seeded and finely chopped
salt and pepper
grated Parmesan cheese to serve

Melt the margarine in a large saucepan and fry the onions for 3 minutes until tender. Stir in the rice, then add the stock and bring to the boil. Cover and simmer for 5–10 minutes until tender and most of the liquid absorbed.

Stir in the carrots, cucumber, radishes and pepper and season to taste with salt and pepper.

Continue cooking, uncovered, for 2–3 minutes more until the vegetables are heated through but still crisp.

Serve hot with plenty of grated Parmesan cheese for sprinkling over the top.

Cook's Tip

Using brown rice in this recipe gives it a slight nutty flavour. Brown rice will require an extra 5–10 minutes cooking time. For even more flavour, stir 3 tablespoons of very finely chopped parsley into the mixture before serving.

289 | Rice Salad Gado Gado

Preparation time
10 minutes, plus 30 minutes to cool

Cooking time
15 18 minutes

Serves 4

Calories
415 per portion

You will need
225 g/8 oz long-grain rice
50 g/2 oz mushrooms, halved
600 ml/1 pint vegetable stock
100 g/4 oz beansprouts
2 tomatoes, peeled and quartered
2 hard-boiled eggs, quartered

For the sauce
100 g/4 oz salted peanuts
4 spring onions, chopped
1 tablespoon soy sauce
1 teaspoon chilli powder

Put the rice, mushrooms and stock into a covered pan, bring to the boil and simmer gently for 15–18 minutes, until the rice is cooked and all the liquid is absorbed. Allow to cool then mix in the beansprouts, tomatoes and hard-boiled eggs.

Put the remaining ingredients in a liquidiser and blend thoroughly, adding enough water to make a smooth sauce. Pour over the rice salad and serve.

Cook's Tip

Made from fermented soya beans, soy sauce is used as extensively in Chinese cookery as salt is in the west. Most commonly dark and pungently flavoured, a more delicate – yet very salty – light soy sauce is also available.

290 | Spiced Rice and Courgette Salad

Preparation time
15 minutes, plus 1 hour to chill

Cooking time
40 45 minutes

Serves 4

Calories
530 per portion

You will need
225 g/8 oz long-grain brown rice
1 teaspoon each turmeric, curry powder, ground cumin and coriander
600 ml/1 pint water
100 g/4 oz courgettes, thinly sliced
2 tablespoons wine vinegar
5 tablespoons groundnut oil
salt
2 carrots, grated
1 onion, finely chopped
100 g/4 oz salted peanuts
1 dessert apple, unpeeled, cored and chopped

Place the rice in a saucepan with the spices and water. Bring to the boil then cover and simmer for 35–40 minutes, until the rice is tender and the liquid has been absorbed.

Meanwhile blanch the courgettes in boiling salted water for 1 minute. Drain, refresh under cold running water and drain again. Turn the rice into a large salad bowl and stir in the vinegar, oil and salt to taste. Cool slightly then add the courgettes, carrots, onion, peanuts and apple. Mix well and chill thoroughly before serving.

Cook's Tip

Flavourless peanut oil is a good choice for salad dressing, as it does not obscure the taste of other ingredients. If you want to cook with it, a pleasant flavour is imparted by first frying several slices of fresh root ginger or garlic in it.

291 | Risotto with Spinach and Herbs

Preparation time
15 minutes

Cooking time
35 minutes

Serves 4—6

Calories
775 520 per portion

You will need
2 tablespoons olive oil
100 g/4 oz butter
1 onion, finely chopped
100 g/4 oz mushrooms, sliced
450 g/1 lb Italian risotto rice (Arborio)
1.5 litres/2¾ pints hot vegetable stock
225 g/8 oz cooked spinach, chopped
1 teaspoon dried oregano
1 clove garlic, crushed
salt and pepper
75 g/3 oz grated Parmesan or Pecorino cheese
lemon wedges to garnish

Heat the oil and half the butter in a large saucepan. Add the onion and mushrooms and cook for a few minutes until the onions are lightly browned. Stir in the rice and cook for 5 minutes. Add the stock, spinach, oregano, garlic and salt and pepper. Stir well and cook for 20–25 minutes or until the rice is tender and has absorbed all the liquid. Stir in the remaining butter and the grated cheese. Serve the risotto garnished with lemon wedges.

292 | Rice and Mushroom Bake

Preparation time
10 minutes

Cooking time
40 45 minutes

Oven temperature
200 C, 400 F, gas 6

Serves 4

Calories
415 per portion

You will need
2 tablespoons vegetable oil
1 large onion, sliced
225 g/8 oz mushrooms, sliced
225 g/8 oz long-grain rice
1 teaspoon cumin powder
1 teaspoon mild chilli powder
1 teaspoon tomato purée
600 ml/1 pint vegetable stock
75 g/3 oz Cheddar cheese, grated
40 g/1½ oz cornflakes

Heat the oil and cook the onion and mushrooms until softened, about 5 minutes. Add the rice and fry until golden brown. Stir in the spices, tomato purée and stock. Bring to the boil and stir once. Reduce the heat, cover the pan and simmer for 15–18 minutes, until the rice is tender and the liquid absorbed. Stir in half the grated cheese and transfer to an ovenproof casserole. Mix the remaining cheese with the cornflakes, sprinkle on top of the rice and bake in a moderately hot oven for 15–20 minutes, until golden brown.

Cook's Tip

Parmesan and pecorino are both grainy, hard, grating cheeses. When young, they are eaten in chunks accompanied by white wine. Straw-coloured Parmesan is made from cows' milk and pecorino from ewes' milk. Buy fresh if possible.

Cook's Tip

Cumin, with its distinctive pungent flavour, is a spice worth investigating both as whole and ground seed. Popular in Mexico, North Africa and the East, it is sold by specialist grocers and some supermarkets. Whole seeds keep their flavour longest and may be ground very easily in an electric coffee grinder.

293 | Fish and Vegetable Rice

Preparation time
8 minutes

Cooking time
12–15 minutes

Serves 4–6

Calories
232 per portion

You will need
225 g / 8 oz haddock fillet
milk
1 tablespoon oil
1 small onion, peeled and finely
   chopped
3 tablespoons water
1 courgette, quartered lengthways
   and chopped
3 mushrooms, wiped and sliced
½ red pepper, cored, seeded and
   finely chopped
½ bunch watercress, stalks
   removed and roughly chopped
1 celery stick, chopped
50 g / 2 oz peeled cooked prawns
150–200 g / 5–7 oz rice, cooked
juice of ½ lemon
salt and pepper

Poach the haddock in milk to cover for 5 minutes or until cooked through and the flesh flakes easily. Drain and flake with a fork, discarding any bones and the skin. Set aside.

Heat the oil and fry the onion for 2 minutes, stirring. Add the water, courgette, mushrooms, red pepper, watercress and celery and stir-fry for 5 minutes.

Add the prawns and continue stir-frying for 1 minute. Add the cooked rice and stir-fry until heated through, then stir in the haddock, lemon juice and salt and pepper to taste. Transfer to warmed serving plates.

Cook's Tip

Haddock fillets are available smoked and unsmoked. Although this recipe uses the unsmoked variety, a smoked fillet will add extra flavour. When buying smoked fillets, avoid the bright yellow ones: these have been dyed.

294 | Nasi Goreng

Preparation time
15 minutes

Cooking time
30 minutes

Serves 4

Calories
342 per portion

You will need
50 g / 2 oz butter
450 g / 1 lb boned shoulder of
   pork, cut into bite-sized strips
2 onions, peeled and sliced
1 red pepper, seeded and
   chopped
50 g / 2 oz shelled peas
50 g / 2 oz cucumber, chopped
50 g /2 oz carrot, grated
4 tablespoons soy sauce
1 teaspoon curry powder
salt and pepper
225 g / 8 oz long-grain rice,
   cooked and drained
1 egg
1 teaspoon cold water
2 tomatoes, cut into wedges
spring onion curls to garnish

Melt the butter and fry the pork for 5–8 minutes until golden. Add the onions and cook for a further 10 minutes. Add the pepper, peas, cucumber and carrot to the pork mixture and cook for a further 5 minutes. Stir in the soy sauce, curry powder and salt and pepper to taste, blending well. Add the rice, tossing well to mix, and reheat.

Meanwhile, beat the egg with the water and salt and pepper to taste. Melt the butter in a small omelette pan and gently cook the egg until the underside is golden. Turn and brown the other side. Cut in wide strips.

Put the rice mixture on a warmed serving dish and top with a lattice of omelette strips. Garnish with tomato wedges and spring onion curls.

Cook's Tip

This is an Indonesian dish that makes an ideal light main course or can be served with a selection of spicy Asian dishes. Add a pinch of five spice powder for a more exotic flavour. The pork can be replaced with shelled cooked prawns for a seafood version. It will keep warm for 30 minutes after cooking if covered.

295 | Brown Rice Ring Mould

Preparation time
5–10 minutes, plus 1½ hours to chill

Cooking time
45 minutes

Serves 4

Calories
400 per portion

You will need
225 g / 8 oz long-grain brown rice
350 ml / 12 fl oz water
salt
100 g / 4 oz walnut halves, roughly chopped
1 (325-g / 11.8-oz) can sweetcorn, drained
1 green pepper, deseeded and diced
¼ teaspoon paprika
pinch of salt
watercress sprigs to garnish

Grease a 1.15-litre / 2-pint ring mould with oil.

Put the rice in a saucepan and pour in the water. Add a little salt, then bring to the boil. Reduce the heat so that the liquid barely simmers. Give the rice a light stir to make sure the grains are not stuck together and cover the pan tightly.

Simmer very gently for 30–40 minutes. At the end of cooking all the liquid should have been absorbed. Mix all the ingredients together and pack the mixture into the ring mould.

Leave the rice to cool and chill thoroughly. Turn out and serve as an accompaniment to a salad.

Cook's Tip

For a more colourful dish, add peas or diced, peeled and deseeded tomatoes to the rice.

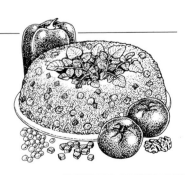

296 | Tomato Rice Mould

Preparation time
10 minutes

Cooking time
15–20 minutes

Serves 4

Calories
295 per portion

You will need
2 (400-g / 14-oz) cans plum tomatoes
2 onions, chopped
1 clove garlic, crushed
1 teaspoon dried or 2 teaspoons chopped fresh basil
salt and pepper
225 g / 8 oz long-grain white rice
450 ml / ¾ pint water
50 g / 2 oz Parmesan cheese, grated
watercress sprigs to garnish

Grease a 1.15-litre / 2-pint ring mould with oil.

For the tomato sauce, blend the tomatoes, onion, garlic, basil and seasoning in a liquidiser until smooth. Cook the rice in the tomato sauce and water for 15–20 minutes or until the liquid has evaporated, stirring occasionally. Stir in the Parmesan cheese.

Press the rice into the mould and leave for 5 minutes. Turn out the rice, and serve with a salad or with grilled meat.

Cook's Tip

For a buffet party dish fill centre of rice ring with lightly cooked cauliflower florets tossed in French dressing.

297 | Pilaf Rice with Cèpe Mushrooms

Preparation time
10 minutes, plus soaking

Cooking time
35–40 minutes

Serves 2
as a light main course

Calories
420 per portion

You will need
450 ml / ¾ pint hot chicken stock
½ teaspoon saffron threads
3 tablespoons olive oil
2 shallots, peeled and finely
    chopped
100 g / 4 oz Italian rice
1 bay leaf
salt and pepper
1 garlic clove, peeled and crushed
100 g / 4 oz cèpe mushrooms,
    sliced and wiped
2 tablespoons white wine
2 teaspoons chopped fresh chives
    to garnish

Pour the hot stock over the saffron threads and leave for 30 minutes.

Heat 2 tablespoons olive oil and fry the shallots for 5 minutes until softened. Stir in the rice and stir until all the grains are evenly coated. Add the stock together with the saffron threads, bay leaf and salt and pepper to taste.

Bring to the boil, reduce the heat, cover and cook gently for 30 minutes until the rice is tender and the stock absorbed.

Meanwhile, heat the remaining oil and cook the garlic for 1 minute. Add the cèpe mushrooms and stir until coated. Add the wine and salt and pepper to taste and cook 15–20 minutes until the mushrooms are tender.

Transfer the rice to a warm serving dish and pour the mushrooms over. Serve hot, sprinkled with chives.

Cook's Tip

Cèpes are wild mushrooms available in the autumn. If you can't find any, dried mushrooms have more flavour than ordinary button mushrooms. To use dried mushrooms, soak for 30 minutes in warm water, then squeeze dry and slice.

298 | Paella

Preparation time
10 minutes

Cooking time
30 minutes

Serves 6

Calories
583 per portion

You will need
200 g / 7 oz long-grain rice
¼ teaspoon powdered saffron
1 tablespoon oil
1 onion, peeled and thinly sliced
1 garlic clove, peeled and crushed
¼ teaspoon paprika
4 tomatoes, skinned and chopped
1 red pepper, cored, seeded and
    finely chopped
100 g / 4 oz petit pois, thawed if
    frozen
4 cooked boneless chicken
    breasts
2 slices lean cooked ham, diced
100 g / 4 oz peeled cooked
    prawns
juice of 1 lemon
1 tablespoon chopped fresh
    parsley
lemon wedges to garnish

Cook the rice in boiling lightly salted water with the saffron until tender. Drain well and keep hot.

Heat the oil and fry the onion, stirring, for 3 minutes. Stir in the garlic, paprika, tomatoes, red pepper and peas and cook, stirring, for 4 minutes. Add the chicken, ham and prawns and heat gently for 3–4 minutes. Stir in the lemon juice and parsley. Mix with the hot rice and turn into a warmed serving dish.

Serve at once, garnished with lemon wedges.

Cook's Tip

Do not be tempted to substitute turmeric for saffron in this Spanish-style dish. Although turmeric will give the rice the characteristic yellow colour, the flavour of the dish will be less delicious.

299 | Mushroom Pasta with Pine Nuts

Preparation time
25 minutes

Cooking time
40 minutes

Serves 4

Calories
480 per portion

You will need
1½ tablespoons vegetable oil
1 medium onion, sliced
450 g/1 lb flat open mushrooms, sliced
salt
1 2 teaspoons green peppercorns
1 tablespoon soy sauce
3 tablespoons water
2 tablespoons double or whipping cream
350 g/12 oz pasta shapes
2 tablespoons pine nuts
chopped parsley to garnish

Heat 1 tablespoon oil in a medium saucepan and cook the onion for about 5 minutes. Add the mushrooms and cook for a further few minutes. Add the salt, green peppercorns, soy sauce and water. Cover the pan and simmer gently for about 20 minutes. Remove lid and cook quickly for 1 minute to reduce liquid. Pour into a liquidiser or food processor and blend very briefly, for just a few seconds. Return to the rinsed-out pan and stir in the cream.

Bring a large pan of salted water to the boil. Add the pasta and boil briskly for 10 minutes then drain.

Meanwhile, heat the remaining oil in a small saucepan and fry the pine nuts for 2 minutes until golden brown. Drain on absorbent kitchen paper. To serve, reheat the sauce without boiling and pour over the pasta. Sprinkle with the pine nuts and parsley.

Cook's Tip

This mushroom sauce has a marvellous taste. Use the flat dark mushrooms for the best flavour. Pine nuts or kernels can be bought in health-food shops.

300 | Brown Rice and Hazelnut Salad

Preparation time
20 25 minutes

Cooking time
40 minutes

Serves 6—8

Calories
245 185 per portion

You will need
175 g/6 oz long-grain brown rice
salt
75 g/3 oz hazelnuts, chopped and toasted
1 red pepper, deseeded and diced
6 spring onions, finely sliced
3 celery sticks, sliced (optional)
50 g/2 oz button mushrooms, sliced
6 tablespoons French dressing (made with 4 tablespoons oil and 2 tablespoons vinegar, 1 teaspoon French mustard, salt and pepper and a pinch of caster sugar)
3 tablespoons chopped parsley

Cook the rice in a saucepan of boiling salted water for 30—40 minutes, until tender. Rinse and drain well.

Place in a salad bowl with the remaining ingredients. Add the dressing and toss thoroughly. Serve cold.

Cook's Tip

Instead of the hazelnuts use toasted cashew nuts instead.

301 | Vegetarian Gumbo

Preparation time
10 minutes

Cooking time
20–25 minutes

Serves 4

Calories
280 per portion

You will need
4 tablespoons corn oil
25 g / 1 oz plain flour
1 large onion, chopped
4 celery sticks, chopped
1 small green pepper, deseeded and chopped
225 g / 8 oz okra, sliced
1 (397-g / 14-oz) can tomatoes
300 ml / ½ pint vegetable stock
1 teaspoon Tabasco sauce
salt and pepper
350 g / 12 oz hot cooked brown rice (100 g / 4 oz uncooked weight)

Place half the oil in a small, heavy-based pan and heat gently. Add the flour and cook over a low heat, stirring frequently until the roux becomes a rich brown colour, but be careful not to let it burn.

In a large saucepan, heat the remaining oil and cook the onion until tender, about 5 minutes. Add the celery, green pepper and okra and sauté for 3 minutes. Stir the tomatoes, stock, Tabasco and roux into the mixture and simmer, covered, for 10 minutes. Season to taste and serve in individual bowls, topped with a portion of hot brown rice.

302 | Pasta Pesto

Preparation time
15 minutes

Cooking time
12 minutes

Serves 4

Calories
600 per portion

You will need
350 g / 12 oz wholewheat caramelli shells, or other pasta shapes
salt and pepper
75 g / 3 oz basil leaves
4 tablespoons olive oil
3 cloves garlic, crushed
50 g / 2 oz pine nuts or blanched slivered almonds
50 g / 2 oz Parmesan cheese, grated
25 g / 1 oz butter, softened
grated Parmesan cheese to serve

Cook the pasta in plenty of boiling, salted water for about 12 minutes, or according to the directions on the packet, until just tender. Drain, refresh in hot water and drain again, tossing to ensure that no water is trapped inside the caramelli. Keep hot.

To make the sauce, blend the basil, oil, garlic and nuts in a liquidiser. Remove the mixture to a bowl, beat in the cheese and butter and season with pepper.

Spoon the sauce over the hot pasta and serve at once, with Parmesan, as an accompaniment to meat and poultry, or on its own.

Cook's Tip

Corn oil, made from the sweetcorn plant, or maize, is among the oils containing polyunsaturated fatty acids, desirable in the diet. Safflower, sunflower, and soya bean oil are others.

Cook's Tip

It is very easy to grow your own basil in a pot. Basil is also excellent sprinkled on salads, particularly tomato.

303 | *Szechuan Noodles*

Preparation time
10 minutes, plus 15 minutes to prepare cucumber

Cooking time
8 minutes

Serves 4

Calories
720 per portion

You will need
½ cucumber, cut into 1-cm/½-in dice
salt
small bunch of radishes, trimmed
1 spring onion, trimmed
450 g/1 lb fresh egg noodles or dried noodles
100 g/4 oz beansprouts
4 tablespoons peanut oil
3-4 tablespoons crunchy peanut butter
1 teaspoon sesame oil
25 g/1 oz salted peanuts, lightly crushed

Sprinkle the cucumber with salt and leave to drain for 15 minutes. Rinse and dry on absorbent kitchen paper. Slice a third of the radishes, leaving the remainder whole. Slice the spring onion diagonally. Meanwhile, cook the fresh noodles for 1 minute in boiling salted water, then drain thoroughly. Cook dried noodles as directed on the packet. Blanch the beansprouts in boiling water for 1 minute. Plunge into cold water, then drain thoroughly.

Fry the drained noodles quickly in 3 tablespoons of the peanut oil, stirring constantly. Transfer to a hot serving plate. Put the remaining oil into a pan with the peanut butter and sesame oil and heat gently. Pour over the noodles and mix lightly.

Arrange the prepared ingredients attractively on top and serve. Serve the remaining radishes in a bowl.

Cook's Tip

Peanut and sesame oil are used in this recipe as they add a distinctive flavour, favoured by the Chinese.

304 | *Rice and Beans*

Preparation time
10 minutes

Cooking time
40 minutes

Serves 4

Calories
475 per portion

You will need
225 g/8 oz long-grain brown rice
750 ml/1¼ pints boiling water
3 tablespoons sunflower oil
1 tablespoon red wine vinegar
salt and pepper
4 spring onions, chopped
1 (415-g/14½-oz) can red kidney beans
50 g/2 oz button mushrooms, sliced
225 g/8 oz tomatoes
4 tablespoons French dressing (see recipe 146)
50 g/2 oz black olives
chopped parsley to garnish

Cook the rice in the water for 40 minutes or until cooked and the water absorbed. Mix together the oil, vinegar and salt and pepper. Fluff up the rice with a fork and stir in the spring onions and oil and vinegar dressing. Cool.

Mix together the kidney beans and mushrooms. Slice the tomatoes and pour over the French dressing. Stir in the olives and salt and pepper to taste.

On a large serving plate, arrange a circle of rice salad round the edge, a circle of bean salad inside, and the tomato mixture in the middle. Scatter over the parsley to garnish.

Cook's Tip

The difference between black and green olives is that the black ones are ripe. Black olives vary from plump and succulent to small and wrinkly specimens. You can sometimes sample them before buying.

305 | Brown Rice Salad

Preparation time
10 minutes, plus 20 minutes to cool

Cooking time
35 minutes

Serves 4

Calories
395 per portion

You will need
100 g/4 oz long-grain brown rice
salt and pepper
100 g/4 oz shelled peas or sliced beans
100 g/4 oz sweetcorn kernels
150 ml/¼ pint Vinaigrette dressing (made up of 6 tablespoons oil, 2 tablespoons vinegar, herbs and salt and pepper)
1 red pepper, deseeded and diced
50 g/2 oz salted peanuts
1 small onion, grated

Cook the rice in a saucepan of boiling salted water for 30 minutes or until tender. Add the peas or beans and sweetcorn and simmer for a further few minutes until just tender. Drain thoroughly.

Transfer to a medium bowl and add half of the dressing while the rice and vegetables are still hot. Toss well to mix, then leave to cool.

Add the remaining ingredients and dressing. Mix well. Taste and adjust the seasoning just before serving. Serve cold with other salad dishes.

Cook's Tip

Brown rice has more protein than polished (white) rice. It also has traces of iron, calcium and vitamin B. When cooked it retains much of its bite and is therefore an ideal basis for salads.

306 | Macaroni Special

Preparation time
5 minutes

Cooking time
20 minutes

Serves 4

Calories
570 per portion

You will need
225 g/8 oz wholewheat macaroni
225 g/8 oz frozen mixed vegetables
25 g/1 oz butter
1 clove garlic, crushed
3 large tomatoes, peeled and chopped
225 g/8 oz mushrooms, sliced
3 tablespoons chopped parsley (optional)
300 ml/½ pint soured cream
50 g/2 oz mozzarella cheese, coarsely grated
4 tablespoons grated Parmesan cheese
4 slices bread, crusts removed, cut into triangles and toasted

Cook the macaroni in plenty of boiling water for about 5 minutes, then add the frozen mixed vegetables and cook for a further 7 minutes. Drain.

Melt the butter in a saucepan, cook the garlic for 1 minute, stir in the tomatoes and mushrooms and cook for 3 minutes. Stir in the macaroni mixture, parsley, if using, soured cream and mozzarella and heat gently until mixture is hot and the cheese just melting. Stir in the Parmesan cheese and serve immediately, garnished with the toast triangles.

Cook's Tip

A soured cream equivalent may be achieved by adding a few drops of lemon juice to fresh double cream.

307 | Seafood Spaghetti

Preparation time
10 minutes

Cooking time
15 minutes

Serves 4

Calories
647 per portion

You will need
4 tablespoons olive oil
4 garlic cloves, peeled and
 crushed
225 g / 8 oz frozen mussels,
 thawed
225 g / 8 oz peeled cooked
 prawns
125 ml / 4 fl oz white wine
salt and pepper
150 ml / ¼ pint double cream
pinch cayenne pepper
350 g / 12 oz spaghetti
2 tablespoons chopped fresh
 parsley

For the garnish
4 unpeeled cooked prawns
quartered lemon slices

Heat 1 tablespoon oil and fry the garlic for 1 minute. Add the mussels, prawns, white wine and salt and pepper to taste, and cook for a further 3 minutes. Stir in the cream and cayenne and heat through.

Meanwhile, cook the spaghetti in a large pan of salted boiling water for 8–10 minutes until just tender.

Drain the spaghetti and mix with the remaining olive oil and the parsley. Serve with the seafood sauce spooned over and garnished with prawns and lemon.

Cook's Tip

Use fresh mussels if they are available instead of frozen. Scrub 225 g / 8 oz mussels well and discard any that are open. Place in a heavy-based pan over a high heat, cover, and cook until the mussels open. Discard any that have **not opened. Remove the mussels from the shells and add to the sauce. Sometimes it is possible to buy fresh mussels that have already been cleaned. The mussel shells make an interesting garnish for this dish.**

308 | Seafood Pasta Salad

Preparation time
30 minutes

Cooking time
10 minutes

Serves 4

Calories
334 per portion

You will need
175 g / 6 oz pasta twists or other
 shapes
1 avocado, peeled, stoned and
 sliced
2 teaspoons lemon juice
175 g / 6 oz peeled cooked
 prawns
1 × 200-g / 7-oz jar mussels in
 brine, rinsed and drained
3 tomatoes, cut into wedges
50 g / 2 oz button mushrooms,
 wiped and sliced
few whole unpeeled cooked
 prawns to garnish

For the dressing
2 tablespoons mayonnaise
2 tablespoons soured cream
1 teaspoon garlic purée
2 teaspoon chopped chives
salt and pepper

Cook the pasta in boiling salted water for 8–10 minutes until just tender. Drain and cool.

Toss the avocado slices in the lemon juice and add the pasta with the prawns, mussels, tomatoes and mushrooms, mixing gently.

To make the dressing, mix the mayonnaise with the soured cream, garlic purée, chives and salt and pepper.

Fold the dressing into the salad and spoon into a serving dish. Chill lightly, then garnish with prawns.

Cook's Tip

Make your own garlic purée by crushing a clove of garlic with the flat part of a knife blade on a chopping board. If you wish place a piece of greaseproof paper over the board so it does not absorb the garlic's strong smell.

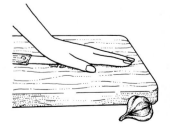

309 | Spaghetti with Tomato Sauce

Preparation time
5 minutes

Cooking time
25 minutes

Serves 4

Calories
480 per portion

You will need
1 onion, finely chopped
2 cloves garlic, crushed
1 tablespoon oil
1 (400-g/14-oz) can chopped
  tomatoes
½ teaspoon dried or 1 teaspoon
  chopped fresh basil
salt and pepper
450 g/1 lb spaghetti

Fry the onion and garlic in the oil for 5 minutes until soft. Add the tomatoes, basil, salt and pepper. Bring to the boil, reduce the heat and simmer gently for 15 minutes or until thickened.

While the sauce is simmering, cook the spaghetti in a large pan of boiling salted water for 10–12 minutes until just tender. Drain, place in a serving bowl and keep hot.

Blend the sauce in a liquidiser. Reheat in a saucepan for a few minutes, pour over the spaghetti and serve immediately.

310 | Spaghetti with Watercress and Walnut Sauce

Preparation time
10 minutes

Cooking time
15 minutes

Serves 4

Calories
615 per portion

You will need
450 g/1 lb wholewheat spaghetti
salt and pepper
1 onion, chopped
1–2 cloves, garlic, crushed
1 tablespoon oil
50 g/2 oz mushrooms, sliced
50 g/2 oz chopped walnuts
bunch of watercress, chopped
300 ml/½ pint soured cream

Cook the spaghetti in a large pan of boiling salted water for 10–12 minutes until just tender.

Meanwhile, make the sauce. Cook the onion and garlic in the oil until transparent. Add the mushrooms and walnuts and cook for a further few minutes. Remove the pan from the heat, stir in the watercress, soured cream and seasoning. Reheat very gently – do not allow the sauce to boil or the cream will curdle.

Drain the spaghetti and place on a serving dish. Pour the sauce over and serve immediately.

Cook's Tip

When fresh tomatoes are cheap and plentiful, use 450 g/1 lb peeled and chopped fresh instead of canned tomatoes and 1 tablespoon tomato purée.

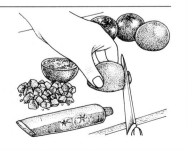

Microwave Tip

To cook sauce in a microwave: cook onion and garlic in oil for 6 minutes. Add mushrooms, walnuts and watercress, cook for 2 minutes. Add cream and cook for 3 minutes.

311 | Pasta with Bolina Cheese Sauce

Preparation time
10 minutes

Cooking time
10–12 minutes

Serves 4

Calories
435 per portion

You will need
275 g/10 oz tagliatelle or pasta shells
125 g/4½ oz Danish Bolina cheese
25 g/1 oz butter
4 tablespoons single cream
2 tablespoons chopped parsley
salt and pepper

Cook the pasta in a large pan of boiling salted water for 10–12 minutes until just tender.

Meanwhile, place the cheese in a bowl. Break it up with a fork, add the butter and set over a pan of boiling water. Cook, stirring occasionally, until the ingredients have melted and blended together. Add the cream and parsley. Season to taste and heat through.

Drain the cooked pasta and place on a heated serving dish. Pour the sauce over the pasta and turn gently with two forks to coat. Serve immediately with a mixed salad and crusty bread.

312 | Gratin of Pasta

Preparation time
15 minutes

Cooking time
25 minutes

Serves 4

Calories
380 per portion

You will need
100 g/4 oz pasta shells
salt and pepper
25 g/1 oz butter
25 g/1 oz plain flour
300 ml/½ pint milk
100 g/4 oz Cheddar cheese, grated
1 (283-g/10-oz) packet frozen Country stir-fry vegetables
2 tablespoons chopped parsley
2 hard-boiled eggs, sliced

Cook the pasta shells in a large saucepan of boiling salted water for 10–12 minutes, until just tender. Melt the butter, add the flour and cook for a minute. Remove from the heat and gradually stir in the milk. Return to the heat and bring to the boil, stirring continually until the sauce bubbles and thickens. Add the cheese, season to taste and leave to cool slightly.

Cook the stir-fry vegetables according to the packet instructions. Toss the cooked pasta shells in parsley and place in a flameproof serving dish. Sprinkle with the stir-fry vegetables and arrange the egg slices on top. Pour over the cheese sauce and brown under a hot grill, if preferred. Serve immediately.

Cook's Tip

Using a big saucepan with plenty of boiling water to cook the pasta is important. The pasta swells and if it is cramped it will tend to clog together in lumps. Adding a few drops of oil to the water helps to prevent this.

Cook's Tip

Pasta shells (conchiglie) are available in a range of sizes and in both plain and wholemeal varieties. They are particularly good with chunky sauces like this one.

313 | Mixed Seafood Stick Noodles

Preparation time
about 15 minutes

Cooking time
about 15 minutes

Serves 4–6

Calories
550–360 per portion

You will need
4 dried Chinese mushrooms (see
 Cook's Tip)
450 g/1 lb rice stick noodles (see
 Cook'sTip)
salt
2 tablespoons oil
4 spring onions, chopped
2 garlic cloves, sliced
5 cm/2 inch piece root ginger,
 peeled and finely chopped
50 g/2 oz peeled prawns
100 g/4 oz squid, sliced (optional)
1 (225-g/7½-oz) can clams,
 drained
2 tablespoons dry sherry
1 tablespoon soy sauce

Soak the mushrooms in warm water for 15 minutes. Squeeze well, discard the stalks, then slice the mushroom caps.

Cook the noodles in boiling salted water for 7–8 minutes until just tender. Drain and rinse in cold water. Set aside.

Heat the oil in a wok or deep frying pan, add the spring onions, garlic and ginger and stir-fry for 30 seconds. Stir in the mushrooms, prawns and squid, if using, then cook for 2 minutes. Stir in the remaining ingredients, then carefully stir in the noodles and heat through.

Pile the mixture into a warmed serving dish and serve at once.

Cook's Tip

Dried Chinese mushrooms are available from specialist shops. They must be soaked in warm water for at least 15 minutes before using and the stalks must be removed before use. Continental dried mushrooms can be used instead, if preferred.

Rice stick noodles are long sticks, like noodles, made from rice flour. They do not require soaking before use.

314 | Noodles Tossed with Meat and Vegetables

Preparation time
20 minutes

Cooking time
about 5 minutes

Serves 4–6

Calories
550–360 per portion

You will need
2 carrots, peeled
3 celery sticks
½ cucumber
2 green chillies, seeded
2 tablespoons oil
1 garlic clove, chopped
350 g/12 oz minced pork
4 spring onions, sliced
1 small green pepper, cored,
 seeded and sliced
1 tablespoon soy sauce
2 tablespoons sweet red bean
 paste (see Cook's Tip)
1 tablespoon dry sherry
350 g/12 oz noodles, cooked

Cut the carrots, celery and cucumber into matchstick lengths. Slice the chillies finely.

Heat the oil in a wok or deep frying pan, add the chillies and garlic and fry quickly for about 30 seconds. Add the pork and cook for 2 minutes. Increase the heat, add the vegetables and cook for 1 minute. Stir in the soy sauce, red bean paste, sherry and noodles. Stir well to mix and heat through.

Pile on to a warmed serving dish and serve at once.

Cook's Tip

Sweet red bean paste is a thick red paste made from soya beans with added sugar and is sold in cans. It is generally used as a dip or as a base for sweet sauces.

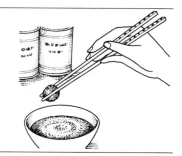

315 | Quick Ravioli Supper

Preparation time
10 minutes

Cooking time
15–20 minutes

Serves 4

Calories
285 per portion

You will need
1 onion, chopped
2 cloves garlic, crushed
1 tablespoon oil
2 (440-g/15½-oz) cans ravioli in
    tomato sauce
50 g/2 oz Cheddar cheese, grated
50 g/2 oz fresh white
    breadcrumbs

Fry the onion and garlic in the oil for a few minutes until the onion is soft and transparent. Add the ravioli and heat gently for 5 minutes. Pour the mixture into a serving dish, then sprinkle over the Cheddar and breadcrumbs and cook under a hot grill until brown.

Serve immediately with a green salad.

316 | Pork Chow Mein

Preparation time
10 minutes

Cooking time
30 minutes

Serves 4

Calories
345 per portion

You will need
225 g/8 oz Chinese egg noodles
salt and pepper
2 tablespoons oil
225 g/8 oz boneless pork, diced
75 g/3 oz spring onions, chopped
2 cloves garlic, crushed
100 g/4 oz button mushrooms
1 tablespoon soy sauce
2 spring onion curls to garnish

Cook the noodles in a saucepan of boiling salted water for 5–10 minutes until just tender. Drain well and set aside.

Heat the oil in a large frying pan or wok, and fry the pork for 5 minutes. Add the onion, garlic and mushrooms and continue cooking for 2–3 minutes, then add the noodles, seasoning to taste and soy sauce. Mix all the ingredients together well and cook for 5 minutes or until the noodles are crispy. Serve immediately garnished as illustrated.

Cook's Tip

Spaghetti in tomato sauce or other shapes of canned pasta can be used in this dish.

Cook's Tip

For chicken chow mein use boneless shredded chicken in place of pork.

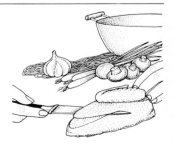

317 | Pasta Bows with Walnuts and Cheese

Preparation time
5 minutes

Cooking time
12–15 minutes

Serves 2

Calories
648 per portion

You will need
175 g / 6 oz pasta bows
1 tablespoon olive oil
1 teaspoon lemon juice

For the garnish
25 g / 1 oz walnut halves, roughly
    chopped
2 teaspoons chopped fresh chives

For the sauce
100 g / 4 oz curd cheese
150 ml / ¼ pint single cream
1 tablespoon grated Parmesan
    cheese
salt and pepper
1–2 tablespoons milk (optional)

Cook the pasta bows in a large pan of boiling salted water for 6–8 minutes until just tender.

Meanwhile, to make the sauce, gently heat the curd cheese until it forms a thick sauce. Stir in the cream, Parmesan cheese and salt and pepper to taste. Heat, stirring, until smooth and creamy. If it seems a little thick add 1–2 tablespoons milk.

Drain the pasta and mix with the oil and lemon juice. Divide between four dishes. Pour over the sauce and serve, sprinkled with walnuts and chives.

Cook's Tip

Pasta is available in a variety of shapes. In Italian, pasta bows are called farfalle. *Other shapes you can try are* fusilli *(twists),* ruoti *(wheels) and* conchiglie *(sea shells).*

318 | Macaroni with Sausage and Tomato Sauce

Preparation time
20 minutes

Cooking time
20 minutes

Serves 4

Calories
394 per portion

You will need
225 g / 8 oz Italian sausages,
    skinned
2 tablespoons olive oil for frying
2 garlic cloves, peeled and
    crushed
2 small onions, peeled and
    roughly chopped
2 small red peppers, cored,
    seeded and cubed
750 g / 1½ lb tomatoes, skinned
    and chopped
2 teaspoons dried oregano
2 tablespoons tomato purée
6 tablespoons Marsala or sherry
salt and pepper
225 g / 8 oz macaroni
25 g / 1 oz butter

Break each sausage into 4 or 5 pieces. Heat the oil and fry the garlic and onions until softened and lightly coloured.

Add the sausages and fry until evenly browned. Add the red peppers, tomatoes, oregano, tomato purée, Marsala or sherry and salt and pepper to taste. Cook gently, uncovered, for 12–15 minutes.

Meanwhile, cook the macaroni in a large pan of salted boiling water for 8–10 minutes until just tender. Drain well and stir in the butter.

Mix together the pasta and sauce and transfer to a warmed serving dish or individual dishes. Serve at once.

Cook's Tip

Prepare the sauce a day ahead. Cool, then cover and chill until the pasta is cooking. Reheat over moderate heat on top of the stove or in a microwave oven.

319 | Tagliatelle alla Carbonara

Preparation time
10–15 minutes

Cooking time
20–25 minutes

Serves 4

Calories
700 per portion

You will need
450 g/1 lb tagliatelle
salt and pepper
100 g/4 oz smoked rindless
 bacon, diced
·2 tablespoons oil or 25 g/1 oz
 butter
2 eggs, lightly beaten
150 ml/¼ pint single cream
2 tablespoons chopped parsley
50 g/2 oz Parmesan cheese,
 grated

Cook the tagliatelle in a large saucepan of boiling salted water for 10–12 minutes until just tender. Drain and place in a serving dish. Keep warm.

Fry the bacon in the oil or butter until crispy, reduce the heat, then add the eggs, cream, parsley, seasoning to taste and half of the Parmesan. Heat gently, without boiling, stirring. Pour the sauce over the pasta, then sprinkle the remaining Parmesan cheese on top and serve immediately.

320 | Tagliatelle with Blue Cheese Sauce

Preparation time
5 minutes

Cooking time
15–20 minutes

Serves 4

Calories
665 per portion

You will need
450 g/1 lb green tagliatelle
salt and pepper
300 ml/½ pint single cream
100 g/4 oz Danish Blue cheese
50 g/2 oz chopped walnuts

Cook the tagliatelle in a large saucepan of boiling salted water for 10–12 minutes until just tender. Drain and place in a serving dish. Keep warm. In a saucepan, over a very low heat, heat the cream. Crumble the Danish Blue with your fingers and add to the cream. Add the chopped walnuts and season well.

Heat until the cheese has melted and the sauce is hot – do not let the sauce boil or it will curdle. Pour the sauce over the tagliatelle and serve immediately.

Cook's Tip

For a really quick and easy pasta dish, stir 100 g/4 oz cream cheese with garlic and herbs into the hot drained pasta.

Cook's Tip

Fresh, chilled pasta is available from many supermarkets and delicatessens. Cook for 3–5 minutes according to type.

321 | Spinach Noodles

Preparation time
10 minutes

Cooking time
15 minutes

Serves 2–3

Calories
780 520 per portion

You will need
225 g/8 oz noodles
1 onion, chopped
50 g/2 oz butter
225 g/8 oz spinach, chopped
150 ml/¼ pint natural yogurt
100 g/4 oz low-fat soft cheese (for
   example Shape cheese)
1 teaspoon lemon juice
salt and freshly ground black
   pepper
¼ teaspoon grated nutmeg

Cook the noodles in boiling salted water for about 12 minutes until tender.

Meanwhile, cook the onion in the butter until soft, but not browned. Add the spinach and continue to cook for 2–3 minutes. Stir in the yogurt, cheese, lemon juice, seasoning and nutmeg and stir over a low heat without boiling. Drain the noodles and add to the hot spinach sauce; toss well then serve immediately.

322 | Pasta with Ratatouille Sauce

Preparation time
15 20 minutes

Cooking time
35 minutes

Serves 4–6

Calories
500 335 per portion

You will need
1 large onion, chopped
1 clove garlic, crushed
450 g/1 lb courgettes, sliced
1 large aubergine, diced
1 green pepper, deseeded and
   diced
450 g/1 lb tomatoes, peeled and
   chopped
1 tablespoon chopped oregano or
   basil
salt and pepper
450 g/1 lb pasta (spaghetti,
   noodles, etc)
1 tablespoon chopped parsley
grated Parmesan cheese to serve

Put all the ingredients, except the pasta, parsley and cheese in a large saucepan. Add enough water to cover vegetables and cook gently for 30 minutes until the vegetables are tender and the juices have thickened slightly, stirring occasionally.

Meanwhile, cook the pasta in a large saucepan in plenty of boiling salted water until just tender (about 5 minutes for freshly made pasta and 15 minutes for dried). Drain and place in a warmed serving dish.

Taste and adjust the seasoning of the sauce, then pour over the pasta. Top with the parsley and grated Parmesan cheese. Serve hot.

Cook's Tip

For special occasions, use a full-fat soft cheese such as Roulé, which is made with a blend of garlic and fine herbs.

Cook's Tip

This dish makes a filling main course. It can also be served cold as a starter, without the pasta. Served in vols-au-vent, it makes an attractive party snack (see Recipe 181 for instructions on cooking vols-au-vent).

323 | Crispy Fried Noodles

Preparation time
15 minutes

Cooking time
about 15 minutes

Serves 4—6

Calories
500—330 per portion

You will need
3 celery sticks
100 g/4 oz spinach leaves, washed
450 g/1 lb egg noodles
salt
1 tablespoon oil
1 garlic clove, sliced
5 cm/2 inch piece root ginger, peeled and finely chopped
3 spring onions, chopped
100 g/4 oz lean pork, sliced
100 g/4 oz boned chicken breast meat, shredded
1 tablespoon soy sauce
1 tablespoon dry sherry
50 g/2 oz peeled prawns

Slice the celery sticks diagonally and shred the spinach leaves.

Cook the noodles in boiling salted water according to the packet instructions until just tender; do not overcook. Drain and rinse with cold water.

Heat the oil in a wok or deep frying pan, add the garlic, ginger and spring onions and fry for 1 minute. Add the pork and chicken and stir-fry for 2 minutes. Add the noodles and remaining ingredients and cook for 3 minutes.

Pile on to a warmed serving dish and serve at once.

324 | Dan-Dan Noodles

Preparation time
15 minutes

Cooking time
about 20 minutes

Serves 4

Calories
500 per portion

You will need
450 g/1 lb noodles
salt
2 tablespoons tahini or sesame seed paste
6 spring onions, chopped
2 garlic cloves, crushed
5 cm/2 inch piece root ginger, peeled and finely chopped
1 tablespoon soy sauce
2 teaspoons red wine vinegar
900 ml/1½ pints beef or chicken stock
2 teaspoons hot pepper oil (see Cook's Tip – optional)

Cook the noodles in boiling salted water according to the packet instructions, until just tender. Drain and keep hot.

Blend the sesame seed paste with 4 tablespoons water and place in a pan, together with the remaining ingredients, except the stock and pepper oil. Cook over a moderate heat, stirring frequently, for about 5 minutes.

Meanwhile, bring the stock to the boil and simmer for 2 minutes. Divide the noodles and hot sauce between 4 individual soup bowls. Spoon over the hot stock and top with the hot pepper oil, if using. Serve at once.

Cook's Tip

There are many different kinds of soy sauce available, both light and dark – the common dark variety is the one used mainly for cooking (unless otherwise stated) while the light kind is generally used as an accompaniment.

Cook's Tip

Hot pepper oil is a hot tasting oil made from hot chilli peppers. It should be used sparingly.

325 | *Nutty Ribbon Pasta*

Preparation time
5 minutes

Cooking time
14 18 minutes

Serves 4

Calories
730 per portion

You will need
350 g/12 oz tagliarini or tagliatelli
300 ml/½ pint single cream
2 large egg yolks
freshly ground black pepper
4 sprigs fresh dill, chopped
175 g/6 oz salted peanuts, roughly
　chopped
chopped fresh dill, to garnish

Cook the pasta in boiling salted water for about 12–15 minutes, until tender but not soft. Meanwhile, combine the cream, egg yolks, black pepper and dill in a bowl. Stir in the peanuts. Drain the pasta and return it to the pan, then immediately add the cream mixture. Heat gently for 2–3 minutes, stirring to mix thoroughly. Serve immediately.

326 | *Pasta al Pomodoro*

Preparation time
10 minutes

Cooking time
25 minutes

Serves 2

Calories
430 per portion

You will need
175 g/6 oz pasta bows
salt and freshly ground black
　pepper
2 tablespoons grated Parmesan or
　other cheese

For the sauce
1 small onion, finely chopped
100 g/4 oz mushrooms, sliced
1 teaspoon sunflower oil
1 (397-g/14-oz) can tomatoes
1 tablespoon chopped fresh basil
　(optional)
salt and pepper

Cook the pasta bows in a large pan of boiling salted water for 10–12 minutes. Drain and keep warm. Meanwhile, sauté the onion and mushrooms in the oil for 5 minutes, stir in the tomatoes and cook gently for 15 minutes to reduce the sauce. Add the basil, if using, and simmer for a further 5 minutes. Season to taste and serve with the pasta bows, topped with Parmesan and freshly ground black pepper.

Cook's Tip

Well known for its affinity with fish, dill deserves to be more widely used. It is especially delicious with eggs, so complements the eggs in this sauce. A herb omelette is another dish in which to use fresh dill.

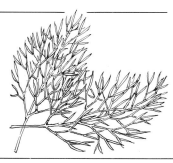

Cook's Tip

This simple dish is ideal for children, who will enjoy it even more if it is made with tri-coloured pasta – plain, spinach and tomato-flavoured.

327 | *Spinach Lasagne*

Preparation time
20 minutes

Cooking time
45 minutes

Oven temperature
200 C, 400 F, gas 6

Serves 4

Calories
530 per portion

You will need
salt and pepper
2 (225-g/8-oz) packets frozen
  spinach, defrosted and drained
$\frac{1}{4}$ teaspoon grated nutmeg
25 g/1 oz pecan nuts, chopped
40 g/1$\frac{1}{2}$ oz butter
40 g/1$\frac{1}{2}$ oz plain flour
600 ml/1 pint milk
200 g/7 oz mature Cheddar
  cheese, grated
$\frac{1}{2}$ teaspoon prepared English
  mustard
175 g/6 oz wholewheat lasagne,
  cooked
paprika to garnish

Season the spinach, add the nutmeg and stir in the nuts. Melt the butter in a saucepan over a low heat, then add the flour. Cook for 2 minutes, stirring. Gradually add the milk and bring the sauce to the boil, stirring constantly. Simmer gently for 2–3 minutes. Add 175 g/6 oz of the cheese and season with salt, pepper and mustard. Layer the spinach and lasagne in an ovenproof dish. Top with the sauce and sprinkle with the reserved cheese. Bake near the top of a moderately hot oven for 20–30 minutes until piping hot and brown on top.

Sprinkle with paprika and serve immediately.

328 | *Courgette and Cauliflower Macaroni*

Preparation time
30 minutes

Cooking time
20 minutes

Serves 4

Calories
605 per portion

You will need
225 g/8 oz macaroni
salt
225 g/8 oz cauliflower, broken into
  small florets
225 g/8 oz courgettes, finely
  chopped

For the sauce
450 ml/$\frac{3}{4}$ pint milk
50 g/2 oz plain flour
50 g/2 oz margarine, cut up
175 g/6 oz Cheddar cheese, grated
salt and pepper
paprika to garnish (optional)

Cook the macaroni in boiling salted water for 15 minutes, then drain. Cook the cauliflower in salted boiling water for 5 minutes, adding courgettes for the final 2 minutes. Drain well and reserve 150 ml/$\frac{1}{4}$ pint of the water. Place the vegetables and macaroni in an ovenproof dish.

Whisk the milk, flour and margarine with the reserved vegetable water in a pan over low heat until boiling and thickened. Stir in most of the cheese with seasoning to taste. Pour over the macaroni, sprinkle with the remaining cheese and a little paprika (if used). Brown under a moderate grill, then serve piping hot.

Cook's Tip

A roasting tin is the best container to use for cooking lasagne as it gives the pasta sheets plenty of room. When cooked, lift each sheet from the water separately with a fish slice and place in a pan or bowl of warm water. Keep the lasagne sheets in the warm water until needed but no longer than necessary, as they can absorb too much water. No-need-to-precook lasagne works very well too, provided there is plenty of sauce.

Cook's Tip

Chop a few sprigs of parsley and stir into the vegetable and macaroni mixture for additional flavour.

329 | *Corsican Cannelloni*

Preparation time
15 minutes

Cooking time
55 minutes

Oven temperature
180C, 350F, gas 4

Serves 4

Calories
275 per portion

You will need
750 ml/1¼ pints boiling water
½ teaspoon vegetable oil
8 sheets 'No-need-to-precook' lasagne verde
225 g/8 oz frozen Ratatouille mix
100 g/4 oz frozen broad beans
2 teaspoons chopped fresh mixed herbs
freshly ground black pepper
1 (397-g/14-oz) can chopped tomatoes
100 g/4 oz mature Cheddar cheese, grated to serve

Pour the boiling water into a suitably shaped large shallow ovenproof dish. Add a few drops of oil. Slide the sheets of lasagne into the dish and leave for 4–5 minutes to soften. Cook the ratatouille and beans in boiling water in a medium saucepan for about 10 minutes or until cooked. Drain well. Add the herbs and freshly ground black pepper to taste.

Lift out the lasagne sheets from the water and drain. Spread out on a clean working surface or large board. Divide the vegetable filling between the lasagne then roll up the strips. Place the cannelloni in a shallow oven-proof dish and spoon over the tomatoes. Cook in a moderate oven for 30 minutes. To serve, sprinkle with grated cheese and place under a preheated hot grill until brown.

330 | *Tropical Salad*

Preparation time
15 minutes

Cooking time
5 minutes

Serves 4

Calories
475 per portion

You will need
275 g/10 oz long-grain brown rice, cooked
50 g/2 oz dried coconut flakes
½ cucumber, unpeeled and cut into 1-cm/½-in cubes
1 small ripe pineapple, peeled, cored and cut into 2.5-cm/1-in pieces
1 tablespoon olive oil
1 teaspoon lemon juice
salt and pepper
2 teaspoons olive oil for shallow frying
50 g/2 oz whole blanched almonds
pineapple leaves to garnish

Put the rice, coconut, cucumber and pineapple into a bowl. Add the oil and lemon juice and a little salt and pepper, taste and adjust the seasoning if necessary. Spoon the salad into a serving dish.

Heat the 2 teaspoons of oil in a small pan and quickly fry the almonds until golden brown. Scatter the almonds over the salad and garnish with the pineapple leaves.

Freezer Tip

Cover the cannelloni with foil and freeze for up to 3 months. Reheat from frozen in a moderate oven (180C, 350F, gas 4) for about 30 minutes, then top with the cheese and place under a hot grill to brown.

Cook's Tip

To remove the centre core from a slice of pineapple, stamp out with a small plain pastry cutter.

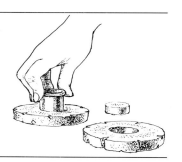

331 | *Marrow Lasagne*

Preparation time
35 minutes

Cooking time
50 minutes

Oven temperature
200 C, 400 F, gas 6

Serves 6

Calories
300 per portion

You will need
1 kg/2 lb whole marrow or squash
2 tablespoons olive oil
1 large onion, chopped
4–6 cardamom pods
2 teaspoons black peppercorns
1 teaspoon caster sugar
salt
225 g/8 oz green lasagne, cooked
225 g/8 oz small round goats'
  cheese, thinly sliced
2 tablespoons cornflour
2 tablespoons milk
450 ml/¾ pint natural yogurt
2 tablespoons grated Parmesan
  cheese

Scoop out the centre of the marrow, or squash, peel and slice the flesh. Cook in boiling water for 15 minutes, or until soft. Drain and mash coarsely.

Heat 1 tablespoon oil in a large pan and cook the onion until soft. Extract the seeds from the cardamom pods and crush with the peppercorns. Stir the ground spices, onion and sugar into the marrow and season. Brush the remaining oil over the base of a 20 × 28-cm/ 8 × 11-in ovenproof dish. Layer the lasagne, marrow and goats' cheese in the dish, ending with a last layer of lasagne.

Mix the cornflour, milk and yogurt in a saucepan. Bring gently to the boil, stirring, and cook for 2–3 minutes. Pour over the lasagne and sprinkle with Parmesan. Bake in a moderately hot oven for about 35 minutes.

Cook's Tip

Green or white cardamom pods have lots of tiny black seeds inside, which should be shiny and highly aromatic. Buy from Indian and Pakistani food stores.

332 | *Vegetable Lasagne*

Preparation time
10 minutes

Cooking time
1½ hours

Oven temperature
180 C, 350 F, gas 4

Serves 4

Calories
800 per portion using
cream cheese
520 per portion using
curd cheese

You will need
2 tablespoons oil
225 g/8 oz French beans, chopped
1 leek or onion, thinly sliced
salt and pepper
1 (397-g/14-oz) can tomatoes
100 g/4 oz lentils
300 ml/½ pint water
pinch of oregano
450 g/1 lb cream or curd cheese
2 eggs, beaten
100 g/4 oz lasagne, cooked
2 tablespoons chopped parsley
2 tablespoons grated Parmesan
  cheese

Heat the oil in a saucepan and fry the beans and leek or onion for 5 minutes. Season to taste. Add the tomatoes, lentils, water and oregano and bring to the boil. Simmer for about 30 minutes or until the lentils are tender.

Mix together the cream or curd cheese and the eggs. Spread half the vegetable mixture in a 1.15-litre/2-pint ovenproof dish and cover with one-third of the lasagne. Spread half the cheese mixture over, then cover with another layer of lasagne. Make a layer with the remaining vegetable mixture, cover with remaining lasagne and finally the remaining cheese mixture. Sprinkle over the Parmesan and bake for 40 minutes.

Cook's Tip

A very popular herb in Italy, oregano, like basil, perfectly complements the flavour of tomatoes. Aubergines and courgettes are also enhanced by its pronounced, aromatic flavour.

333 | Spinach Noodle Salad

Preparation time
5 minutes, plus cooling

Cooking time
15 minutes

Serves 6

Calories
252 per portion

You will need
225 g / 8 oz green spinach noodles
salt
150 ml / ¼ pint French dressing
small garlic clove, crushed
100 g / 4 oz mushrooms, wiped and thinly sliced
100 g / 4 oz cooked ham, thinly sliced
25 g / 1 oz Parmesan cheese, grated

Cook the noodles in a large pan of boiling salted water for 10–15 minutes until just tender. Drain.

Pour the French dressing into a large bowl and add the garlic and mushrooms and toss well. Add the noodles while still warm and toss again.

Cut the ham into ribbons about the same width as the noodles, add to the salad and toss together.

To serve, transfer to a large bowl and sprinkle with the grated Parmesan cheese.

334 | Pasta, Cucumber and Radish Salad

Preparation time
25 minutes

Serves 4

Calories
163 per portion

You will need
100 g / 4 oz pasta shapes, such as shells, bows or spirals
salt
175 g / 6 oz radishes, sliced
½ cucumber, diced
150 ml / ¼ pint soured cream
pepper
1 Cos lettuce, washed
2 spring onions, finely chopped, to garnish

Cook the pasta in a large pan of boiling salted water for 10 minutes or until just tender. Rinse with cold water and drain.

Put the radishes and cucumber into a bowl and add the pasta.

Stir in the soured cream, adding plenty of black pepper and a little salt. Toss to coat thoroughly.

Arrange the lettuce leaves on a serving dish and spoon the salad into them. Serve, garnished with spring onions.

Cook's Tip

Green spinach noodles get their colour, as the name implies, from the spinach added to the pasta dough. For variety, you can also use red noodles made from beetroots or yellow ones coloured with saffron.

Cook's Tip

This salad makes a complete light meal if served with hot garlic and herb bread. Combine 75 g / 3 oz butter with 3 crushed garlic cloves and 2 tablespoons finely chopped fresh herbs. Slice a French stick at 5 cm / 2 inch intervals without cutting all the way through. Spread the butter mixture in the slashes, then wrap the loaf in foil and bake for 10 minutes at 220C, 425F, Gas 7.

335 | Stuffed Pasta Shells

Preparation time
15 minutes, plus time to cool the pasta

Cooking time
10–12 minutes

Serves 4

Calories
525 per portion

You will need
1 avocado, peeled and diced
1 tablespoon lemon juice
1 (198-g 7-oz) can tuna, drained and flaked
100 g/4 oz cottage cheese
1 onion, chopped
1 green pepper, deseeded and chopped
2 tablespoons mayonnaise
salt and pepper
225 g/8 oz large pasta shells
crisp lettuce to serve

Brush or dip the avocado in the lemon juice, then mix with the tuna, cottage cheese, onion, pepper and mayonnaise in a bowl, and season well.

Cook the pasta shells in a large saucepan of boiling salted water for 10–12 minutes until just tender. Drain and leave to cool. Stuff the shells with the filling and serve on a bed of crisp lettuce. This dish can be served either as a starter or a light lunch.

336 | Pasta Salad

Preparation time
15 minutes, plus time to cool the pasta

Cooking time
10–12 minutes

Serves 4

Calories
495 per portion

You will need
225 g/8 oz pasta bows
salt and pepper
bunch of spring onions, chopped
1 red pepper, deseeded and chopped
1 green pepper, deseeded and chopped
2 celery sticks, sliced
1 tablespoon chopped parsley
150 ml/$\frac{1}{4}$ pint natural yogurt
150 ml/$\frac{1}{4}$ pint mayonnaise
1 teaspoon honey
$\frac{1}{4}$ teaspoon freshly grated nutmeg

Cook the pasta bows in a large saucepan of boiling salted water for 10–12 minutes until just tender. Drain and leave to cool.

In a large mixing bowl, combine all the salad ingredients. Add the pasta. Mix together the yogurt, mayonnaise, honey and nutmeg. Transfer the salad to a serving bowl, and pour over the dressing. Serve with crisp lettuce leaves.

Cook's Tip

These stuffed pasta shells can be served as a tasty first course, with a light tomato dressing. Arrange the shells on individual plates. Stir 1 tablespoon tomato purée and a generous dash of Worcestershire sauce into 150 ml/$\frac{1}{4}$ pint soured cream. Season to taste with garlic salt and pepper. Spoon this dressing over the pasta shells and serve with crisp toast or French bread.

Cook's Tip

Add cooked or canned fish or meat to this salad for a more substantial lunch or supper dish. If adding fish use small pasta shells instead of bows.

DESSERTS AND PUDDINGS

No matter how simple, a pudding is still something of a treat, whether it's hot Rhubarb Crumble for the family or classy Champagne Water Ice to end a special dinner party. The beauty of most desserts is that they can be prepared in advance, and if necessary kept warm, until you are ready to serve. The choice is enormous: hot puddings are usually thought of as comforting winter fare, and there's certainly a welcoming warmth to Apple and Apricot Charlotte, Gourmet Bread and Butter Pudding or Pineapple Upside Down Pudding. As well as old favourites like these, this chapter includes some tempting ideas for enlivening family meals, such as Doughnut Spirals in Syrup and Baked Ginger Pudding with Lemon Sauce. Hot puddings can be sophisticated too: none of your guests will be able to resist Pears Brûlée or Black Cherry Clafouti.

Many delicious desserts are based on fruit. It's best to use fruits in season to get the best quality and value. In the colder months, make Autumnal Pudding, Orchard Tart and Apple Strudel — irresistible with custard, cream or fromage frais. When summer comes, make the most of soft fruits with Fruit Baskets, Chocolate Fondue with Fresh Fruit and Summer Pudding. Cold desserts come into their own now, and you'll find some unusually refreshing ideas here: try Indian Ice Cream and Bean and Kiwi Fool or Amaretto Ice Bombe.

No selection of desserts would be complete without some chocolate-based recipes: this chapter offers a delectable choice, including scrumptious Overnight Chocolate Cake. With these and other inspiring ideas, you'll find a dessert for every occasion.

337 | Quick Lemon Mousse

Preparation time
10 minutes, plus 1
hour to chill

Cooking time
2–3 minutes

Serves 4

Calories
250 per portion

You will need
2 lemons
1 lemon jelly
150 ml/¼ pint water
1 (410-g/14.5-oz) can
  evaporated milk
angelica to decorate

Reserve four slices of lemon for decoration. Grate the rind from one lemon and extract the juice from both. Melt the jelly in the water over a gentle heat. Remove the pan from the heat, add the lemon rind and juice. Pour into a small bowl and leave to cool.

Whisk the evaporated milk until thick and doubled in volume. Carefully fold in the jelly mixture and pour into a large glass dish. Chill for about an hour or until set. Decorate with the lemon slices and pieces of angelica.

338 | Citrus Syllabub

Preparation time
15 minutes, plus 1
hour to marinate and 1
hour to chill

Serves 6

Calories
290 per portion

You will need
grated rind and juice of 1 orange
grated rind and juice of 1 lemon
4 tablespoons sweet white wine
75 g/3 oz caster sugar
300 ml/½ pint double cream,
  whipped

Place the fruit rinds and juices in a bowl with the wine and marinate for at least 1 hour. Strain the liquid through a fine sieve, reserving a few strands of rind for decoration.

Gently fold the strained liquid and sugar into the cream. Spoon into six glass serving dishes. Decorate with the citrus rind and chill for an hour before serving. Serve with brandy snaps or sweet biscuits of your choice.

Freezer Tip

Double or whipping cream can be frozen in its whipped state. Spoon the whipped cream into a plastic container and label with the quantity of unwhipped cream. Defrost and use as required.

Cook's Tip

Syllabub makes a luscious topping for a traditional trifle. Swirl it over the top of the custard, or it can even be used instead of the custard.

339 | *Orange Russe*

Preparation time
30 minutes, plus several
hours to set

Serves 6

Calories
350 per portion

You will need
about 21 sponge fingers
grated rind and juice of 2 oranges
1 teaspoon lemon juice
2 teaspoons agar-agar or 3
   teaspoons powdered gelatine
150 g/5 oz Blue Brie cheese
100 g/4 oz curd cheese
50 g/2 oz caster sugar
2 egg whites
150 ml/¼ pint whipping cream
few strips of blanched orange rind
   to decorate

Base-line an 18-cm/7-in loose-bottomed cake tin. Trim the sponge fingers to 7.5 cm/3 in lengths. Stand the fingers, trimmed side down and sugar side out, around the edge of the tin (see Cook's Tip).

Heat the orange and lemon juice to just below boiling, add the agar-agar and stir until dissolved. Set aside to cool. Thinly de-rind the Blue Brie. Beat with the curd cheese, sugar and orange rind until smooth. Gradually add the cooled gelatine mixture. Leave until on the point of setting.

Whisk the egg whites until stiff but not dry, then whip the cream until it holds its shape. Fold just over half the cream into the setting cheese mixture, then add the egg whites. Pour into the biscuit-lined tin and level the surface. Refrigerate until set.

Remove from the tin to serve and decorate with the reserved cream and strips of blanched orange rind.

340 | *St Clement's Cheesecake*

Preparation time
30 minutes, plus 1½
hours to chill

Cooking time
5 minutes

Serves 8—10

Calories
390 315 per portion

You will need
75 g/3 oz unsalted butter
175 g/6 oz digestive or gingernut
   biscuits, crushed

For the filling
2 eggs, separated
50 g/2 oz caster sugar
350 g/12 oz low-fat cream cheese,
   lightly creamed
150 ml/¼ pint whipping cream,
   lightly whipped
1 (135-g/4¾-oz) packet lemon jelly
200 ml/7 fl oz boiling water

To decorate
1 large peeled orange, segmented
1 small peeled lemon, segmented
sprig of fresh mint

Lightly grease a 20-cm/8-in loose-bottomed cake tin. Melt the butter in a saucepan, mix in the crushed biscuits and press on to the base of the tin. Chill. Beat the egg yolks and sugar together until very thick and pale. Fold in the cheese and cream. Dissolve the jelly in the boiling water. Cool, then stir into the cheese mixture. Whisk the egg whites stiffly, and fold into the mixture. Pour over the biscuit base and chill until firm.

Remove the cheesecake from the tin and decorate as shown.

Cook's Tip

If the sponge fingers slither sideways in the tin, stand them upright and secure each to the tin with a tiny knob of butter.

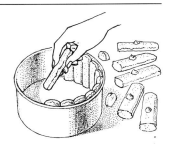

Cook's Tip

If a loose-bottomed tin is not available, grease and line a 20-cm/8-in deep cake tin and place double thickness foil strips in a cross to lift out set cheesecake.

341 | Apricot and Orange Glories

Preparation time
20 minutes, plus 2 hours to set

Serves 4

Calories
245 per portion

You will need
2 (185-g 6½-oz) cans apricot halves in fruit juice
1 orange jelly tablet (see Cook's Tip)
150 ml ¼ pint boiling water
300 ml ½ pint natural yogurt
2 tablespoons clear honey
4 fresh cherries with stalks

Drain the juice from the apricots and make up to 300 ml/½ pint with water. Reserve four apricot halves and slice the remainder. Dissolve the jelly tablet in the boiling water then stir in the fruit juice. Pour into a shallow container and chill until set.

Turn the jelly out on to a wet work surface and with a wet knife chop it into small dice. Mix the yogurt and honey together, then layer the jelly, yogurt and apricot slices in four individual glass dishes. Top each with an apricot half, hollow side up and holding a cherry as a final touch.

342 | Fruit Baskets

Preparation time
30 minutes, plus 1½ 2 hours to stand

Cooking time
10 minutes

Oven temperature
180 C, 350 F, gas 4

Serves 4

Calories
315 per portion

You will need
100 g/4 oz plain flour
100 g/4 oz icing sugar
3 egg whites
few drops of orange essence
25 g/1 oz flaked almonds
1 ripe pear, cored and sliced
a little lemon juice

For the sauce
2 slices fresh pineapple, peeled, cored and chopped
120 ml/4 fl oz pineapple juice
1 2 drops yellow food colouring
120 ml/4 fl oz natural yogurt

Filling and decoration
350 g/12 oz seasonal fruit
1 tablespoon icing sugar

Sift the flour and icing sugar, then beat in the egg whites until smooth. Stand for 1–2 hours. Stir in the essence and almonds. Mark four 18-cm/7-in circles on baking trays lined with non-stick baking parchment. Spread the batter in the marked circles. Cook in a moderate oven for 8 minutes until pale golden. Allow to cool for about a minute, then ease off the baking trays with a palette knife and mould (see Cook's Tip). Simmer the pineapple, juice and colouring for 2 minutes then blend in the liquidiser. Chill then mix in the yogurt. Place each basket on a pool of pineapple sauce. Fill and decorate the biscuit baskets as shown.

Cook's Tip

Vegetarian table jelly crystals are available in 100 g/3½ oz tubs. To use, place the powdered crystals in a large bowl, pour in 200 ml/⅓ pint boiling water, stir briskly, then add the fruit juice. Proceed as in the recipe above.

Cook's Tip

Shaping the biscuits: cut a fine slice off 4 oranges, so they stand well. Grease with oil. Carefully slide a biscuit off the tray and lift over an orange. Press gently and flute the edges. Lift off when cold.

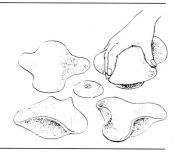

343 | Blackcurrant Kissel

Preparation time
5 minutes

Cooking time
15 minutes

Serves 4

Calories
231 per portion

You will need
750 g / 1½ lb blackcurrants,
   removed from stems, thawed if
   frozen
75 g / 3 oz soft light brown sugar
4 tablespoons red wine
juice and grated rind of ½ orange
1 tablespoon arrowroot
2 tablespoons caster sugar
4 tablespoons blanched almonds
whipped cream to serve

Cook the blackcurrants with the sugar, wine and orange juice and rind over low heat for 8–10 minutes, or until just tender.

Stir a little of the juice from the fruit into the arrowroot to make a smooth paste. Stir this into the fruit and simmer gently, stirring constantly for 2 minutes until the mixture thickens.

Pour the kissel into a heatproof serving dish and sprinkle with the caster sugar.

Toast the almonds on a baking sheet under a hot grill for 4 minutes, shaking occasionally to brown them evenly.

Decorate the kissel with the almonds. Serve at once or cover and chill. Serve with whipped cream.

344 | Strawberries in Butterscotch Sauce

Preparation time
5 minutes

Cooking time
10 minutes

Serves 4

Calories
433 per portion

You will need
750 g / 1½ lb fresh strawberries,
   hulled

For the sauce
150 g / 5 oz soft light brown sugar
150 g / 5 oz golden syrup
125 ml / 4 fl oz double cream
3–4 drops vanilla essence

To make the sauce, heat the sugar and syrup over a low heat, stirring occasionally, until the sugar has dissolved. Cook for a further 5 minutes.

Remove from the heat and stir in the cream and vanilla essence. Beat for 2 minutes, until the sauce is smooth and glossy.

Serve the strawberries with the sauce, hot or cold.

Cook's Tip

Sprinkling the top of the kissel with caster sugar prevents a skin from forming on the surface. Stir the sugar in before serving.

Cook's Tip

The sauce can be made a day ahead and stored in the refrigerator. If you do this, however, serve the sauce at room temperature because it doesn't reheat well.

345 | Fresh Fruit Pavlova

Preparation time
30 minutes

Cooking time
1 hour

Oven temperature
150 C, 300 F, gas 2

Serves 6

Calories
410 per portion

You will need
3 egg whites
175 g / 6 oz caster sugar
1 teaspoon cornflour
1 teaspoon vinegar
½ teaspoon vanilla essence

For the filling
300 ml / ½ pint double cream
2 bananas, sliced and brushed
   with lemon juice
2 kiwi fruits, peeled and sliced
100 g / 4 oz green grapes, halved
   and deseeded
2 oranges, peeled and segmented

Mark a 20-cm/8-in circle on a piece of non-stick baking parchment and place on a baking tray. Whisk the egg whites until they stand in stiff peaks. Gradually whisk in half the sugar. Fold in the remaining sugar with the cornflour, vinegar and vanilla. Spoon or pipe the meringue on to the marked circle and bake in the centre of a cool oven for 1 hour. Leave to cool in oven. Remove paper and place on a plate.

Whip the cream until stiff. Spoon over the pavlova base, arrange the prepared fruit on top and chill before serving.

346 | Meringues with Chocolate Sauce

Preparation time
15 minutes

Cooking time
2½ hours

Oven temperature
110 C, 225 F, gas ¼

Serves 6

Calories
265 per portion

You will need
4 egg whites
225 g / 8 oz caster sugar

For the chocolate sauce
150 ml / ¼ pint water
50 g / 2 oz sugar
4 tablespoons golden syrup
4 tablespoons cocoa powder

Grease three baking trays thoroughly or line with non-stick baking parchment. Whisk the egg whites until stiff and standing in peaks. Add the sugar, a tablespoon at a time, whisking continuously. Fit a piping bag with a large star nozzle and fill the bag with the meringue mixture.

Pipe 36 rosettes on to the baking trays or spoon on if preferred. Bake in a very cool oven for 2½ hours or until the meringues are crisp. Remove from the oven and cool on a wire rack.

To make the chocolate sauce, put all the ingredients into a pan and heat very gently. Bring to the boil, reduce the heat and cook for 1 minute, stirring all the time. Spoon over the meringues just before serving.

Cook's Tip

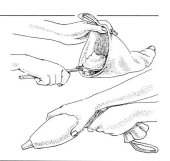

To pipe meringue, use a large piping bag fitted with a large plain nozzle.

Microwave Tip

To make the chocolate sauce in the microwave, put all the ingredients in a measuring jug and microwave on full power for 5 minutes, stirring once.

347 | Indian Ice Cream with Pistachios

Preparation time
10 minutes, plus 3–4 hours freezing time

Cooking time
45 minutes

Serves 6–8

Calories
370–280 per portion

You will need
300 ml/½ pint double cream
300 ml/½ pint milk
1 (400-g/14-oz) can condensed milk
1 tablespoon clear honey
2 tablespoons chopped pistachios
2 teaspoons rose water
green food colouring (optional)

Heat the cream, milk, condensed milk and honey together in a heavy-based pan. Bring gently to the boil, stirring constantly, then simmer for 45 minutes over a very low heat. Remove from the heat, sprinkle in the pistachios and rose water, then add a little food colouring if liked. Allow to cool.

Pour the mixture into a shallow 900-ml/1½-pint freezer container or 6–8 kulfi moulds and freeze for 3–4 hours. Remove from the freezer and leave to stand at room temperature for 20–30 minutes to soften.

To serve, turn out of the kulfi moulds (see Cook's Tip) or cut into squares.

348 | Chinese Fruit Salad

Preparation time
20–25 minutes, plus 2 hours chilling time

Serves 4

Calories
100–200 per portion

You will need
1 large honeydew melon
4–5 types fresh or canned fruit, with the syrup from the can (see Cook's Tip)

Cut the honeydew melon in half and scoop out and discard the seeds. Cut the flesh into small chunks and reserve the shell.

Prepare the other fruit, leaving it whole if small, otherwise separating it into segments or cutting it into small chunks as with the melon.

Mix the pieces of melon with the fruit and canned syrup. Pack the melon shell with this mixture, then cover tightly with cling film. Chill for at least 2 hours in the refrigerator before serving.

Cook's Tip

This recipe calls for the inclusion of condensed milk, and to make it even richer, double cream. Traditionally, this Indian ice cream would be served in kulfi moulds, which are small and conical in shape and available from most specialist cook shops. To turn out the ice cream, briefly dip the kulfi mould, upside down, in warm water, then invert on to a serving dish.

Cook's Tip

Choose from kiwi fruit, lychees, strawberries, pineapple, pears, apples, peaches, grapes, cherries and tangerines. For the best effect you should have at least 4 different types of fruit.

349 | Marbled Gooseberry Fool

Preparation time
12 minutes, plus
cooling and chilling

Cooking time
30 minutes

Serves 6

Calories
324 per portion

You will need
750 g / 1½ lb gooseberries,
  thawed if frozen, topped and
  tailed
175 g / 6 oz caster sugar
1 teaspoon powdered gelatine
2 tablespoons water
150 ml / ¼ pint whipping cream
1 × 425-g / 15-oz can custard
a few drops green food colouring
  (optional)

Put the gooseberries and sugar in a pan and heat gently until the sugar has dissolved. Simmer, uncovered, until the fruit forms a thick pulp, stirring occasionally.

Purée the mixture in a liquidizer or food processor, then sieve to remove the seeds. Leave to cool for 30 minutes.

Meanwhile, sprinkle the gelatine over the water in a heatproof basin and leave to soften for 5 minutes. Stand the basin in a pan of hot water until the gelatine has dissolved.

Whip the cream until it forms soft peaks. Stir in the cool, but still liquid, gelatine. Lightly fold in the custard.

Tint the gooseberry purée with green colouring if liked. Put alternate spoonfuls of the gooseberry purée and custard mixture into individual glasses, finishing with the custard. Chill for at least 1 hour before serving.

Cook's Tip

To make the attractive 'marbled' effect, before chilling push the handle of a teaspoon from the top to the base at 2.5 cm / 1 inch intervals all around each serving glass.

350 | Grapefruit Mousse

Preparation time
25 minutes, plus
chilling and setting

Cooking time
3 minutes

Serves 6

Calories
148 per portion

You will need
4 eggs, separated
100 g / 4 oz caster sugar
3 tablespoons cold water
3 teaspoons powdered gelatine
finely grated rind of 1 grapefruit
150 ml / ¼ pint freshly squeezed
  grapefruit juice

For the decoration
shredded grapefruit rind
fresh mint sprigs

Whisk egg yolks and sugar in a bowl until the mixture is light and fluffy.

Put the water into a heatproof bowl. Sprinkle the gelatine over the water and leave to soften for 5 minutes. Stand the bowl in a pan of gently simmering water until the gelatine dissolves. Remove from the heat. Stir in the grapefruit rind and juice, then leave to cool but not set.

Add the gelatine mixture in a thin steady stream to the egg and sugar mixture, whisking constantly. Chill for 10 minutes or until it is just beginning to set around the edges.

Whisk the egg whites until stiff, then fold into the grapefruit mixture. Whisk very lightly for a few seconds to give a smooth mixture.

Spoon the mixture into individual glass dishes and leave to set for several hours. To serve, decorate with grapefruit rind and mint.

Cook's Tip

When grating the grapefruit rind be careful to grate only the outer part known as the zest; this contains the best flavour. If you push too hard, you will include the white pith which will give a bitter taste to the mousse.

351 | Frozen Raspberry Delight

Preparation time
10 minutes, plus 2
hours to freeze

Serves 4

Calories
595 per portion

You will need
1 Swiss roll
3 tablespoons brandy
300 ml/½ pint raspberry yogurt
100 g/4 oz fresh or frozen
  raspberries, hulled or defrosted
300 ml/½ pint double or whipping
  cream
whipped cream to decorate

Slice the Swiss roll thinly and use to line the base and sides of a 900-ml/1½-pint pudding basin. Carefully spoon over the brandy.

In a bowl, mix together the yogurt and raspberries. Whip the cream until thick and fold into the yogurt mixture. Pour over the Swiss roll and freeze for 2 hours or until firm.

Dip the basin briefly in warm water to help turn out the pudding. Decorate with piped whipped cream and serve immediately.

352 | Chocolate Orange Soufflé

Preparation time
30 minutes, plus 1
hour to chill

Cooking time
5 minutes

Serves 6

Calories
480 per portion

You will need
3 eggs, separated
75 g/3 oz caster sugar
  grated rind and juice of 2 oranges
15 g/½ oz gelatine
3 tablespoons hot water
300 ml/½ pint whipping cream
175 g/6 oz plain chocolate,
  grated

Lightly grease a 600-ml/1-pint soufflé dish. Cut a double strip of greaseproof paper, equal in width to the height of the dish plus 5 cm/2 in and long enough to go right round the outside of the dish. Lightly grease the top 5 cm/2 in and tie securely with string around the dish.

Place the egg yolks and sugar in a bowl over a saucepan of simmering water and whisk until thick and creamy. Whisk in the orange rind and juice. Dissolve the gelatine in the water over simmering water.

Whisk the egg whites until they stand in soft peaks and whip the cream until stiff. Fold the cooled gelatine into the orange mixture, followed by half the cream, the egg whites and two-thirds of the grated chocolate. Pour into the soufflé dish, smooth the top and chill until set.

Peel the paper away from the soufflé using the back of a knife. Press grated chocolate around the sides of the soufflé. With the remaining cream pipe swirls on the top and decorate with a sprinkle of grated chocolate.

Freezer Tip

Pipe swirls of whipped cream on to a cling film lined baking tray. Open freeze, pack carefully in rigid containers and use from frozen to decorate cakes or puddings.

Microwave Tip

Gelatine can be dissolved in the water, in a small basin in the microwave. Allow about 1 minute on full power.

353 | Bean and Kiwi Fool

Preparation time
10 minutes, plus overnight soaking time and chilling time

Cooking time
45–60 minutes

Serves 8

Calories
260 per portion

You will need
175 g/6 oz moong beans, soaked in cold water overnight
100 ml/4 fl oz milk
300 ml/½ pint double cream
1½ tablespoons brown sugar
2 tablespoons sake (rice wine)
1 teaspoon vanilla flavouring
2 kiwi fruit, peeled and puréed, to decorate

Drain the beans and rinse, then place in a large pan and cover with fresh cold water. Bring to the boil, half cover and cook for 45–60 minutes until tender. Drain well.

Put the cooked beans in a liquidizer or food processor and work to a purée. Add the milk and 100 ml/4 fl oz of the cream and mix to a thick batter, then add the sugar, rice wine and vanilla. Pour into 8 individual glasses or bowls and chill for at least 2 hours.

To serve, pour a little of the kiwi fruit purée on top of each pudding. Whip the remaining cream until thick, then spoon or pipe on top. Serve well chilled.

Cook's Tip

It is possible to buy moong beans with the husks removed, but the texture given by the moong bean skins is good in this Vietnamese pudding.

354 | Caramel Custards with Lime

Preparation time
20 minutes, plus chilling time

Cooking time
about 1 hour

Oven temperature
160 C, 325 F, gas 3

Makes 8

Calories
280 per portion

You will need
225 g/8 oz granulated sugar

For the custard
1 (410-g/14½-oz) can evaporated milk
300 ml/½ pint milk
5 eggs
1 tablespoon caster sugar
finely grated rind of 2 limes

Put the sugar in a pan, add 8 tablespoons water and heat to dissolve. Boil, without stirring until the mixture turns a rich golden caramel colour. Immediately pour a little into 8 warmed 150-ml/¼-pint ramekins and swirl to coat the base and sides.

Warm the evaporated milk and milk together in a pan, without boiling. Whisk the eggs with the sugar, then slowly whisk in the warmed milk. Strain, then stir in the lime rind and pour into the ramekin dishes.

Stand in a roasting tin with cold water to come halfway up the sides of the dishes and bake for about 45 minutes or until set. Remove from the water and leave to cool, then chill for at least 2 hours.

Turn out to serve on individual serving dishes, or serve in the ramekins.

Cook's Tip

This variation of crème caramel shows a glimpse of the Spanish influence on Philippino cuisine. It has a delicious bitter-sweet flavour that makes an ideal dessert to serve after a robust or rich main course dish.

355 | Rum and Chocolate Desserts

Preparation time
25 minutes, plus
overnight chilling

Cooking time
5 minutes

Serves 4

Calories
347 per portion

You will need
butter
225 g / 8 oz Madeira cake or plain
     sponge cake, thinly sliced
4 tablespoons dark rum
225 ml / 8 fl oz strong black coffee
2 tablespoons caster sugar
100 g / 4 oz plain chocolate
2 eggs, separated
300 ml / ½ pint double or
     whipping cream
crystallized fruit slices to decorate

Lightly butter four small bowls or large cups. Line the bowls with cake, cutting the pieces to fit. Reserve enough cake to cover the bowls.

Mix together the rum, coffee and sugar. Sprinkle over the cake in the bowls, reserving a little.

Melt the chocolate in a bowl over simmering water. Remove from the heat, cool slightly and stir in the egg yolks. Whisk the egg whites and fold into the chocolate. Pour into the bowls.

Cover the mixture with the reserved cake and sprinkle with the reserved coffee mixture. Cover and chill overnight.

To serve, whip the cream until stiff. Turn out the desserts onto serving plates and cover with piped rosettes of cream. Decorate the top with crystallized fruit.

Cook's Tip

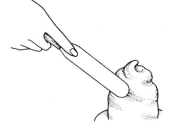

If you don't have a piping bag, or are in a hurry, spread the whipped cream over the dessert and swirl with the back of a palette knife.

356 | Overnight Chocolate Cake

Preparation time
20 minutes, plus
overnight chilling

Serves 10

Calories
435 per portion

You will need
225 g / 8 oz unsalted butter, diced
225 g / 8 oz plain chocolate,
     broken into pieces
2 eggs
25 g / 1 oz caster sugar
12 oblong semi-sweet biscuits,
     such as Nice or Afternoon Tea
50 g / 2 oz glacé cherries,
     chopped
50 g / 2 oz walnut halves,
     chopped
double cream and glacé lemon or
     orange slices to decorate

Line a 450 g / 1 lb loaf tin with greaseproof paper.

Place the chocolate and butter in a heatproof bowl over a pan of simmering water until melted, stirring occasionally.

Meanwhile, whisk the eggs and sugar together until thick and creamy. Gradually stir this into the melted chocolate.

Spoon a little chocolate mixture into the prepared tin, then add a layer of biscuits, then a layer of cherries and walnuts. Continue layering like this until all the ingredients are used, ending with a chocolate layer.

Cover with cling film and chill for at least 12 hours.

To serve, turn the cake out onto a serving dish. Whip some cream until stiff, then pipe decoratively on the top. Add the glacé fruit slices.

Cook's Tip

This flourless cake is ideal to have on hand for afternoon tea or when friends drop in. For special occasions, sprinkle the biscuits with kirsch, a cherry-flavoured liqueur.

357 | Cream Cheese Balls in Syrup

Preparation time
15 minutes, plus
making panir

Cooking time
2¼ hours

Makes 12–15

Calories
400 per ball

You will need
1 recipe Panir (see Cook's Tip)
75 g/3 oz blanched almonds,
 chopped
115 g/4½ oz semolina
12–15 cubes sugar

For the syrup
1 litre/1¾ pints water
200 g/8 oz sugar
pinch of cream of tartar
½ teaspoon rose water

Stir the panir to a smooth paste, then add the almonds and semolina. Knead well until smooth.

When the palm of the hand is greasy, mould the paste. Break the dough into 12–15 pieces, about the size of walnuts. Shape into balls, moulding each one around a sugar cube.

To make the syrup, put all the ingredients except the rose water in a heavy-based pan and heat gently until the sugar dissolves. Bring to the boil, add the balls of dough, then lower the heat and simmer very gently for 2 hours. Stir in the rose water, then serve hot or cold.

358 | Almond Junket

Preparation time
15 minutes, plus 2–3
hours chilling time

Cooking time
about 5–10 minutes

Serves 4

Calories
280 per portion

You will need
15 g/½ oz agar-agar or isinglass
 (see Cook's Tip)
4 tablespoons sugar
300 ml/½ pint milk
1 teaspoon almond flavouring
1 (400-g/14-oz) can apricots or
 mixed fruit salad
50 g/2 oz white grapes, peeled
 and seeded

Dissolve the agar-agar or isinglass in 300 ml/½ pint water over a gentle heat. Dissolve the sugar in 300 ml/½ pint water in a separate saucepan, then combine with the dissolved setting agent and add the milk and almond flavouring. Pour into a large serving bowl and leave until cold. Chill for at least 2–3 hours until set.

To serve, cut the junket into small cubes and place in a serving bowl. Pour the canned fruit and syrup over the junket, add the grapes and mix well. Serve chilled.

Cook's Tip

To make panir, a simple curd cheese, put 2.4 litres/4 pints milk in a pan and bring to the boil. Remove from the heat, leave to cool to 37C/98F. Beat in 500 ml/17 fl oz natural yogurt, 4 teaspoons lemon juice and 1 tablespoon salt.

Leave in a warm place for 12 hours. Strain through muslin for 30 minutes, then squeeze out as much liquid as possible. Shape in the cloth and place under a heavy weight for 3 hours; cut into cubes to use.

Cook's Tip

Agar-agar or isinglass is used as a setting agent. It is possible to use gelatine instead. Use 25 g/1 oz powdered gelatine and dissolve in the water according to the packet instructions.

359 | Chocolate Mint Cheesecake

Preparation time
30 minutes, plus 1½ hours to chill

Cooking time
5–10 minutes

Serves 8

Calories
630 per portion

You will need
75 g / 3 oz butter
225 g / 8 oz plain chocolate digestive biscuits, crushed

For the topping
450 g / 1 lb cream cheese
50 g / 2 oz caster sugar
100 g / 4 oz plain chocolate, melted
2 eggs, separated
few drops peppermint essence
3 tablespoons hot water
15 g / ½ oz gelatine
150 ml / ¼ pint double cream to decorate

Lightly grease a 20-cm/8-in loose-bottomed cake tin. Melt the butter in a saucepan, add the crushed biscuits and mix well to coat evenly. Press evenly over the base of the tin and chill until set.

In a mixing bowl beat the cream cheese with the sugar, melted chocolate, egg yolks and peppermint essence. Place the hot water in a small bowl and sprinkle over the gelatine. Stand over a saucepan of simmering water and stir until dissolved. Cool slightly and stir into the cream cheese mixture. Whisk the egg whites until standing in soft peaks and fold in. Pour over the biscuit base and chill until firm.

Remove the cheesecake from the tin. Whip the cream until stiff and pipe around the top of the cheesecake.

360 | Profiteroles

Preparation time
20 minutes

Cooking time
25–30 minutes

Oven temperature
220 C, 425 F, gas 7

Serves 4

Calories
860 per portion

You will need
150 ml / ¼ pint water
50 g / 2 oz butter
75 g / 3 oz plain flour
pinch of salt
2 eggs, lightly beaten

For the filling
300 ml / ½ pint whipping cream

For the chocolate sauce
100 g / 4 oz plain chocolate
75 g / 3 oz butter
3 tablespoons golden syrup

Put the water and butter in a saucepan and heat gently until the butter melts, then bring rapidly to the boil. Remove from the heat and quickly stir in the flour and salt until the mixture leaves the sides of the pan clean. Allow to cool slightly, then beat in the eggs a little at a time. Beat well until the paste is smooth and glossy. Spoon teaspoon-sized balls on to a greased baking tray. Bake in a hot oven for 20–25 minutes until well risen, golden and crisp. Remove from the oven and split each profiterole. Cool on a wire rack.

Whip the cream, then use to fill the profiteroles. Place on a serving plate. Melt the chocolate, butter and syrup over a gentle heat. Pour over the profiteroles and serve immediately.

Cook's Tip

If a loose bottomed tin is not available grease and line a 20-cm/8-in deep cake tin and place double thickness foil strips in a cross to lift out set cheesecake.

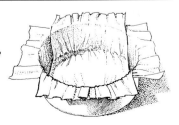

Cook's Tip

Choux pastry items should be cut open immediately they are removed from the oven to allow steam to escape and prevent them becoming soft.

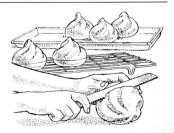

361 | Mocha Soufflé

Preparation time
30 minutes, plus
cooling and setting

Cooking time
6–8 minutes

Serves 8

Calories
344 per portion

You will need
3 teaspoons instant coffee
    granules
3 tablespoons boiling water
3 teaspoons powdered gelatine
100g / 4 oz plain chocolate, broken
    in pieces
5 eggs, separated
150 g / 5 oz caster sugar
300 ml / ½ pint double cream
25 g / 1 oz chocolate vermicelli
150 ml / ¼ pint whipping cream
crystallized rose petals

Dissolve the coffee in the boiling water in a heatproof bowl and leave to cool. Sprinkle the gelatine over the coffee and leave to soften for 5 minutes, then stand the bowl in a pan of simmering water and leave until the gelatine dissolves. Allow to cool, but not set.

Meanwhile, melt the chocolate in a heatproof bowl over a pan of simmering water. Whisk the egg yolks and sugar until creamy and pale. Take the bowl off the pan and whisk in the chocolate until cold. Whisk in the gelatine mixture until combined. Leave the mixture in the refrigerator for 5–10 minutes, or until just beginning to set.

Whisk the egg whites until stiff. Whip the cream until soft peaks form. Fold the egg whites, then the cream into the chocolate mixture. Turn into the prepared dish and smooth. Chill for several hours or overnight.

To serve, peel away the greaseproof paper or foil. Coat the exposed sides of the soufflé with chocolate vermicelli. Decorate the top with 8 swirls of whipped cream with rose petals between.

362 | Chestnut Mousse

Preparation time
15 minutes, plus setting

Cooking time
10–15 minutes

Serves 4

Calories
451 per portion

You will need
2 eggs, separated
150 ml / ¼ pint milk
2 teaspoons powdered gelatine
2 tablespoons water
1 × 225-g / 8-oz can sweetened
    chestnut purée
150 ml / ¼ pint double cream
75 ml / 3 fl oz double cream,
    whipped, to decorate

Place the egg yolks and milk in a bowl over a pan of hot water and stir constantly until the mixture thickens and coats the back of a spoon. Do not let the water boil.

Dissolve the gelatine in the water over a gentle heat. Beat the gelatine into the purée with the custard. Set aside to cool slightly.

Whip the cream until soft peaks form, then fold into the chestnut mixture. Whisk the egg whites until stiff, then lightly fold in. Place in four small bowls or a large serving bowl. Chill until set.

Just before serving, top with whipped cream.

Cook's Tip

To prepare the soufflé dish, tie a band of double thickness greaseproof paper or foil around the outside of a 1.2 litre / 2 pint soufflé dish to stand 5 cm / 2 inches above the rim.

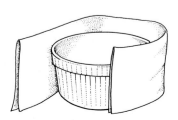

Cook's Tip

Add extra flavour to this creamy dessert by replacing 1 tablespoon water with orange juice and stirring the finely grated rind of 1 orange into the chestnut purée.

363 | Pineapple Ice Cream

Preparation time
15 minutes, plus 4 hours to freeze

Serves 4

Calories
275 per portion

You will need
450 g/1 lb fresh or canned pineapple
50 g/2 oz caster sugar
150 ml/¼ pint water
150 ml/¼ pint double or whipping cream
2 egg whites

Blend the pineapple in a liquidiser or food processor until smooth. Dissolve the sugar in the water over a gentle heat. Add to the pineapple mixture. When cool, pour into a rigid plastic container and freeze for 1 hour or until half frozen.

Turn out into a large mixing bowl and mash with a fork. Whip the cream until stiff and fold into the pineapple mixture. Finally whisk the egg whites until stiff but not dry and fold in. Pour the ice cream back into the plastic container and freeze for 3 hours, whisking twice more during the freezing process to achieve a really smooth texture.

364 | Creamy Coffee Ice Cream

Preparation time
15 minutes, plus 3–4 hours to freeze

Serves 6

Calories
440 per portion

You will need
300 ml/½ pint milk
2 tablespoons instant coffee powder
3 eggs, lightly beaten
50 g/2 oz caster sugar
1 (410-g/14.5-oz) can evaporated milk
300 ml/½ pint double or whipping cream, whipped

Place the milk, coffee, eggs and sugar in a bowl over a pan of simmering water and cook, stirring continuously, until the mixture coats the back of the spoon. Pour the mixture into a large rigid plastic container, cool and freeze for 1 hour or until half frozen.

Whisk the evaporated milk until doubled in volume. In another bowl whisk the half-frozen coffee mixture until smooth. Whisk the evaporated milk into the coffee mixture. Return to the freezing container and freeze until just firm. Remove from the freezer, whisk the ice cream until smooth, whisk in the whipped cream and freeze again until firm. Accompany with cigarette russes or other sweet biscuits and, if you like, serve with a hot chocolate sauce.

Cook's Tip

If using fresh pineapple, cut off the leafy top and scoop out the inside. Fill the fruit shell with the ice cream, replace the lid and freeze for about 1 hour before serving on a doily-lined cake stand.

Cook's Tip

To make a very quick hot chocolate sauce, melt Mars bars in a basin over a saucepan of hot water, or in the microwave.

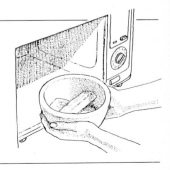

365 | Champagne Water-Ice

Preparation time
15 minutes, plus
freezing

Serves 8

Calories
136 per portion

You will need
225 g / 8 oz caster sugar
300 ml / ½ pint water
300 ml / ½ pint champagne
juice of 1 lemon
juice of 1 orange

Dissolve the sugar in the water, then add the champagne and fruit juices. Pour into shallow trays and freeze.

When frozen round the edges but still soft in the centre, tip into a chilled bowl and whisk until smooth. Refreeze.

Repeat the whisking at intervals until creamy, smooth and white. Serve in chilled bowls or glasses.

366 | Amaretto Ice Bombe

Preparation time
15 minutes, plus
freezing

Serves 6

Calories
170 per portion

You will need
50 g / 2 oz Italian macaroons,
  crushed
4 tablespoons Amaretto liqueur
600 ml / 1 pint vanilla ice cream
300 ml / ½ pint double or
  whipping cream
2 crushed macaroons

Place a circle of greaseproof paper in the base of a wetted 600 ml / 1 pint basin. Chill the basin.

Mix together the macaroons and liqueur.

Press a little ice cream over the base of the basin. Spread half the macaroon mixture over the top. Cover with a layer of ice cream, then the remaining macaroon mixture. Spread the remaining ice cream over the top. Place in the freezer for 1 hour.

Whip the cream until stiff. Turn out the bombe onto a chilled plate and cover with cream.

Sprinkle the top with crushed macaroons and return to the freezer for 15 minutes.

Cook's Tip

The Spanish version of champagne is a sparkling wine known as 'cava'. Using cava will give an equally delicious dessert. Set your freezer to its coldest setting 30 minutes before beginning.

Cook's Tip

Amaretto liqueur is an almond-flavoured liqueur from Italy. It is available from most off-licences.

367 | Tropical Pancakes

Preparation time
20 minutes

Cooking time
30 minutes

Oven temperature
180 C, 350 F, gas 4

Serves 4

Calories
475 per portion

You will need
100 g/4 oz plain flour
pinch of salt
1 egg, lightly beaten
300 ml/½ pint milk
oil for frying

For the filling
50 g/2 oz butter
25 g/1 oz dark soft brown sugar,
    plus extra for sprinkling
6 ripe bananas, roughly chopped
2 tablespoons dark rum
juice of 1 lemon
25 g/1 oz flaked almonds

Sift the flour and salt into a bowl. Add the egg, then gradually add half the milk, beating well to make a smooth batter. Beat in the remaining milk.

Heat a little oil in a frying pan. Pour in a little batter, tilting the pan so the batter covers the base, and cook until the underside is golden. Turn and cook the second side, then remove and keep warm. Repeat with the remaining batter.

Melt the butter in a frying pan with the sugar. Stir in the bananas and cook until softened, add the rum and lemon juice and mix thoroughly. Place one pancake on a greased ovenproof plate. Cover with a little banana mixture and then another pancake. Continue layering in this way, and sprinkle the last pancake with sugar and flaked almonds. Bake in a moderate oven for 12–15 minutes. Serve hot, cut into wedges.

Cook's Tip

If you want to create the pyramid effect in the photograph, cook each pancake slightly smaller than the last, by using a little less batter. When assembling, start with the largest pancake.

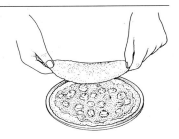

368 | Pineapple and Apricot Fritters

Preparation time
15 minutes

Cooking time
5 minutes

Serves 4

Calories
415 per portion

You will need
1 (425-g/15-oz) can pineapple
    rings
1 (410-g/14-oz) can apricot
    halves
flour for dusting
oil for deep frying

For the batter
100 g/4 oz plain flour
pinch of mixed spice
pinch of salt
1 large egg, separated
150 ml/¼ pint water
1 tablespoon oil
caster sugar to sprinkle

Drain the pineapple rings and apricot halves, pat dry with absorbent kitchen paper and dust with flour. Sift the flour, mixed spice and salt into a bowl. Gradually beat in the egg yolk, water and oil to form a smooth batter. Whisk the egg white until stiff and fold in.

Heat the oil for deep frying to 180 C/350 F, or until a cube of bread dropped in becomes golden in 30 seconds. Dip the pieces of fruit into the batter to coat well and fry the fritters for 4–5 minutes or until golden. Drain on absorbent kitchen paper. Sprinkle with sugar and serve immediately with cream.

Cook's Tip

Use peeled bananas, cut in half, instead of the canned fruit. Serve with a little warmed golden syrup poured over.

369 | *Doughnut Spirals in Syrup*

Preparation time
15 minutes, plus
overnight standing

Cooking time
about 10 minutes

Makes 20—24

Calories
270 per spiral

You will need
275 g/10 oz plain flour
40 g/1½ oz rice flour
pinch of baking powder
½ teaspoon salt
175 ml/6 fl oz water
vegetable oil for deep frying

For the syrup
1 litre/1¾ pints water
200 g/8 oz sugar
pinch of cream of tartar
½ teaspoon rose water
½ teaspoon yellow or red food
    colouring (optional)

Sift the flours, baking powder and salt into a bowl. Gradually add the water and beat to a smooth batter. Cover and
chill overnight.

To make the syrup, put the water, sugar and cream of
tartar in a heavy-based pan and heat to dissolve the
sugar. Add the rose water and food colouring if used.

Heat the oil, put the batter in a piping bag fitted with a
large plain nozzle and pipe spirals, about 10 cm/4 inches
in diameter, into the hot oil. Deep fry for about 3 minutes
until crisp, then drain on absorbent kitchen paper.

Immerse the spirals in the syrup for 30 seconds while
still warm. Serve warm or cold.

370 | *Deep-Fried Sweet Potato Balls*

Preparation time
10 minutes

Cooking time
about 25 minutes

Serves 4—6

Calories
450—350 per portion

You will need
450 g/1 lb sweet potatoes
100 g/4 oz glutinous or sweet rice
    flour
50 g/2 oz brown sugar
50 g/2 oz sesame seeds
oil for deep frying

Put the potatoes in a pan, cover with water and bring to
the boil. Reduce the heat and simmer for 15—20 minutes
or until tender. Drain and peel. Mash the potatoes, then
beat in the rice flour and sugar.

With dampened hands, form the mixture into walnut-
sized balls. Roll each ball in sesame seeds.

Heat the oil to 160 C/325 F and deep fry the potato balls
until golden. Drain on absorbent kitchen paper, then
serve hot.

Cook's Tip

**These pretzel-like sweets or
dessert are a joy if eaten
sweet and warm. In Indian
cities, they are sold at open
stalls where, by the light of a
hissing Tilley lamp, the spirals
are deep-fried especially for
you.**

Cook's Tip

**This recipe can also be made
from yams instead of the
sweet potatoes. A yam is a
large sweet tuberous root
with a moist texture. It
resembles a sweet potato and
is cooked in the same way.**

371 | Pineapple Upside-Down Pudding

Preparation time
15 minutes

Cooking time
50 minutes

Oven temperature
180C, 350F, gas 4

Serves 4

Calories
610 per portion

You will need
25 g/1 oz butter
50 g/2 oz soft brown sugar
1 (227-g/8-oz) can pineapple rings, drained
4 glacé cherries, halved

For the sponge
100 g/4 oz butter, softened
100 g/4 oz caster sugar
2 eggs, lightly beaten
$\frac{1}{4}$ teaspoon mixed spice
175 g/6 oz self-raising flour, sifted

Lightly grease a 15-cm/6-in round cake tin. Melt the butter in a saucepan, add the sugar and pour over the base of the tin. Arrange the pineapple rings and cherries decoratively in the base, placing the cherries rounded side down.

To make the sponge mixture, beat the butter and sugar until soft and creamy. Gradually beat in the eggs and using a metal spoon, fold in the spice and flour. Spoon the mixture over the fruit in the tin, carefully smooth the top and bake in a moderate oven for about 50 minutes or until the sponge is firm and golden.

Turn out the sponge on to a serving plate, and serve immediately with custard or cream.

Cook's Tip

Other canned fruits can be used in this recipe. Try apricot halves, peach halves or slices, or pear halves.

If you like, make a quick jam sauce to serve with the pudding. Heat 225 g/8 oz jam in a saucepan with the juice from the fruit. Stir to prevent sticking, then strain before serving.

372 | Prune and Apricot Pudding

Preparation time
10 minutes

Cooking time
1 hour

Oven temperature
180C, 350F, gas 4

Serves 4

Calories
550 per portion

You will need
100 g/4 oz no-need-to-soak stoned dried prunes
100 g/4 oz no-need-to-soak dried apricots
4 tablespoons water
50 g/2 oz chopped walnuts

For the sponge
100 g/4 oz soft margarine
100 g/4 oz soft brown sugar
2 eggs, lightly beaten
100 g/4 oz self-raising wholemeal flour

Arrange the prunes and apricots in the base of a 1.15-litre/2-pint ovenproof dish. Sprinkle over the water and add the walnuts. Beat the margarine and sugar together until creamy. Gradually beat in the eggs, then fold in the flour. The mixture should be a soft dropping consistency. Cover the fruit with the sponge mixture and bake for about an hour in a moderate oven. Serve hot with custard.

Microwave Tip

Cover dried fruit with water or fruit juice, cover with cling film and microwave on full power for about 18 minutes instead of soaking.

373 | Blackberry and Apple Crumble

Preparation time
15 minutes

Cooking time
35 45 minutes

Oven temperature
190 C, 375 F, gas 5

Serves 4

Calories
350 per portion

You will need
225 g 8 oz blackberries
450 g 1 lb cooking apples, peeled,
    cored and thinly sliced
25 g 1 oz unrefined sugar (golden
    granulated or molasses)

For the crumble
100 g 4 oz wholemeal flour
75 g 3 oz polyunsaturated
    margarine
50 g 2 oz fruit 'n fibre cereal, lightly
    crushed
15 g ½ oz unrefined sugar

Mix together the fruit and sugar and place in a 1.15-litre/
2-pint ovenproof dish.

Put the flour into a mixing bowl and rub in the fat. Stir
in the cereal and sugar. Spread this topping evenly over
the fruit and bake in a moderately hot oven for 35–45
minutes, until the crumble is crisp and the fruit soft.
Serve warm with custard.

374 | Autumnal Pudding

Preparation time
20 minutes, plus 2
hours to chill and set

Cooking time
10 minutes

Serves 4

Calories
225 per portion

You will need
oil for brushing
8 thin slices wholewheat bread
150 ml/¼ pint apple juice
50 g/2 oz granulated sugar
juice of ½ lemon
2 dessert apples, peeled, cored
    and sliced
1 dessert pear, peeled, cored and
    sliced
75 g/3 oz blackberries
pinch of ground cinnamon
1½ teaspoons agar-agar or 2
    teaspoons powdered gelatine
6 tablespoons water

For the sauce
225 g/8 oz blackberries
3 tablespoons icing sugar
juice of ½ lemon
fresh fruit to decorate

Brush the insides of four individual pudding basins with
oil. Cut the bread into circles and fingers to line them.

Stir the apple juice, sugar and lemon juice over low
heat until dissolved. Add the apple and pear slices and
poach gently for 4 minutes. Stir in the blackberries and
cinnamon; cool. In a small saucepan, dissolve the agar-
agar in the cold water, then bring to the boil, stirring constantly. Add to the cooled fruits. Spoon into the basins
and chill. Poach the sauce ingredients gently, blend in a
liquidiser and serve with the puddings, as shown.

Cook's Tip

**All berry fruits taste good with
a crumble topping. Try
cranberries, loganberries,
tayberries or raspberries,
varying the quantity of sugar
as required.**

Cook's Tip

**Agar-agar, which is derived
from seaweed, is the preferred
setting agent for many
vegetarians. If using gelatine
dissolve it in a little water in a
basin over a saucepan of hot
water. Stir frequently.**

375 | Summer Pudding

Preparation time
20 minutes, plus
overnight chilling

Cooking time
5 minutes

Serves 6

Calories
205 per portion

You will need
225 g/8 oz blackcurrants, topped
   and tailed
225 g/8 oz raspberries
225 g/8 oz redcurrants, topped
   and tailed
175 g/6 oz sugar
3 tablespoons water
8–10 thin slices white bread,
   crusts removed

Put the prepared fruit in a large saucepan with the sugar and water, bring to the boil and simmer gently for 5 minutes. Leave to cool.

Line a 900-ml/1½-pint pudding basin with slices of bread, cutting the slices to fit and making sure that there are no gaps. Spoon the fruit mixture into the basin, and top with more bread slices cut to fit. Cover the pudding with a plate with a weight on it and chill in the refrigerator overnight so that the juices can penetrate through the bread.

To serve, turn out the pudding and accompany with clotted cream or hot custard.

376 | Black Forest Gâteau

Preparation time
30 minutes

Cooking time
40 minutes

Oven temperature
180 C, 350 F, gas 4

Makes 1 cake

Total calories
4060

You will need
3 eggs
75 g/3 oz caster sugar
50 g/2 oz plain flour
25 g/1 oz cocoa powder
3 tablespoons kirsch
600 ml/1 pint double or
   whipping cream
1 (390-g/13¾-oz) can blackberry
   pie filling

For the glacé icing
225 g/8 oz icing sugar, sifted
25 g/1 oz cocoa powder
2 tablespoons water
chocolate curls to decorate

Line and grease a deep 18-cm/7-in round cake tin. Whisk the eggs and sugar until pale and thick. Fold in the flour and cocoa powder. Pour the mixture into the tin and bake in a moderate oven for about 40 minutes. Cool on a wire rack. Cut into three layers horizontally, and soak each layer with 1 tablespoon kirsch.

Whip the cream until thick. Sandwich the cake together with some of the cream and the pie filling. Pipe the remaining cream on to the side of the cake and a border on the top.

Mix the icing sugar, cocoa powder and water until smooth and pour over the top. Decorate with chocolate curls.

Cook's Tip

When turning out any
moulded dish, place a plate
over the mould, making
sure that it is in exactly the
right position. Invert the
mould and the plate and
give them both a firm jerk.

Cook's Tip

To make chocolate curls,
spread melted chocolate on
a level smooth surface and
leave to set. Hold a knife at
an angle of 45° and draw
across chocolate to make
curls.

377 | Crunchy Pear Layer

Preparation time
10 15 minutes

Cooking time
35 minutes

Oven temperature
180 C, 350 F, gas 4

Serves 4

Calories
305 per portion

You will need
450 g 1 lb cooking pears, peeled, cored and quartered
3 tablespoons water
1 2 teaspoons ground ginger
150 g 5 oz demerara sugar
50 g 2 oz butter
50 g 2 oz fresh breadcrumbs
150 ml ¼ pint single cream, to serve

Cook the pears gently in the water with the ginger and 50 g/2 oz of the sugar until tender. Slice one of the poached pear quarters; reserve for decoration. Melt the butter in a frying pan and fry the breadcrumbs with the remaining sugar until crisp. Layer the pears and crunchy crumbs in a buttered ovenproof dish, finishing with a layer of crumbs.

Bake in a moderate oven for 30 minutes and serve hot or cold. Decorate with the reserved pear slices and serve with cream.

Cook's Tip

Use crushed ginger biscuits instead of the breadcrumbs, or try hazelnut biscuits for a delicious combination of flavours.

378 | Winter Fruit Compote

Preparation time
15 minutes, plus overnight to soak

Cooking time
30 minutes

Oven temperature
190 C, 375 F, gas 5

Serves 4

Calories
305 per portion

You will need
225 g/8 oz dried apricots
100 g/4 oz stoned dried prunes
600 ml/1 pint unsweetened orange juice
2 oranges
100 g/4 oz raisins
2 small bananas, thickly sliced
natural yogurt, to serve

Place the apricots and prunes in a bowl and pour over the orange juice. Cover and leave to soak overnight.

Using a serrated knife, peel the oranges and remove all the pith. Cut in between the membranes to separate the orange segments. Stir into the fruit mixture with the raisins and bananas and turn into an ovenproof dish. Cover and cook in a moderately hot oven for about 30 minutes. Serve warm with natural yogurt.

Cook's Tip

The fruit may be plumped in a microwave oven, if preferred. Combine the apricots, prunes, raisins and orange juice in a bowl, cover lightly and cook for 5 minutes on Full power. Cool slightly before adding the oranges and bananas.

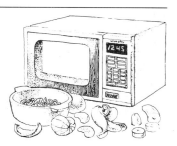

379 | *Banana Fritters*

Preparation time
10 minutes

Cooking time
about 5 minutes

Serves 8

Calories
250 per portion

You will need
100 g/4 oz self-raising flour
40 g/1½ oz rice flour
½ teaspoon salt
finely grated rind of 1 lime
   (optional)
vegetable oil for deep frying
8 small bananas
lime wedges for serving
caster sugar for serving

Sift the flours and salt into a bowl. Add about 200 ml/
7 fl oz water to make a smooth coating batter, then stir in
the grated lime rind, if using.

Heat the oil in a wok or deep fat frier. Meanwhile, peel
the bananas, spear them one at a time with a skewer and
dip into the batter until evenly coated. Deep fry, in
batches, in the hot oil until crisp and golden. Drain on
absorbent kitchen paper.

Serve hot with lime wedges and sprinkled over with
caster sugar.

380 | *Rice Fritters*

Preparation time
10 minutes

Cooking time
about 5–10 minutes

Makes about 20

Calories
100 per fritter

You will need
160 g/5½ oz cooked medium-
   grain rice
2 eggs, beaten
3 tablespoons sugar
½ teaspoon vanilla essence
50 g/2 oz plain flour
1 tablespoon baking powder
pinch of salt
25 g/1 oz desiccated coconut
vegetable oil for deep frying
sifted icing sugar for sprinkling

Put the rice, eggs, sugar and vanilla in a bowl and mix
well. Sift together the flour, baking powder and salt, then
stir into the rice mixture. Stir in the coconut.

Heat the oil in a deep-fat frier to 180 C/350 F (just
before it starts to sizzle). Drop tablespoonfuls of the mixture into the hot oil, one at a time, and deep fry until
golden on all sides. Drain on absorbent kitchen paper.

Transfer to a warmed serving dish and sprinkle with a
generous amount of icing sugar. Serve hot.

Cook's Tip

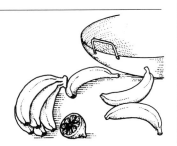

*If possible, buy very small
bananas – sometimes called
'apple bananas' – for these
fritters: they look better than
the larger ones and are
usually sweeter in flavour.*

Cook's Tip

*In many Asian countries rice is
often used as an ingredient for
desserts. These are not
always eaten after a meal, in
the western manner, but may
be served as a snack between
meals.*

381 | Chocolate Pudding

Preparation time
20 minutes

Cooking time
1½ hours

Serves 4

Calories
715 per portion

You will need
100 g/ 4 oz soft margarine
100 g/ 4 oz caster sugar
2 eggs, lightly beaten
25 g/ 1 oz cocoa powder
100 g/ 4 oz self-raising flour
50 g/ 2 oz plain chocolate, grated

For the mocha sauce
25 g/ 1 oz butter
25 g/ 1 oz plain flour
600 ml/ 1 pint milk
50 g/ 2 oz caster sugar
1 tablespoon cocoa powder
1 tablespoon instant coffee

Grease a 1-litre/2-pint pudding basin.

Beat the margarine and sugar until soft and creamy, then gradually beat in the eggs. Fold in the sifted cocoa, flour and chocolate. Pour the mixture into the prepared basin and cover with greased greaseproof paper and a piece of greased cooking foil, pleated to allow for rising. Secure with string. Steam on a trivet or upturned saucer in a saucepan half-full of water for 1½ hours.

To make the sauce, melt the butter over a low heat, add the flour and, stirring continuously, cook for 2 minutes, then gradually add the milk and bring to the boil. Reduce the heat to simmer gently, add the sugar, cocoa and coffee, and cook until dissolved.

Turn out the pudding and pour over the hot sauce to serve.

382 | Baked Ginger Pudding with Lemon Sauce

Preparation time
20 minutes

Cooking time
45–50 minutes

Oven temperature
180 C, 350 F, gas 4

Serves 4

Calories
545 per portion

You will need
100 g/ 4 oz soft margarine
100 g/ 4 oz soft brown sugar
2 eggs, lightly beaten
175 g/ 6 oz self-raising flour, sifted
2 teaspoons ground ginger

For the sauce
grated rind and juice of 2 lemons
25 g/ 1 oz cornflour
50 g/ 2 oz sugar
300 ml/ ½ pint water
25 g/ 1 oz butter

Grease a deep 15-cm/6-in square cake tin. Beat the margarine and sugar together until creamy, gradually beat in the eggs, then fold in the flour and ginger. Pour into the tin and bake in a moderate oven for 40–45 minutes. Turn out of the tin.

To make the sauce, mix the lemon rind and juice with the cornflour and sugar. Gradually add the water, transfer to the hob and bring to the boil, stirring continuously. Stir in the butter. Cut the pudding into squares and serve hot with the sauce.

Microwave Tip

Steamed puddings microwave well. Cover with cling film instead of foil. Microwave on full power for 5 minutes

Microwave Tip

To make the lemon sauce in the microwave, mix the ingredients until smooth, adding all the liquid. Microwave on full power for 6 minutes, whisking twice.

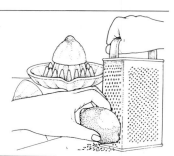

383 | *Fruity Yule Pudding*

Preparation time
25 minutes

Cooking time
3–4 hours, plus 2 hours
on the day of serving

Serves 8

Calories
295 per portion

You will need
100 g/4 oz self-raising wholemeal
   flour
100 g/4 oz fresh wholewheat
   breadcrumbs
1 teaspoon mixed spice
1 teaspoon ground cinnamon
1 teaspoon grated nutmeg
100 g/4 oz polyunsaturated
   margarine
75 g/3 oz light soft brown sugar
2 eggs, beaten
1 dessert apple, peeled, cored and
   grated
1 carrot, grated
225 g/8 oz raisins
grated rind and juice of 1 orange

Mix together the flour, breadcrumbs and spices. Beat the margarine with the sugar for about 5 minutes until soft and light, then beat in the eggs, apple, carrot, raisins, orange rind and juice. Stir in the flour mixture until evenly blended.

Press lightly into a greased 1.15-litre/2-pint pudding basin and cover with double thickness greaseproof paper, tied down securely. Steam for 3–4 hours, topping up the water as necessary, then for a further 2 hours on the day of serving.

384 | *Choux Ring*

Preparation time
45 minutes

Cooking time
40–45 minutes

Oven temperature
220 C, 425 F, gas 7
then
190 C, 375 F, gas 5

Serves 8

Calories
435 per portion

You will need
300 ml/½ pint water
100 g/4 oz butter
150 g/5 oz plain flour
3–4 eggs, lightly beaten
300 ml/½ pint double cream
1 tablespoon sweet sherry
1 (225-g/8-oz) can sweetened
   chestnut purée
a little cocoa powder

Make the choux pastry, using the first four ingredients and following the instructions in the Cook's Tip below. Transfer to a piping bag fitted with a large nozzle. Dampen a large baking tray and pipe a 25-cm/10-in circle of paste on it. Pipe another circle immediately inside. Bake for 10 minutes at the higher setting, then reduce the temperature and cook for a further 35–40 minutes, until well puffed, crisp and brown. Split the choux ring in half immediately it is removed from the oven; cool.

Whip the cream and sherry together and fold into the chestnut purée. Spread the choux base with the chestnut cream and cover with the choux top. Dust with cocoa.

Cook's Tip

Dried and fresh fruit replaces much of the sugar in this light Christmas pudding; an ideal alternative for the health and weight conscious.

Cook's Tip

To make choux pastry, heat the water and butter gently until the fat melts, then bring to a rapid boil. Off the heat, immediately add all the flour. Beat vigorously, return to the heat and continue beating until the mixture forms a ball **which leaves the sides of the pan clean. Cool to lukewarm, beat in enough egg to give a piping consistency, then beat until glossy.**

385 | Treacle Tart

Preparation time
15 minutes

Cooking time
35 minutes

Oven temperature
190 C, 375 F, gas 5

Serves 4

Calories
575 per portion

You will need
225 g / 8 oz plain flour
pinch of salt
100 g / 4 oz margarine
2–3 tablespoons cold water

For the filling
8 tablespoons golden syrup
2 teaspoons grated lemon rind
50 g / 2 oz fresh white
  breadcrumbs

Sift the flour and salt into a bowl. Cut the margarine into small pieces and rub in until the mixture resembles fine breadcrumbs. Sprinkle over the water and mix to form a dough. Knead very lightly, roll out three-quarters of the pastry on a lightly floured surface and use to line a 23-cm/ 9-in ovenproof pie plate. Leave to chill in the refrigerator while preparing the filling.

Gently heat the syrup and mix in the lemon rind and breadcrumbs. Pour into the pastry shell. Roll out the remaining pastry and cut into thin strips to form a lattice pattern on top of the tart. Bake in a moderately hot oven for about 30 minutes and serve with a custard sauce.

386 | Custard Jam Tart

Preparation time
20 minutes

Cooking time
1 hour 10 minutes

Oven temperature
200 C, 400 F, gas 6
160 C, 325 F, gas 3

Serves 4

Calories
625 per portion

You will need
225 g / 8 oz plain flour
pinch of salt
100 g / 4 oz margarine
2–3 tablespoons cold water

For the filling
2 tablespoons jam
600 ml / 1 pint milk
50 g / 2 oz caster sugar, plus extra
  to sprinkle
4 egg yolks
few drops vanilla essence
$\frac{1}{2}$ teaspoon grated nutmeg

Sift the flour and salt into a bowl. Cut the margarine into small pieces and rub in until the mixture resembles fine breadcrumbs. Add the water and mix to form a dough. Knead very lightly, roll out on a lightly floured surface and use to line a 20-cm/8-in fluted flan ring placed on a baking tray. Prick the base with a fork and bake blind in a moderately hot oven for 10 minutes.

Spread the jam evenly over the pastry. Heat the milk over a low heat until lukewarm, then beat in the sugar, egg yolks and vanilla. Pour over the jam, sprinkle the nutmeg on top and bake in a moderate oven for about 1 hour until firm. Serve either hot or cold, sprinkled with a little extra caster sugar.

Microwave Tip

Put the syrup in a basin and microwave on full power for 1½–2 minutes, then mix in the lemon rind and breadcrumbs.

Freezer Tip

Open freeze an extra pastry flan case, then pack the middle with crumpled absorbent kitchen paper, put in a polythene bag and freeze. Cook from frozen when required.

387 | *Orchard Tart*

Preparation time
25 minutes

Cooking time
35 40 minutes

Oven temperature
200 C, 400 F, gas 6

Serves 6

Calories
355 per portion

You will need
For the pastry
100 g/4 oz plain flour
50 g/2 oz concentrated butter,
    softened
50 g/2 oz ground hazelnuts
25 g/1 oz soft brown sugar
1 egg, beaten

For the filling
4 large pears, peeled, cored and
    chopped
2-cm/$\frac{3}{4}$-in piece fresh root ginger,
    peeled and chopped
2 tablespoons clear honey
100 g/4 oz demerara sugar
3 tablespoons water
4 dessert apples, peeled, cored
    and nalved

Place the flour in a mixing bowl and add the concentrated butter; rub in until very fine. Add the hazelnuts and sugar, bind with the egg. Roll out to line a 20-cm/8-in loose-bottomed flan tin.

Place the pears in a pan with the ginger, honey, sugar and water and cook over a moderate heat for 5 minutes. Remove the pears with a slotted spoon, drain well and place in the flan case, crushing them slightly. Slice the apple halves almost through but keeping in shape and arrange rounded side up over the flan. Reduce the pan juices until thick enough to coat then spoon over the apples. Bake in a moderately hot oven for 30 minutes and serve warm with cream.

388 | *Gourmet Bread and Butter Pudding*

Preparation time
15 minutes

Cooking time
30 40 minutes

Oven temperature
180 C, 350 F, gas 4

Serves 4

Calories
455 per portion

You will need
8 large slices white or granary
    bread
50 g/2 oz concentrated butter,
    melted
50 g/2 oz demerara sugar
$\frac{1}{2}$ teaspoon mixed spice
100 g/4 oz sultanas
2 eggs, beaten
1 teaspoon vanilla essence
450 ml/$\frac{3}{4}$ pint milk
1 tablespoon sherry (optional)

Remove the crusts and cut the bread into fingers or desired shapes for one large (1.15-litre/2-pint) pudding or four individual (300-ml/$\frac{1}{2}$-pint) puddings.

Brush a little melted butter inside the ovenproof dishes and cover the base with bread. Mix the sugar, spice and sultanas together and sprinkle half over the bread, drizzle with a little of the melted butter and repeat the layers, finishing with bread and melted butter. Beat the eggs, vanilla, milk and sherry together and carefully pour over. Bake in a moderate oven for 30–40 minutes until set.

Cook's Tip

To slice the apples evenly without cutting right through place the halves, cut side down, on a work surface in front of a thin chopping board. Use a large knife held horizontally so that the board halts the descending blade.

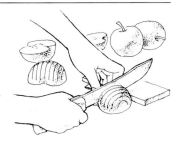

Cook's Tip

The texture and flavour of this updated old favourite will be even better if the pudding is allowed to stand for 1 hour before cooking.

389 | Poached Pears with Chocolate Sauce

Preparation time
5 minutes

Cooking time
25 minutes

Serves 4

Calories
285 per portion

You will need
450 ml / ¾ pint water
75 g / 3 oz sugar
¼ teaspoon vanilla essence
4 large ripe dessert pears, peeled
100 g / 4 oz plain bitter chocolate, broken into pieces

Bring the water, sugar and vanilla essence to the boil. Add the pears and poach over moderately low heat for 5–10 minutes, turning them occasionally, until they are really tender. Carefully lift the pears from the syrup and keep warm.

Melt the chocolate in the syrup over low heat. Beat the mixture well, then simmer for 10 minutes, until the sauce is thick enough to coat the spoon.

Serve the pears warm, with the sauce separately.

390 | Pears Brûlée

Preparation time
20 minutes, plus cooling and chilling

Cooking time
15 minutes

Serves 4

Calories
350 per portion

You will need
4 ripe pears, peeled, stoned and each cut into 8 pieces
300 ml / ½ pint red wine
75 g / 3 oz soft light brown sugar
2 teaspoons arrowroot or cornflour
2 tablespoons water
300 ml / ½ pint double or whipping cream
150 ml / ¼ pint yogurt
100 g / 4 oz soft light brown sugar

Place the pears, wine and sugar in a large pan and bring slowly to the boil until the sugar has dissolved. Simmer, covered, for 10 minutes until the pears are just tender.

Remove the pears with a slotted spoon and arrange in four small ovenproof dishes.

Boil the wine syrup quickly to reduce to 150 ml / ¼ pint. Blend the arrowroot or cornflour with the water and stir into the syrup. Boil for 1 minute until the syrup clears and thickens.

Spoon some syrup over each dish of pears and chill for 1 hour.

Whip the cream until soft peaks form. Beat the yogurt until smooth, then fold into the cream. Spoon the cream and yogurt onto the pears, covering them completely. Cover and chill for at least 4 hours.

Sprinkle the sugar evenly over each dish and place under a preheated grill for 2 minutes until the sugar is caramelized. Cool and chill again for 2 hours or more before serving.

Cook's Tip

You can also prepare the pears in advance, then chill and serve them cold. Serve with whipped cream and hot or cold chocolate sauce.

Cook's Tip

If you don't have four flameproof dishes, make this dessert in one dish, such as a gratin dish. It must be flameproof so it doesn't crack under the grill.

391 | Apple and Apricot Charlotte

Preparation time
20 minutes

Cooking time
50–60 minutes

Oven temperature
180 C, 350 F, gas 4

Serves 4

Calories
300 per portion

You will need
7 (1-cm/½in) slices white bread
50 g/2 oz butter
2 large cooking apples
1 (425-g/15-oz) can apricot pie
  filling
50 g/2 oz soft brown or demerara
  sugar
½ teaspoon ground cinnamon
knob of butter

Remove the crusts from the bread and use two slices to make breadcrumbs. Butter the remaining slices and use to line a 1.15-litre/2-pint ovenproof dish (buttered sides against the dish), cutting them to fit.

Peel, core and chop the apples. Mix with the apricot pie filling and spoon into the lined dish. Mix together the breadcrumbs, sugar and cinnamon and sprinkle over the top. Dot a knob of butter over the top and bake in a moderate oven for 50–60 minutes. Serve hot with custard or fresh cream.

392 | Rhubarb Crumble

Preparation time
15 minutes

Cooking time
40 minutes

Oven temperature
180 C, 350 F, gas 4

Serves 4

Calories
445 per portion

You will need
450 g/1 lb rhubarb
75 g/3 oz soft brown sugar
grated rind of 1 orange

For the crumble
75 g/3 oz butter
175 g/6 oz plain flour
75 g/3 oz soft brown sugar

Wash and trim the rhubarb. Cut the stalks into 2.5-cm/1-in lengths and put into a buttered 900-ml/1½-pint pie dish. Sprinkle over the sugar and orange rind.

To make the crumble, rub the butter into the flour until the mixture resembles fine breadcrumbs. Stir in the sugar and spread the crumble over the rhubarb mixture, smoothing it over to cover the fruit completely. Bake in a moderate oven for about 40 minutes or until the crumble is crunchy and golden and the fruit is cooked. Serve hot with vanilla ice cream.

Cook's Tip

Instead of using the apricot pie filling, double the quantity of apples and add 50 g/2 oz raisins to make a simple apple charlotte.

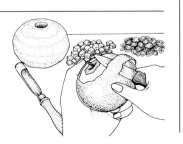

Cook's Tip

Ginger complements rhubarb. Chop about 4 pieces crystallised or preserved stem ginger and add to the rhubarb.

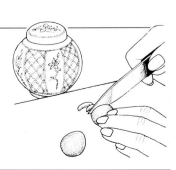

393 | Apple Strudel

Preparation time
20 minutes

Cooking time
25–30 minutes

Oven temperature
200 C, 400 F, gas 6

Serves 4

Calories
540 per portion

You will need
1 (212-g/7½-oz) packet frozen
  puff pastry, defrosted
icing sugar to sprinkle

For the filling
50 g/2 oz fresh white
  breadcrumbs
50 g/2 oz chopped walnuts
100 g/4 oz mixed dried fruit
50 g/2 oz caster sugar
450 g/1 lb cooking apples,
  peeled, cored and sliced
1 teaspoon mixed spice
grated rind of 1 orange
50 g/2 oz butter, melted

Roll out the pastry very thinly on a lightly floured board to make an oblong shape.

Mix the breadcrumbs, walnuts, dried fruit, sugar, apples, mixed spice and orange rind together, and spread over one end of the pastry to within 1 cm/½ in of the edges. Brush the edges with the melted butter and roll up like a Swiss roll. Place on a baking tray and brush with the remainder of the butter. Bake in a moderately hot oven for 25–30 minutes or until golden.

Dust with icing sugar, slice and serve hot with custard.

394 | Stuffed Baked Apples

Preparation time
10 minutes

Cooking time
40–50 minutes

Oven temperature
180 C, 350 F, gas 4

Serves 4

Calories
160 per portion

You will need
4 large cooking apples
50 g/2 oz currants or sultanas
25 g/1 oz soft brown sugar
4 teaspoons golden syrup
½ teaspoon ground ginger
25 g/1 oz butter

Remove the cores from the apples using a corer. Slit the skin round the centre of each apple with the tip of a sharp knife to prevent the apples bursting during cooking. Place in an ovenproof dish. Mix together the fruit and sugar, and stuff the apple centres with the mixture. Pour one teaspoon of syrup over each apple, sprinkle over a little ginger and top with a knob of butter.

Bake in a moderate oven for 40–50 minutes. Serve immediately with hot custard.

Cook's Tip

For an authentic strudel, use phyllo instead of puff pastry. Sold frozen in delicatessens, phyllo pastry is in paper-thin sheets. Brush each sheet with melted butter and use two or three sheets thickness.

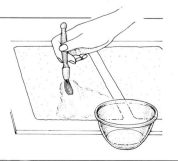

Cook's Tip

If the apple core does not run straight through the middle, push the corer through from one end first, then from the other to remove all the bits.

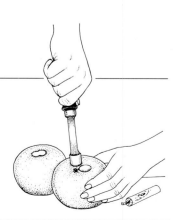

395 | Chocolate Fondue with Fresh Fruit

Preparation time
15 minutes

Cooking time
3–5 minutes

Serves 4

Calories
570 per portion

You will need
2 kiwi fruit
225 g/8 oz fresh strawberries
225 g/8 oz grapes
100 g/4 oz fresh or canned
   pineapple segments
100 g/4 oz fresh or canned
   satsuma segments

For the fondue
225 g/8 oz plain chocolate
150 ml/¼ pint double cream
2 tablespoons brandy

Peel the kiwi fruit and cut each into four. Hull the strawberries. Arrange all the fruit attractively in serving bowls.

Melt the chocolate gently either in a fondue pan or in a basin over simmering water, and when completely melted gradually add the cream and brandy, stirring well. Transfer the fondue to the table and keep hot over a burner.

Dip the fruit in the fondue, using fondue forks.

Microwave Tip

Melt the chocolate in a basin in the microwave on full power for about 3–4 minutes. Stir in the cream and brandy, microwave for 30 seconds and serve.

396 | Black Cherry Clafouti

Preparation time
15 minutes

Cooking time
50–60 minutes

Oven temperature
190 C, 375 F, gas 5

Serves 4

Calories
545 per portion

You will need
2 (411-g/14.5-oz) cans stoned
   black cherries, well drained
175 g/6 oz plain flour
100 g/4 oz caster sugar, plus
   extra to sprinkle
4 eggs
600 ml/1 pint milk

Lightly grease a 1.5-litre/2½-pint shallow ovenproof dish. Spread the drained cherries over the bottom.

Place the flour and sugar in a bowl, make a well in the centre and add the eggs and milk. Gradually work the flour into the liquid to make a smooth batter. Pour over the cherries and bake in a moderately hot oven for 50–60 minutes, or until golden brown and firm to the touch. Sprinkle with caster sugar and serve warm with cream.

Cook's Tip

To make batter in the food processor, put in the flour, eggs and a little milk. Process until smooth, then gradually add the remaining milk as the machine works.

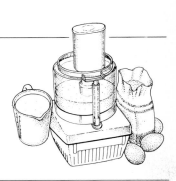

HOME BAKING

Can anyone resist the smell of home-baked bread, scones fresh from the oven, a proudly risen cake all sweet and spicy? And as well as being good to eat, all these are fun to make, whether you enjoy kneading dough or the creative effort of decorating a cake. For these reasons baking is the most satisfying branch of cooking. It is one of the most varied, too. That variety is well represented in this chapter, first with a selection of breads both sweet and savoury. Savoury Cheese Flowerpot Bread is wonderful with hot soup and perfect for picnics, while Spiced Tea Bread is just right for teatime. For tea or elevenses, nothing's nicer than Plain Scones with jam and cream or smooth Drop Scones with Bilberry Sauce.

A cake makes every occasion special. If the family's gathered round a winter fireside, they'll love a slice of Battenburg Cake or Cherry and Coconut Cake; summer teas on the lawn call for a Strawberry Choux Ring and a selection of sweet mouthfuls like Nutty Angelica Fancies and Lemon Treacle Tarts. Small cakes are great for children's parties too: treat them to Chocolate Macaroon Fingers and Peanut Cookies.

This chapter includes some recipes for gorgeous gâteaux which are ideal with coffee after a good meal, such as Pineapple Blitz Torte and Ice Cream Coffee Gâteau. And the year's most important celebration is honoured with the very special California Christmas Cake.

397 | Grainy Bread

Preparation time
25 minutes, plus 2½ hours to rise and prove

Cooking time
35–40 minutes

Oven temperature
220C, 425F, gas 7
190C, 375F, gas 5

Makes 2 loaves

Calories
1295 per loaf

You will need
15 g/½ oz dried yeast
1 teaspoon caster sugar
450 ml/¾ pint warm water and milk mixed
275 g/10 oz plain wholewheat flour
275 g/10 oz strong plain white flour
2 teaspoons salt
15 g/½ oz butter or margarine
150 g/5 oz cracked wheat
50 g/2 oz wheatgerm
2 tablespoons malt extract

Grease two 450-g/1-lb loaf tins. Place the yeast, sugar and water and milk mixture in a jug and mix well. Leave in a warm place until frothy, about 10 minutes.

Sift the flours and salt into a bowl. Rub in the butter or margarine, then add 100 g/4 oz of the cracked wheat and the wheatgerm. Mix in the yeast liquid and malt extract.

Turn out on to a lightly floured surface and knead until smooth and elastic, about 10 minutes. Place in an oiled bowl, cover with cling film and leave to rise in a warm place until doubled in size, about 1–1½ hours.

Turn the dough on to a lightly floured surface, knock back and knead again for 2–3 minutes. Shape into two loaves, place in the tins. Cover and leave to rise. Sprinkle with the remaining cracked wheat and bake in a hot oven for 15 minutes. Reduce to moderately hot and bake for a further 20–25 minutes. Cool on a wire rack.

398 | Soda Bread

Preparation time
15 minutes

Cooking time
35 minutes

Oven temperature
220C, 425F, gas 7

Makes 1 loaf

Total calories
1805

You will need
450 g/1 lb plain flour
½ teaspoon cream of tartar
1 teaspoon salt
1½ teaspoons bicarbonate of soda
350 ml/12 fl oz milk
flour to sprinkle

Grease a baking tray. Sift the flour, cream of tartar, salt and bicarbonate of soda into a bowl. Add the milk and mix to a smooth soft dough. Knead gently on a lightly floured surface, then shape into a round. Place on the baking tray and mark the top quite deeply into four sections with a sharp knife.

Sprinkle with flour and bake in a hot oven for 35 minutes. Allow to cool on a wire rack. Break into quarters and serve sliced, with butter if liked.

Freezer Tip

Home-made bread freezes well. Put the cold fresh bread in polythene bags and suck out all the air with a pump. Seal, label and store for up to 6 months.

Cook's Tip

For a change, divide the dough into 8 pieces and make round rolls, cutting a cross in each. Bake at the same temperature as the loaf for about 15 minutes. Serve warm.

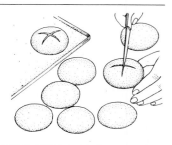

399 | Herb Bread

Preparation time
20 minutes, plus 30
minutes to prove

Cooking time
25–30 minutes

Oven temperature
200 C, 400 F, gas 6

**Makes 1 (450-g/
1-lb) loaf**

Total calories
1615

You will need
25 g/1 oz fresh yeast
250 ml/8 fl oz warm milk
1 egg, beaten
2 teaspoons dried tarragon
2 teaspoons caster sugar
2 teaspoons salt
350 g/12 oz strong plain white
   flour, sifted
1 tablespoon oil
2 teaspoons fennel seeds

Cream the yeast with half the milk. Put the remaining milk in a large bowl and mix in the egg, tarragon, sugar and salt. Add the yeast mixture and 275 g/10 oz of the flour. Beat well to form a creamy dough. Add the remaining flour and oil and beat until thoroughly blended.

Place the mixture in a well-greased 450-g/1-lb loaf tin, brush with water and sprinkle with the fennel seeds. Cover with cling film and leave in a warm place for 30 minutes to rise.

Bake for 25–30 minutes until golden brown and the bread sounds hollow when tapped. Cool on a wire rack.

400 | Ploughman's Pinwheel Loaf

Preparation time
20 minutes, plus about
2–2½ hours to prove

Cooking time
30 minutes

Oven temperature
220 C, 425 F, gas 7

**Makes 1 (450-g/
1-lb) loaf**

Total calories
1345

You will need
½ tablespoon dried yeast
1 teaspoon caster sugar
100 ml/4 fl oz warm milk
225 g/8 oz strong plain white flour
½ teaspoon salt
25 g/1 oz butter or margarine
1 egg, beaten
½ onion, grated
50 g/2 oz Cheddar cheese, grated
1 tablespoon sweet pickle or
   chutney

Mix the yeast with the sugar and milk and leave for 10 minutes. Sift the flour and salt into a bowl and rub in the butter. Add the yeast and half of the egg and mix to a smooth dough. Knead for 10 minutes until smooth and elastic. Place in an oiled bowl, cover and leave to rise in a warm place until doubled in size.

Knead on a floured surface for a few minutes then roll out to a 23 × 13-cm/9 × 5-in rectangle.

Mix the onion with three-quarters of the cheese and pickle. Spread over the dough, almost to the edges. Roll up from a long side like a Swiss roll. Place, seam-side down, in a greased 450-g/1-lb loaf tin. Cover and leave in a warm place until doubled in size.

Glaze with the remaining egg and sprinkle with the remaining cheese. Bake for 30 minutes until golden.

Cook's Tip

You can make this herb bread with fresh tarragon when available but use 4 teaspoons of the chopped herb. It is delicious toasted and served with pâté.

Cook's Tip

This bread is best served warm straight from the oven. Serve with soups, salads and savoury dishes, remembering to choose a complementary pickle or chutney for the filling.

401 | *Savoury Cheese Flowerpot Bread*

Preparation time
30 minutes plus about 3 hours for rising

Cooking time
45 minutes

Oven temperature
200 C, 400 F, gas 6

Makes 1 (675-g/ 1½-lb) flowerpot loaf

Total calories
1680

You will need
350 g/12 oz strong wholemeal flour
¼ teaspoon salt
15 g/½ oz butter
1 sachet easy-blend dried yeast
25 g/1 oz walnuts, chopped
100 g/4 oz low-fat hard cheese, finely grated (for example Shape cheese)
75 g/3 oz celery, chopped
150 ml/¼ pint warm water
beaten egg to glaze
1 tablespoon kibbled wheat

Mix the flour and salt together. Rub in the butter and stir in the yeast. Thoroughly mix in the walnuts, cheese and celery. Add the water to make a dough and knead for 10 minutes. Leave to rise in a large bowl, covered with a lightly oiled plastic bag, in a warm place, until double in size – about 2 hours.

Knock back, knead and shape to fit a well greased unused flowerpot measuring about 15 cm/6 in in depth and width. Cover with plastic again and leave to rise for about 1 hour. Glaze and sprinkle with kibbled wheat. Bake for 45 minutes until golden. The bottom of the bread should sound hollow when tapped. Cool on a wire rack and serve sliced, lightly spread with butter.

Cook's Tip

Season the flowerpot before use by brushing the inside very thoroughly with oil. Place the empty pot in a moderately hot oven (200 C, 400 F, gas 6) for 15 minutes. Allow to cool completely before use.

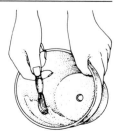

402 | *Peanut Cookies*

Preparation time
10 minutes

Cooking time
12 minutes

Oven temperature
180 C, 350 F, gas 4

Makes 12

Calories
95 per cookie

You will need
50 g/2 oz butter, softened
50 g/2 oz soft brown sugar
50 g/2 oz salted peanuts, roughly chopped
½ teaspoon mixed spice
75 g/3 oz self-raising flour
1 tablespoon orange juice

Cream the butter and sugar together until light and fluffy, then stir in the peanuts, spice, flour and juice to form a soft, not sticky, dough. Break the mixture into 12 equal-sized pieces and roll each into a ball. Place well apart on greased baking trays, flattening them slightly with a fork. Bake for 10–12 minutes or until firming. Leave on trays until firm enough to transfer to a wire rack to cool completely.

Cook's Tip

Mixed spice usually includes cinnamon, cloves and nutmeg, but Jamaica pepper or coriander may be added.

403 | *Cheesy Digestive Biscuits*

Preparation time 20 minutes	**You will need** 175 g/6 oz wholemeal flour 25 g/1 oz medium oatmeal
Cooking time 25–30 minutes	½ teaspoon salt 75 g/3 oz lard 1 tablespoon demerara sugar
Oven temperature 180 C, 350 F, gas 4	40 g/1½ oz Cotswold cheese with chives, finely grated 1 egg, beaten
Makes about 20	2 tablespoons water

Calories
80 per biscuit

Sift the flour, oatmeal and salt into a bowl and discard any bran that remains in the sieve. Rub in the lard, stir in the sugar and cheese, mixing well. Add two-thirds of the egg and water and mix to a firm dough. Roll out on a floured surface and cut out about 20 rounds with a 7.5-cm/3-in cutter. Place on greased baking trays and prick with a fork. Brush with the remaining egg.

Bake for 25–30 minutes or until lightly golden. Cool on a wire rack. Serve with cheese and pickles or as a savoury snack.

404 | *Cheese and Chive Shortbread*

Preparation time 15–20 minutes	**You will need** 150 g/5 oz plain flour 25 g/1 oz ground rice
Cooking time 1 hour	¼ teaspoon grated nutmeg ⅛ teaspoon mustard powder pinch of salt
Oven temperature 150 C, 300 F, gas 2	100 g/4 oz butter or margarine 100 g/4 oz Cheddar cheese, finely grated
Makes 8	2 teaspoons snipped chives 1 tablespoon single cream

Calories
220 per slice

Sift the flour, ground rice, nutmeg, mustard and salt into a bowl. Rub in the butter, stir in the cheese and chives, mixing well. Bind together with the cream to make a firm dough.

Press evenly into a floured 18-cm/7-in loose-bottomed flan tin. Make a decorative edge by pressing around with the prongs of a fork. Prick thoroughly.

Bake for about 1 hour or until golden brown and crisp. Cut into eight segments while still hot, then leave to cool in the tin.

Cook's Tip

For a special savoury topping sprinkle the biscuits with a little sea salt after glazing and before baking.

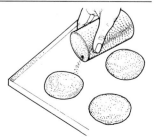

Cook's Tip

This shortbread is good served instead of bread or biscuits with cheese, soups and salads.

405 | *Muffins*

Preparation time
25 minutes, plus 2
hours to rise and prove

Cooking time
15–25 minutes

Makes 10

Calories
205 per muffin

You will need
15 g/½ oz dried yeast
½ teaspoon caster sugar
300 ml/½ pint warm milk
1 egg, beaten
25 g/1 oz butter, melted
450 g/1 lb strong plain white
    flour
1 teaspoon salt

Flour two baking trays. Whisk together the yeast, sugar and half the milk in a jug. Leave in a warm place until frothy, about 10 minutes.

Mix the egg with the remaining milk and the butter. Sift the flour and salt into a bowl. Add the yeast and egg mixtures and mix to a soft dough. Turn on to a lightly floured surface and knead until smooth and elastic, about 10 minutes. Place in an oiled bowl, cover with cling film and leave to rise in a warm place until doubled in size, about 1½ hours.

Turn out the dough on a lightly floured surface and knead for 2 minutes. Roll and stamp out 10 rounds with a 7.5-cm/3-in plain cutter, re-rolling as necessary. Place on the floured trays, cover with cling film and leave to prove for 30 minutes.

Lightly grease a griddle or heavy frying pan. Cook the muffins a few at a time over a moderate heat for 5–8 minutes each side, until well risen. Leave to cool on a wire rack. Serve split and toasted with butter.

406 | *Croissants*

Preparation time
1 hour, plus 2–2½ hours
to rise and time to chill

Cooking time
10–15 minutes

Oven temperature
220 C, 425 F, gas 7

Makes 12

Calories
200 per croissant

You will need
25 g/1 oz fresh yeast
3 tablespoons water
200 g/7 oz butter
2 teaspoons salt
1½ tablespoons sugar
150 ml/¼ pint milk
350 g/12 oz plain flour
beaten egg to glaze

Cream the yeast with water. Put 25 g/1 oz of the butter into a bowl with the salt and sugar and pour over the milk. Cool to lukewarm, then add yeast and flour and knead until smooth. Cover and leave to rise until doubled in size. Knead the dough, wrap in an oiled polythene bag and chill thoroughly. Roll out on a floured board into a rectangle 13 × 38 cm/5 × 15 in. Dot a third of the remaining butter over the top two-thirds of dough. Fold in three and roll out, then fold again. Chill for 30 minutes, then repeat twice more.

Roll out dough to three 30-cm/12-in squares. Cut squares into four triangles. Roll up each and form into crescents. Put on a floured baking tray. Prove for 30 minutes. Brush with glaze and bake in a hot oven for 10–15 minutes.

Freezer Tip

Muffins freeze well. Pack them in a polythene bag when cold. Defrost in the microwave on full power, allowing about 15 seconds for 1, 30 seconds for 2 and 1 minute for 4.

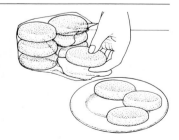

Cook's Tip

When rolling fat into dough for croissants, flaky or puff pastry, do not allow the dough to become greasy during rolling. Chill it frequently between rolling. To do this quickly, put it in the freezer for 10 minutes.

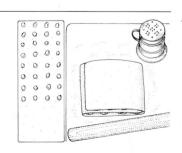

407 | Spiced Tea Bread

Preparation time
10 minutes plus
overnight to macerate
fruit

Cooking time
1¼ hours

Oven temperature
180 C, 350 F, gas 4
then
160 C, 325 F, gas 3

Makes 1 lb loaf

Total calories
2005

You will need
175 g / 6 oz mixed dried fruit
grated rind and juice of ½ orange
1 teaspoon mixed spice
1 teaspoon ground cinnamon
freshly made tea
175 g / 6 oz self-raising flour
50 g / 2 oz wholemeal flour
2 teaspoons baking powder
50 g / 2 oz caster sugar
1 egg, beaten
4 tablespoons oil
1 tablespoon chopped nuts

Place fruit, orange rind and spices in a basin. Make the orange juice up to 150 ml / ¼ pint with tea and stir into the fruit. Leave overnight. Line and grease a 450-g / 1-lb loaf tin. Mix the dry ingredients in a bowl. Beat in the egg, oil and macerated fruit mixture. Pour into the prepared tin and sprinkle the nuts on top. Bake at the hotter temperature for 45 minutes, then reduce the temperature for a further 30 minutes or until bread is firm and a skewer comes out clean. Leave for 5 minutes in the tin, then cool on a wire rack.

408 | Banana and Walnut Loaf

Preparation time
20 minutes

Cooking time
1 hour

Oven temperature
180 C, 350 F, gas 4

Makes 1 loaf

Total calories
2790

You will need
100 g / 4 oz soft margarine
175 g / 6 oz light muscovado sugar
2 ripe bananas
2 eggs
225 g / 8 oz self-raising flour
1 teaspoon baking powder
50 g / 2 oz walnuts, chopped
2 tablespoons milk

Cream the margarine with the sugar until soft and light. Mash the bananas and mix in well. Break the eggs into the mixture and beat well. Gently fold in the sifted flour and baking powder, then stir in the walnuts and milk. Turn into a lined and greased 1-kg / 2-lb loaf tin and bake in a moderate oven for 1 hour, until well risen and golden brown. Turn out and cool on a wire rack. Serve sliced, spread with butter if liked.

Cook's Tip

If a cake or loaf such as this one begins to brown too much before it is fully cooked, cover loosely with a piece of foil.

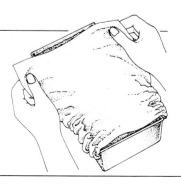

Cook's Tip

A great favourite with children, this, and so easy to make that even a relatively young child could attempt it with suitable supervision.

409 | *Naan*

Preparation time
2¼ hours, including
resting time

Cooking time
10 minutes

Oven temperature
240 C, 475 F, gas 9

Makes 6

Calories
360 per naan

You will need
15 g/½ oz fresh yeast
¼ teaspoon sugar
2 tablespoons warm water
450 g/1 lb self-raising flour
1 teaspoon salt
150 ml/¼ pint tepid milk
150 ml/¼ pint natural yogurt (at
   room temperature)
2 tablespoons melted butter or
   cooking oil

For the garnish
2–3 tablespoons melted butter
1 tablespoon poppy or sesame
   seeds

Mix the yeast with the sugar and water and leave in a warm place for 15 minutes.

Sift the flour and salt into a bowl, make a well in the centre and pour in the yeast liquid, milk, yogurt and butter or oil. Mix to a smooth dough and knead for 10 minutes until smooth and elastic. Place in a bowl, cover and leave to rise in a warm place for 1–1½ hours.

Knead on a floured surface, then divide into 6 pieces. Pat or roll each piece into an oval. Place on warmed baking trays and bake for 10 minutes. Brush with the melted butter and sprinkle with the poppy or sesame seeds. Serve warm.

410 | *Puri*

Preparation time
about 20 minutes, plus
30 minutes standing
time

Cooking time
about 5–10 minutes

Makes 16

Calories
100 per puri

You will need
225 g/8 oz wholemeal flour
¼ teaspoon salt
about 150 ml/¼ pint warm water
2 teaspoons melted ghee
oil for deep frying

Mix the flour with the salt in a bowl. Make a well in the centre, add the water gradually and work to a dough. Knead in the ghee, then knead for 10 minutes, until smooth and elastic. Cover and set aside for 30 minutes.

Divide the dough into 16 pieces. With lightly oiled hands, pat each piece into a ball. Lightly oil a pastry board and rolling pin and roll out each ball into a thin circular pancake.

Deep fry the puris very quickly, turning them over once, until deep golden in colour. Drain well and serve at once, hot.

Cook's Tip

Naan is a north Indian bread traditionally baked in a clay oven called a tandoor. The leavened dough is rolled or slapped into an oval shape, then stuck inside the heated oven so that it hangs free; its weight stretches the naan into *a teardrop shape. It is usually served with tandoori chicken and kebabs, but is good with any of the drier curries.*

Cook's Tip

Puris are delicious served with vegetable curries. They can be made with half wholemeal and half plain white flour if preferred.

411 | Cheese and Pineapple Scones

Preparation time
20 minutes

Cooking time
15 minutes

Oven temperature
200 C, 400 F, gas 6

Makes 12 scones

Calories
145 per scone

You will need
275 g/10 oz wholemeal flour
4 teaspoons baking powder
pinch of salt
65 g/2½ oz butter
50 g/2 oz low-fat hard cheese,
    finely grated (for example Shape cheese)
1 (227-g/8-oz) can crushed
    pineapple, drained
3 tablespoons milk
1 large egg, beaten
milk to glaze

Mix the flour, baking powder and salt together. Rub in the butter until the mixture resembles fine breadcrumbs. Stir in the cheese and pineapple. Bind to a dough with the milk and egg.

Roll out 1 cm/½ in thick and cut out twelve 6-cm/2½-in rounds. Place on a greased baking tray. Brush with milk and bake for about 15 minutes, until risen and golden. Cool on a wire rack. Serve split, spread with butter and pineapple jam.

412 | Nut Flapjacks

Preparation time
5 minutes

Cooking time
40 minutes

Oven temperature
160 C, 325 F, gas 3

Makes 12

Calories
215 per flapjack

You will need
100 g/4 oz vegetable margarine
4 tablespoons golden syrup
75 g/3 oz soft brown sugar
225 g/8 oz rolled oats
75 g/3 oz walnuts, chopped
grated rind of 1 orange
¼ teaspoon salt

For the decoration
fromage frais or quark (optional)
orange slices (optional)

Grease a 19-cm/7½-in square, shallow tin.

Put the margarine and syrup in a pan and melt over low heat. Remove from the heat and stir in the sugar, oats, walnuts, orange rind and salt until well mixed. Turn the mixture into the tin and bake for 40 minutes or until just starting to bubble at the edges. Cool for 5 minutes to firm up slightly. Cut into squares and leave until stiff enough to lift out on to a wire rack to cool completely.

Decorate as shown, if liked.

Cook's Tip

Baking powder loses its potency if stored for a long time. If dubious about that tin at the back of the cupboard, sprinkle 1 teaspoon of the baking powder into a little hot water. It should fizz enthusiastically.

Cook's Tip

Coconut makes a very good addition to these flapjacks. Reduce the amount of oats by 75 g/3 oz and substitute desiccated coconut.

413 | Plain Scones

Preparation time
15 minutes

Cooking time
10–12 minutes

Oven temperature
220 C, 425 F, gas 7

Makes 8

Calories
170 per scone

You will need
225 g / 8 oz plain flour
3 teaspoons baking powder
pinch of salt
50 g / 2 oz butter or margarine
25 g / 1 oz caster sugar
scant 150 ml / ¼ pint milk plus
milk to glaze

Sift the flour, baking powder and salt in a bowl. Rub in the butter or margarine until the mixture resembles fine breadcrumbs, then stir in the sugar. Mix in enough milk to make a soft dough. Turn on to a floured surface and knead very lightly.

Roll out the dough to about 1 cm / ½ in thick and cut out 8 rounds using a 6-cm / 2½-in cutter, re-rolling the dough as necessary. Place on a greased baking tray and brush with milk. Bake in a hot oven for 10–12 minutes or until well risen and golden brown. Cool on a wire rack. Serve with butter or whipped cream and jam.

414 | Cheese Scones

Preparation time
15 minutes

Cooking time
12–15 minutes

Oven temperature
220 C, 425 F, gas 7

Makes 8

Calories
190 per scone

You will need
225 g / 8 oz plain flour
3 teaspoons baking powder
pinch of salt
½ teaspoon mustard powder
40 g / 1½ oz butter or margarine
1 onion, finely chopped
75 g / 3 oz mature Cheddar
cheese, grated
scant 150 ml / ¼ pint milk
beaten egg or milk to glaze

Sift the flour, baking powder, salt and mustard into a bowl. Rub in the butter or margarine until the mixture resembles fine breadcrumbs. Stir in the onion and Cheddar, then mix in enough milk to make a soft dough. Roll out on a lightly floured surface to about 1 cm / ½ in thick. Cut out 8 rounds using a 6-cm / 2½-in cutter, re-rolling the dough as necessary. Place on a greased baking tray and brush with a little egg or milk. Bake in a hot oven for 12–15 minutes or until well risen and golden. Cool on a wire rack.

Cook's Tip

To make fruit scones, stir 50 g / 2 oz sultanas into the rubbed-in mixture. Combine as above.

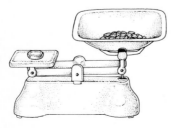

Freezer Tip

For a delicious cobbler topping for casseroles, remove the scones from the oven when they are two-thirds cooked, cool and freeze. Arrange the frozen scones on the casserole and cook for 15–20 minutes.

415 | Cotswold Scone Ring

Preparation time
10 – 15 minutes

Cooking time
15 – 20 minutes

Oven temperature
220 C, 425 F, gas 7

Makes 8

Calories
265 per scone

You will need
225 g/8 oz self-raising flour
1 teaspoon baking powder
pinch of salt
1 teaspoon mustard powder
40 g/1½ oz butter or margarine
100 g/4 oz Cotswold cheese with
  chives, grated
about 150 ml/¼ pint milk
beaten egg to glaze

For the filling
2 (62.5-g/2.2-oz) packets soft
  cream cheese
2 tablespoons snipped chives
½ teaspoon garlic granules

Sift the flour, baking powder, salt and mustard into a bowl. Rub in the butter until the mixture resembles fine breadcrumbs. Stir in the cheese and add enough milk to mix to a soft dough.

Turn onto a floured surface and knead until smooth. Roll out to 1 cm/½ in thickness. Using a 7.5-cm/3-in plain cutter, cut out 8 scones. Arrange them in a circle, overlapping slightly, on a greased baking tray. Brush with egg to glaze. Bake for 15–20 minutes, or until firm and golden. Cool on a wire rack.

To make the filling, mix the cream cheese with the chives and garlic granules. Break the scones apart while still warm, split each one and spread with the cheese mixture. Serve immediately.

416 | Fruit Scone Round

Preparation time
15 minutes

Cooking time
15 – 20 minutes

Oven temperature
200 C, 400 F, gas 6

**Makes 1 (18-cm/
7-in) round**

Total calories
1455

You will need
225 g/8 oz self-raising flour
1 teaspoon baking powder
50 g/2 oz butter or margarine
25 g/1 oz caster sugar
75 g/3 oz mixed dried fruit
about 150 ml/¼ pint milk
milk to glaze

Sift the flour and baking powder into a bowl and rub in the butter until the mixture resembles fine breadcrumbs. Stir in the sugar and fruit and add enough milk to mix to a soft dough.

Turn onto a floured surface, knead lightly then form into an 18-cm/7-in round and place on a floured baking tray.

Score the round into 8 sections, then brush with milk to glaze.

Bake for 15–20 minutes until golden brown. Cool on a wire rack. Serve with butter and jam.

Cook's Tip

**This savoury scone is a boon
for packed lunches, picnics or
buffet lunches. Vary the
topping occasionally by
sprinkling with grated cheese,
poppyseeds, sesame seeds or
coarse sea salt, instead of the
plain egg glaze.**

Cook's Tip

**It is thought that scones
probably originated in
Scotland, forming part of the
traditional high tea. The
recipe above is a good basic
fruit mixture baked in a round
ready for pulling or slicing
apart for serving.**

417 | Almond Scones

Preparation time
15 minutes

Cooking time
10 minutes

Oven temperature
200C, 400F, Gas 6

Makes 10

Calories
123 per scone

You will need
175 g / 6 oz plain flour
½ teaspoon salt
4 teaspoons baking powder
2 tablespoons ground almonds
50 g / 2 oz chilled butter, cut into
   chunks
50 g / 2 oz sultanas
150 ml /¼ pint milk
few drops almond essence
milk to glaze

Sift the flour, salt and baking powder together in a bowl, then stir in the ground almonds. Rub in the butter until the mixture resembles fine breadcrumbs, then stir in the sultanas.

Make a well in the centre, then pour in the milk and almond essence. Mix lightly until a soft dough is formed.

Turn the dough onto a floured surface and knead gently until smooth. Roll out the dough to 1 cm / ½ inch thick and cut into rounds with a 6 cm / 2½ inch cutter.

Place the scones on a lightly greased baking sheet and brush the tops lightly with milk. Bake in a preheated oven for 7–10 minutes, until the scones are well risen and golden brown. Remove from the oven and cool on a wire tray. Store in an airtight container until ready to use.

Cook's Tip

Make these luscious scones extra special by serving with strawberry jam and clotted or whipped cream. Peach jam would also be delicious.

418 | Drop Scones with Bilberry Sauce

Preparation time
10 minutes

Cooking time
4–6 minutes

Makes about 12

Calories
80 per portion

You will need
100 g /4 oz plain flour
2 teaspoons baking powder
pinch salt
1 egg, beaten
150 ml / ¼ pint milk
oil for greasing
150 ml / ¼ pint soured cream to
   serve

For the sauce
225 g / 8 oz bilberries or
   blueberries, thawed if frozen
2 tablespoons blackberry jelly
1 teaspoon lemon juice
1 tablespoon sugar (optional)

Sift the flour, baking powder and salt together, then stir in the egg. Gradually pour on the milk, beating constantly until the batter is smooth.

Lightly oil a heavy frying pan, and when hot, drop the batter on to it, 2 teaspoons at a time, well apart.

Cook the scones over moderate heat for 2–3 minutes, or until the surface starts to bubble. Flip them over and cook the other side for 2–3 minutes until golden brown. Keep warm in a folded tea towel.

To make the sauce, stir together the bilberries, fruit jelly and lemon juice and bring to the boil. Simmer for 2 minutes. Sweeten with the sugar, if necessary.

Serve the drop scones warm, and the sauce and soured cream separately.

Cook's Tip

Bilberries are small blue berries that grow on moors and in mountain woods. Blueberries are easier to find, being in season from mid-July until October. Frozen ones should be thawed before using in this recipe.

419 | Chelsea Buns

Preparation time
40–45 minutes, plus 1½ hours to rise and prove

Cooking time
30–35 minutes

Oven temperature
190 C, 375 F, gas 5

Makes 9

Calories
185 per bun

You will need
2 teaspoons dried yeast
5 tablespoons warm milk
½ teaspoon sugar
225 g / 8 oz strong plain flour
½ teaspoon salt
1 egg, beaten
15 g / ½ oz butter, melted
golden syrup to glaze

For the filling
15 g / ½ oz butter, melted
50 g / 2 oz soft brown sugar
100 g / 4 oz mixed dried fruit

Blend the yeast with the warm milk, sugar and 50 g / 2 oz of the flour. Leave until frothy, about 20 minutes.

Mix the remaining flour and the salt together. Add to the yeast mixture with the beaten egg and melted butter. Mix well and knead the dough on a lightly floured board for about 10 minutes. Put to rise in a large greased polythene bag, loosely tied, until doubled in size, about 1 hour.

Knead the dough on a lightly floured surface. Roll into a rectangle about 23 × 30 cm / 9 × 12 in, brush with the melted butter and sprinkle on the sugar and fruit. Roll up as for a Swiss roll and cut into 9 slices. Place in a greased 23-cm / 9-in square cake tin. Leave to rise inside a greased polythene bag until the buns feel springy.

Remove the polythene bag and bake the buns in a moderately hot oven for 30–35 minutes. Place on a wire rack and brush the hot buns with the syrup.

420 | Jam Doughnuts

Preparation time
15 minutes, plus 1½ hours to rise and prove

Cooking time
10–15 minutes

Makes 16

Calories
210 per doughnut

You will need
450 g / 1 lb strong plain flour
pinch of salt
50 g / 2 oz butter or margarine
15 g / ½ oz fresh yeast
50 g / 2 oz caster sugar
300 ml / ½ pint warm milk
2 eggs, beaten
2–3 tablespoons jam
oil for deep frying

Sift the flour and salt into a bowl, then rub in the butter or margarine. Cream the yeast with 15 g / ½ oz of the sugar. Make a well in the centre of the flour, pour in the warm milk and beaten eggs. Add the yeast, mix to a light dough, cover and leave to rise in a warm place for 1 hour.

Divide the dough into 16 and shape into rounds. Place a small teaspoonful of jam in the centre of each round and draw up the edges to form a ball, pinching the dough together to seal. Put into oiled tartlet tins to prove in a warm place for 20–30 minutes.

Heat the oil to 180 C / 360 F. Deep fry the doughnuts for 3–5 minutes, drain on absorbent kitchen paper and roll in the remaining caster sugar.

Cook's Tip

Leave yeast doughs to rise in a warm place; near a central heating boiler, radiator or in front of a fire. Alternatively warm the grill compartment of the cooker but make sure that it is not too hot or the dough will dry out on top and begin to cook instead of rise.

Cook's Tip

To make jam and cream doughnuts, shape the unfilled dough into long doughnuts. Deep fry and roll in sugar. Split when cool and fill with jam and whipped cream.

421 | Tea Cakes

Preparation time
25 minutes, plus 1½–2 hours to rise and prove

Cooking time
20–22 minutes

Oven temperature
220C, 425F, gas 7

Makes 8

Calories
270 per tea cake

You will need
450 g / 1 lb plain flour
1 teaspoon salt
2 teaspoons sugar
100 g / 4 oz currants
25 g / 1 oz fresh yeast
300 ml / ½ pint warm milk
melted butter to brush

Sift together the flour and salt. Add the sugar and currants. Cream the yeast with a little extra sugar and some of the warm milk. Pour this mixture into a well in the centre of the flour, scatter flour lightly over the yeast and leave in a warm place for 10 minutes. Add the rest of the milk, mix to a light dough and knead well. Cover the bowl with cling film or a cloth, and put in a warm place to rise, until doubled in size, about 1–1½ hours.

Knead again, divide into eight, roll and shape into round tea cakes. Prick each one with a fork. Put on a warmed greased tin, cover with a cloth and stand in a warm place to prove for 30 minutes. Bake in a hot oven for 10–12 minutes, brush with melted butter and return to the oven for 10 minutes. Serve each cake split in half, lightly toasted and spread with butter.

422 | Hot Cross Buns

Preparation time
40 minutes, plus 1½–2 hours to rise and prove

Cooking time
20–25 minutes

Oven temperature
220C, 425F, gas 7

Makes 12

Calories
250 per bun

You will need
450 g / 1 lb strong plain flour
1 teaspoon salt
1 teaspoon ground mixed spice
½ teaspoon ground cinnamon
50 g / 2 oz butter
1 sachet easy-blend dried yeast
50 g / 2 oz caster sugar
100 g / 4 oz currants
50 g / 2 oz chopped mixed peel
150 ml / ¼ pint warm milk
4 tablespoons warm water
1 egg, beaten

For the glaze
50 g / 2 oz granulated sugar
3 tablespoons milk

Sift the flour, salt and spices into a bowl. Rub in the butter. Stir in the yeast, sugar, currants and peel. Make a well in centre and add the milk, water and egg. Mix to form a soft dough. Turn out on to a lightly floured surface and knead until smooth and elastic. Place in an oiled bowl, cover with cling film and leave to rise in a warm place until doubled in size, 1–1½ hours.

Knock back the dough, then shape into 12 balls. Place well apart on greased baking trays and flatten slightly. Cover with oiled cling film and leave to prove for 30 minutes. Remove cling film, slash a cross in each bun. Bake in a hot oven for 20–25 minutes.

Bring the sugar and milk to the boil, stirring. Brush over the buns. Cool on a wire rack.

Freezer Tip

Fresh yeast can be frozen. Wrap small pieces in cling film, then pack in a polythene bag. Store for up to 6 months.

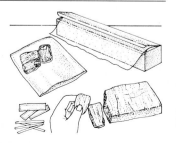

Freezer Tip

Make the buns in advance and freeze them unglazed. When defrosted, put them in a hot oven for 2–3 minutes, then glaze them.

423 | Dundee Cake

Preparation time
15 minutes

Cooking time
3½ hours

Oven temperature
150 C, 300 F, gas 2

Makes 1 cake

Total calories
5385

You will need
225 g / 8 oz butter or margarine
225 g / 8 oz caster sugar
5 eggs, lightly beaten
350 g / 12 oz self-raising flour, sifted
675 g / 1½ lb mixed dried fruit
100 g / 4 oz glacé cherries, washed and quartered
1 teaspoon mixed spice
50 g / 2 oz whole blanched almonds

Line and grease a deep 20-cm/8-in round cake tin. Cream the butter or margarine with the sugar until light and fluffy. Gradually beat in the eggs, adding a little flour if necessary to prevent the mixture from curdling. Mix the dried fruit and cherries with a spoonful of the flour. Fold the remaining flour and the mixed spice into the creamed mixture. Stir in the dried fruit and glacé cherries. Spoon the mixture into the prepared tin and level the surface. Top with concentric circles of almonds.

Bake in a cool oven for 3½ hours or until a skewer inserted into the centre of the cake comes out clean. Leave to cool in the tin for about 10 minutes, then turn out on to a wire rack to cool completely.

424 | Quick Fruit Cake

Preparation time
15 minutes

Cooking time
1–1¼ hours

Oven temperature
180 C, 350 F, gas 4

Makes 1 cake

Total calories
2410

You will need
100 g / 4 oz butter or margarine
100 g / 4 oz caster sugar
2 eggs, lightly beaten
225 g / 8 oz self-raising flour, sifted
100 g / 4 oz mixed dried fruit
50 g / 2 oz glacé cherries, washed and sliced

Line and grease a deep 18-cm/7-in round cake tin. Cream the butter or margarine with the sugar until light and fluffy. Gradually beat in the eggs, adding a little of the flour to prevent curdling. Mix the dried fruit and cherries with a spoonful of the flour. Fold the remaining flour into the creamed mixture, then fold in the fruit. Spoon the mixture into the prepared tin.

Level the top of the cake and bake in a moderate oven for 1–1¼ hours or until a skewer inserted into the centre of the cake comes out clean. Leave to cool in the tin for 5 minutes, then turn out and cool completely on a wire rack.

Cook's Tip

If you have whole almonds with peel on, then cover them with boiling water and leave for 1 minute. Drain and rub off the skins between your thumb and forefinger. Weigh the nuts without skins.

Cook's Tip

To level the surface of a fruit cake mixture, dampen a large metal spoon in hot water, shake off the water and use the rounded side to level the mixture. Dampen the spoon again if the mixture begins to stick.

425 | Mid-morning Coffee-time Cake

Preparation time
15 minutes

Cooking time
55 minutes

Oven temperature
18iC, 350 F, gas 4

Makes 1 (18-cm/ 7-in) square cake

Total calories
3165

You will need
100 g/4 oz butter
200 g/7 oz caster sugar
2 eggs, beaten
1 teaspoon vanilla essence
300 ml/½ pint soured cream
175 g/6 oz self-raising flour
1 teaspoon bicarbonate of soda
75 g/3 oz hazelnuts or walnuts, coarsely chopped

Cream the butter with the sugar until light and fluffy. Gradually beat in the eggs. Stir in the vanilla essence and soured cream. Sift the flour with the soda and fold into the creamed mixture. Add 50 g/2 oz of the nuts and mix well. Spoon into a greased and lined 18-cm/7-in deep, square cake tin.

Bake for 30 minutes or until a skewer inserted into the centre comes out clean. Without removing the cake from the oven, carefully sprinkle the remaining nuts on top. Bake for a further 25 minutes. Turn out and allow to cool on a wire rack. Serve warm or cold.

426 | Passion Cake

Preparation time
20 minutes

Cooking time
1 hour 5 minutes

Oven temperature
180 C, 350 F, gas 4

Makes 1 (23-cm/ 9-in) cake

Total calories
5430

You will need
50 g/2 oz walnuts, coarsely chopped
2 ripe bananas, mashed
175 g/6 oz Muscovado sugar
3 eggs, beaten
275 g/10 oz plain flour
1 teaspoon salt
1 teaspoon bicarbonate of soda
2 teaspoons baking powder
175 ml/6 fl oz corn oil
175 g/6 oz grated carrot
walnut halves to decorate (optional)

For the icing
75 g/3 oz butter, softened
75 g/3 oz cream cheese
175 g/6 oz icing sugar, sifted
½ teaspoon vanilla essence

Mix the walnuts with the banana. Add the sugar and eggs and mix well. Sift the flour with the salt, soda and baking powder. Add to the nut mixture with the oil and beat well. Fold in the carrot. Spoon into a greased and lined 23-cm/9-in deep, round cake tin.

Bake for about 1 hour 5 minutes until golden and a skewer inserted into the centre comes out clean. Cool on a wire rack.

To prepare the icing, beat the butter with the cream cheese until light. Beat in the icing sugar and vanilla essence. Spread over the cake and mark with a fork to give a rough-textured finish. Decorate with walnut halves, if liked.

Cook's Tip

To prevent the bowl from slipping while the mixture is being creamed, place the bowl on a damp teatowel or sponge.

Cook's Tip

It is essential to use ripe bananas for this recipe. Choose bananas without a hint of green and those that have brownish streaks to their skins.

427 | Coconut Cake

Preparation time
15 minutes, plus 30
minutes standing time

Cooking time
45–50 minutes

Oven temperature
190 C, 375 F, gas 5

**Makes 1 (450-g/
1-lb) loaf cake**

Total calories
2505

You will need
2 eggs
about 6 tablespoons milk
100 g/4 oz caster sugar
75 g/3 oz desiccated coconut
175 g/6 oz plain flour
2 teaspoons baking powder
100 g/4 oz butter or margarine

For the topping
2 tablespoons desiccated coconut
1 tablespoon demerara sugar

Break the eggs into a measuring jug, beat lightly, then add the milk to make up to 150 ml/¼ pint. Mix in half the sugar and the coconut and leave to stand for 30 minutes.

Sift the flour and baking powder together into a bowl, then stir in the remaining sugar. Rub in the butter until the mixture resembles fine breadcrumbs, then add the coconut mixture. Mix gently but thoroughly together.

Turn the mixture into a greased and floured 450-g/ 1-lb loaf tin. Mix together the coconut and sugar for the topping and sprinkle over the top.

Bake for 45–50 minutes or until firm to the touch. Cool on a wire rack.

428 | Cherry and Coconut Cake

Preparation time
15 minutes

Cooking time
45–50 minutes

Oven temperature
180 C, 350 F, gas 4

**Makes 1 (450-g/
1-lb) loaf cake**

Total calories
2300

You will need
150 g/5 oz self-raising flour
¼ teaspoon salt
100 g/4 oz caster sugar
75 g/3 oz butter or margarine
1 egg
5 tablespoons milk
175 g/6 oz glacé cherries, halved
50 g/2 oz desiccated coconut
1 tablespoon demerara sugar

Sift the flour and salt into a bowl. Stir in the caster sugar then rub in the butter until the mixture resembles fine breadcrumbs.

Beat the egg and milk together and toss the cherries with the coconut. Add both to the flour mixture and fold in gently.

Place in a greased and floured 450-g/1-lb loaf tin and sprinkle with the demerara sugar. Bake for 45–50 minutes or until firm to the touch. Turn out to cool on a wire rack.

Cook's Tip

If you are unsure about the size or capacity of your baking tins then why not paint the measurement on the base or side with nail varnish so that you needn't check or measure time and time again.

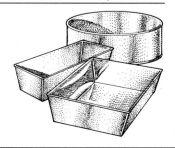

Cook's Tip

Remember when spooning a cake mixture into a baking tin to level the surface with the back of a spoon or palette knife so that the cake rises evenly during baking.

429 | Apple and Almond Layer Cake

Preparation time
20 minutes

Cooking time
1½ hours

Oven temperature
160 C, 325 F, gas 3

Makes 1 cake

Total calories
3190

You will need
150 g 5 oz soft margarine
2 large eggs, beaten
225 g 8 oz golden granulated
　　sugar
1 teaspoon almond essence
225 g 8 oz self-raising flour, sifted
1½ teaspoons baking powder
350 g 12 oz cooking apples,
　　peeled, cored and sliced
25 g 1 oz flaked almonds

Place the margarine, eggs, sugar, almond essence, flour and baking powder in a bowl and beat thoroughly until well combined. Alternatively use a mixer or food processor.

Spread half the cake mixture in the base of a greased 20-cm/8-in loose-bottomed cake tin. Cover with the sliced apples and put the remaining cake mixture on top of the apples in blobs. Sprinkle over the flaked almonds and bake in a moderate oven for about 1½ hours, until evenly golden and the edges shrink away from the sides of the tin. Turn out and cool on a wire rack.

Cook's Tip

This is especially delicious served warm with whipped cream for dessert, though equally good as a lovely teatime cake.

430 | California Christmas Cake

Preparation time
30 minutes, plus 1 hour
to macerate fruit

Cooking time
2 2¼ hours

Oven temperature
160 C, 325 F, gas 3

Makes 1 cake

Total calories
4650

You will need
350 g / 12 oz raisins
50 g / 2 oz glacé cherries, quartered
50 g / 2 oz dried apricots, chopped
3 tablespoons sherry
175 g / 6 oz margarine
175 g / 6 oz light soft brown sugar
3 eggs, beaten
50 g / 2 oz ground almonds
50 g / 2 oz almonds, chopped
few drops of almond essence
225 g / 8 oz self-raising wholemeal
　　flour
1 teaspoon mixed spice
whole nuts for topping
clear honey to glaze

Soak the fruit in the sherry for 1 hour. Beat together the margarine and sugar until fluffy, beat in the eggs, then stir in the fruit mixture, ground and chopped almonds and essence. Fold in the flour and spice. Turn into a greased and double-lined 20-cm/8-in round cake tin and smooth the top. Arrange rows of nuts over the top of the cake to completely cover it. Bake in a moderate oven for 2–2¼ hours, until firm to the touch and a skewer inserted in the centre of the cake comes out clean. Cool in the tin for 30 minutes, then turn out, remove the paper and cool on a wire rack. Brush the cake with melted honey when cold and fix a ribbon around the side.

Cook's Tip

The easiest way to quarter the cherries and chop the apricots is to use clean kitchen scissors, frequently dipping the blades in a jug of hot water.

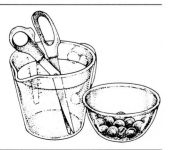

431 | *Autumn Gâteau*

Preparation time
40 minutes

Cooking time
1¾ hours

Oven temperature
160 C, 325 F, gas 3

**Makes 1 (18-cm/
7-in) square
gâteau**

Total calories
5170

You will need
175 g/6 oz butter or margarine
175 g/6 oz caster sugar
3 eggs
2 medium cooking apples, peeled,
   cored and grated
200 g/7 oz self-raising flour
75 g/3 oz desiccated coconut

For the filling and decoration
2 tablespoons cornflour
2 tablespoons clear honey
250 ml/8 fl oz apple juice
1 large red dessert apple
juice of ½ lemon
300 ml/½ pint double cream
shredded coconut

Cream the butter with the sugar until pale and fluffy. Gradually beat in the eggs and stir in the grated apples. Fold in the flour with the coconut and turn into a greased and base-lined 18-cm/7-in square cake tin. Bake for 1¾ hours then cool on a wire rack.

Blend the cornflour with the honey and a little apple juice. Heat the remaining juice until warm then stir in the cornflour mixture. Return to the pan, bring to the boil, stirring constantly, and cook for 3–4 minutes. Cool.

Core and slice the apple and sprinkle with the lemon juice. Cut the cake in half. Whip the cream and reserve a little for piping. Gradually add the cornflour mixture to the cream and chill. Spread the base with some of this mixture, cover with the second layer and spread with the remaining mixture. Sprinkle the cake with shredded coconut, pipe the cream and decorate as shown.

Cook's Tip

*If preferred you could use
150 ml/¼ pint double cream
and 150 ml/¼ pint whipping
cream for this recipe. This
mixture will still whip and
holds its shape and will be a
little less expensive.*

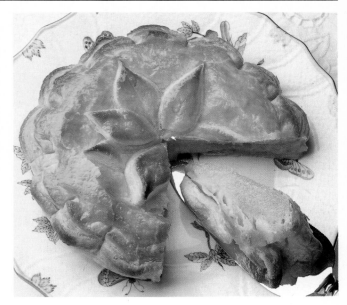

432 | *Gâteau Pithiviers*

Preparation time
25 minutes

Cooking time
30–45 minutes

Oven temperature
230 C, 450 F, gas 8
200 C, 400 F, gas 6

**Makes 1 (23-cm/
9-in) gâteau**

Total calories
3335

You will need
1 (398-g/14-oz) packet frozen puff
   pastry, defrosted
100 g/4 oz ground almonds
100 g/4 oz caster sugar
40 g/1½ oz unsalted butter, melted
2 egg yolks
2 tablespoons double cream
2 tablespoons dark rum
beaten egg to glaze
1 tablespoon icing sugar, sifted

Roll out the pastry on a floured surface to make two 23-cm/9-in circles. Line a 20-cm/8-in pie plate with one.

Cream the almonds with the sugar, butter, egg yolks, cream and rum and spoon into the pie plate. Brush the pastry rim with water then top with the second pastry circle. Seal and crimp the edges and push up to make petal shapes. Decorate the top with any pastry trimmings. Glaze with beaten egg and bake at the higher temperature for 10–15 minutes. Reduce the oven temperature and cook for a further 20–30 minutes, or until golden and cooked through.

Remove from the oven, dust with icing sugar and place under a hot grill to caramelize the sugar.

Cook's Tip

*This is a delicious gâteau to
serve with single cream or
natural yogurt or even a
scoop of ice cream.*

433 | Battenburg Cake

Preparation time
25 minutes

Cooking time
35–40 minutes

Oven temperature
180 C, 350 F, gas 4

Makes 1 cake

Total calories
4990

You will need
175 g/ 6 oz butter or margarine
175 g/ 6 oz caster sugar
3 eggs
175 g/ 6 oz self-raising flour
grated rind of 1 lemon
a few drops of pink food
  colouring
2 tablespoons lemon curd
450 g/ 1 lb marzipan
caster sugar for dredging

Line and grease a deep 18-cm/7-in square cake tin and divide down the middle with a strip of folded greaseproof paper. Cream the fat and sugar until pale and fluffy. Gradually beat in the eggs, then fold in the flour.

Halve the mixture. Add the lemon rind to one portion and colouring to the other. Put mixtures separately in the tin. Bake in a moderate oven for 35–40 minutes or until a skewer inserted into the cake comes out clean. Cool on a wire rack.

Trim the edges, cut each piece of cake in half lengthways, making four strips. Sandwich alternate colours together with lemon curd in two layers. Roll the marzipan to a 20 × 37-cm/8 × 15-in oblong. Spread the outside of the cake with lemon curd. Place in the middle of the marzipan. Ease the marzipan around the cake. With join underneath, pinch the edges and dust with caster sugar.

434 | Devil's Food Cake

Preparation time
20 minutes

Cooking time
2 hours

Oven temperature
150 C, 300 F, gas 2

Makes 1 cake

Total calories
4505

You will need
175 g/ 6 oz butter or margarine
175 g/ 6 oz caster sugar
3 eggs
4 tablespoons golden syrup
50 g/ 2 oz ground almonds
50 g/ 2 oz cocoa powder
175 g/ 6 oz self-raising flour
150 ml/¼ pint milk
grated chocolate to decorate

For the frosting
1 egg white
175 g/ 6 oz icing sugar
1 tablespoon golden syrup
3 tablespoons water

Line and grease a deep 20-cm/8-in round cake tin. Cream the butter or margarine and sugar until light and fluffy. Gradually beat in the eggs, then thoroughly stir in the syrup, almonds and cocoa powder. Carefully fold in the flour and add enough milk to make a mixture with a dropping consistency. Spoon into the tin, smooth the top and bake in a cool oven for about 2 hours. Turn out on to a wire rack to cool.

Make the frosting: place all the ingredients in a basin over boiling water and whisk until the icing stands in soft peaks. Remove from the heat and continue whisking until cool, then quickly spread it over the cake. Decorate with grated chocolate.

Microwave Tip

To make lemon curd: cook the juice of 3 lemons with 100 g/ 4 oz butter and 350 g/ 12 oz caster sugar on full power for 6 minutes. Meanwhile, whisk 3 eggs and the grated rind of 3 lemons. Whisk in the hot butter. Cook for about 12–14 minutes, whisking every 2 minutes. Strain and pot.

Cook's Tip

To line a cake tin. Cut circles of greaseproof paper the size of base of tin. Cut a double thickness strip of paper 5 cm/ 2 in wider than height of tin and the length of circumference. Fold up 1 cm/½ in along length. Snip at 1 cm/½ in intervals. Grease tin with melted lard. Place one circle in tin. Place strip around edge with folded edge on bottom of tin. Place second circle in tin. Grease paper.

435 | Marbled Almond Cake

Preparation time
20–25 minutes

Cooking time
1¼ hours

Oven temperature
160 C, 325 F, gas 3

**Makes 1 (18-cm/
7-in) cake**

Total calories
3690

You will need
75 g/3 oz ground almonds
200 g/7 oz caster sugar
3 eggs, beaten
150 g/5 oz butter or margarine,
  softened
150 g/5 oz plain flour, sifted
225 g/8 oz glacé cherries, halved
25 g/1 oz desiccated coconut

Mix the ground almonds with 75 g/3 oz of the sugar. Mix to a paste with 2 tablespoons of the egg and set aside.

Cream the butter and remaining sugar together until light and fluffy. Beat in the remaining egg, a little at a time, adding 2 tablespoons of the flour when half of the egg is used. Fold in the remaining flour.

Mix the cherries with the coconut and fold into the creamed mixture, stirring gently to distribute evenly.

Turn half the mixture into a greased 18-cm/7-in deep, round cake tin. Roll out the almond paste to fit just inside the tin and place on top of the mixture, pressing down gently. Place the remaining cake mixture on top.

Bake for 1¼ hours, covering with foil for the last 30 minutes to prevent over-browning. Leave in the tin for 5 minutes, then cool on a wire rack.

Cook's Tip

You can make your own wonderfully fresh ground almonds if you have a blender or food processor. Simply grind or process a quantity of blanched almonds equal to that which you want ground, using the metal blade, until *finely ground, about 20–25 seconds.*

436 | Fruit 'n' Nut Cake

Preparation time
20 minutes

Cooking time
1¾–2 hours

Oven temperature
150 C, 300 F, gas 2

**Makes 1 (18-cm/
7-in) square cake**

Total calories
4375

You will need
150 g/5 oz butter or margarine
6 tablespoons golden syrup
100 g/4 oz dried apricots
50 g/2 oz sultanas
225 g/8 oz raisins
100 g/4 oz currants
50 g/2 oz almonds, chopped
10 tablespoons milk
225 g/8 oz plain flour
pinch of grated nutmeg
grated rind of 1 orange
2 eggs, beaten
½ teaspoon bicarbonate of soda

For the topping
50 g/2 oz dried apricots
50 g/2 oz whole almonds
25 g/1 oz glacé cherries
2 tablespoons honey

Place the butter, syrup, fruit, nuts and milk in a pan and melt over a low heat. Simmer gently for 5 minutes. Cool slightly. Place the flour, nutmeg and orange rind in a bowl and add the eggs. Stir the bicarbonate of soda into the cooled fruit mixture and add to the dry ingredients. Mix well and place in a greased and lined 18-cm/7-in deep, square cake tin. Smooth the surface.

Bake for 1¾–2 hours then turn out to cool on a wire rack.

To make the topping, place all the ingredients in a saucepan and heat until thoroughly mixed. Spread on top of the cake.

Cook's Tip

You can test a fruit cake to see if it is cooked by inserting a fine skewer or wooden cocktail stick into the centre of the cake – if the skewer or stick comes out clean of mixture then the cake is cooked – if not, cook longer.

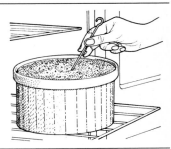

437 | Chocolate Cake

Preparation time
30 minutes

Cooking time
25–30 minutes

Oven temperature
160 C, 325 F, gas 3

Makes 1 cake

Total calories
4180

You will need
100 g/4 oz butter or margarine
100 g/4 oz caster sugar
2 eggs, lightly beaten
100 g/4 oz self-raising flour, sifted
50 g/2 oz cocoa powder, sifted
2 tablespoons boiling water
100 g/4 oz butter
450 g/1 lb icing sugar, sifted
50 g/2 oz plain chocolate, grated
2–3 tablespoons water
brown food colouring

Base-line and grease two 18-cm/7-in sandwich tins. Cream the butter or margarine with the sugar until light and fluffy. Gradually beat in the eggs. Fold in the flour and 25 g/1 oz cocoa. Divide the mixture between the tins. Bake in a moderate oven for 25–30 minutes. Cool on a wire rack.

Mix the remaining cocoa powder and boiling water together. Beat the butter and 225 g/8 oz icing sugar until pale, beat in the cocoa. Use one-third of the buttercream to sandwich the cakes together. Spread another third over the side of the cake. Press the grated chocolate on the side. Mix the remaining icing sugar and water. Colour a few teaspoons brown and place in a piping bag fitted with a small plain nozzle. Spread the rest over the cake and pipe on parallel rows of brown. Draw the point of a skewer across the rows to give a feathered effect. Pipe a border with the remaining buttercream.

438 | Coffee and Almond Cake

Preparation time
25 minutes

Cooking time
30 minutes

Oven temperature
160 C, 325 F, gas 3

Makes 1 cake

Total calories
3845

You will need
100 g/4 oz butter or margarine
100 g/4 oz caster sugar
2 eggs, lightly beaten
100 g/4 oz self-raising flour
½ teaspoon baking powder
50 g/2 oz ground almonds
1 tablespoon instant coffee, dissolved in 1 tablespoon hot water

For the filling and decoration
100 g/4 oz butter
225 g/8 oz icing sugar, sifted
1 tablespoon instant coffee, dissolved in 1 tablespoon hot water
50 g/2 oz flaked almonds

Base-line and grease two 18-cm/7-in sandwich tins. Cream the fat and sugar until light and fluffy. Gradually beat in the eggs. Fold in the flour, baking powder, ground almonds and coffee. Divide the mixture between the tins. Bake in a moderate oven for 30 minutes or until well risen and firm to the touch. Cool on a wire rack.

Cream the butter and icing sugar until light and fluffy. Stir in the coffee. Use one-third of the mixture to sandwich the cakes together. Use the remainder to spread over the top and sides of the cake and to pipe a border on top of the cake. Press the flaked almonds on the side of the cake.

Cook's Tip

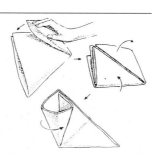

For fine piping, fold a 20-cm/8-in paper square in half. Fold the corners of the long side up towards the point and crease the fold lines. Unfold, form into a cone and secure. Snip off corner to take a nozzle.

Cook's Tip

To level out a creamed cake mixture in sandwich tins, tap the base of the tin firmly on the edge of a table or work surface. The mixture will level in the tin.

439 | Strawberry Choux Ring

Preparation time
40 minutes

Cooking time
35–40 minutes

Oven temperature
220 C, 425 F, gas 7

**Makes 1 (25-cm/
10-in) gâteau**

Total calories
4365

You will need
1 recipe Choux Pastry (see
    Introduction)
50 g/2 oz flaked almonds
3 tablespoons strawberry jam
300 ml/½ pint double cream,
    whipped with the finely grated
    rind and juice of 1 small orange
450 g/1 lb strawberries, halved

For the icing
225 g/8 oz icing sugar
1–2 tablespoons orange juice

Spoon or pipe the choux pastry mixture onto a dampened baking tray to form a 25-cm/10-in ring, with sides about 2.5 cm/1 in high. Sprinkle with almonds. Bake for 35–40 minutes, split in half horizontally and leave to cool.

Spread the jam inside the bottom of the choux ring. Fill with the cream and strawberries, then replace the top half of the ring.

Mix the icing sugar with enough orange juice to make a coating consistency and drizzle over the ring. Allow to set.

440 | Pineapple Blitz Torte

Preparation time
30–40 minutes

Cooking time
30–35 minutes

Oven temperature
180 C, 350 F, gas 4

**Makes 1 (20-cm/
8-in) gâteau**

Total calories
3505

You will need
100 g/4 oz plain flour
2 teaspoons baking powder
75 g/3 oz butter
225 g/8 oz caster sugar
3 eggs, separated
½ teaspoon vanilla essence
6 tablespoons milk
100 g/4 oz flaked almonds
    (optional)

For the filling
150 ml/¼ pint double cream,
    whipped
1 (227-g/8-oz) can pineapple
    pieces, drained

Sift the flour with the baking powder. Cream the butter and half of the sugar until light and fluffy. Beat in the egg yolks then the vanilla essence. Fold in the flour mixture with the milk and divide between two greased and floured 20-cm/8-in sandwich tins.

Whisk the egg whites until stiff, then whisk in the remaining sugar, a tablespoon at a time, until stiff. Spoon into a piping bag fitted with a large star-shaped nozzle and pipe a layer of stars over each sponge. Sprinkle with almonds, if using, and bake for 30–35 minutes. Leave in the tins for 10 minutes.

Place one cake, meringue side up, on a serving plate. Cover with the whipped cream and pineapple then top with the second cake layer, meringue side up.

Cook's Tip

You can use any kind of soft berry fruit to make this gâteau – try replacing the strawberries with raspberries, redcurrants, blackcurrants, loganberries or blackberries if liked.

Cook's Tip

It is necessary to drain the pineapple pieces thoroughly for this recipe or the cream will separate or curdle and the cake layers will become soggy. Drain well and dry slightly on absorbent kitchen paper.

441 | Tipsy Ring

Preparation time
25 minutes

Cooking time
40–50 minutes

Oven temperature
160 C, 325 F, gas 3

**Makes 1 (23-cm/
9-in) ring cake**

Total calories
3785

You will need
100 g/4 oz butter or margarine
100 g/4 oz caster sugar
5 tablespoons ginger wine
2 eggs
100 g/4 oz self-raising flour
25 g/1 oz cocoa powder

For the icing and decoration
175 g/6 oz plain chocolate
50 g/2 oz butter
150 ml/¼ pint double cream
few pieces of cystallized ginger

Cream the butter with the sugar and 2 tablespoons of the ginger wine until fluffy. Gradually beat in the eggs then fold in the flour sifted with the cocoa. Turn into a greased 23-cm/9-in ring tin and bake for 40–50 minutes. Turn out to cool on a wire rack. Whilst the cake is still warm drizzle the remaining ginger wine over it.

Melt the chocolate with the butter. Allow to cool slightly then drizzle over the cake. Whip the cream until stiff and pipe around the top edge of the cake. Decorate with crystallized ginger.

442 | Praline Gâteau

Preparation time
45 minutes

Cooking time
15–20 minutes

Oven temperature
180 C, 350 F, gas 4

**Makes 1 (20-cm/
8-in) gâteau**

Total calories
3690

You will need
100 g/4 oz caster sugar
3 eggs
75 g/3 oz plain flour
40 g/1½ oz butter or margarine,
   melted
grated rind of 1 lemon

For the praline
100 g/4 oz split almonds
150 g/5 oz caster sugar

For the filling and decoration
300 ml/½ pint double cream

Whisk the sugar and eggs in a bowl over a pan of hot water until thick. Fold in the flour, butter and lemon rind and divide between two greased and base-lined 20-cm/8-in sandwich tins. Bake for 15–20 minutes. Allow to cool slightly then turn out onto a wire rack.

Place the almonds and sugar in a pan and heat to melt the sugar. Cook until the sugar caramelizes and turns golden. Pour onto an oiled tin and allow to set. Crush finely.

Whip the cream and mix some with a little of the praline to sandwich the cake layers together. Spread the sides with more cream and coat with the praline. Spread the remaining cream on top and pipe around the cake edge with rosettes. Sprinkle with any remaining praline.

Cook's Tip

Use 1 tablespoon coffee essence instead of the cocoa powder and rum instead of ginger wine if liked. Soak the cake in rum instead of ginger wine but ice and decorate as above.

Cook's Tip

The praline is best crushed in a polythene bag with a rolling pin. Prepared praline can be kept for a good few weeks in an airtight tin.

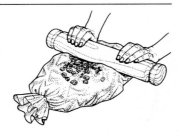

443 | Chocolate Mallow Gâteau

Preparation time
20 minutes

Cooking time
15–20 minutes

Oven temperature
180 C, 350 F, gas 4

Makes 1 (20-cm/ 8-in) gâteau

Total calories
3375

You will need
5 eggs, separated
175 g/6 oz caster sugar
175 g/6 oz plain chocolate, melted
2 tablespoons very hot water

For the filling and decoration
300 ml/½ pint double cream
icing sugar

Beat the egg yolks with the sugar until pale and creamy. Whisk in the chocolate, then the water. Whisk the egg whites until stiff and fold gently into the egg yolk mixture. Turn into two greased and lined 20-cm/8-in sandwich tins. Bake for 15–20 minutes, until firm to the touch. Leave the cakes to cool in their tins.

Whip the cream until it stands in stiff peaks then use to sandwich the cake layers together. Dust with icing sugar to finish.

444 | Brandy Torte

Preparation time
30 minutes

Cooking time
1–1¼ hours

Oven temperature
160 C, 325 F, gas 3

Makes 1 (23-cm/ 9-in) gâteau

Total calories
3895

You will need
5 eggs, separated
200 g/7 oz caster sugar
4 tablespoons grated chocolate
2 teaspoons ground cinnamon
finely grated rind and juice of 1 lemon
100 g/4 oz ground almonds
4 tablespoons brandy
100 g/4 oz dried breadcrumbs
2 teaspoons baking powder

For the decoration
300 ml/½ pint double cream
grated chocolate
chocolate leaves

Beat the egg yolks with the sugar until light and creamy. Stir in the chocolate, cinnamon, lemon rind and juice, almonds and brandy. Whisk the egg whites until stiff and fold into the mixture. Mix the breadcrumbs with the baking powder and fold into the mixture. Turn into a greased 23-cm/9-in loose-bottomed cake tin and bake for 1–1¼ hours until firm. Cool on a wire rack.

Whip the cream until thick. Spread the top and sides of the cake thinly with cream. Press chocolate over the sides. Pipe any remaining cream on top and decorate with chocolate leaves.

Cook's Tip

The cakes will sink a little in their tins during cooling and the tops may crack – don't worry if this happens to yours – both results are characteristic of the gâteau.

Cook's Tip

Dry the breadcrumbs for this recipe in a cool oven – they will take up to 1 hour depending upon temperature. For economy, dry whilst cooking another dish at a low temperature. Freeze for up to 3 months if liked.

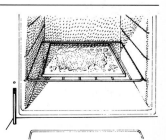

445 | Ice Cream Coffee Gâteau

Preparation time
30 minutes, plus 6 hours freezing time

Makes 1 (15-cm/6-in) gâteau

Total calories
1560

You will need
2 tablespoons apricot jam
10 sponge fingers, halved
2 eggs, separated
2 tablespoons coffee essence
1 tablespoon medium dry sherry
4 tablespoons icing sugar
150 ml/¼ pint double cream
melted chocolate and whipped cream to decorate

Gently heat the jam and brush the edges of the sponge fingers. Use to line the sides of a 15-cm/6-in round cake tin lined with greaseproof paper. Stand the biscuits around the edge, sugared sides facing out, pressing the biscuits close together.

Beat the egg yolks with the coffee essence and sherry. Whisk the egg whites until stiff. Gradually whisk in the icing sugar and whisk until thick and glossy. Fold into the coffee mixture. Whip the cream and fold in. Pour into the prepared tin and freeze until firm, about 6 hours.

To serve, turn out of the tin and decorate with drizzled melted chocolate and whipped cream.

Cook's Tip

Remove the gâteau from the freezer to the refrigerator about 30 minutes before serving to allow the ice cream to soften slightly for easy cutting.

446 | Sachertorte

Preparation time
50 minutes

Cooking time
50–60 minutes

Oven temperature
180 C, 350 F, gas 4

Makes 1 (23-cm/9-in) gâteau

Total calories
6590

You will need
100 g/4 oz butter
175 g/6 oz caster sugar
175 g/6 oz plain chocolate, melted
1 teaspoon vanilla essence
6 egg yolks
75 g/3 oz plain flour
8 egg whites
6 tablespoons apricot jam, warmed

For the chocolate icing
225 g/8 oz plain chocolate
100 ml/4 fl oz double cream
350 g/12 oz icing sugar, sifted
whipped cream and chocolate curls to decorate

Cream the butter with the sugar until light and fluffy. Beat in the melted chocolate and vanilla. Gradually add the egg yolks and fold in the flour. Whisk the egg whites until stiff and fold in. Spoon into a greased and floured 23-cm/9-in loose-bottomed cake tin and bake for 50–60 minutes. Leave to cool in the tin for 30 minutes then turn out onto a wire rack.

Slice the cake horizontally and sandwich together with the warmed apricot jam.

Melt the chocolate in a bowl over hot water, then beat in the cream and icing sugar. Allow to cool for 10 minutes then spread over the top and sides of the cake. Leave to set for 30 minutes then decorate with swirls of cream and chocolate curls.

Cook's Tip

A smooth finish to the icing can be achieved if a wet palette knife is smoothed across the surface after spreading.

447 | Raspberry Cream Squares

Preparation time
25 minutes

Cooking time
10–12 minutes

Oven temperature
220 C, 425 F, gas 7

Calories
675 per square

You will need
1 (368-g/13-oz) packet puff pastry
2 tablespoons raspberry jam, sieved
300 ml/½ pint double or whipping cream
50 g/2 oz raspberries
100 g/4 oz icing sugar
1 tablespoon water

Grease two baking trays. Roll out the pastry thinly and cut into two 7.5 × 30-cm/3 × 12-in strips. Place on the prepared baking trays and bake in a hot oven for 10–12 minutes or until well risen and golden. Leave to cool on a wire rack. Heat the jam until runny and brush on to one strip of pastry. Whip the cream until thick, then fold in the raspberries. Spread the cream filling over the pastry slice without the jam. Top with the jam-coated pastry slice, jam side up. Carefully cut into four. Beat the icing sugar and water until smooth and pour over the jam.

448 | Ginger Snaps

Preparation time
25 minutes

Cooking time
8–10 minutes

Oven temperature
190 C, 375 F, gas 5

Makes 12

Calories
130 per ginger snap

You will need
50 g/2 oz butter or margarine
2 tablespoons syrup
50 g/2 oz soft brown sugar
50 g/2 oz plain flour
1 teaspoon ground ginger

For the filling
150 ml/¼ pint double or whipping cream
chopped stem ginger and angelica to decorate

Grease as many wooden spoon handles as possible. Thoroughly grease two baking trays. Melt the butter or margarine, syrup and sugar over a low heat, then stir in the flour and ginger. Drop teaspoonsful of the mixture well apart on a baking tray to allow room for spreading.

Cook in a moderately hot oven for 8–10 minutes, then leave the biscuits to cool for a few seconds. Use a palette knife to lift them off very carefully, then roll around the wooden spoon handles with the top of the biscuit on the outside. Hold in position for a few minutes until set. Slip the biscuits from the handles and place on a wire rack to cool. Bake the biscuits in batches. If they set too quickly return them to the oven to melt for a few seconds.

Whip the cream until thick and use to fill the ginger snaps. Decorate with stem ginger and angelica.

Cook's Tip

To make custard slices: cook pastry as above. Spread both slices with jam and thick custard with whipped cream folded in, then sandwich together, jam sides in. Cut into 5-cm/2-in slices.

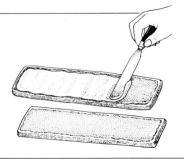

Cook's Tip

To make cups to hold ice cream or sorbet, mould hot biscuits over oiled oranges and leave to cool.

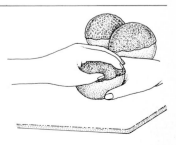

449 | Lemon Treacle Tarts

Preparation time
20–25 minutes

Cooking time
35 minutes

Oven temperature
180 C, 350 F, gas 4

Makes 6

Calories
585 per tart

You will need
225 g/8 oz plain flour
150 g/5 oz butter
grated rind of 1 small lemon
1 egg yolk
2 tablespoons water
beaten egg to glaze
caster sugar to dust

For the filling
175 g/6 oz fresh white
   breadcrumbs
375 g/13 oz golden syrup
finely grated rind of 1 lemon
1 tablespoon lemon juice

Sift the flour into a bowl. Rub in the butter then stir in the lemon rind. Mix the egg yolk with the water and add to the dry ingredients and bind to a firm dough. Roll out on a floured surface and use to line six greased 10-cm/4-in individual flan cases. Reserve any dough trimmings.

Mix the breadcrumbs with the golden syrup, lemon rind and juice. Spoon into the pastry cases and decorate with pastry leaves made from the trimmings. Glaze the leaves with beaten egg and dust with caster sugar.

Bake for 35 minutes or until golden. Cool on a wire rack.

Cook's Tip

These delicious tarts make a very good pudding too if served with cream, ice-cream or custard.

450 | Festive Mince Pies

Preparation time
20 minutes

Cooking time
20–25 minutes

Oven temperature
200 C, 400 F, gas 6

Makes 24

Calories
140 per pie

You will need

For the pastry
275 g/10 oz plain flour
25 g/1 oz ground almonds
175 g/6 oz butter or margarine
75 g/3 oz icing sugar
grated rind of 1 lemon
1 egg yolk
3 tablespoons milk

For the filling
225 g/8 oz mincemeat
1 tablespoon brandy
grated rind of 1 small orange
icing sugar to dust

Mix the flour with the ground almonds, rub in the butter then mix in the icing sugar and lemon rind. Mix the egg yolk with the milk and stir into the flour mixture, binding to make a firm dough. Chill for 30 minutes.

Roll out two-thirds of the pastry on a floured surface and cut 24 rounds with a 7.5-cm/3-in fluted cutter. Use to line greased tartlet tins. Mix the mincemeat with the brandy and orange rind and spoon into the cases.

Roll out the remaining pastry and, using a star-shaped cutter, cut out 24 stars for the pie lids. Place in position and bake for 20–25 minutes until pale golden. Cool on a wire rack.

Serve warm, dusted with icing sugar.

Cook's Tip

You could top the mince pies with other festive cut-out shapes – bells, reindeer, and Christmas trees, for example.

451 | Strawberry Palmiers

Preparation time
20–25 minutes

Cooking time
20 minutes

Oven temperature
220C, 425F, gas 7

Makes 8

Calories
550 per palmier

You will need
150 g/5 oz caster sugar
1 (368-g/13-oz) packet frozen puff
  pastry, defrosted
225 g/8 oz strawberries
450 ml/¾ pint double cream
2 teaspoons icing sugar, sifted

Sprinkle a board with 25 g/1 oz of the sugar and roll out the pastry to a 30-cm/12-in square. Trim the edges square, brush with water and sprinkle with 50 g/2 oz of the sugar. Fold two opposite sides together to meet in the centre, brush again with water and sprinkle with the remaining sugar. Fold again in the same way and press down lightly. Finally fold the two sides up together to produce a single roll that when cut across will form heart-shaped slices. Cut into 16 (1-cm/½-in) slices and place on a baking tray.

Bake for 10 minutes, turn over with a spatula and bake for a further 10 minutes. Cool on a wire rack.

Halve the strawberries and reserve a few to decorate. Whip the cream with the sugar until thick. Sandwich the palmiers with the cream and strawberries. Decorate the tops with the reserved strawberries.

Cook's Tip

Pastry palmiers will keep fresh in an airtight tin for several days without their filling. For best results fill at the very last moment to appreciate the crisp pastry with the creamy soft and fruity filling.

452 | Blackberry and Apple Jalousie

Preparation time
30 minutes

Cooking time
25–30 minutes

Oven temperature
220C, 425F, gas 7

Serves 6

Calories
385 per portion

You will need
675 g/1½ lb cooking apples,
  peeled, cored and thickly sliced
25 g/1 oz butter
1½ teaspoons ground mace
100 g/4 oz blackberries, hulled
75 g/3 oz demerara sugar
1 (368-g/13-oz) packet frozen puff
  pastry, defrosted
beaten egg to glaze

Place the apples in a pan with the butter and 1 teaspoon of mace and cook until just softened. Add the blackberries and cook for a further 2 minutes. Stir in 50 g/2 oz of the sugar and leave to cool.

Divide the pastry in half and roll out each piece on a floured surface to a 28 × 20-cm/11 × 8-in rectangle. Place one on a dampened baking tray. Fold the second in half lengthways and cut diagonal slits through the folded edge at 1-cm/½-in intervals to within 2.5 cm/1 in of the cut edges. Open out for use.

Place the apple mixture on the pastry, brush the edges with beaten egg and cover with the cut pastry top, sealing the edges well. Glaze with egg and sprinkle with the remaining sugar and mace. Bake for 25–30 minutes until golden. Serve warm or cold.

Cook's Tip

This jalousie is doubly delicious if served with Calvados cream. To prepare this, whip 300 ml/½ pint double cream with 2 tablespoons Calvados until softly stiff. Chill before serving.

453 | Baked Cherry Cheesecake

Preparation time
25–30 minutes

Cooking time
1 hour 5–1 hour 10 minutes

Oven temperature
200 C, 400 F, gas 6
180 C, 350 F, gas 4

Serves 6–8

Calories
525–390 per portion

You will need
½ recipe rich shortcrust pastry (see Introduction)

For the filling
4 eggs
4 tablespoons caster sugar
finely grated rind and juice of 1 lemon
225 g/8 oz cottage cheese, sieved
300 ml/½ pint soured cream
1 tablespoon plain flour

For the decoration
1 (397-g/14-oz) can cherry pie filling
150 ml/¼ pint double cream

Roll out the pastry on a lightly floured surface and use to line a 20-cm/8-in deep, loose-bottomed cake tin. Bake 'blind' at the higher temperature for 20 minutes, removing the paper and beans after 15 minutes.

To make the filling, beat the eggs with the sugar until light and fluffy, then beat in the remaining filling ingredients. Pour into the pastry case.

Reduce the oven temperature and bake for 45–50 minutes. Turn off the oven and leave the cheesecake in the oven to cool.

To serve, remove from the tin and place on a serving plate. Top with the cherry pie filling and decorate with whipped cream.

Cook's Tip

This baked cheesecake can be topped with any number of different flavoured pie fillings. Try blackcurrant, redcurrant or blackberry and apple for example.

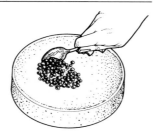

454 | Lemon Sponge Cheesecake

Preparation time
25 minutes

Cooking time
1½ hours

Oven temperature
160 C, 325 F, gas 3

Serves 6

Calories
540 per portion

You will need
50 g/2 oz butter or margarine
50 g/2 oz caster sugar
1 egg, beaten
50 g/2 oz self-raising flour

For the filling
350 g/12 oz cottage cheese, sieved
150 ml/¼ pint double cream
25 g/1 oz plain flour
50 g/2 oz caster sugar
3 eggs, beaten
finely grated rind of 2 lemons
juice of 1 lemon

For the topping
100 g/4 oz sugar
2 lemons, peeled and sliced
50 g/2 oz butter
25 g/1 oz flaked almonds

Beat the first four ingredients until smooth. Pour into a greased and lined 18-cm/7-in cake tin. Bake for 15 minutes. Mix the filling ingredients together and pour over the sponge. Return to the oven and cook for 1¼ hours. Turn off and leave the cheesecake in the oven for a further 30 minutes to cool. Remove and cool.

Place the sugar in a pan and heat until caramelized. Dip in the lemon slices then cool on a wire rack. Add the butter and almonds to the pan and cook until the mixture thickens. Turn onto waxed paper and leave to set, then crumble over the cheesecake with the lemon slices.

Cook's Tip

To line a deep cake tin, cut a piece of greaseproof paper long enough to go around the inside of the tin and about 5 cm/2 in taller than the height of the tin. Fold up about 2.5 cm/1 in of the strip, creasing it well and snip the folded edge at regular intervals. Cut 2 rounds to line the base of the tin. Place one round on the base of the tin. Position the strip around the tin, then cover and secure in place with the second round base paper.

455 | Nutty Angelica Fancies

Preparation time
15−20 minutes

Cooking time
25−30 minutes

Oven temperature
180 C, 350 F, gas 4

Makes 12

Calories
295 per cake

You will need
100 g/4 oz butter or margarine
100 g/4 oz caster sugar
2 eggs, lightly beaten
100 g/4 oz self-raising flour
100 g/4 oz walnuts, chopped
75 g/3 oz angelica, chopped

For the icing and decoration
225 g/8 oz icing sugar, sifted
2 tablespoons water
25 g/1 oz walnuts, chopped
50 g/2 oz angelica, chopped

Cream the butter with the sugar until light and fluffy. Gradually beat in the eggs and fold in the flour, using a metal spoon. Mix together the walnuts and angelica and fold into the cake mixture. Divide the mixture between 12 greased dariole moulds.

Bake for 25−30 minutes then turn out to cool on a wire rack.

To make the icing, mix the icing sugar with the water until thick and smooth. Drizzle over the top of each cake and sprinkle with a mixture of the chopped walnuts and angelica.

456 | Almond Clusters

Preparation time
10 minutes

Cooking time
35 minutes

Oven temperature
160 C, 325 F, gas 3

Makes 24

Calories
95 per meringue

You will need
3 egg whites
175 g/6 oz caster sugar
225 g/8 oz flaked almonds
few drops of almond essence
50 g/2 oz plain chocolate, melted

Whisk the egg whites until stiff then gradually whisk in all the sugar until thick and glossy. Fold in the almonds and a few drops of almond essence. Place small mounds of the mixture on a baking tray lined with non-stick cooking parchment.

Bake for 35 minutes then remove and cool on a wire rack.

Place the melted chocolate in a small greaseproof piping bag, cut a tiny hole in the point of the bag and pipe swirls of chocolate over the tops of the cakes.

Cook's Tip

Place the filled dariole moulds on a baking tray for cooking to ease the lifting in and out of the oven.

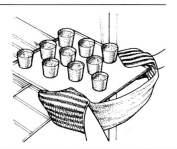

Cook's Tip

These little cakes make an ideal base for a dessert. They may be served in individual dishes with scoops of ice cream and topped with a light fruit sauce.

457 | Almond Macaroons

Preparation time
15 minutes

Cooking time
15–20 minutes

Oven temperature
160 C, 325 F, gas 3

Makes 20–22

Calories
50–45 per macaroon

You will need
2 egg whites
100 g/4 oz caster sugar
100 g/4 oz ground almonds
1 teaspoon ground rice
few drops of almond essence
halved almonds

Whisk the egg whites until stiff. Gradually whisk in the sugar and continue whisking until the mixture is thick and glossy. Stir in the ground almonds, ground rice and a few drops of almond essence

Place the mixture in a piping bag fitted with a large plain nozzle. Pipe small circles of the mixture onto baking trays lined with rice paper. Place an almond on top of each.

Bake for 15–20 minutes. Carefully remove as much rice paper from around the macaroons as possible and cool on a wire rack.

458 | Shortbread

Preparation time
15 minutes, plus 1 hour chilling time

Cooking time
40 minutes

Oven temperature
160 C, 325 F, gas 3

Makes 8

Calories
195 per biscuit

You will need
150 g/5 oz plain flour
pinch of salt
1 teaspoon ground cinnamon
25 g/1 oz ground rice
50 g/2 oz caster sugar
100 g/4 oz butter
caster sugar to dust

Sift the flour, salt, cinnamon and rice into a bowl and stir in the sugar. Rub in the butter then knead until smooth but not sticky. Wrap in clingfilm and chill for 30 minutes.

Press the dough out to an 18-cm/7-in round and place on a greased baking tray. Flute the edge and prick all over with a fork. Mark into 8 portions and chill for 30 minutes.

Bake for about 40 minutes or until pale golden. Leave on the baking tray for 10 minutes, then transfer to a wire rack to cool. Dust with sugar to serve.

Cook's Tip

To pipe out the mixture, hold the piping bag at a right angle to the baking tray and squeeze gently for the required amount of mixture. Pull away quickly to break the mixture or cut away with a knife for a clean break.

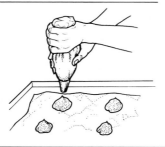

Cook's Tip

If liked the mixture can be pressed into a decorative shortbread mould. If this is liberally dusted with caster sugar before the mixture is added it will help the release properties when unmoulding onto the baking tray.

459 | Chocolate Macaroon Fingers

Preparation time
20 minutes

Cooking time
15 minutes

Oven temperature
180 C, 350 F, gas 4

Makes about 18

Calories
115 per finger

You will need
175 g/6 oz caster sugar
150 g/5 oz ground almonds
2 tablespoons ground rice
2 egg whites
$\frac{1}{3}$ teaspoon almond essence
75 g/3 oz plain chocolate, melted

Mix the sugar, almonds and ground rice together. Beat the egg whites lightly, add the dry ingredients and almond essence and beat to a smooth, firm consistency.

Leave the mixture to stand for 5 minutes, then place in a piping bag fitted with a 2-cm/$\frac{3}{4}$-in plain nozzle. Pipe 7.5-cm/3-in lengths on baking trays lined with silicone paper.

Bake for 15 minutes. leave to cool on the baking trays then remove from the silicone paper.

Dip each end of the macaroons in melted chocolate, then place on a piece of greaseproof paper to set.

460 | Coconut Macaroons

Preparation time
10 minutes, plus cooling time

Cooking time
20 minutes

Oven temperature
180 C, 350 F, gas 4

Makes 18

Calories
145 per macaroon

You will need
225 g/8 oz desiccated coconut
275 g/10 oz sugar
5 egg whites
glacé cherries, halved, to decorate

Mix the coconut, sugar and egg whites together in a saucepan. Heat gently, stirring carefully with a wooden spoon until the mixture is warm but not hot – about 60 C/140 F. Remove from the heat and leave until cold.

Divide the mixture into 18 mounds, setting them down on greased and floured baking trays. Top each mound with a half glacé cherry.

Bake for 20 minutes until pale golden brown. Cool on a wire rack.

Cook's Tip

For a different flavour occasionally why not dip the fingers in a coffee, orange or mint flavoured chocolate.

Cook's Tip

These macaroons can be topped with coloured glacé cherries for a children's party – try green and yellow as well as red.

461 | Walnut Coffee Trumpets

Preparation time
15 minutes

Cooking time
about 30 minutes

Oven temperature
180C, 350F, gas 4

Makes 20

Calories
125 per biscuit

You will need
50 g/2 oz butter or margarine
25 g/1 oz golden syrup
50 g/2 oz soft brown sugar
50 g/2 oz walnuts, chopped
40 g/1½ oz plain flour

For the filling
300 ml/½ pint double cream
2 tablespoons golden syrup
1 tablespoon coffee essence

Place the butter, syrup and sugar in a saucepan and stir over a gentle heat until melted and well mixed. Stir in the nuts and flour. Place teaspoonfuls of this mixture onto greased baking trays.

Bake, in batches, for 8–10 minutes, until well spread, bubbling and a dark golden colour. Allow to cool on the trays for a minute then carefully remove with a palette knife and wrap around greased cream horn tins. Leave to cool on a wire rack then carefully remove the tins.

To make the filling, whip the cream with the syrup until thick then stir in the coffee essence. Spoon or pipe the cream into the horns and serve at once.

462 | Cinnamon Rings

Preparation time
15 minutes

Cooking time
10–15 minutes

Oven temperature
180C, 350F, gas 4

Makes 24

Calories
105 per biscuit

You will need
175 g/6 oz plain flour
100 g/4 oz butter or margarine
50 g/2 oz caster sugar
½ teaspoon ground cinnamon
grated rind of 1 orange
1 egg yolk

For the decoration
225 g/8 oz icing sugar, sifted
2–3 tablespoons orange juice
coarsely grated orange rind

Sift the flour into a bowl and rub in the butter. Add the sugar, cinnamon, orange rind and egg yolk and mix to a smooth dough. Knead lightly then roll out thinly. Use a 6-cm/2½-in cutter to cut out 24 biscuits. Cut the middle out of each biscuit using a 2.5-cm/1-in fluted cutter. Place on greased baking trays.

Bake for 10–15 minutes until golden then cool on a wire rack.

To decorate the rings, mix the icing sugar with the orange juice until smooth. Carefully coat the top of the biscuits with the icing and sprinkle with the orange rind. Leave to set.

Cook's Tip

These biscuits may be stored unfilled for 2–3 weeks in an airtight container and make an ideal accompaniment to cold desserts.

Cook's Tip

Any leftover centres of the rings that cannot be re-rolled to make more biscuits can be baked separately as small biscuits for children or small appetites.

463 | *Sponge Bites*

Preparation time
15 minutes

Cooking time
10 minutes

Oven temperature
190 C, 375 F, gas 5

Makes about 24

Calories
100 per cake

You will need
3 eggs
100 g/4 oz caster sugar
100 g/4 oz plain flour
caster sugar to dust

For the filling
2 tablespoons raspberry jam
300 ml/½ pint double cream,
   whipped

Whisk the eggs with the sugar until pale and thick. Gently fold in the flour.

   Place the mixture in a piping bag fitted with a 1-cm/½-in plain nozzle. Pipe into discs, 4 cm/1½ in in diameter, on lined baking trays, 5 cm/2 in apart. There should be enough mixture for 48 discs. Sift over a little sugar.

   Bake for 10 minutes or until light golden brown. Allow to cool on the baking trays. When cold, dampen the underside of the paper and carefully peel off the discs.

   Sandwich together in pairs with the jam and cream.

464 | *Maids of Honour*

Preparation time
20 minutes

Cooking time
15 – 20 minutes

Oven temperature
190 C, 375 F, gas 5

Makes 12

Calories
200 per cake

You will need
½ recipe easy flaky pastry (see
   Introduction)
40 g/1½ oz butter, softened
50 g/2 oz caster sugar
finely grated rind of 1 lemon
1 egg, lightly beaten
50 g/2 oz ground almonds
1 tablespoon double cream
1 tablespoon raspberry jam

Roll out the pastry thinly on a floured surface and use to line 12 (6-cm/2½-in) patty tins.

   Cream the butter and sugar together, without beating. Add the lemon rind and egg, then the almonds and cream. Stir gently until smooth.

   Place about ¼ teaspoon jam in each pastry case. Cover with the filling to three-quarters fill the cases.

   Bake for 15 – 20 minutes or until golden. Cool on a wire rack.

Cook's Tip

These tempting little bites can be frozen without their filling. Open freeze until firm then place in a rigid box. Freeze for up to 3 months. Defrost at room temperature for about 1 hour before filling as above.

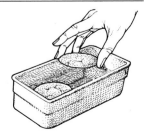

Cook's Tip

These small cakes were first made during Henry VIII's reign and were popular at Hampton Court Palace. The story goes that they were popular with the Queen's maids of honour and so were named after them.

465 | Danish Spiced Apricot Whirls

Preparation time
20 minutes

Cooking time
45 minutes

Oven temperature
220 C, 425 F, gas 7

Makes 6

Calories
495 per whirl

You will need
1 (411-g/14½-oz) can apricot
    halves, drained and chopped
75 g/3 oz dried figs, chopped
75 g/3 oz raisins
50 g/2 oz walnuts, chopped
3 tablespoons chopped mixed peel
50 g/2 oz soft light brown sugar
1 teaspoon ground ginger
½ teaspoon ground cloves
1 tablespoon lemon juice
1 (368-g/13-oz) packet frozen puff
    pastry, defrosted
caster sugar to dust

Mix the apricots with the figs, raisins, walnuts, peel, sugar, ginger, cloves and lemon juice, mixing well.

Roll out the pastry on a lightly floured surface to a 30 × 60-cm/12 × 24-in rectangle. Cut into six equal strips crossways. Divide the filling into six portions and spread down the centre of each pastry strip. Dampen the edges with water and roll up from the short end to make pinwheels, sealing the edges carefully. Place in a greased and lined 20-cm/8-in round cake tin. Brush with a little water and dust with caster sugar.

Bake for about 45 minutes, remove from the tin, then carefully separate the six pinwheels for serving.

466 | Apple Crescents

Preparation time
20 minutes

Cooking time
15 minutes

Oven temperature
220 C, 425 F, gas 7

Makes about 10

Calories
185 per crescent

You will need
1 (215-g/7½-oz) packet frozen puff
    pastry, defrosted
275 g/10 oz cooking apples,
    peeled, cored and finely
    chopped
1 tablespoon caster sugar

For the decoration
caster sugar
175 ml/6 fl oz double cream,
    whipped

Roll out the pastry on a floured surface to 3 mm/⅛ in thickness. Cut out as many 10-cm/4-in rounds as possible, re-rolling as necessary. Roll the rounds across the centre to make them slightly oval.

Mix the apple and sugar together, and place a tablespoon of the mixture in the centre of each pastry round. Dampen the edges with water and fold to make half moons, sealing the edges. Brush with water and sprinkle with sugar. Place on baking trays.

Bake for 15 minutes or until golden brown. Transfer to a wire rack and leave until cold.

Carefully split the crescents along the join and pipe in whipped cream.

Cook's Tip

These delicious spiced pastry whirls are best served warm. Try them with a little clotted cream for a really sinful treat!

Cook's Tip

Any rounds made from rolled and re-rolled pastry trimmings will not rise quite as well as first rolled ones, so try and cut out as many rounds from the first pastry rolling as possible.

Index